C000137095

Encrypting the Past

The German-Jewish Holocaust Novel
of the First Generation

KIRSTIN GWYER

OXFORD
UNIVERSITY PRESS

OXFORD

UNIVERSITY PRESS

Great Clarendon Street, Oxford, OX2 6DP,
United Kingdom

Oxford University Press is a department of the University of Oxford.
It furthers the University's objective of excellence in research, scholarship,
and education by publishing worldwide. Oxford is a registered trade mark of
Oxford University Press in the UK and in certain other countries

© Kirstin Gwyer 2014

The moral rights of the author have been asserted

First Edition published in 2014

All rights reserved. No part of this publication may be reproduced, stored in
a retrieval system, or transmitted, in any form or by any means, without the
prior permission in writing of Oxford University Press, or as expressly permitted
by law, by licence or under terms agreed with the appropriate reprographics
rights organization. Enquiries concerning reproduction outside the scope of the
above should be sent to the Rights Department, Oxford University Press, at the
address above

You must not circulate this work in any other form
and you must impose this same condition on any acquirer

Published in the United States of America by Oxford University Press
198 Madison Avenue, New York, NY 10016, United States of America

British Library Cataloguing in Publication Data
Data available

Library of Congress Control Number: 2013957452

ISBN 978–0–19–870993–0

Links to third party websites are provided by Oxford in good faith and
for information only. Oxford disclaims any responsibility for the materials
contained in any third party website referenced in this work.

For Matthew, Zoë and Luke

Acknowledgements

This book is a revision of my thesis, which was begun on an Oxford Clarendon Fund Bursary, and a Graduate Scholarship at St Hugh's College, Oxford, continued on a Hanseatic Scholarship awarded by the Alfred Toepfer F.V.S. Stiftung, completed on lectureships at St John's College, Oxford, and St Edmund Hall, Oxford, and reworked for publication on a Junior Research Fellowship at Merton College, Oxford. My heartfelt thanks go to all these institutions and to their representatives, as well as to Oxford's Modern Languages Faculty, for their assistance and the opportunities they have afforded me.

At a personal level, thanks are due, first and foremost, to my DPhil supervisor, Dr Tom Kuhn, whose commitment, insight, and counsel have been invaluable. Several other members of the Oxford German Sub-Faculty have offered advice and encouragement at various stages. I am particularly obliged to Professor Ritchie Robertson for his warm interest in this project from its inception, and to Dr David Groiser for his helpful remarks on a very early draft proposal. Special thanks are due to the examiners of my thesis, Professor Karen Leeder and Professor Stuart Taberner, for their critical engagement, constructive advice, and generous support. Two anonymous readers at OUP have offered valuable suggestions that have enriched the final version of this project. I am also very grateful for the efforts and input of the OUP editorial team, especially Rachel Platt, Rebecca Stubbs, and Rowena Anketell.

Material for this book has come from sources both public and private. I welcome this opportunity to express my gratitude to the staff of the Bodleian and Taylor Institution Libraries in Oxford, especially to Jill Hughes and Helen Buchanan at the Taylorian. I am also indebted to the staff of the Deutsche Nationalbibliothek, and of the Universitätsbibliothek and the Bibliothekszentrum Geisteswissenschaften at the Johann Wolfgang Goethe-Universität in Frankfurt am Main, as well as to the staff of the exile archive at the Letterkundig Museum Den Haag, and to Martin Decking at the Universität Paderborn for introducing me to the Jenny-Aloni-Archiv. Karen Cappel-Augustin, and Lisette Buchholz at Persona-Verlag in Mannheim, generously supplied information and indicated resources on Elisabeth Augustin that would otherwise have eluded me.

A comprehensive list of family, friends, and colleagues who have been there for me would exceed the scope of these acknowledgements. Special thanks must go to Christine and Colin Gwyer and Julia Weber, as well as the following, for their unwavering support and friendship, and for unfailingly providing distraction to prevent me from being driven to it: Rebecca Braun, Steffan and Vicky Davies, Nicola Esbester, Chris Fricker, Matthew Kempshall, Stephan Keuck, Tom Kuhn, Myfanwy Lloyd, Alastair Matthews, Stephen Mossman, Katharina Smith-Müller, Charlotte Ryland, Marie Isabel Matthews-Schlinzig, Marcel Schneider, Tim Senior, Jan and Karina Stráský, Rowan Tomlinson, Ailsa Wallace and Robin White. I am greatly obliged to Hanspeter Trauffer and Catherine Trümpy for their kind encouragement in the pre-Oxford days, and to Andrew Kahn and Wes Williams at Teddy Hall, and Ian Maclachlan and Jonathan Thacker at Merton College, for their forbearance and for being a source of support and entertainment in the final stages of thesis and book respectively. Matthew, Zoë and Luke have been infinitely caring and tireless (unsleeping, even) in their support. It is to them that I dedicate this, with all my love.

Contents

Introduction

Mapping a Blind Spot: The German-Jewish Holocaust Novel of the First Generation

There is no established referential framework for what will be provisionally referred to here as first-generation German-Jewish Holocaust fiction. Very little about this conceptual constellation, in fact, is unproblematic. Concerns of terminological unwieldiness aside, the designations 'Holocaust fiction' and 'German-Jewish' each denote areas of considerable scholarly dispute.[1] The Holocaust novel, with its apparently irreconcilable dual objective of historical testimony and literary fabrication, persistently defies delineation and has been referred to as 'an entangled battlefield, criss-crossed by ideological minefields and rhetorical quagmires'.[2] Much the same can be claimed of the epithet German-Jewish, and maybe never more so than when it is applied to citizens of German-speaking countries who were compelled to identify with Judaism *ex negativo*, after the atrocities committed against them and their families in the name of National Socialism had obliterated their individual identities and appropriated their language.[3] Finally, while both the Holocaust novel and

---

[1] The use of the term Holocaust, with its connotations of religious sacrifice, to refer to the National Socialist persecution and mass murder of Jews is itself far from uncontested. Indeed, it has become something of a commonplace to denounce, and seek to improve on, existing terminology in this field. However, 'Holocaust' has established itself as the designation commonly employed in anglophone research, and, since none of the other terms in use, including Shoah, Churban, or, synecdochally, Auschwitz, are unassailable, I have, for the most part, followed standard practice. For an elaboration on current nomenclature, see e.g. James E. Young, *Writing and Rewriting the Holocaust: Narrative and the Consequences of Interpretation* (Bloomington: Indiana University Press, 1988), 85–9.

[2] Efraim Sicher, *The Holocaust Novel* (New York: Routledge, 2005), p. xiii.

[3] On the virtual impossibility of finding 'an agreed definition of the concept "German-Jewish"', see e.g. Pól O'Dochartaigh, who in consequence proposes a broadly inclusive definition of German-Jewish culture and literature in his 'Introduction: German-Jewish Literature?', in O'Dochartaigh (ed.), *Jews in German Literature Since 1945: German-Jewish Literature?* (= *German Monitor* 53) (Amsterdam: Rodopi, 2000), pp. iii–x (p. iii).

German-Jewish writing independently have received a fair amount of
critical attention, their earliest convergence—in post-war texts by
German-language nationals who were persecuted as Jews during the
Holocaust, survived in captivity, hiding, or exile, and went on to produce
works of prose narrative rooted in both imagination and personal
experience—marks something of a blind spot in academic research.

Literary scholarship in Germany came late to studying German-Jewish
survivor writing in any form and to this day rarely gives consideration to
the Holocaust novel (as it has established itself internationally, particularly
in the US) as a genre in its own right. As recently as 1992, Dieter Lamping
lamented the absence in Germany of an 'Auseinandersetzung mit dem
Holocaust, wie er in der Literatur dargestellt wird, [. . .] mit der Literatur
angesichts des Holocaust', adding: 'Diese Diskussion zu führen ist längst
an der Zeit. In Israel und den USA wird sie auch seit längerem schon
geführt. Den Studien [. . .] ist hierzulande jedoch kaum etwas an die Seite
zu stellen.'[4] From the outset, there was simply no context in Germany in
which to situate such literature. Any form of German-Jewish post-war
writing, especially if it was produced abroad, was often not published in
Germany until years later, and sometimes not at all. As a result of the
pressures of *Vergangenheitsbewältigung*, a great deal of non-Jewish writing
in German engaging with National Socialism and its after-effects on life
and literature has been published since the late 1950s and early 1960s, but
it has almost exclusively been presented from the perspective of the
perpetrators and not the persecuted. The inclusion in the German literary
canon of no more than a handful of writers representing the latter
viewpoint occasionally had the flavour of a political gesture, a demonstra-
tion of the 'Kräfte zur kritischen Selbsteinsicht, die der deutsche literarische Betrieb, stellvertretend für die Deutschen, hatte aufbringen
können', as, for example, in the case of the poet Nelly Sachs.[5] More
commonly, whenever an author's biographical circumstances, his or her
self-perception, or the nature of his or her work appeared to allow for it, as,
for instance, in the case of Peter Weiss, such inclusion took the form of a
tacit subsumption of the author's work under the general heading of
Nachkriegsliteratur. Meanwhile, non-Jewish German writing since 1945

[4] 'Nachwort', in Lamping (ed.), *Dein aschenes Haar Sulamith: Dichtung über den Holocaust* (Munich: Piper, 1992), 271–92 (288). Four years later, Lamping's verdict remained
tellingly unchanged: 'Die Literatur über den Holocaust ist in der deutschsprachigen
Literaturwissenschaft bislang kaum untersucht worden.' In Lamping, *Literatur und Theorie:
Über poetologische Probleme der Moderne* (Göttingen: Vandenhoeck & Ruprecht, 1996),
134.
[5] Stephan Braese, *Die andere Erinnerung: Jüdische Autoren in der westdeutschen Nachkriegsliteratur* (Berlin: Philo, 2001), 10.

that has attempted to identify if not with the survivors' experiences, then with their position has been described as engaging in a 'Verallgemeinerung der Opferperspektive' as a means, conscious or unconscious, of avoiding a 'Beschäftigung mit der Täterperspektive'.[6]

Recent efforts to counter this incorporative or appropriative trend and make space for the viewpoint of the excluded *other* have, paradoxically, often only succeeded in preserving German-Jewish alterity by defining it as what it is not in relation to non-Jewish Germanness. Even progressive studies such as Stephan Braese's compelling *Die andere Erinnerung*, which set out to make German-Jewish literature their focal point, are not entirely free of this impulse. For instance, Braese's definition of the position of German-Jewish authors in German post-war literature relative to their 'Erinnerungs*differenz* zur Majorität der deutschen Schriftsteller und ihres Publikums hinsichtlich der Jahre 1933–1945', resulting from their 'Nicht-Teilhabe an der kollektiven Erfahrung der Mehrheit der Deutschen', puts a definite slant on the study's fundamental contention that the relation between Jewish and non-Jewish authors should be conceived of as an objective '*Gegenüber*' and '*Konkurrenz* der Erinnerungen'.[7] Such a discrepancy may well be rooted in an underlying sentiment that we encounter more explicitly phrased in earlier critical writing, for example in the introduction to a collection of articles written on the occasion of a symposium in Osnabrück in 1991 on Jewish contributions to German literature after 1945: 'Im Hinblick auf den Holocaust liegt der Kontakt mit den Menschen, die sich sowohl der jüdischen als auch der deutschen Geschichte und Kultur verbunden wissen, gerade im deutschen Interesse.'[8] Indeed, Braese cites this very collection in his study as an example of constructive scholarship marked by a 'genuin politisches Ethos'.[9] Born of the tension between the effort to compensate for a cultural and literary neglect and the concurrent attempt to render such compensation somehow sociopolitically productive, and even ethically significant, for the present, such a bias in these volumes conceived by non-Jewish Germans is understandable, and can prove fruitful, but it has so far largely precluded an approach that views first-generation German-Jewish post-war fiction as an autonomous category

---

[6] Stefan Krankenhagen, *Auschwitz darstellen: Ästhetische Positionen zwischen Adorno, Spielberg und Walser* (Cologne: Böhlau, 2001), 93.

[7] *Die andere Erinnerung*, 11, 30, 29, 11; original emphasis. See also Stephan Braese et al. (eds), *Deutsche Nachkriegsliteratur und der Holocaust* (Frankfurt a.M.: Campus, 1998), 9–16.

[8] Jens Stüben and Winfried Woesler (eds), *'Wir tragen den Zettelkasten mit den Steckbriefen unserer Freunde': Beiträge jüdischer Autoren zur deutschen Literatur seit 1945* (Darmstadt: Häusser, 1993), 15.

[9] *Die andere Erinnerung*, 26.

and aspires to an independent analysis of its literary features. This holds true even for the few German-language publications that have recently sought to promote the study of Holocaust representation in Germany, such as *Shoah—Formen der Erinnerung* or *Shoah in der deutschsprachigen Literatur*.[10] Drawing heavily on international research and introducing articles by non-German scholars, both collections examine texts by assorted German-Jewish authors not just in comparison with, and in contrast to, non-Jewish German writing, but also independently as well as in an international context. However, not least because their compilational form does not lend itself to the development of an overarching argument, the individual authors presented in them are not considered in conjunction, and a comprehensive view of a possible corpus of (first-generation) German-Jewish Holocaust writing and its characteristics fails to emerge. In Germany, literary representations of the past and its effects on the present from a 'Jewish' perspective become an exclusively and exhaustively explored subject matter only where the focus is on texts by non-Germans and/or authors of a generation born too late to have personal memories of the Holocaust.[11]

Internationally, the study of Holocaust literature was also slow to take off, though this is easily forgotten in the face of the sheer volume of recent scholarship devoted to the subject. Earliest efforts to establish the literature of the Holocaust as a distinct genre date back only to the 1970s and early 1980s, and were for the most part undertaken by Jewish scholars such as Lawrence Langer, Sidra DeKoven Ezrahi, Alvin Rosenfeld, Alan Mintz, or David Roskies.[12] Since then, Holocaust fiction has become a

---

[10] Nicolas Berg, Jess Jochimsen, and Bernd Stiegler (eds), *Shoah—Formen der Erinnerung: Geschichte, Philosophie, Literatur, Kunst* (Munich: Fink, 1996), and Norbert Otto Eke and Hartmut Steinecke (eds), *Shoah in der deutschsprachigen Literatur* (Berlin: Schmidt, 2006), with the latter acknowledging its debt to the former. See also the bilingual Walter Schmitz (ed.), *Erinnerte Shoah: Die Literatur der Überlebenden/The Shoah Remembered: Literature of the Survivors* (Dresden: Thelem, 2003).

[11] See e.g. Thomas Nolden, *Junge jüdische Literatur: Konzentrisches Schreiben in der Gegenwart* (Würzburg: Königshausen & Neumann, 1995); or Hartmut Steinecke, *Literatur als Gedächtnis der Shoah: Deutschsprachige jüdische Schriftstellerinnen und Schriftsteller der 'zweiten Generation'* (Paderborn: Schöningh, 2005) on second-generation German-Jewish literature. See e.g. Beate Wolfsteiner, *Untersuchungen zum französisch-jüdischen Roman nach dem Zweiten Weltkrieg* (Tübingen: Niemeyer, 2003); Susanne Düwell, '*Fiktion aus dem Wirklichen': Strategien autobiographischen Erzählens im Kontext der Shoah* (Bielefeld: Aisthesis, 2004); or Birgit Schlachter, *Schreibweisen der Abwesenheit: Jüdisch-französische Literatur nach der Shoah* (Cologne: Böhlau, 2006) for analyses of writing in languages other than German.

[12] Lawrence L. Langer, *The Holocaust and the Literary Imagination* (New Haven: Yale University Press, 1975); Sidra DeKoven Ezrahi, *By Words Alone: The Holocaust in Literature* (Chicago: University of Chicago Press, 1980); Alvin H. Rosenfeld, *A Double Dying: Reflections on Holocaust Literature* (Bloomington: Indiana University Press, 1980); Alan Mintz, *Hurban: Responses to Catastrophe in Hebrew Literature* (New York: Columbia

rather well-ploughed field of literary studies, especially in the US. Yet of all the many internationally published studies whose focus is the Holocaust as literary inspiration very few consider novels by the first generation in any language.[13] Even fewer include German-language texts in their considerations.[14] This again holds true especially where works of the first generation are concerned, but even contemporary German-Jewish writing remains a marginal area of anglophone research.[15] In part, the neglect of the first generation can be put down to the fact that very few of its texts have been translated into English. This, in turn, is symptomatic of the particular place, or, rather, non-place, that those authors have come to occupy who, by choice, or through lack of choice, continued to write in German even after the language had apparently been irreversibly corrupted, and after any notion of a productive German-Jewish cultural and societal symbiosis had been rendered at least temporarily absurd by the events of history. They represent a point of view that is too Jewish for the German literary canon but at the same time too German for any international canon of Holocaust fiction, even though both the trigger for, and the conditions of, their writing would absolutely warrant inclusion in the latter. Or as Norbert Eke puts it:

> Einerseits kann die deutschsprachige Shoah-Literatur nur schwerlich in ihrer Entwicklung aus dieser weltliterarischen Erscheinung herausgelöst werden

University Press, 1984); David G. Roskies, *Against the Apocalypse: Responses to Catastrophe in Modern Jewish Culture* (Cambridge, MA: Harvard University Press, 1984).

[13] Though recent efforts in related disciplines to refute the widely held fallacy of the absence of Holocaust representations before the 1960s, such as David Cesarani and Eric Sundquist (eds), *After the Holocaust: Challenging the Myth of Silence* (London and New York: Routledge, 2011), will hopefully contribute towards paving the way for further such explorations.

[14] Though see Dagmar C. G. Lorenz, *Verfolgung bis zum Massenmord: Holocaust-Diskurse in deutscher Sprache aus der Sicht der Verfolgten* (New York: Lang, 1992), published in German in the United States, for a comprehensive overview of German-Jewish writing since 1933, including a number of first-generation works of fiction on pp. 153–231, and Pascale R. Bos, *German-Jewish Literature in the Wake of the Holocaust: Grete Weil, Ruth Klüger, and the Politics of Address* (New York: Palgrave Macmillan, 2005).

[15] Among the few exceptions to this are Leslie Morris and Karen Remmler (eds), *Contemporary Jewish Writing in Germany: An Anthology* (Lincoln, NB and London: University of Nebraska Press, 2002), a collection of excerpts from primary texts in translation, and the volumes Leslie Morris and Jack Zipes (eds), *Unlikely History: The Changing German-Jewish Symbiosis, 1945–2000* (New York and Basingstoke: Palgrave, 2002); Hillary Hope Herzog, Todd Herzog, and Benjamin Lapp (eds), *Rebirth of a Culture: Jewish Identity and Jewish Writing in Germany and Austria Today* (New York and Oxford: Berghahn, 2008); and Vivian Liska and Thomas Nolden (eds), *Contemporary Jewish Writing in Europe: A Guide* (Bloomington: Indiana University Press, 2008), which set out to situate contemporary German-Jewish culture and writing in relation to its countries of origin.

(insofern stellt sich beispielsweise die Frage nach Verflechtungen und Wech-
selwirkungen zwischen den Literaturen [. . .]). Andererseits nimmt sie im
internationalen Rahmen aufgrund der Rolle Deutschlands (und Österreichs)
in der Geschichte eine Sonderstellung ein: das gilt für nichtjüdische Schriftsteller, insbesondere aber für jüdische Autoren, weil sie als deutschsprachige
Autoren in der 'Sprache der Täter' schreiben.[16]

This unexplored area—where considerations of identity and idiom, of
memory, imagination, and history converge, and where disciplines intersect yet have a hard time coming together—is where this book will
venture. In considering these authors writing without addressees during
the approximately thirty-year period from 1945 to 1975, between the end
of the war and the beginnings of Holocaust literary studies, as a category
unto themselves, it is not my intention to gloss over their marginalized
social, cultural, or even geographical position relative to their former and
their adopted countries. However, I do want to avoid situating their work
in a primarily relational way, for instance in terms of a continuing
'negative symbiosis', as defined by Dan Diner, between German Jews
and non-Jews, or indeed as a minority literature viewed from a Germano-
centric perspective.[17] To consider their writing as peripheral in this way
both segregates it and renders it definitionally dependent on the centre
from which it is excluded. What I intend to put forward instead is a
reading of a number of texts from within first-generation German-Jewish
Holocaust fiction that defines these texts first and foremost in respect of
their own literary traits and techniques, as a corpus in their own right as
well as a potential constituent of a supranational and transgenerational
canon. This reading will draw on texts by H. G. Adler, Elisabeth Augustin, Jenny Aloni, Erich Fried, and Wolfgang Hildesheimer. These authors
have never been treated as a set before and, for reasons that will become
clear further on, many of them might not be included in a category of
Holocaust fiction even if one existed for German-language literature.
What they have in common, aside from their native language, is the
experience of persecution and exile in adulthood, and a more fundamental
feeling of displacement brought on by the sense of not having ended up at
their supposed destination, of having survived 'Auschwitz' despite it
being, as Peter Weiss puts it, 'eine Ortschaft, für die ich bestimmt war',

---

[16] 'Shoah in der deutschsprachigen Literatur – Zur Einführung', in Eke and Steinecke
(eds), *Shoah in der deutschsprachigen Literatur*, 7–18 (15).
[17] 'Negative Symbiose: Deutsche und Juden nach Auschwitz', in Micha Brumlik et al.
(eds), *Jüdisches Leben in Deutschland seit 1945* (Frankfurt a.M.: Athenäum, 1986), 243–57.

and despite their names having been 'auf den Listen derer, die dorthin für immer übersiedelt werden sollten'.[18]

Yet the assumption that these correspondences would have produced enough literary parallels in their texts to warrant consideration of them as a corpus seems, at first glance, no less problematic than the terminology I use to refer to them. Where German-Jewish fiction produced after 1945, and especially that written outside Germany, is concerned, it stands to reason that since its authors hailed from different backgrounds, had experienced the events of the past in very different ways, and, even after the war, continued to live and work in vastly diverse environments, exposed to distinct political, religious, social, cultural, and literary influences, their creative responses to the Holocaust would be reflective above all of these dissimilarities. This study, however, is predicated on the premise that the quest for adequate representational approaches to the trauma of the past, and its aftermath in the present, has, against all the odds and notwithstanding the authors' contrasting circumstances, resulted in the adoption of verifiably similar literary strategies across a thus far under-researched segment of German-Jewish post-war fiction. Given the situational absence of almost any direct form of contact or exchange among the authors under discussion, proving this will involve demonstrating that in the case of at least some of first-generation Holocaust fiction, the theme of the writing has come to shape its form.

Moreover, I contend that the very isolation of most of these German-Jewish writers not only from the literary establishment but also from one another, the very fact that they have 'kaum eine gemeinsame Disposition—*außer* der der jüdischen Verfolgungserfahrung', makes them a perfect test case by which to assess the validity of this premise for Holocaust fiction more generally.[19] In thus regarding them as both a set unto themselves and, as it were, a potential control group in the study of Holocaust fiction internationally, I aim not only to draw attention to a neglected area of German literary studies, but also to suggest how conceptions of the Holocaust novel as it is studied internationally might be constructively reconfigured by the inclusion of these German-Jewish authors.

To this end, Chapter 1 outlines the theoretical context from which the proposed category is absent. It shows that the first-generation Holocaust novel is an under-researched area in Holocaust representation studies not only where Jewish writing in German is concerned but more generally.

---

[18] 'Meine Ortschaft', in Weiss, *Rapporte* (Frankfurt a.M: Suhrkamp, 1968), 113–24 (114).
[19] Braese, *Die andere Erinnerung*, 31; original emphasis.

Focusing on either documentary writing by eyewitnesses, which as testimony is commonly regarded as unassailable, or on fictional recreations by authors born after the Holocaust, which tend to be problematized on account of their lack of historical accuracy and authenticity, literary scholarship has largely ignored the convergence of the testimonial and the literary in first-generation survivor writing. One reason for this may be that, unlike Holocaust 'faction' or fictions of the Holocaust, the first-generation prose narratives in question are not straightforwardly descriptive; they do not write 'about' the past, as a result of which they are not necessarily even recognized as Holocaust writing. It will be shown that this refusal of direct representation is the consequence of the authors' attempt to do justice to a paradox that affects not just the survivors' but also cultural and scholarly perceptions and representations of the Holocaust: the fact that while the Holocaust is conceived of as an empirical historical reality and an atrocious, but relatable, succession of past events on a chronological timeline, it at the same time makes itself felt as trauma, with lastingly disruptive effects on the present, and as such resists being consigned to the past but keeps returning to haunt us in the present. The authors discussed here attempted to convey in, or rather through, their writing that the 'truth' of the Holocaust consists not only in the atrocious facts we know about it but also in the way that the experience of these facts, and their enduring effects, challenges straightforward understanding and representation. This manifests itself by the fact that the texts in question do not try to explain or describe the events of the past but, as it were, enact them structurally, by mimicking their continuing disruptive impact in the present on time, space, and self through the form of the narrative. Indeed, it will be shown that, in their effort to convey that which simultaneously demands testimony yet defies description, this set of authors was employing what we would today think of as (post)modernist and trauma-theoretical representational strategies, before either of the corresponding theories had been established, and before the National Socialist persecution and mass murder had attained their discursive and conceptual status as 'the Holocaust'.

In thus framing the analysis of narrative strategies adopted by these individuals in the broader debate on the ethics and aesthetics of Holocaust writing, as well as setting it against the backdrop of the (post)modern, this chapter also outlines to what extent treating these writers as a set, and their body of work as a hitherto unacknowledged category of Holocaust fiction, has implications that go well beyond simply drawing attention to a number of important but critically neglected authors. In revealing how certain kinds of testimony have been privileged above others in international Holocaust studies, this book raises questions of a more general nature concerning canon formation and our theoretical responses to the Holocaust. In considering foremost among these responses (those informed by) the theory of deconstruction and trauma theory, it invites a re-examination of the relationship between the (post)modern and trauma. In reading the first-generation texts under discussion as Holocaust novels *avant la lettre*, it finally suggests that they proleptically anticipate a preoccupation with afterwardsness and belatedness that will become a main characteristic of the times in which they are (still not being) received, as well as the very thing precluding them from entering any contemporary literary canon.

In Chapters 2 to 4, I proceed to a close text-based reading of four of these first-generation authors: Adler, Augustin, Aloni, and Fried. In the course of this analysis, it will become clear that even though they were drawing not only on the experience of persecution but on other, earlier or contemporaneous, personal crises—many of which, triggered by questions of identity, gender, or migration, were generally prevalent at the time—it was only after 1945, and in the effort to respond to the events of the Holocaust, that the aesthetic forms (not just the themes) of their writing were altered to reflect the experience of crisis and trauma. The analyses presented in these chapters will demonstrate that in these early Holocaust novels the theme of the writing not only came to shape its form but was in fact expressed through the form: that the upheaval of the Holocaust came to be encrypted in the fabric of the text. At the same time, these works are already imbued with a sense that they are responding not just to a personal crisis but to a hyper-crisis of modernity.

Chapter 5 is devoted to the fifth author, Hildesheimer. Though he is a member of the outlined category on the basis of the representational strategies employed in his works, Hildesheimer's writing approaches the Holocaust from a greater remove than that of the other authors discussed here. In consequence of his having been exposed to the atrocities of the Holocaust in a less immediate way, and having embarked on his writing career at a slightly later stage, his work comes to mark the point where individual and personal trauma crosses over into collectively transmittable (non-)'memory'.

Out of this observation arises my Conclusion, which glances forward to where, depending on one's point of view, literary scholarship either finally removes, or emphatically cements, the parenthesis bracketing the German-Jewish Holocaust novel. It does so by attempting to catch up to the first-generation German-Jewish perspective and literary response through later, non-Jewish attempts to view the past through their eyes: most notably, perhaps, in and through the works of W. G. Sebald. Our response to Sebald's response exemplifies that, as suggested in Chapter 1, the most important single cause for the neglect experienced by the first-generation Holocaust novel, especially but by no means exclusively in German, may well be the way in which it clashes with our self-understanding as guardians of the past and keepers of the Holocaust legacy, a self-understanding that has left little room for considering the (literary) contributions of the first generation.

1

An Absence in Context

Holocaust Representation in Testimony,
Scholarship, and Literature

It is necessary to speak, to write, and keep on speaking and writing
(lest we forget) about the Jewish Holocaust during the Nazi period
even if words cannot express this monstrous event.

It is impossible to speak or write about the Holocaust because words
cannot express this monstrous event.

(Raymond Federman, *The Necessity and Impossibility of Being a*
Jewish Writer)

I have indicated that the term 'Holocaust novel' denotes a contentious
area and alluded to why this may have been exacerbated in the case of
Holocaust survivors writing in German, who, because of their uniquely
marginalized positions in politically or culturally unreceptive climates,
often had a particularly hard time getting their work acknowledged, let
alone appreciated. What I have not addressed is what may have caused the
Holocaust novel to become 'an entangled battlefield' to begin with.[1]
Because in what follows I suggest that the especially difficult standing of
representations of the Holocaust that aspire to be literary first, and
documentary only indirectly, is indissociable from the already problematic
reception of Holocaust representation more generally, it will be necessary
first to give a brief overview of this contested greater field in which
questions of facticity, authenticity, and legitimacy are foregrounded, yet
which is at the same time haunted by the figures of the unknowable, the
unspeakable, and the unimaginable. As will be shown, the discussion of
primary texts has from the outset risked being displaced in our study
of Holocaust representation by an uneasy negotiation between views of
the Holocaust as irrecoverable cataclysm (which cannot or must not be

[1] Efraim Sicher, *The Holocaust Novel* (New York: Routledge, 2005), p. xiii.

recreated through the imagination) and the past as inescapable legacy (which we can, should, or cannot help but, keep re(-)presenting). This chapter will propose that the particular blind spot we have where the first-generation Holocaust novel not only in German but in any language is concerned is a product of this displacement itself, as well as of the fact that, especially in the past two decades, there has been a strong tendency, both at a critical and a cultural level, towards privileging the legacy that can be known over the event that is felt to elude understanding.

SPEAKING THE UNSPEAKABLE: HOLOCAUST SURVIVOR TESTIMONY

The question of the fundamental representability of the Holocaust, of whether it can be, and should be, spoken, or not, is as old as the earliest witness testimonies by its now largely deceased survivors. It is in these that the essential paradox afflicting any attempts at a narrative representation of the Holocaust first manifests itself: the apparent irreconcilability, as summed up in the epigraph to this chapter by Raymond Federman, of the imperative to preserve the events of the past in memory and transmit what we know about them, lest the facts be forgotten, and the no-less-urgent sense that there is something beyond these facts that falls outside language, and that no words can therefore do justice to the full extent of the atrocity—the simultaneous 'necessity and impossibility' of representing the Holocaust.[2]

Insight into the presence of these contradictory concerns in oral witness testimony, and into the consequences this has for the witnesses' accounts, goes back to Holocaust scholar and literary critic Lawrence L. Langer. Drawing on videotaped witness statements collected in the Fortunoff Video Archive for Holocaust Testimonies, which was established at Yale in 1982, Langer has identified what he refers to as a struggle between 'two contending voices', each of which 'competes for control of the narrative', in these spoken representations of the Holocaust.[3] The first voice, born of the necessity to transmit, speaks in what Langer calls 'chronicle mode'.[4] This mode treats the Holocaust 'as an event sandwiched between prewar and postwar periods' and seeks to order the events of the past into a sequential, chronological narrative and to provide a 'detached portrait',

---

[2] 'The Necessity and Impossibility of Being a Jewish Writer' (2001), <http://www.federman.com/rfsrcr0.htm> [accessed 23 Apr. 2008] (para. 1 of 30).
[3] *Holocaust Testimonies: The Ruins of Memory* (New Haven: Yale University Press, 1991), 65.
[4] *Holocaust Testimonies*, 65.

offered 'from the vantage point of today'.[5] Not least, this mode ultimately aims 'to reconstruct a semblance of continuity in a life that began as, and now resumes what we would consider, a normal existence'.[6] However, this first voice is continually drowned out by a second, which, in its struggle 'to detach "the way it was" from how we think it was', resorts to 'a lexicon of disruption, absence, and irreversible loss', and reveals 'a break [...] that telling cannot mend'.[7] In this second mode of witnessing, survivors 'do not search for the historicity of experience' or 'try to recapture the dynamic flow of events', for they are 'concerned less with the past than with a sense of that past in the present'.[8] Elsewhere, Langer has therefore also referred to these modes as the 'chronological current', which can be channelled into 'historical narrative', and the 'durational persistence' of 'Holocaust time', 'which cannot overflow the blocked reservoir of its own moment and hence never enters what we call the stream of time'.[9]

Torn between these two narrative voices that 'vie for primacy', 'each honest, each incomplete', the survivors' testimony comes to be marked by a sense of 'cotemporality': it is 'trapped between the realities of then and now'.[10] This, in turn, reflects the nature of the survivors' experience of their 'post'-Holocaust existence, in which, as one witness puts it, they go about the business of 'daily living' as best they can, but 'what happened' is 'always there' and risks becoming 'so overwhelming that it will make so-called normal life unable to function'.[11] In other words, they are constantly threatened by the resurgence of what Langer terms 'deep memory', in analogy to Charlotte Delbo's distinction between the unpredictably and uncontrollably resurfacing *mémoire profonde* of the Holocaust and the *mémoire ordinaire* of everyday life, which attempts to re-establish linearity and chronology and into which the *mémoire profonde* irrupts.[12] As both they and their testimony remain torn between 'the revelations of deep memory and the consolations of common memory', the survivors have the impression that they are inhabiting two worlds at once: the present and the past-in-the-present, or as Langer puts it, a 'life after "death" called survival', and a 'life within death for which we have no name'.[13] Finally, this 'coalescing' of 'time-and-place frames', with 'neither one negating or affirming the other', also threatens the survivors' identity and fractures their sense of self.[14]

---

[5] *Holocaust Testimonies*, 66, 6.   [6] *Holocaust Testimonies*, 2–3.
[7] *Holocaust Testimonies*, pp. 65, xi, 50.   [8] *Holocaust Testimonies*, 40.
[9] Lawrence L. Langer, *Admitting the Holocaust: Collected Essays* (New York: Oxford University Press, 1995), 15–16.
[10] *Holocaust Testimonies*, 3, 30.   [11] *Holocaust Testimonies*, 30, 61.
[12] *Holocaust Testimonies*, 5.   [13] *Holocaust Testimonies*, 23, 35.
[14] *Holocaust Testimonies*, 25.

Though the content of the survivors' accounts is harrowing, it is through their form that the competing demands of 'common memory' and 'deep memory', the experience of leading an existence both 'after "death"' and 'within death', and the resultant 'necessity and impossibility' of testifying adequately to a past-that-is-not-past, are expressed most clearly: in their fragmented speech patterns, disarticulated structures, and abortive attempts to impose narrative sequence and order. What Langer says with regard to one witness seems to hold true across the board: 'The witness does not *tell* the story; he reenacts it.'[15] Yet what is being re-enacted through the formal breakdown of the witnesses' testimonies is not the story of the event itself but that of its aftermath, not the experience as it was then but the experience of reliving the past in the present.

SPEAKING OF SPEAKING THE UNSPEAKABLE: THE STUDY OF HOLOCAUST REPRESENTATION

As narratives that 'do not function in time like other narratives' are 'doomed on one level to remain disrupted' and, 'instead of leading to further chapters in the autobiography of the witnesses', simply 'exhaust themselves in the telling', oral Holocaust testimonies could not be further removed from the metanarratives of scientific detachment we might expect to find in scholarly studies of the Holocaust and its literature or literary history.[16] Yet the patterns and structures we encounter in the discourse of these academic disciplines may appear in many respects strikingly similar to those that characterize these fragmentary and sequentially and structurally disrupted tales of testimony.

Apparently, the Holocaust has come to lead a dual existence not only in survivors' accounts of it but also in our collective cultural and academic awareness. We study it as an empirical historical reality, speak of it as an atrocious but relatable succession of past events on a chronological time-line, situate representations of it within literary historical developments, yet at the same time we may feel that it resists being consigned to the past and haunts us in the present as a spectral figure that has fallen outside history and memory and is perceived not by the shape it took but by the shadow it still casts and the absence it has left: as an 'anwesende Abwesenheit'.[17] Unlike its historical aspect, this spectral persistence of the

---

[15] *Holocaust Testimonies*, 27; original emphasis.   [16] *Holocaust Testimonies*, p. xi.
[17] Daniel Libeskind, 'trauma/void', in Elisabeth Bronfen et al. (eds), *Trauma: Zwischen Psychoanalyse und kulturellem Deutungsmuster* (Cologne: Böhlau, 1999), 3–26 (18).

Holocaust 'refuses to be bounded by two dates' and defies notions of historical continuity and coherent narration.[18] Saul Friedlander hints at this split perception of the Holocaust in contemporary scholarship when, in his search for a definition of the 'intangible but nonetheless perceived boundaries' that affect its representation, he speaks of the Holocaust as being 'as accessible to both representation and interpretation as any other historical event', yet concedes that while 'we feel the obligation of keeping the record of this past through some sort of "master-narrative"', we may struggle to establish 'the elements of such a master-narrative' because we are hampered by 'the impression that this event, perceived in its totality, may signify more than the sum of its components'.[19]

Not unlike witness testimony, the entire field of Holocaust representation has consequently come to be marked by a contention between two 'voices', one reminding us of the necessity to keep speaking of the Holocaust, the other suggesting that such representation may not be straightforwardly possible. At one end of the spectrum, Berel Lang, for instance, has denounced claims of the unrepresentability of the Holocaust as a rhetorical device: a means for scholarship to draw attention, by indirection and praeterition, to the enormity of its task:

> Virtually all [such] claims [. . .]—in those variations on the unspeakable which encompass the indescribable, the unthinkable, the unimaginable, the incredible—come embedded in yards of writing which attempt to overcome the inadequacy of language in representing moral enormity at the same time that they assert it.[20]

Worse still, the 'unsayability' argument has been accused of being an avoidance strategy, of serving as a pretext for the lazy or a refuge for the cowardly, or as Jorge Semprún puts it: 'On peut toujours tout dire, en somme. L'ineffable dont on nous rebattra les oreilles n'est qu'alibi. Ou signe de paresse.'[21] In fact, Lang states: 'the Holocaust *is* speakable, *has* been spoken, *will* be spoken [. . .], and, most of all, *ought* to be'.[22]

Yet at the opposite end of the spectrum, there are those who insist, with George Steiner, that: 'It is by no means clear that there can be, or that there ought to be, any form, style, or code of articulate, intelligible expression

---

[18] Andrew Leak and George Paizis, 'Introduction', in Leak and Paizis (eds), *The Holocaust and the Text: Speaking the Unspeakable* (Basingstoke: Macmillan, 2000), 1–16 (1).

[19] 'Introduction', in Friedlander (ed.), *Probing the Limits of Representation: Nazism and the 'Final Solution'* (Cambridge, MA: Harvard University Press, 1992), 1–21 (2–3).

[20] 'Holocaust Genres and the Turn to History', in Leak and Paizis (eds), *The Holocaust and the Text*, 17–31 (18).

[21] *L'Écriture ou la vie* (Paris: Gallimard, 1997), 26.

[22] 'Holocaust Genres', 18; original emphasis.

somehow adequate to the facts of the Shoah.'[23] Alongside, and often encroaching on, the array of documentary and scholarly material that incorporates the Holocaust into a narrative with a beginning, middle, and end, as a cataclysm with a build-up and fallout, there stands a vast, and well-rehearsed, store of writing that appears to be responding to a sense of it as ungraspable excess and insurmountable glitch in the fabric of reality. Examples of critical writing evoking the Holocaust's defiance of epistemological mastery and its disruption of metanarratives abound. Typically, it is cast as a caesura, irrevocably separating the post-Holocaust present from any pre-Holocaust past, and precipitating a historical crisis. Yet at the same time, this breach does not mark a Zero Hour, or a clean break with the past and end of an era followed by a new beginning, but stands for an indefinite hiatus with ongoing implications for the present. Amir Eshel has outlined a concept, albeit with regard to rhetoric employed in Holocaust poetry, of a 'Zeit der Zäsur', which would appear to capture this sense and of which he says: 'Nicht nur die vergangenen Schrecken umfaßt diese Rhetorik, sondern ihre Fortdauer. Sie gilt auch nicht nur einem Moment, nämlich dem des "Bruches", der "Katastrophe". Vielmehr entwirft sie eine [...] *Zeit der Zäsur*.'[24] This impression of being trapped in an interminable caesura is reminiscent of the 'durational persistence' of the Holocaust in the lives of survivors, as outlined by Lawrence Langer. Indeed, Langer also refers to the Holocaust as 'a permanent hole in the ozone layer of history'.[25] Anticipating the image of 'life within death' employed by Langer in his analysis of survivor testimony, Edith Wyschogrod figures the Holocaust as the persistence of a 'death-world' in the 'life-world' that has altered the very fabric of our reality:

> Present experience is not comparable to life before the advent of the death event of which the death-world is a part. The life-world, such as it is, now and in the future, includes in collective experience and shared history the death event of our times, which is the death-world of the slave labor and concentration camps and the other means of man-made mass death. Once the death-world has existed, it continues to exist, for eternity as it were; it becomes part of the sediment of an irrevocable past, without which contemporary experience is incomprehensible.[26]

---

[23] 'The Long Life of Metaphor: An Approach to the Shoah', in Berel Lang (ed.), *Writing and the Holocaust* (New York: Holmes & Meier, 1988), 154–71 (155).

[24] *Zeit der Zäsur: Jüdische Dichter im Angesicht der Shoah* (Heidelberg: Winter, 1999), 21; original emphasis.

[25] *Holocaust Testimonies*, p. xv.

[26] *Spirit in Ashes: Hegel, Heidegger, and Man-Made Mass Death* (New Haven: Yale University Press, 1985), 34.

Though we may treat it as a historical event, this past-as-sediment is perceived through its continuing effects on the present, or as Werner Hamacher puts it:

> We do not just write 'after Auschwitz'. There is no experiential 'after' to an absolute trauma. The historical continuum being disrupted, any attempt to restore it would be a vain act of denegation. The 'history' of Auschwitz, of what made it possible, supported it, and still supports it in all its denials and displacements—this 'history' cannot enter into history.[27]

This sense of living and thinking in a 'post'-Holocaust 'Zeit der Zäsur' is persistent. In 1999, Nicola King stated: 'The Holocaust remains a contemporary concern [...] because the event itself has come to represent a rupture in historical continuity, problematising the relationship between past and present.'[28]

Not just historical continuity but 'the credibility of all pre-existing epistemologies' is felt to have been permanently and irreversibly damaged by this 'Zäsur, durch die sämtliche Grundlagen der westlichen Zivilisation und Humanität in Zweifel gezogen wurden'.[29] As Adorno put it: 'Gelähmt ist die Fähigkeit zur Metaphysik, weil, was geschah, dem spekulativen metaphysischen Gedanken die Basis seiner Vereinbarkeit mit der Erfahrung zerschlug.'[30] Maurice Blanchot speaks of the Holocaust as a 'toute-brûlure où toute l'histoire s'est embrasée, où le mouvement du Sens s'est abîmé'.[31] Not only is our sense of being-in-the-world and existing in a continuum felt to have been disrupted in its wake, but so are the tools at our disposal for countering or coming to terms with such a disruption, which, famously, prompted Jean-François Lyotard to liken the Holocaust to an earthquake, 'un séisme', that destroys 'pas seulement des vies, des édifices, des objets, mais aussi les instruments qui servent à mesurer directement et indirectement les séismes'.[32] In this view, the aftermath of the catastrophe is widely and deeply felt, but the catastrophe itself

---

[27] 'Journals, Politics: Notes on Paul de Man's Wartime Journalism', in Werner Hamacher et al. (eds), *Responses: On Paul de Man's Wartime Journalism* (Lincoln, NB: University of Nebraska Press, 1989), 438–67 (458–9).

[28] ' "We come after": Remembering the Holocaust', in Roger Luckhurst and Peter Marks (eds), *Literature and the Contemporary: Fictions and Theories of the Present* (Harlow: Longman, 1999), 94–108 (94).

[29] George M. Kren and Leon Rappoport, *The Holocaust and the Crisis of Human Behavior* (New York: Holmes & Meier, 1980), 128; Michael Hofmann, *Literaturgeschichte der Shoah* (Münster: Aschendorff, 2003), 7.

[30] Theodor W. Adorno, *Gesammelte Schriften*, ed. Rolf Tiedemann et al., 20 vols (Frankfurt a.M.: Suhrkamp, 1970–86), xi. *Noten zur Literatur*, ed. Tiedemann (1974), 409–30 (352).

[31] *L'Écriture du désastre* (Paris: Gallimard, 1980), 80.

[32] *Le Différend* (Paris: Minuit, 1983), 91.

cannot be adequately described or indeed fully comprehended except in the negative, as a major force exceeding our means of reflection and description. Dan Diner, for instance, speaks of 'Auschwitz' as

> ein Niemandsland des Verstehens, ein schwarzer Kasten des Erklärens, ein historiographische Deutungsversuche aufsaugendes, ja, *außerhistorische* Bedeutung annehmendes Vakuum. Nur ex negativo, nur durch den ständigen Versuch, die Vergeblichkeit des Verstehens zu verstehen, kann ermessen werden, um welches Ereignis es sich bei diesem Zivilisationsbruch gehandelt haben könnte.[33]

Here, as in survivor testimony, the black hole of the disaster itself is felt to be impossible to comprehend and recover, as it has subverted the very tools we would use to master it in this way, yet nor, therefore, can the breach it has caused be overcome.

However, the tension between voices in the study of Holocaust representation, between the voice asserting the necessity of representation and the voice claiming its impossibility, as embodied by the earlier Lang and Steiner quotations, does not necessarily split the field into two separate factions. Rather, it often manifests itself, as it did in survivor testimony, within a single individual's thought and writing. Frequently, scholars aiming to establish the kind of 'master-narrative' mentioned by Friedlander shift abruptly from Lang's to Steiner's perspective of the Holocaust and back in their writing, without necessarily being aware of the contradictions this seems to produce, as the destructuring effects of the Holocaust irrupt into their reflections on its facts. Arthur A. Cohen, for example, attempts to give an overview of developments in the field of Holocaust representation and identifies different stages in the quest of finding a language for the events of the past:

> The first decade after the revelation of the murder of the Jews [...] was passed in defining the language of formal description and formal judgment. It was the time of the statistical accounting, the development of an accurate historical language, the numbering of the victims, the definition of the grammar of genocide [...]. The second period saw the rescue of a literature, the beginnings of the controversies of interpretation, the publication of fictional accounts of the camps and autobiographic documents [...]. The task of this literature was neither to astonish nor to amaze, neither to exalt

---

[33] 'Zwischen Aporie und Apologie: Über Grenzen der Historisierbarkeit der Massenvernichtung', *Babylon: Beiträge zur jüdischen Gegenwart*, 2 (1987), 23–33 (33); original emphasis.

nor to abase, but to provide a vivifying witness to the mortal objectivity of the statistics.[34]

Yet in the same chapter that presents this description of the traits and motivations of different forms of Holocaust representation, Cohen reveals himself as entirely ambivalent about the very possibility of conceptualizing the Holocaust, which he conceives of as being a part of a historical continuum yet also as a menace to memory and consequently representation. In stark contrast to the orderly structure of the paragraph outlining Holocaust representation in general, this other paragraph not only reflects on but actually seems to mirror the breakdown in communication to which it alludes:

> The death camps are a reality which, by their very nature, obliterate thought and the human program of thinking. We are dealing, at the very outset, therefore, with something unmanageable and obdurate—a reality which exists, which is historically documented, which has specific beginnings and ends, located in time, the juncture of confluent influences which run from the beginnings of historical memory to a moment of consummating orgy, never to be forgotten, but difficult to remember, a continuous scourge to memory and the future of memory and yet something which, whenever addressed, collapses into tears, passion, rage.[35]

As in the earlier examples of spoken witness testimony, there appear to be two separate currents vying for dominance in Cohen's essay: a conventionally flowing one that tries to establish one possible metanarrative for the Holocaust, in this case by giving a literary-historical account of its evolution in representation, and a counter-current in the shape of the structure of its experience, or, to be precise, the structural collapse it produces as it irrupts into and works against the overarching narrative. The Cohen example suggests that Steiner's and Lang's positions are not so much diametrically opposed as two sides of the same coin, each standing for only one perceived aspect of the Holocaust: one representing the historical events of the past, the other the insurmountable traumatic caesura these have opened up; one integrated in a chronological continuum, the other a threat to it; one speakable, the other elusive. To exclude one aspect from consideration would then, it seems, mean to avoid fully engaging with the subject matter.

---

[34] *The Tremendum: A Theological Interpretation of the Holocaust* (New York: Crossroad, 1981), cited in *An Arthur A. Cohen Reader: Selected Fiction and Writings on Judaism, Theology, Literature, and Culture*, ed. David Stern and Paul Mendes-Flohr (Detroit: Wayne State University Press, 1998), 235.
[35] *An Arthur A. Cohen Reader*, ed. Stern and Mendes-Flohr, 234–5.

The failure of Holocaust representation studies to integrate more comprehensively these vying voices has produced a critical discourse largely preoccupied with either drawing on or trying to dismantle such oxymoronic notions as thinking the unthinkable, imagining the un-imaginable, and speaking the ineffable. As a result, the entire discipline may appear both self-curtailing and somewhat self-absorbed. Unlike other areas of research, which are devoted to establishing and examining the different shapes the object or objects of their scrutiny may take, the study of Holocaust writing can get so caught up in probing the very possibility and/or legitimacy of Holocaust representation, and thus of its own *raison d'être*, that there is a danger of it exhausting itself in a contemplation of its own capacity and limitations instead of exploring the potential inherent in its subject matter. In what follows, I shall suggest that the particularly difficult standing of literary, non-documentary representations of the Holocaust, especially in the first generation, originates here: in the schol-arly focus not on the object of study on which its field is founded but on its own reception of that object, a focus which, again surprisingly not unlike Holocaust survivor testimony, shows a concern 'less with the past than with a sense of that past in the present'.[36]

IMAGINING THE UNSPEAKABLE: HOLOCAUST FICTION

Compared to the purportedly factual and unmediated accounts provided by historical writing or (oral) witness testimony, fiction of the Holocaust has a history of being viewed with suspicion and treated as an at best limited but at worst morally reprehensible mode of reflecting on the past. As a result, those who produce it have at times been reluctant to have their work considered as belonging to the genre. A famous example is Art Spiegelman's insistence, in a letter to the *New York Times Book Review*, that they not categorize *Maus I* and *II* as fiction since: 'to the extent that "fiction" indicates that the work isn't factual, I feel a bit queasy'.[37] It has been argued that the distrust of fiction of the Holocaust above all other forms of Holocaust representation stems from our propensity to conflate

---

[36] Langer, *Holocaust Testimonies*, 40.
[37] Cited in Sara R. Horowitz, *Voicing the Void: Muteness and Memory in Holocaust Fiction* (Albany, NY: State University of New York Press, 1997), 2. See also e.g. Gillian Banner, *Holocaust Literature: Schulz, Levi, Spiegelman and the Memory of the Offence* (London: Vallentine Mitchell, 2000), 131, and Sicher, *The Holocaust Novel*, p. xii.

the imagined with the fabricated.[38] In as much as fictitious is regarded as synonymous with untrue, or untruthful, a work of fiction may be felt to be incompatible with, or even harmful to, historical facts. Yet this does not explain why we seem to be so much more acutely aware of the potential for such incompatibility when the facts in question pertain to the Holocaust rather than any other event in history. Another reason that has been given for the perceived dubiousness of fiction is the fear that a literary treatment of the Holocaust could aestheticize the facts and thereby anaesthetize the reader to them, or even allow him or her to draw pleasure from the work of art instead of plumbing the atrocity out of which it arose. In this, as in many respects, the scholarship of Holocaust representation has been inclined to defer to Adorno's verdict and refer to his assessment: 'Die sogenannte künstlerische Gestaltung des nackten körperlichen Schmerzes der mit Gewehrkolben Niedergeknüppelten enthält, sei's noch so entfernt, das Potential, Genuß herauszupressen.'[39] In other words, it may be accepted that, again to speak with Adorno, 'Das perennierende Leiden [. . .] soviel Recht auf Ausdruck [hat] wie der Gemarterte zu brüllen', but any presentation of such suffering in any but the most directly testimonial and least literary forms risks being termed not only inadequate but somehow improper or even unethical.[40] Saul Friedlander has proposed that though we cannot pinpoint the limits imposed on the representation of the Holocaust, we can tell when they have been transgressed, by the 'intractable criterion' of 'a kind of uneasiness' that we experience at this point.[41] It would seem that when it comes to representing the Holocaust, literary assessment is hard to separate from moral judgement.

Friedlander's 'intractable criterion' informs even studies such as Efraim Sicher's *The Holocaust Novel*, which concludes its preface by stating unequivocally that 'in the final analysis, the Holocaust novel must stand the test [. . .] of whether it is good literature'.[42] As Sicher points out:

> No story can be told with any degree of coherence without being reordered, emplotted, and retold from a point of view that will allow imaginative empathy. Imagination and fantasy do not necessarily impair authenticity. Fiction and history are not exclusive. Both, in fact, are narrative constructions. Rather, the 'invention' of a past could be profitably distinguished from its fabrication and falsification.[43]

---

[38] See e.g. Horowitz, *Voicing the Void*, 1–32.

[39] *Gesammelte Schriften*, ed. Tiedemann et al., xi. *Noten zur Literatur*, 423.

[40] *Gesammelte Schriften*, ed. Tiedemann et al., vi. *Negative Dialektik*, ed. Tiedemann (1973), 355.

[41] Friedlander, 'Introduction', in Friedlander (ed.), *Probing the Limits of Representation*, 3.

[42] Sicher, *The Holocaust Novel*, p. xxiii.   [43] Sicher, *The Holocaust Novel*, p. xiii.

And yet the texts discussed in Sicher's monograph are clearly held accountable to standards beyond that of their literary quality, on the grounds that 'Trivialization and appropriation of the Holocaust [...] seem so much more morally inappropriate and offensive' than those of any other historical event.[44] The analysis of Martin Amis's *Times Arrow*, for instance, suggests that 'the postmodern play with language and meaning could be thought insensitive or irreverent to the memory of the six million victims of a real misuse of language that was neither imagined nor playful'.[45] Emily Prager's *Eve's Tattoo* and Sherri Szeman's *The Kommandant's Mistress* are both accused of 'moral impropriety', with Sicher commenting on the latter text that 'the attempt to make imaginable the most intimate moments of real life in the camps, to go beyond the literary presentation of historical material [...] raises serious ethical questions'.[46] In the final analysis, the ethical appraisal of a text counts at least as much as its qualitative assessment. As Lawrence Langer has observed, it seems that,

> When the Holocaust is the theme, history imposes limitations on the supposed flexibility of artistic license. We are confronted by the perplexing challenge of the reversal of normal creative procedure: instead of Holocaust fictions liberating the facts and expanding the range of their implications, Holocaust facts enclose the fictions, drawing the reader into an ever-narrower area of association, where history and art stand guard over their respective territories, wary of abuses that either may commit upon the other.[47]

At the same time, the Holocaust itself, 'the most radical form of genocide encountered in history', was nothing if not excessive and transgressive, and in order to capture that sense of it, we might need our representations to be the same, which is why the Holocaust is also 'an event which tests our traditional conceptual and representational categories'.[48] Thus, on the one hand, the excesses of the Holocaust limit how transgressive any given representation can be with regard to the facts it relates, which in the eyes of some automatically disqualifies fictional accounts of it. On the other hand, however, its excess, that in it which refuses to stay put in its place in history and returns to haunt us in the present, and the limitations this excess imposes on straightforward representation, guarantee that even a 'truthful' rendering will fail to be 'true' to the full extent of the experience if it provides simply an accurate factual account. This has led some scholars of Holocaust representation to conclude that imaginative literature of the Holocaust may be no worse placed—and perhaps indeed better

---

[44] Sicher, *The Holocaust Novel*, p. xxiii.   [45] Sicher, *The Holocaust Novel*, 180.
[46] Sicher, *The Holocaust Novel*, 183, 184.   [47] *Admitting the Holocaust*, 75–6.
[48] Friedlander, 'Introduction', in Friedlander (ed.), *Probing the Limits of Representation*, 3.

able—to communicate its subject matter than any other form of representation. Lawrence Langer even claims, in one of the earliest of only a handful of studies devoted to the topic of Holocaust literature in the first generation, that 'the power of the imagination to evoke an atmosphere does far more than the historian's fidelity to fact to involve the uninitiated reader in the atmosphere of the Holocaust', though he also acknowledges, in the volume's first chapter, that it 'would be presumptuous to argue that only art can convey the fullest meanings of the Holocaust experience'.[49]

Still it remains that within the already disputed practice of finding words for what may anyway defy expression there are perceived degrees of contentiousness. While any writing relating (to) the Holocaust may come into question for its representational adequacy, accusations of inappropriateness tend to be reserved for those texts whose aspirations are not predominantly documentary but also, or fundamentally, literary. Barring very few exceptions, scholars of Holocaust representation, regardless of their stance on the possibility of representation, have never challenged the survivor's right to bear witness or the historian's duty to reconstruct the past in declaredly (auto)biographical, documentary, 'factual' forms, even while querying whether any such expression can fully convey the extent of the horror and the depth of the experience of which it is born. Only where representations of the Holocaust that aspire to literariness, rather than literalness, are concerned have these doubts tended to become a negative certainty, and do the witness's right or the historian's duty somehow become the author's transgression.

As Sara Horowitz has observed, the view of Holocaust fiction as a 'weaker, softer kind of testimony' if not 'a misleading, dangerous confusion of verisimilitude with reality' appears to be a persistent one, and this holds true for both German and international Holocaust representation studies.[50] In Germany, which was preoccupied initially with the *Wiederaufbau*, and later with the task of facing up to and working through the past from the perpetrators' perspective, with establishing guilt and apportioning and accepting blame, Holocaust writing in general received very little attention until well into the 1980s, and even then only under the influence of international scholarship. Since then, the silence of the early years is said to have given way to prolific and well-rehearsed discussions of the Holocaust and how to convey and commemorate it:

[49] *The Holocaust and the Literary Imagination* (New Haven: Yale University Press, 1975), 79, 7.
[50] *Voicing the Void*, 1.

Indem die Shoah seit dem Schweigen der Nachkriegszeit Stück für Stück in den Diskurs überführt wurde, trat eine Rederoutine ein, in der das Zurück-zucken, welches mit der Tabuisierung verbunden war [...], einer souve-ränen Rhetorik des Gedenkens wich [...]. Nicht die Sprachlosigkeit kennzeichnet mehr die Auseinandersetzung mit dem Thema, sondern die Diskurswucherung.[51]

However, as Kramer's phrasing implies, these discussions, for all their eloquence, may not necessarily get any closer to the point than the silence did. Few and far between are the studies in German that manage to move beyond a discussion of Adorno's famous statement about poetry after Auschwitz, 'nach Auschwitz ein Gedicht zu schreiben ist barbarisch, und das frißt auch die Erkenntnis an, die ausspricht, warum es unmöglich ward, heute Gedichte zu schreiben', applied in truncated form but sweep-ingly to cover any writing striving for artistic merit.[52] As recently as 1995, Thomas Nolden lamented that even where German-language Jewish literature by later generations is concerned, the literary debate still revolves around the notion of representability rather than the forms of representa-tion, around 'Darstellbarkeit' not 'Darstellungen':

Im deutschsprachigen Raum beschränkt sich die Debatte um die junge jüdische Literatur—wenn überhaupt von einer Debatte die Rede sein kann—auf die ästhetische Darstellbarkeit der Shoah, wobei hier erst vom amerikanischen Kontinent neue Einsichten importiert werden mußten, um die deutsche Diskussion von ihrem Ausgangs- und oft auch schon Endpunkt des Diktums Adornos [...] fortzubewegen.[53]

Yet, for all the influence international scholarship may recently have exerted on German scholarship, the establishment of Holocaust literature studies internationally experienced a similar, if shorter, delay to that in Germany. James Berger speaks, with particular reference to the US and France, of a 'moratorium' or 'latency period' in this context that extended into the 1970s.[54] Having spent the first two post-war decades in the

---

[51] Sven Kramer, *Auschwitz im Widerstreit: Zur Darstellung der Shoah in Film, Philosophie und Literatur* (Wiesbaden: Deutscher Universitätsverlag, 1999), 1–2.

[52] *Gesammelte Schriften*, ed. Tiedemann et al., x. *Kulturkritik und Gesellschaft*, ed. Tie-demann (1977), 30.

[53] *Junge jüdische Literatur: Konzentrisches Schreiben in der Gegenwart* (Würzburg: Königshau-sen & Neumann, 1995), 86. Though see Dagmar C. G. Lorenz, *Verfolgung bis zum Massenmord: Holocaust-Diskurse in deutscher Sprache aus der Sicht der Verfolgten* (New York: Lang, 1992), published in German in the United States, for an overview of German-Jewish writing since 1933, including a number of first-generation works of fiction on pp. 153–231, and Pascale R. Bos, *German-Jewish Literature in the Wake of the Holocaust: Grete Weil, Ruth Klüger, and the Politics of Address* (New York: Palgrave Macmillan, 2005).

[54] *After the End: Representations of Post-Apocalypse* (Minneapolis: University of Minnesota Press, 1999), 107.

shadow of historical scholarship, which was consulting representations of the Holocaust—oral and written witness testimony for the most part—to ascertain the substance of what had happened, literary scholarship was uncharacteristically loath to emerge from that shadow and consider material written about and/or after the Holocaust in terms of anything other than its documentary, 'informational' value, let alone explore any of the alternative forms of representation that were emerging alongside the historical and testimonial. Since then, as in Germany, literary scholarship internationally has expended most of its energy debating the question of representability rather than the forms of representation.

This has prompted Horowitz to comment: 'As I see it, the early discomfort regarding the confluence of fiction and history and literature and atrocity continues to inform the contemporary critical discourse, diminishing the evaluation of literary projects.'[55] While Horowitz is absolutely right where the diminished evaluation of literary projects is concerned, the enduring discomfort she observes is in fact less uniform than it may seem. While the 'confluence of fiction and history' in more contemporary texts is indeed often regarded with unease, the same confluence in the first generation of Holocaust writing is apparently so discomfiting as to be rarely regarded at all. The very premise of Holocaust literature, in the narrow, artistically ambitious sense of the term, by survivors is often simply overlooked, or avoided, by the scholarship of Holocaust writing. Consciously or not, theoreticians of Holocaust representation tend to want to impose a strict divide between testimonial accounts and literary representations, ascribing the former to survivors and the latter to later generations, generally esteeming the former and problematizing the latter, without allowing for the possibility of a crossover in the form of a literary treatment of the Holocaust in the first generation. The first-generation Holocaust novel, despite in a sense being the origin of their field and foundation of their studies, often figures only as an absence in their criticism, which focuses instead on texts by later generations and on the impact the Holocaust has on us today. As a result of what appears as a simultaneous, irreconcilable inclination to validate first-generation testimony and to revile fictional Holocaust writing for lacking a 'claim to "truth"', the few early examples of a literature of the Holocaust that have been discussed are often simply not considered as literary works at all but are interpreted metaphysically and monumentally, as a testament to the resilience of the human spirit, which renders them unimpeachable but at the same time precludes—or perhaps dispenses with

---

[55] *Voicing the Void*, 28–9.

the need for—a closer engagement with their specific forms.[56] As, for instance, David Patterson has stated:

> Let it be said, then, at the outset, that the Holocaust novel is not primarily an attempt to recount the details of a particular occurrence, to depict a reality that transcends the imagination, or to describe a horror inaccessible to a limited language. It is, rather, an event and an endeavor to fetch the word from the silence of exile and restore it to its meaning; it is an attempt to resurrect the dead soul or self of the human being.[57]

Since the advent of more recent and more overtly fictional works, produced by members of generations born too late to remember the Holocaust, scholarship has moved rapidly from (skirting) the literary aspects of the fiction of the first generation to examining the literature of later generations and, commonly, dismissing or criticizing it for its fictionality.

As a result of this surprisingly swift relegation, within just a decade, of the concept of Holocaust fiction to the fictions of younger authors, who are not granted—or do not have thrust on them—what Maxim Biller has ironically referred to as the 'Auschwitz-Bonus' conferred by personal experience, the Holocaust novel has become something of a conceptual irreconcilability.[58] The particular form of 'faction' it stands for now poses a greater taxonomical conundrum than ever. As Sicher observes, since Holocaust fiction first established itself as a distinct genre in the 1970s and early 1980s, no real attempt has been made to put forward anything resembling a conclusive definition of it.[59] Generic delineation is usually undertaken tacitly or even posited as being somehow self-explanatory, with the result that the designation 'Holocaust novel' has been adduced to refer to prose works as diverse as Elie Wiesel's *La Nuit* (1958), Myriam Anissimov's *Comment va Rachel?* (1973), D. M. Thomas's *The White Hotel* (1981), Thane Rosenbaum's *Second Hand Smoke* (1999), or W. G. Sebald's *Austerlitz* (2001), though it is far more likely to be used for the later, non-witness texts.[60]

---

[56] Friedlander, 'Introduction', in Friedlander (ed.), *Probing the Limits of Representation*, 3.

[57] *The Shriek of Silence: A Phenomenology of the Holocaust Novel* (Lexington: University Press of Kentucky, 1992), 4–5.

[58] Maxim Biller, 'Harlem Holocaust', in *Wenn ich einmal reich und tot bin* (Cologne: Kiepenheuer & Witsch, 1990), 89–143 (134).

[59] *The Holocaust Novel*, p. xii.

[60] *La Nuit* (Paris: Minuit, 1958), adapted from Wiesel's memoirs *Un di velt hot geshvigen* (1956), published in English as *Night*, trans. Stella Rodway (New York: Hill & Wang, 1960); *Comment va Rachel?* (Paris: Denoël, 1973); *The White Hotel* (Harmondsworth: Penguin, 1981); *Second Hand Smoke: A Novel* (New York: St Martin's Press, 1999); *Austerlitz* (Munich: Hanser, 2001).

The displacement of first-generation Holocaust literature by more contemporary writing is clearly in evidence in the critical response to these different texts. While Langer, as one of the earliest advocates of an independent discipline dedicated to a literature, in the narrow sense of the term, of the Holocaust, proposed to enquire into the literary imagination of, and the techniques adopted by, authors with personal experience of the Second World War and the Holocaust in his 1975 monograph, more recent studies on the Holocaust and the imaginary, such as Sue Vice's *Holocaust Fiction* (2000), overwhelmingly concentrate on novels where such experience is absent or has been distorted or faked.[61] Sicher, whose own monograph on the Holocaust novel comprises an overview of 'the changing face of Holocaust fiction', argues that Vice's study might more appropriately have been titled 'Holocaust fictions', since it deals with texts whose authority and legitimacy have been called into question as a result of charges levelled against their authors of relying too heavily on anterior sources or claiming a false autobiography for themselves. At the same time, Sicher acknowledges that it is becoming increasingly difficult to defend what he calls, albeit with no further elaboration, 'a "purist" definition' of the Holocaust novel and that 'many critics and public figures' have been 'quick to denounce each new assault they perceived on the memory of the victims in novels, movies, and art shows', but that in doing so they merely 'demonstrated how unstable and questionable existing conventions of representation were'.[62] Sicher's objection notwithstanding, the title of Vice's study is absolutely representative of scholarly practice, which has indeed become to reserve the designation 'Holocaust fiction' for Sicher's 'Holocaust fictions', for often controversial texts by authors with no, or no authentic, testimonial claim. James Young, for example, applies the term 'Holocaust Documentary Fiction' to texts where the novelists fabricate an eyewitness authority and 'testimony is adopted rhetorically'.[63] Robert Eaglestone similarly distinguishes between the 'Texts of Testimony' and 'Holocaust Fiction', and the earliest text of which he provides a detailed analysis in the latter section is Emily Prager's novel *Eve's Tattoo* from 1991, which appears alongside readings of three other contemporary novels as well as Binjamin Wilkomirski/Bruno Dössekker's fabricated autobiography *Fragments*.[64] Even Langer, who asserts 'a symbiotic kinship between actual and imaginative truth in the literature of the Holocaust',

---

[61] Langer, *The Holocaust and the Literary Imagination*; Vice, *Holocaust Fiction* (London: Routledge, 2000).
[62] Sicher, *The Holocaust Novel*, pp. 205, xvi.
[63] *Writing and Rewriting the Holocaust: Narrative and the Consequences of Interpretation* (Bloomington: Indiana University Press, 1988), 51.
[64] *The Holocaust and the Postmodern* (Oxford: Oxford University Press, 2004), 42, 101.

refers to the 'separate efforts' of 'those who were determined to record for posterity the details of their often unbearable ordeals' and 'the writers whose creative talents have helped us to imagine the unthinkable' in the preface to the 1995 collection that includes the essay containing that assertion.[65]

I would suggest that the apparent impossibility of moving the debate beyond the question of 'Darstellbarkeit' where the Holocaust novel is concerned, and the bracketing of literature by the first generation in favour of a, broadly negative, focus on post-Holocaust authors, are both grounded in the same phenomenon that affects Holocaust representation studies more generally and is revealed in phrases such as Langer's 'have helped us to imagine the unthinkable': when it comes to the Holocaust and its literature, we would appear to be preoccupied not just with the past as it was, and has been represented, but also, and increasingly so, with the past as it remains present, and is represented, today. In literary terms, this means that we have come to be at least as interested in the reception of a text as we are in its contents and form, and, as I shall propose, we may have more invested in the former. Perhaps unsurprisingly, therefore, even studies aiming to present close critical analyses direct their attention to how we read the texts in question at least as much as to how they are written. Sometimes this is deliberate and acknowledged. Vice's *Holocaust Fiction*, for instance, sets out to look not only at the texts themselves but at 'the violently mixed receptions of these books, and what can be concluded from their reception about the ethics and practice of millennial Holocaust literature', as we read in the back-cover blurb. Eaglestone enquires into how 'Holocaust fiction [. . .] names not only texts, but a way of reading'.[66] Often, however, the shift in focus happens tacitly, or the slippage from text to reception appears to be unconscious. This seems to be the case for Langer. Even as he calls for the debate on Holocaust representation to be moved away from the premise itself and onto the forms in which it has been attempted, with the intention of drawing our attention to seminal texts of the first generation in the process, his writing betrays a greater interest in critical response than in literary form, threatening to eclipse the very authors he is supposedly validating:

> The fundamental task of the critic is not to ask whether it should or can be done, since it already has been, but to evaluate *how* it has been done, judge its effectiveness, and analyze its implications for literature and for society. It may seem presumptuous, but perhaps it is time to begin thinking of such

---

[65] *Admitting the Holocaust*, 75.
[66] Eaglestone, *The Holocaust and the Postmodern*, 107.

literature and such writers as a 'movement', and to speak, however hesitantly, of an aesthetics of atrocity.[67]

In his or her role as mediator between text and society, the critic is apparently of unsurpassable importance in Langer's eyes, for, by the end of the study, he or she, or perhaps only Langer himself, would seem to be in a position to do the work of not only the Holocaust author but even the Holocaust survivor for them. The volume's final chapter, dedicated to a reading of Jorge Semprún's *Le Grand Voyage*, closes tellingly with the phrase: 'And once having left the world of the living to make this vicarious long voyage through the pages of art ourselves, who among us can ever return the same?'[68] Not only does imagined experience take the place of actual experience in this statement, but the implication is that it is our reading that makes these texts work, that if we read in the (methodologically and ethically) right way, we can overcome not only the representability problem but along with it the very need for living memory and the first generation. This suggestion is even clearer in the essays that make up Langer's *Admitting the Holocaust*. Here, Langer again expresses the hope that the time may have come for a move towards a greater acceptability of Holocaust fiction, which suggests that in the two decades since the publication of *The Holocaust and the Literary Imagination* this had still not happened, but now Langer is also clearly no longer referring to first-generation writing but to the literature of later generations and, more to the point, to how we read that literature:

> Perhaps [. . .] we have finally begun to enter the second stage of Holocaust response, moving from what we know of the event (the province of histor-ians), to how to remember it, which shifts the responsibility to our own imaginations and what we are prepared to admit there.[69]

While in 1975, in his assertion 'the power of the imagination to evoke an atmosphere does far more than the historian's fidelity to fact to involve the uninitiated reader', Langer had seemed to invest the survivor's 'power of the imagination' with the ability to 'involve the uninitiated reader' (though in retrospect, his phrasing turns out to be ambiguous), he now explicitly credits 'our own imaginations', along with what appears to be our moral courage, our preparedness to 'admit' the worst there, with the ability to bridge what elsewhere he has referred to as 'the vast imaginative space separating what [the survivor] has endured from our capacity to

---

[67] *The Holocaust and the Literary Imagination*, 22; original emphasis.
[68] *The Holocaust and the Literary Imagination*, 296.
[69] *Admitting the Holocaust*, 13.

absorb it'.[70] Again, Langer has not just moved from the response of the first to that of more contemporary generations; he is practically dispensing with the need for the first generation's recollection, and representations, in the first place. This curiously pervasive self-absorption in the study of Holocaust representations, resulting from a preoccupation less with the past itself than with its legacy, manifests itself again and again, in different guises, in the post-Holocaust period and up to the present day. The remaining sections of this chapter will look more closely at the forms this has taken and at how not only our blind spot regarding the first-generation Holocaust novel, but also the enduringly difficult standing of literary Holocaust representations more generally, might be traced back to this preoccupation and to the overwhelming sense of existing in an aftermath that is implicit in it.

THE PAST AS TRACE: POSTMODERNISM

Since the 1990s, a number of Holocaust scholars have asserted that a sea change, such as that called for by Langer in 1975, has finally taken place in the field of Holocaust representation and that debates over the fundamental question of 'representability' have given way to an examination of the different forms in which representation has been attempted. Or as Nicolas Berg, Jess Jochimsen, and Bernd Stiegler state in the prologue to *Formen der Erinnerung* (1996):

> Die Infragestellung der Aussagbarkeit und Tradierbarkeit der Shoah wurde abgelöst durch eine Reflexion über die Darstellungsformen und ihre Voraussetzungen und Konsequenzen. An die Stelle der Problematisierung von Darstellbarkeit überhaupt trat eine Analyse der verschiedenen Formen des Ausgesagten und Dargestellten.[71]

Two apparently separate theoretical approaches informing the field of Holocaust studies in recent decades have individually been credited with enabling this paradigm shift, which tends to be presented as a liberation from the shackles of the 'unsayable' and a vindication of Holocaust fiction. What sets these approaches apart from previous ways of thinking about representation is that they are, at least in theory, each in their own way founded on, and engaged in, an effort to cogitate that tension between the ungraspable excess of an original event and the disruptive but describable

---

[70] *The Holocaust and the Literary Imagination*, 79; *Holocaust Testimonies*, 19.
[71] 'Vorwort', in Berg et al. (eds), *Shoah—Formen der Erinnerung: Geschichte, Philosophie, Literatur, Kunst* (Munich: Fink, 1996), 7–11 (7).

effects of its durational persistence that has been the undoing of other modes of reflecting (on) the Holocaust. In practice, their potential re-habilitation of non-documentary modes of representation notwithstand-ing, both schools of thought, as we shall see, can in fact be regarded as performing a shift in focus away from the cataclysm of the Holocaust as it happened and towards its impact in the present, a shift that is largely analogous to the bracketing of inconceivable catastrophe in favour of measurable fallout that we encounter elsewhere. The theoretical ap-proaches in question are postmodernism—or, more precisely, what Rob-ert Eaglestone has called 'a "postmodern turn" in contemporary thought, focusing on testimony, literature, history, and philosophy'—and trauma theory, specifically the trauma-theoretical turn in recent thinking about memory and the legacy of the Holocaust.[72]

The first of these, postmodernism, especially as informed by decon-structive and post-structuralist thought, is characterized by a general preoccupation with the limits of conceptualization and communicability, and with what falls outside these limits. Postmodernism is concerned with the absence of origin: with how no object or event can ever be known other than through the traces it leaves behind, and how language gives the illusion of presence but can in fact never indicate the 'here and now', because linguistic signs are always already separate from their referent and divided in themselves. Jacques Derrida has coined the term *différance*, meaning simultaneously 'to differ' and 'to defer', in evocation of this process whereby traces arise without an origin, because any 'origin' is itself also already different and deferred.[73] As James Berger describes it:

> *Differance* [...] is the reason the world is the way it is—irremediably non-unitary, divided and differing from itself in every particle, ungraspable in itself and having, as it were, no self to grasp. What is primary and original is *differance*, which cannot be an origin, which is by definition not-present.[74]

In this world, 'no origin will ever be recovered intact; only scattered fossils can be inferred'.[75] These scattered fossils—or traces—are 'a presence that marks an absence', and they are crucial to deconstruction.[76] Trace 'is not one concept or thing because it is outside what concepts can cover or ideas about what "things" are'. Rather, it constitutes 'the disruption of intelli-gibility (it interrupts systems of thought) and the limit of intelligibility (it cannot be described)'. 'It marks the infinite appearing in the finite, the

[72] Eaglestone, *The Holocaust and the Postmodern*, 339.
[73] 'Différance', in *Marges de la philosophie* (Paris: Minuit, 1972), 1–29.
[74] Berger, *After the End*, 111.
[75] Berger, *After the End*, 111.
[76] Eaglestone, *The Holocaust and the Postmodern*, 287.

ethical in the material', and without it, Eaglestone points out, 'deconstruction would be impossible'.[77] The idea of an irrecoverable origin
which manifests itself as trace corresponds closely, at least at a superficial
level, to the sense of that excess in the Holocaust which cannot be
cogitated and integrated into narrative, and which reveals itself as sedi-
ment of the past in the present.

At the same time, deconstruction's dismantling of the illusion created
by language 'that one can tell a true history of events; that events,
understood as discrete occurrences that can be narrated, indeed take
place in the way that language presents them', redeems literary representations of the past.[78] If historical accounts can be regarded as no more
objective or unmediated than any other form of narrative, but rather as
just another 'verbal structure in the form of a narrative prose discourse',
shaped by 'epistemological, aesthetic, and moral' requirements and 'implicit, precritical sanctions', they are no more capable of directly accessing
any 'reality' or 'truth' than any other linguistic construct, including
fiction.[79] This rethinking of historical referentiality emphasizes that
what knowledge we gain of events of the past is entirely dependent on,
and inseparable from, the forms in which it is conveyed to us. As James
Young puts it specifically with reference to the Holocaust: 'None of us
coming to the Holocaust afterwards can know these events outside the
ways they are passed down to us.'[80] Moreover, by considering all narratives equally as constructions of worlds rather than descriptions of 'the
world', and in the process calling into question the notions of authenticity,
faithfulness, or imitation that have so powerfully informed Holocaust
representation debates, this reconfiguration of historical writing theoretically casts fiction not only as a more acceptable but even as the least
deceitful form of representation available to us in that it is the one most
upfront about its fictional status.[81]

What renders the deconstructionist insight into representational relativity problematic in the eyes of some scholars is that inherent in the
hermeneutic approach it encourages is the potential of this becoming a
hermetic view that loses sight of what falls outside narrative framing. As

---

[77] Eaglestone, *The Holocaust and the Postmodern*, 286.

[78] Berger, *After the End*, 111.

[79] Hayden White, *Metahistory: The Historical Imagination in Nineteenth-Century Europe*
(Baltimore: Johns Hopkins University Press, 1973), pp. ix–x.

[80] Young, *Writing and Rewriting the Holocaust*, p. vii.

[81] For proponents of a paradigm shift in Holocaust representation studies inspired by the
notion of representational relativity, see e.g. Hans Otto Horch, 'Edgar Hilsenrath: Provo-
kation der Erinnerungsrituale', in Norbert Otto Eke and Hartmut Steinecke (eds), *Shoah in
der deutschsprachigen Literatur* (Berlin: Schmidt, 2006), 267–73.

Young points out, the question that arises 'if Holocaust narrative is nothing but a system of signs merely referring to other signs' is where that leaves 'the events themselves'.[82] 'Unlimited deconstruction of the Holocaust' comprises 'the hypothetical possibility that events and texts never existed outside each other and that all meanings of events created in different representations are only relative'.[83] Especially in light of the de Man affair, for some scholars, such as David Hirsch, deconstruction stands not for an acknowledgement but for a denial of the Holocaust.[84] Robert Eaglestone, on the other hand, argues that 'deconstruction concerns the relationship between what can be discussed, the text, and the "exorbitant" which lies outside the text but forms its context'.[85] To Eaglestone, postmodernism is not ahistorical; it merely takes issue with the unexamined belief in history as grand narrative.[86] Indeed, Eaglestone proposes that while 'our way of thinking, criticizing, doing history itself, the discourses that our debates inhabit and the horizons which orient these debates, are still striving to respond to the Holocaust', 'postmodern thought, especially that of Emmanuel Levinas and Jacques Derrida or inspired by them, marks the most profound attempt to do this', precisely because it arises out of 'an awareness of "the trace", of that otherness which escapes the limits of systems of thought and language but is made manifest in them'.[87]

Indeed, the emphasis on the trace left by an 'absent referent' in deconstruction echoes so closely the references to an ungraspable excess and durational persistence, or to a black hole and insurmountable caesura, we encounter in survivor testimony, as well as in a great deal of Holocaust scholarship, that it does not seem implausible to consider deconstruction as another, albeit more mediated and belated, reaction that 'stems' from the Holocaust.[88] Dominick LaCapra has suggested: 'Postmodernism can also be defined as post-Holocaust; there's an intricate relation between the two.'[89] Robert Eaglestone proposes that 'postmodernism in the West begins with thinking about the Holocaust', that 'postmodernism—understood as

---

[82] Young, *Writing and Rewriting the Holocaust*, 3.

[83] Young, *Writing and Rewriting the Holocaust*, 3.

[84] *The Deconstruction of Literature: Criticism after Auschwitz* (Hanover, NH: University Press of New England, 1991).

[85] Eaglestone, *The Holocaust and the Postmodern*, 191.

[86] Eaglestone, *The Holocaust and the Postmodern*, 3.

[87] Eaglestone, *The Holocaust and the Postmodern*, 2–3. A similar point is made by Dominick LaCapra in *Representing the Holocaust: History, Theory, Trauma* (Ithaca, NY: Cornell University Press, 1994), 223.

[88] Eaglestone, *The Holocaust and the Postmodern*, 280.

[89] *Writing History, Writing Trauma* (Baltimore: Johns Hopkins University Press, 2001), 179.

poststructuralism, a still developing tradition of post-phenomenological philosophy—is a response to the Holocaust'.[90]

Yet the 'intimate relationship' between postmodernism and 'that great trauma of the twentieth century', does not, at least initially, appear to have been a conscious one on the part of postmodernist theoreticians.[91] Certainly, it was not a connection that was made explicit until many years after the initial rise of postmodernism, and Eaglestone may be closer to the truth when, elsewhere in *The Holocaust and the Postmodern*, he refers to postmodernism not as a deliberate response to the Holocaust but as having 'its roots in the experience of and thought about the Holocaust, though these are often unacknowledged'.[92] As we know, from studies by Eaglestone himself but also by James Berger or Colin Davis, the writing of, for instance, Lévinas and Derrida can be shown to be haunted by the spectres of the Holocaust, right down to a linguistic and structural level.[93] Yet it was two decades after Derrida first developed the concept of trace, in *De la grammatologie* and *L'Écriture et la différence* (1967), before he himself conceded as much by, as it were, updating his vocabulary and proposing, as more precise refigurations of his 'origin' and 'trace', the terms 'Holocaust' and 'ashes', as in the following quotation, in which he refers to himself in the third person:

> J'ai maintenant l'impression que le meilleur paradigme de la trace, pour lui, ce n'est pas, comme certains l'ont cru, et lui aussi peut-être, la piste de chasse, le frayage, le sillon dans le sable, le sillage dans la mer, l'amour du pas pour son empreinte, mais la cendre (ce qui reste sans rester de l'holocauste, du brûle-tout, de l'incendie l'encens).[94]

This belated revision has prompted James Berger to comment that 'poststructuralist theory in the late 1960s and early 1970s (both in France and the United States) [. . .] neglected the Holocaust' and that 'poststructuralism's move toward Holocaust theory' did not take place until the 1980s, coinciding with the return of the Shoah 'to general public consciousness'.[95] However, as Berger points out, 'this neglect of the central, most traumatic violence of the century coincided with a rhetoric that was intensively apocalyptic, filled with invocations of rupture, decentering,

---

[90] Eaglestone, *The Holocaust and the Postmodern*, 2.

[91] Gideon Ofrat, *The Jewish Derrida*, trans. Peretz Kidron (Syracuse, NY: Syracuse University Press, 2001), 152. Cited in Eaglestone, *The Holocaust and the Postmodern*, 280.

[92] Eaglestone, *The Holocaust and the Postmodern*, 340.

[93] For compelling explorations of the Holocaust as trace in post-structuralist writing see Berger, *After the End*; Eaglestone, *The Holocaust and the Postmodern*; and Davis, *Haunted Subjects: Deconstruction, Psychoanalysis and the Return of the Dead* (Basingstoke: Palgrave Macmillan, 2007).

[94] *Feu la cendre* (Paris: Des Femmes, 1987), 27.   [95] Berger, *After the End*, 108.

fragmentation, irretrievably lost identity, the shattering of origins and ends'. The questions Berger consequently sets out to answer are:

> How could a discourse so attuned to rhetorics of obliteration entirely overlook that act of overwhelming obliteration in its still recent past? And why, a decade or so later, did the Holocaust come so suddenly to occupy explicitly a discourse that previously had seemed to describe its violence while not mentioning its name?[96]

The answers Berger comes up with suggest that, ironically for a theory that denies the very possibility of an original event, there does appear to have been a specific trigger to postmodernism, a point of origin it was initially unable to recognize and only gradually came to acknowledge, belatedly struggling to accommodate its unsettling effects on the very theoretical framework to which it first gave rise. Berger concludes that 'the Shoah retrospectively reappears' in the earlier stages of postmodernism 'as an absent, or repressed, historical referent', and that

> the explicit and belated entry of this century's central historical catastrophe into a philosophical discourse characterized by powerful but unspecified imagery of rupture, disintegration, and erasures of history should help us rethink poststructuralism as a post-apocalyptic genre that has begun to remember its catastrophe only in the wake of its fall from grace in the academy.[97]

The terminology in which this view of post-structuralism's belated response to the Holocaust is couched makes this response sound as much symptomatic as analytical. It suggests that the postmodernists' enterprise is one of 'partly work[ing] through and partly act[ing] out the past that haunts them', which is reinforced by Berger's description of specifically Derrida's work as an oeuvre that 'begins in and continually returns to attempts to respond—even by avoiding, disguising, blurring that response—to the most traumatic historical event of Derrida's lifetime'.[98]

While postmodernist theory does provide a framework within which to think about the problems of representation raised by the Holocaust as 'that event that most resists and yet most requires representation', it apparently remains that, far from constituting a move away from the 'Problematisierung von Darstellbarkeit überhaupt', as Berg, Jochimsen, and Stiegler suggested, the stance adopted by postmodernism merely shifts the focus from the impossibility of representing the event itself to a reflection on that impossibility and to the epistemologies of our (post-Holocaust)

---

[96] Berger, *After the End*, 107.   [97] Berger, *After the End*, pp. 108, xvii.
[98] Berger, *After the End*, pp. xv, 130.

present.[99] The Holocaust is thus essentially recast as marking an epistemological crisis for those who come to it afterwards, as 'a traumatic breach in our uncritical belief in the kinds of knowledge we have of it'.[100]

THE PAST AS SYMPTOM: TRAUMA THEORY

The other development in literary scholarship, which has even more recently been credited with valorizing fictional representations of the Holocaust and bringing about a paradigm shift in the question of 'Darstellbarkeit', is trauma theory.[101] Trauma studies first emerged in 1980, when post-traumatic stress disorder came to be recognized as a separate diagnostic category, owing largely to the efforts of Vietnam veterans campaigning to raise awareness of the consequences of the war and the psychological effects of combat. By the early 1990s, scholars of trauma had begun to recognize the interdisciplinary import of their field, and the emphasis in trauma studies started to shift from the medical and scientific evaluation and cataloguing of the symptoms of trauma to the exploration of its cultural and ethical implications, at which point trauma theory also became of interest to literary studies.

In many respects, the implications of trauma-theoretical conceptions for the documentation of traumatic events closely recall postmodernist conclusions about representation. As Ana Douglass and Thomas A. Vogler have argued: 'The traumatic event bears a striking similarity to the always absent signified or referent of the poststructuralist discourse, an object that can by definition only be construed retroactively, never observed directly.'[102] Dominick LaCapra makes a similar point in proposing that the other way of formulating the view that 'postmodernism can also be defined as post-Holocaust' is 'to see the post-Holocaust in terms of the post-traumatic'.[103] Trauma theorists believe that trauma is characterized principally by the fact that it does not register, or, more precisely, registers only as a lacuna, at the moment of its initial occurrence, or as Dori Laub states in terms reminiscent of those used by Lyotard in his earthquake analogy: 'Massive trauma precludes its registration; the observing and recording mechanisms of the human mind are temporarily knocked out,

---

[99] Berger, *After the End*, p. xvii.
[100] Young, *Writing and Rewriting the Holocaust*, 98.
[101] See e.g. Bos, *German-Jewish Literature in the Wake of the Holocaust*.
[102] Douglass and Vogler (eds), *Witness and Memory: The Discourse of Trauma* (New York and London: Routledge, 2003), 5.
[103] *Writing History, Writing Trauma*, 179.

malfunction.'[104] In consequence, trauma is experienced only belatedly, when it returns in flashbacks, hallucinations, or dreams to haunt its sufferers, who thus do not possess the traumatic event to recall and relate at will but are themselves possessed by it. The pathology of trauma is therefore not the result of a particular type of event but the product of 'the *structure of its experience* or reception'.[105] The absent origin in postmodernism, which manifests itself through trace, becomes a mental lacuna in trauma theory and manifests itself as symptoms. Like the origin in deconstruction, the source of the trauma is held by trauma theorists to resist narrativization. Bessel A. van der Kolk and Onno van der Hart, for instance, assert that traumatic experience 'is not transformed into a story, placed in time, with a beginning, a middle and an end (which is characteristic for narrative memory)'.[106] In terms that again echo vocabulary favoured by deconstructionists, Laub expands on what makes trauma fall outside narrative sequence:

> The traumatic event, although real, took place outside the parameters of 'normal' reality, such as causality, sequence, place and time. The trauma is thus an event that has no beginning, no ending, no before, no during and no after. This absence of categories that define it lends it a quality of 'otherness', a salience, a timelessness and a ubiquity that puts it outside the range of associatively linked experiences, outside the range of comprehension, of recounting and of mastery.[107]

However, unlike postmodernists, or indeed the survivors and a number of scholars of the Holocaust, trauma theorists do not consider the origin of trauma to be inherently and permanently inaccessible. They relate its incomprehensibility and resultant incommunicability to the breakdown of witnessing suffered by its victims during the original traumatic occurrence, and they believe that, with the help of a listener, a witness to their disrupted testimony, sufferers may be able belatedly to restore the traumatic event to the order of narrative and be 'cured'. Thus, while postmodernists perceive the silence imposed by the Holocaust as a sign that 'quelque chose reste à phraser qui ne l'est pas' and, moreover, 'ne peut pas l'être dans les idiomes admis', trauma theorists argue that theirs

---

[104] Shoshana Felman and Dori Laub, *Testimony: Crises of Witnessing in Literature, Psychoanalysis, and History* (New York: Routledge, 1992), 57.
[105] Cathy Caruth, 'Introduction', in Caruth (ed.), *Trauma: Explorations in Memory* (Baltimore: Johns Hopkins University Press, 1995), 3–12 (4); original emphasis.
[106] 'The Intrusive Past: The Flexibility of Memory and the Engraving of Trauma', in Caruth (ed.), *Trauma: Explorations in Memory*, 158–82 (177).
[107] Felman and Laub, *Testimony*, 69.

is a more productive understanding of the 'record that has yet to be made'.[108]

While postmodernism regards the Holocaust as having irreversibly undermined conventional epistemologies, such as the unconditional belief in a historical master narrative, Cathy Caruth suggests that in the encounter with trauma 'we can begin to recognize the possibility of a history that is no longer straightforwardly referential (that is, no longer based on simple models of experience and reference)', and that through the notion of trauma we can therefore 'understand that a rethinking of reference is aimed not at eliminating history but at resituating it in our understanding, that is, at precisely permitting *history* to arise where *immediate understanding* may not'.[109] The implication of this 'Wiedereinführung des Historischen über die Unmöglichkeit der Repräsentation', as Birgit Erdle puts it, for the evolving view of the Holocaust as caesura is then picked up by Sigrid Weigel, who elaborates:

> Nicht um die *Störung* des Geschichtsbegriffs durch die Einsicht in die Unmöglichkeit eines unmittelbaren Verstehens geht es, sondern Geschichte entspringt dort und nur dort, wo ein unmittelbares Verstehen ausgeschlossen ist. Das impliziert eine Inversion jener Betrachtungsweise des Schnitts, der Zäsur, des Einbruchs oder der Störung, wie sie vor allem im europäischen Kontext eines 'Denkens nach Auschwitz' bei Adorno bzw. einer 'Posthistoire' in der Nach-Geschichte der Shoah z.B. bei Lyotard, Derrida, Lévinas und Kofman erscheint.[110]

This explains why trauma theorists feel that their take on the Holocaust as caesura has been able to bring about the paradigm shift ascribed to, but not achieved by, postmodern views of representation, as we see, for example, in Weigel's statement that trauma theory has come 'die Philosophie über das Schweigen, über die Lücke und die Zäsur durch Lektüren und Deutungen der diskursiven und literarischen Erinnerungen und der vielfältigen Symbolisierungsweisen im Gedächtnis der Nachgeschichte abzulösen'.[111]

Again, however, I would argue that what we encounter here is not an 'Ablösung' but simply a displacement of the philosophy of silences and caesuras. As I suggested was the case with deconstruction, trauma theory

---

[108] Lyotard, *Le Différend*, 91; Laub, in Felman and Laub, *Testimony*, 57.

[109] *Unclaimed Experience: Trauma, Narrative, and History* (Baltimore: Johns Hopkins University Press, 1996), 11; original emphasis.

[110] Erdle, 'Die Verführung der Parallelen: Zu Übertragungsverhältnissen zwischen Ereignis, Ort und Zitat', in Bronfen et al. (eds), *Trauma*, 27–50 (30). Weigel, 'Téléscopage im Unbewußten: Zum Verhältnis von Trauma, Geschichtsbegriff und Literatur', in Bronfen et al. (eds), *Trauma*, 51–76 (54); original emphasis.

[111] 'Téléscopage im Unbewußten', in Bronfen et al. (eds), *Trauma*, 71.

focuses much and, as time passes, ever more of its attention on post-Holocaust generations, as becomes apparent even from the Weigel reference just cited to the 'Gedächtnis der Nachgeschichte'. To an extent, this is inevitable, given that the recasting of the Holocaust as trauma automatically positions it within a continuum—while at the same time supposedly preserving its status as an epistemological breach and limit-event—by providing a category within which to think of the Holocaust as simply another, albeit extreme, crisis in a long list of crises constituting a 'Narrativ verketteter Dekonstruktivitäten und vervielfältigter Zivilisationsbrüche'.[112] As Erdle explains:

> Über eine Universalisierung des Traumas läßt sich demnach ein Kontinuum stiften, ein Kontinuum menschlicher Destruktivität und katastrophischer Einbrüche—also gerade das, was das Trauma radikal zunichte macht. Das so gestiftete Kontinuum ist aber nicht (mehr) im Sinn einer *longue durée* zu verstehen, sondern es stellt eher ein Netz von Symmetrien oder Ähnlichkeiten dar. [. . .] Auschwitz ist in diesem Netz lose assoziiert, gewissermaßen zu einem Extremfall unter Extremfällen geworden [. . .]. Dies deutet auf eine paradoxe Denkfigur: einerseits ist der Holocaust in dieser Konzeption zum Paradigma *der* Geschichte des 20. Jahrhunderts geworden, um aber andererseits aufgelöst zu werden in der Universalisierung, die über den Trauma-Begriff möglich wird.[113]

However, in addition to this universalization already partly inherent in a concept that cannot be defined by the content of the events that trigger it, trauma theory dilutes the 'Extremfall' of the Holocaust further still by concentrating on its after-effects on contemporary society almost to the exclusion of the trauma's origin and the very unnarratable excess in it that renders it traumatic. Indicative of this is, for example, the recent surge in popularity of the work of psychoanalysts Nicolas Abraham and Maria Torok, which has been (re)discovered and appropriated by trauma theory and also literary studies. Revealingly, the main focus in this has not been on Abraham and Torok's work on primary traumatization but on their essay collection *L'Écorce et le noyau*, which explores the possibility of a transgenerational transmission of trauma through the concept of the *fantôme*. *Fantômes*, according to Abraham and Torok, are the ghosts of deceased ancestors come to haunt their descendants not as spirits as such but in the shape of the lacunae left in later generations by the unresolved traumas of previous ones, causing symptoms that derive not from the

---

[112] Erdle, 'Die Verführung der Parallelen', in Bronfen et al. (eds), *Trauma*, 30.
[113] 'Die Verführung der Parallelen', in Bronfen et al. (eds), *Trauma*, 31–2; original emphasis.

individual's own life experience but from somebody else's.[114] Sigrid
Weigel, for instance, has taken 'Abrahams Hinweis auf die Phantome
und Vergegenständlichungen als Form, in der sich das Unausgesprochene,
die Familiengeheimnisse und die "Lücke im Aussprechbaren" bei den
nachfolgenden Generationen fortsetzen' as a sign of it being time for the
paradigm of the unspeakable in writing about the Holocaust to be
abolished.[115]

The attraction of Abraham and Torok's phantom theory to contemporary scholarship resides in its broadening of the application of trauma to
include those who suffer from it vicariously and secondarily. Yet this
broadening appeals not because it promises to ensure that the absent-
present memory of the Holocaust will be preserved even when, not many
years from now, every last survivor will have passed away, but, on the
contrary, because it offers a view of the Holocaust in which, increasingly,
what matters is no longer its original unintelligibility, which, in fact,
remains undisputed, but only its present transmittability, and with it,
the possibility of continuity and even a (pseudo-)cure. Indeed, the concept
of traumatic transmission is taken far beyond the idea of a secondary
traumatization of the survivors' descendants proposed by Abraham and
Torok. The notion that it is possible to be traumatized indirectly is
extended further to include, for instance, the listeners to or readers of
trauma testimony. Laub states that 'for the testimonial process to take
place, there needs to be a bonding, the intimate and total presence of an
other—in the position of one who hears', and that, in consequence of this
bonding, 'the listener to trauma comes to be a participant and a co-owner
of the traumatic event: through his very listening, he comes to partially
experience trauma himself'.[116] This, in turn, echoes an assertion by
Lawrence Langer, who proposed that 'a statement like "to understand,
you have to go through with it," however authentic its inspiration,
underestimates the sympathetic power of the imagination' and suggested
that 'perhaps it is time to grant that power the role it deserves'.[117] While
empathy is without a doubt an important quality in a witness to testimony, especially in a clinical setting where it becomes 'a desirable affective
dimension of inquiry which complements and supplements empirical
research and analysis', this stance risks bringing about the kind of dubious

---

[114] *L'Écorce et le noyau* (Paris: Flammarion, 1978).
[115] 'Téléscopage im Unbewußten', in Bronfen et al. (eds), *Trauma*, 71. For very similar
reasons, the idea of transgenerational trauma is also important to postcolonial studies. For
an application of Abraham and Torok to postcolonial fiction see e.g. Erica L. Johnson,
'Unforgetting Trauma: Dionne Brand's Haunted Histories', *Anthurium: A Caribbean
Studies Journal*, 2 (2004), 1–14.
[116] Felman and Laub, *Testimony*, 70–1, 57.   [117] *Holocaust Testimonies*, p. xv.

scenario outlined by Dominick LaCapra in which the secondary witness comes to 'identify with the victim' to the extent of making himself or herself 'a surrogate victim who has a right to the victim's voice or subject position'.[118] Kalí Tal has made a similar point more forcefully about Felman and Laub, in whose work, she argues, 'the survivor's experience has been completely replaced by the experience of those who come in contact with the survivor's testimony—an appropriative gambit of stunning proportions'.[119] Increasingly, or increasingly overtly, the crisis of witnessing experienced by survivors of the Holocaust is being displaced in trauma theory by a focus on the recipients of testimony. Even LaCapra's own writing is not entirely free of this impulse. Though evidently highly critical of the tendency towards 'surrogate victimage', he does speak of the historian or empathetic observer as a 'secondary witness' who through the act of 'testimonial witnessing' may belatedly gain 'secondary memory' and even experience 'transmission of the traumatic nature of the event', albeit 'not a full reliving or acting out of it'.[120]

Again close in effect, if not in intention, to the *post factum* epistemological crisis proclaimed by postmodernism, such displacement suggests a view of contemporary culture in its entirety as living in a post-apocalyptic, post-traumatic age in which, as Ruth Klüger has put it: 'alle, die nach Auschwitz leben, vor allem die, die in westlichen Ländern leben, Auschwitz in ihrer, in Europas Geschichte haben, so daß wir alle, selbst die Nachgeborenen, gewissermaßen Überlebende des Holocaust sind'.[121] Not only has the concept of trauma generally been watered down to the point where it has become almost evacuated of meaning in recent years, but the trauma of specifically the Holocaust appears to have become something of a free-for-all. If we are all survivors of the Holocaust, then any distinction between those who lived through it and those who live after it, even between perpetrators and victims, dissolves at the ill-defined site of what everyone alive today supposedly has in common: the trauma of history; history as trauma. LaCapra picks up on this tendency in trauma theory to equate history or culture in their entirety with trauma and to generalize the category of the survivor, and he refers to trauma as 'an occasion for rash amalgamations or conflations (for example, in the idea that contemporary culture, or even all history, is essentially traumatic or

---

[118] *Writing History, Writing Trauma*, 78.
[119] *Worlds of Hurt: Reading the Literature of Trauma* (New York: Cambridge University Press, 1996), 53–4.
[120] *History and Memory after Auschwitz* (Ithaca, NY: Cornell University Press, 1998), 182, 11, 20–1.
[121] *Von hoher und niedriger Literatur* (Göttingen: Wallstein, 1996), 31.

that everyone in the post-Holocaust context is a survivor)'.[122] In a similar vein, Ruth Leys has criticized about Cathy Caruth's work in particular that 'in her account the experience (or nonexperience) of trauma is characterized as something that can be shared by victims and nonvictims alike, and the unbearable sufferings of the survivor as a pathos that can and must be appropriated by others'.[123] Others have argued, with reference particularly to Germany, that the blurring of victim and perpetrator positions entailed by a non-specific approach to trauma accommodates Germans who hope that trauma might somehow come to take the place of the 'negative symbiosis', which still defines German–Jewish relations, by enabling 'die Stiftung eines gemeinsamen Ortes, der aus der Position der Nachträglichkeit begründet wird', or even that it might bring about an 'Umschuldung', a 'Tausch der Positionen von "Opfern" und "Tätern"'.[124]

The dubiousness of, and the problems arising from, an indiscriminate application of the concept of trauma are undeniable, yet while it would be hard to argue with the various objections just cited, what they fail to address is that the unreflecting usage of the term trauma to denote also (and increasingly above all) secondary and indirect psychological disturbances—the uncritical equation, in other words, of the term trauma with Abraham and Torok's *fantôme*—is not proof of an inherent flaw in the concept of trauma as much as an indication that, in attending not to the original trauma of the Holocaust but only to its secondary symptoms, trauma theory is apparently attempting to enact and 'work through' a displaced version of the patterns of post-traumatic repetition that affect its analysands. What has come to be trauma theory's main preoccupation, the lacunae left in an individual by Abraham and Torok's phantoms, is, evidently, not the same as the original non-experience of an overwhelmingly traumatic situation, as Weigel implies in the conclusion of her article by raising the question 'ob jene obsessiven und phantomatischen Formen, in denen sich die traumatischen Erinnerungen und die Lücken im Gedächtnis der vorausgegangenen Generation bei den Heutigen fortzeugen, noch als Variante des Traumas zu fassen sind?'[125] What Abraham and Torok's *fantômes* stand for is the return of the repressed: the haunting of the analysand by the traumas and troubling experiences of which his or her ancestors never spoke, but which were nonetheless in the air and have left their mark in the analysand as perceived shameful, unmentionable secrets.

---

[122] *Writing History, Writing Trauma*, p. x.
[123] *Trauma: A Genealogy* (Chicago: University of Chicago Press, 2000), 305.
[124] Erdle, 'Die Verführung der Parallelen', in Bronfen et al. (eds), *Trauma*, 32, 43.
[125] 'Téléscopage im Unbewußten', in Bronfen et al. (eds), *Trauma*, 76.

Unlike the spirits of traditional ghost stories, the *fantômes* then consider it their task not to reveal something hidden or forgotten but actively to prevent the secrets of the past from coming to light.[126] Contrary to the never-known traumatic event itself, these secrets can, and in Abraham and Torok's opinion should, be restored to knowledge by the analysand. Once this takes place and the secrets have been narrated and thus dispelled, the patient is cured. As Colin Davis explains:

> The secrets of Abraham and Torok's lying phantoms are unspeakable in the restricted sense of being a subject of shame and prohibition. It is not at all that they cannot be spoken; on the contrary, they can and should be put into words so that the phantom and its noxious effects on the living can be exorcised.[127]

This is precisely what trauma theory appears to have been attempting to do, by embarking on something akin to a talking cure designed to work through not the original trauma but the after-effects it has had on contemporary society. The *fantômes* are not the same as the trauma that originally gave trauma theory its name, and trauma theory's focus on them is tantamount not to an analysis but to a displacement of trauma proper. This, as a result, comes to occupy a very similar position in trauma theory to that of the original caesura in the postmodernist view of the Holocaust. It becomes a spectre that haunts the writing of trauma theorists without its essence being touched on, and trauma theory's assertions of the potential inherent in the 'report yet to be made' are overshadowed by its overriding concern for its own response. Unlike postmodernism, however, trauma theory draws attention to the Holocaust as 'absent referent' not by emphasizing its inaccessibility but, on the contrary, by the very fact that it attempts to 'overcode the accounts of the Holocaust with a discourse of healing analysis or therapy' and to cover the gaps in its own knowledge by means of inappropriately and misleadingly precise terms to refer to the incomprehensible excess that in fact eludes its grasp.[128] Cathy Caruth, for example, says with reference to trauma: 'And it is, indeed, at the *specific* point at which knowing and not knowing intersect that the language of literature and the psychoanalytic theory of traumatic experience *precisely* meet', though there is nothing specific or precise about that

---

[126] For an excellent study on 'hauntology', including a chapter on Abraham and Torok's phantoms and how they differ not only from 'conventional' ghosts but also from the spectres of deconstruction, see Davis, *Haunted Subjects*, esp. the chapter on 'Lying Ghosts in Deconstruction and Psychoanalysis', 66–92.

[127] Davis, *Haunted Subjects*, 13.

[128] Eaglestone, *The Holocaust and the Postmodern*, 33.

site whatsoever.[129] As LaCapra has pointed out, with reference to Caruth's application of trauma theory to the literary, 'the language of literary theory [...] itself seems to repeat, whether consciously or unconsciously, the disconcertingly opaque movement of post-traumatic repetition in a seeming attempt to elucidate that movement'.[130]

This displacement of the trauma of the Holocaust in favour of a focus on the secondary witnesses' afflictions—the descendants' phantoms or the transference of trauma to the listener of testimony—highlights how the Holocaust, despite psychoanalysis's categorization of it as just another, if extreme, trauma, in fact differs from other kinds of traumatic events, where a 'cure' of post-traumatic stress disorder in the survivor himself or herself is conceivable in trauma theory. With trauma as it is generally defined, the reality of the event is thought to be encrypted within the mind of the survivor. Psychoanalysis holds that while this reality is blocked off from the traumatized, it can be accessed and decrypted by a witness to their testimony such as a psychiatrist. Abraham and Torok's other important work, *Cryptonymie: Le Verbier de l'homme aux loups*, a reworking of Freud's 'Wolfsmann' case study from 'Aus der Geschichte einer infantilen Neurose', which in this respect would be more apposite to thinking about the trauma of the Holocaust than their concept of *fantôme*, puts forward the concept of the *crypte* as a site in the analysand's mind where unremembered and unarticulated experience of his or her own resides inaccessibly to the analysand himself or herself. In Abraham and Torok's theory, the encrypted experience may manifest itself in *cryptonymes*, linguistic indicators that allude to the crypts without unlocking them, and which are described by Abraham and Torok as 'des mots qui cachent' by means of which the analysand engages in the process of 'le dire sans le dire', 'montrer-cacher', and 'promener un rébus et le donner comme indéchiffrable'.[131] While the analysand himself or herself is incapable of entering the crypt, the analyst is not, in Abraham and Torok's view. Indeed, they append a detailed dictionary to their study of possible interpretations of the wolfman's cryptonyms. Yet from trauma theory's bracketing of the traumatic event of the Holocaust in favour of a concentration on the phantoms of the past in the present, it would appear that such a cure does not seem possible, at least not within its own theoretical

---

[129] *Unclaimed Experience*, 3; my emphasis. For the insight into the extensive use of the words 'precisely' and 'paradoxically' as possible 'marker or trace of post-traumatic effects that may not be sufficiently worked through' in the writing of both Caruth and Felman, I am indebted to LaCapra's *Writing History, Writing Trauma*, 106.
[130] *Writing History, Writing Trauma*, 184.
[131] *Cryptonymie: Le Verbier de l'homme aux loups* (Paris: Aubier Flammarion, 1976), 115, 122.

framework, when it comes to the Holocaust. As was the case with postmodernism, the Holocaust might be viewed as an unacknowledged 'proto-trauma' for contemporary trauma studies. Certainly, it serves its theorists as an archetype and yardstick while at the same time appearing as 'a historical irreducible that tests and disrupts their previous theorizing'.[132]

THE PAST AS LEGACY: 'POST-MEMORY'

Whether we think of the continual bracketing of event in favour of after-effect—of origin in favour of trace or of trauma in favour of symptom—since the post-war period as the product of a (secondary and displaced) 'movement of post-traumatic repetition' or find a different conceptual framework for it, it remains that the concern 'less with the past than with a sense of that past in the present' is not exclusive to the traumatized survivors.[133] The earlier discussion of literary-theoretical, postmodernist, and trauma-theoretical contributions to Holocaust studies suggests that a preoccupation with the present as aftermath, in the form of a sense of coming after an always-already-absent origin, has become the cornerstone of our contemporary responses to the Holocaust. If trauma theory in some respect appears as a rejoinder to postmodernism, and an attempt to overcome some of its theoretical aporias, in particular that of referentiality, what it has in common with the postmodernist reaction to the Holocaust is the importance it attaches to this sense of afterwardsness or belatedness. Not only are both postmodernism and trauma theory founded on notions of deferral that, for all the ways in which both theories have abandoned Freud, are heavily informed by the mechanism of *Nachträglichkeit*—the retroactive logic of which subverts causality and denies the primacy of an originary moment—but as a result of this they have come to rehabilitate belatedness to the point where, especially in trauma theory, it appears as a position of privilege and as paradoxically original. As we have seen, in recent developments in trauma theory, such as the rapidly growing interest in the effects of transgenerational transmission of trauma, belatedness is now commonly regarded as a vantage point from which the secondary witness to primary testimony is supposedly able to gain an understanding of the event that eluded the primary witness.

Owing not least to the influence of these trauma-theoretical developments, the concentration on, and importance attached to, the notion of 'coming after' has in recent years also been highly visible at a broader social

[132] Berger, *After the End*, p. xvii.
[133] LaCapra, *Writing History, Writing Trauma*, 184; Langer, *Holocaust Testimonies*, 40.

and cultural level. Here, the shift in focus from the experience of trauma
and latency in the first generation to the belatedness and traumatic legacy
of its descendants has manifested itself in the form of a displacement of
memory by what Marianne Hirsch has called 'postmemory': as an ever-
growing interest in the experience of, and literature by, 'postmemorial'
generations, as well as an increasing investment in what these may be in a
position to achieve.[134] Under the sway of modern-day trauma theory, an
entire collective identity has been constructed around the sense of suffering from the condition of 'coming after', from living in the shadow of the
Holocaust without having lived through or even during it. Eva Hoffman,
herself the daughter of Polish Holocaust survivors, speaks of 'a sort of
relief' provided by the realization 'that there were others for whom a
Holocaust inheritance was both meaningful and problematic; that living
with it was a palpable enough experience to be overtly recognizable; that it
was in fact an experience; and that, in some way, it counted'.[135] She
describes the second generation as being haunted by what it did not
witness, and does not know, directly:

> The paradoxes of indirect knowledge haunt many of us who came after. The
> formative events of the twentieth century have crucially informed our
> biographies and psyches, threatening sometimes to overshadow and over-
> whelm our own lives. But we did not see them, suffer through them,
> experience their impact directly. Our relationship to them has been defined
> by our very 'post-ness', and by the powerful but mediated forms of know-
> ledge that have followed from it.[136]

Yet, as we have seen, the condition of 'post-ness' tends to be extended well
beyond the offspring of survivors. Not only these immediate descendants
but all of us in the Western hemisphere may be felt to exist in a post-
apocalyptic, post-traumatic age, defined by an earlier generation's experience to which we can only respond indirectly and belatedly. What started
out as a primary trauma that was having a secondarily traumatic effect on
those closest to the survivors has now apparently become vicariously
traumatic for those whose lives it has not affected at all: as a result not
of the (immediate or belated) impact it has had, but of the impact it never
will have. In other words, while for the survivor generation, and indirectly
its descendants, the experience that keeps returning in the present is
that of unintegratable persecution, loss, and suffering, what is apparently

---

[134] *Family Frames: Photography, Narrative, and Postmemory* (Cambridge, MA: Harvard University Press, 1997).
[135] Eva Hoffman, *After Such Knowledge: A Meditation on the Aftermath of the Holocaust* (London: Vintage, 2005), 27; original emphasis.
[136] Hoffman, *After Such Knowledge*, 25.

unintegratable for the rest of us is the absence of such an experience. At the same time, as has happened in trauma theory, the seemingly incurable condition of belatedness has come to be rehabilitated: the disadvantaged position of 'coming after', and being excluded from immediate knowledge, is being transformed into an asset and is even becoming exclusive. In the course of this development, first-hand knowledge of events is increasingly not only being supplemented with but being supplanted by an emphasis on the 'power' of the 'mediated forms of knowledge' of the past referred to by Hoffman. This becomes very clear if we look at the evolving definition of the concept of 'postmemory', which goes back to Marianne Hirsch:

> Thus postmemory characterizes the experience of those who [...] have grown up dominated by narratives that preceded their birth, whose own belated stories are displaced by the powerful stories of the previous generation, shaped by monumental traumatic events that resist understanding and integration.[137]

This is not Hirsch's original definition but a reworded later one, and the changes she has made are particularly interesting in this context. For one thing, Hirsch has softened her early assessment of the power of the 'stories of the previous generation' over the 'belated stories' of the 'postmemory' age by substituting 'displaced' for what originally read 'evacuated'.[138] Hirsch's rewording of the end of the sentence redresses the power balance further still. In the original definition, the traumatic events that shape the belated stories of the 'postmemory' generations 'can be neither understood nor recreated'.[139] In the 2001 article, there is a clear suggestion that such a recreation may take place even while the events themselves remain resistant to understanding: by means of the imagination. The importance of the imagination in the 'postmemorial' relationship to the past was already stressed in *Family Frames*, where we are told: 'Postmemory is a powerful [...] form of memory precisely because its connection to its object or its

---

[137] 'Surviving Images: Holocaust Photographs and the Work of Postmemory', in Barbie Zelizer (ed.), *Visual Culture and the Holocaust* (London: Athlone, 2001), 214–46 (221). It is not at all my intention here to detract from the potential inherent in the concept of 'postmemory' when it is applied in consideration of its limitations. Both that potential and its restrictions have been comprehensively and convincingly discussed elsewhere. See e.g. J. J. Long, 'Monika Maron's *Pawels Briefe*: Photography, Narrative, and the Claims of Postmemory', in Anne Fuchs, Mary Cosgrove, and Georg Grote (eds), *German Memory Contests: The Quest for Identity in Literature, Film, and Discourse since 1990* (Rochester, NY: Camden House, 2006), 147–65; Anne Fuchs, *Phantoms of War in Contemporary German Literature, Films and Discourse: The Politics of Memory* (Basingstoke: Palgrave Macmillan, 2008), esp. ch. 3.

[138] *Family Frames*, 22.   [139] *Family Frames*, 22.

source is mediated not through recollection but through imaginative
investment and creation.'[140] 'Surviving Images' goes beyond this to propose that not only can the absence of recollection be compensated for, but
that it is in fact an advantage: that it is only in mediated form, and
therefore only in the 'postmemorial' generation, that the past can be
witnessed and even healed:

> If indeed one of the signs of trauma is its delayed recognition, if trauma is
> recognizable only through its aftereffects, then it is not surprising that it is
> transmitted across generations. Perhaps it is *only* in subsequent generations
> that trauma can be witnessed and worked through, by those who were not
> there to live it but who received its effects, belatedly, through the narratives,
> actions, and symptoms of the previous generation.[141]

We find a similar hope expressed in a number of other critical studies, all
of which place their faith in the potential of our 'imaginative investment'
to mend ruptures and restore continuity. In Erin McGlothlin's insightful
examination of the Holocaust novel in the second generation, the survivors' descendants are credited with the ability to 'provide a referent for
the signifier of traumatic effect'.[142] Efraim Sicher suggests, with reference
specifically to American-Jewish 'postmemorial' authors, though his obser-
vations are more generally applicable, that they are

> in effect attempting a rescue of memory, and in the return to a past which
> they have not experienced they are reconstructing their biographies and life
> histories in narratives of identity which can then be transmitted to the next
> generation. Their return journey, real or imagined, confronts the past in
> order to do the necessary mourning for working-through.[143]

The 'postmemorial' generation is invested with the power to mend the
memory chain that is felt to have ruptured with the Holocaust generation,
but its 'return' is to a past that never existed outside its members'
imagination and its 'rescue' of memory seems to be achieved at the cost
of excising the first generation and its recollections from the histories
created for transmission.

Since the 1970s, but peaking in the 1990s and at the beginning of this
century, such investment in, and absorption by, those who 'come after' to
the detriment of those who came first has, at its extreme, fostered what
David Cesarani, after Hasia Diner, has called the 'myth of silence': the

---

[140] *Family Frames*, 22.   [141] 'Surviving Images', 222; original emphasis.
[142] *Second-Generation Holocaust Literature: Legacies of Survival and Perpetration* (Rochester, NY: Camden House, 2006), 55.
[143] 'The Future of the Past: Countermemory and Postmemory in Contemporary American Post-Holocaust Narratives', *History & Memory*, 12 (2000), 56–91 (70).

'comfortable consensus' that up to that point, there had been widespread reluctance, including among survivors, to engage, in whatever form, with the events of the recent past and that, as a result, 'the years 1945 to 1970 were a desert as far as testimony, memoirs, historiography, films and other forms of representation were concerned'.[144] In this view, members of the 'postmemorial' generation step into the breach and do what their ancestors could not. The vocabulary used to describe their valiant efforts and potential for 'working through' ranges, as we see, for instance, in the Sicher comment quoted earlier, from the hopeful and uplifting to the redemptive and even heroicizing. This could be seen as indicative of a desire on the part of the 'postmemorial' generation to be cured of the traumatic effects of the past if not, in fact, of the traumatic past itself. Again, the displacement in focus from event to legacy suggests an underlying sense of ongoing traumatization, of something having remained unresolved, in the shape of the belief that the past is inherited by the post-traumatic generation 'in the form of traumatic repetition' and can be accessed 'only through the constant replay, or, more accurately, reimagining, of traumatic events', as Mary Cosgrove has described it with reference to W. G. Sebald.[145] This lack, or impossibility, of resolution may be the result of vicarious traumatization by an earlier generation's experiences, as, for instance, Andreas Huyssen proposes in his reading of Sebald's *Luftkrieg und Literatur* essay as 'a kind of secondary traumatic repetition'.[146] If, however, we read the unsettling legacy as consisting not in another's traumatic experience but in the absence of such experience, then the desire for a cure for the 'postmemorial' condition may, paradoxically, be a desire for more, rather than less, suffering, a thesis on which Gary Weissman has founded his thought-provoking study *Fantasies of Witnessing*.[147] At its most extreme, the displacement and appropriation of the original victims' history and memories might be the result not of a

---

[144] 'Introduction', in Cesarani and Eric J. Sundquist (eds), *After the Holocaust: Challenging the Myth of Silence* (London and New York: Routledge, 2012), 1–14 (1, 4). For his terminology, Cesarani is in turn drawing on Hasia R. Diner, *We Remember with Reverence and Love: American Jews and the Myth of Silence after the Holocaust, 1945–1962* (New York: New York University Press, 2009).

[145] 'Melancholy Competitions: W. G. Sebald Reads Günter Grass and Wolfgang Hildesheimer', *German Life and Letters*, 59 (2006), 217–32 (221).

[146] 'On Rewritings and New Beginnings: W. G. Sebald and the Literature about the *Luftkrieg*', *Zeitschrift für Literaturwissenschaft und Linguistik*, 124 (2001), 72–90 (83).

[147] *Fantasies of Witnessing: Postwar Efforts to Experience the Holocaust* (Ithaca, NY: Cornell University Press, 2004). On the subject of Holocaust envy and vicarious victimhood, and on how these are encouraged by the way in which 'popular culture products incite audiences to engage in fantasies of witnessing the pain of others', see also Anne Rothe, *Popular Trauma Culture: Selling the Pain of Others in the Mass Media* (New Brunswick, NJ: Rutgers University Press, 2011), 6.

desire to be closer to and better understand them, but to 'be' them and better them, or it might fall somewhere in between the two on the scale between staking a claim of proximity and one of proxy.

Whether the cause is over- or under-exposure to an earlier generation's trauma, resulting either in secondary traumatization or in a particular form of victim envy, born, perhaps, of the feeling 'that we do not have our own history, that we are secondary not only chronologically but, so to speak, ontologically', and manifested in suggestions that 'postmemory' may be a better response to, and receptacle for, the traumatic past than memory, the displacement of memory by 'postmemory' may go a long way towards explaining our blind spot for the 'original' Holocaust novel.[148] Maybe, then, it is not that we are suspicious of the imaginary because we equate it with the fictitious where Holocaust writing in the first generation is concerned, but that, on the contrary, we on some level consider access to the past through the imagination to be the prerogative of those who come after and that this renders us unwilling, or unable, fully to consider its role in the generation in which it appears conjoined with experience.

'A REAL FICTITIOUS DISCOURSE': THE HOLOCAUST NOVEL IN THE FIRST GENERATION

The neglect of the first-generation Holocaust novel resulting from our focus on the nature and status of our own belated response is compounded by the fact that the response we encounter in these first fictional texts is not only early but in a number of respects ahead of its time. For one thing, the authors in question were writing Holocaust fiction not just before such a category had been designated, and before debates over the fundamental representability of the Holocaust were under way, but before the events themselves had even entered public consciousness and parlance as 'the Holocaust'. At the same time, these first-generation authors were already demonstrating an acute awareness of their own 'afterwardsness': a sense that their own experience of the past was not as complete as that of those who did not survive and that even as members of the first generation they were therefore going to lead the rest of their lives in the shadow of an event of which they could never have comprehensive first-hand, unmediated knowledge. As Primo Levi famously put it:

---

[148] Hoffman, *After Such Knowledge*, 28.

we are those who by their prevarications or abilities or good luck did not touch bottom. Those who did so, those who saw the Gorgon, have not returned to tell about it or have returned mute, but they are [. . .] the complete witnesses, the ones whose deposition would have a general signifi- cance.[149]

Decades before the establishment of modern-day trauma theory, these members of the first generation were already considering themselves secondary witnesses, speaking in the survivors' stead, 'by proxy, as pseudo-witnesses' and 'bear[ing] witness to a missing testimony'.[150] They, too, felt they were preserving and transmitting memories not fully owned by them, but they saw it as their task to do so without appropri- ating someone else's experience or placing a premium on either their own belatedness or on our belated belatedness. Or as Elie Wiesel has put it: 'The past belongs to the dead and the survivor does not recognize himself in the words linking him to them. We speak in code, we survivors, and this code cannot be broken, cannot be deciphered, not by you no matter how much you try.'[151]

Both postmodernism and trauma theory have since found ways of theorizing this impression of an absent or irretrievable origin that mani- fests itself vestigially and cryptically. In postmodernism, vestiges are all there is, whereas trauma theory would conceive of Wiesel's 'code' as the result of unremembered experience that is encrypted in the survivor's mind, inaccessible to himself and therefore destined to be passed on to witnesses after the fact who may be able to decode it for him. To survivors like Wiesel, the truth appears to lie somewhere between the two. While Wiesel makes it very clear that his 'code' can be decrypted by neither the survivor nor anyone else, he also says that words, however impenetrable, do provide a link to the dead. The same is true of the other authors examined here. The absence of testimony by what Levi calls the 'complete witness' seems to have acted as an ethical injunction in their writing to transmit the past but to ensure that in transmission it remained 'encoded', as an event that represents at once an irrecoverable caesura and an inescapable legacy. Any attempt on their part to evoke the Holocaust in the present consequently had to involve negotiating the incommensurable and traumatic in a manner that both conveyed and preserved, both addressed and remained silent about the past, without encouraging any

---

[149] *The Drowned and the Saved*, trans. Raymond Rosenthal (London: Abacus, 1989), 64.
[150] Giorgio Agamben, *Remnants of Auschwitz: The Witness and the Archive*, trans. Daniel Heller-Roazen (New York: Zone, 1999), 34.
[151] 'The Holocaust as Literary Inspiration', in Wiesel et al., *Dimensions of the Holocaust* (Evanston, IL: Northwestern University Press, 1990), 5–19 (7).

view that would lead to either a bracketing of the event, or to its dissolution in a narrative cast as a talking cure.

These authors' response to the challenge of 'encrypting' the past in writing was proleptic not only in content but also as regards the narrative techniques they developed and deployed in rising to it. As will be demonstrated in Chapters 2–5, the task with which they were faced, and the textual strategies they adopted, suggest that these authors of the first-generation Holocaust novel are where the 'surprising realignment of reference with what is not fully masterable by cognition' that we have come to associate with post-structuralism and trauma theory first came about.[152] It has been argued that, where their representational strategies are concerned, 'trauma fiction emerges out of postmodernist fiction and shares its tendency to bring conventional techniques to their limit'.[153] It is undoubtedly true that trauma fiction 'overlaps with and borrows from' postmodern fiction 'in its self-conscious deployment of stylistic devices as modes of reflection or critique', while at the same time the 'rise of trauma theory' has provided authors 'with new ways of conceptualising trauma', as Anne Whitehead persuasively demonstrates in her close readings of texts such as Toni Morrison's *Jazz* (1992), Anne Michaels's *Fugitive Pieces* (1997), or Pat Barker's *Another World* (1998).[154] Yet the works analysed by Whitehead are shaped primarily by the theoretical background informing them. The theory provides the authors with templates for evoking trauma. In the texts by first-generation Holocaust novelists, however, it is the experience of trauma that provides the template, even when, as will be shown, the authors discussed here do turn, in varying degrees, to trauma theory's precursor in Freudian thought in an attempt to elucidate, contextualize, or suggest a theoretical underpinning for the experience they are seeking to recreate. In what follows, it will become apparent that, before the establishment of postmodernism, of modern-day trauma theory, or of postmodern or trauma literature as recognized categories, the authors of the first-generation Holocaust novels examined here had already taken to adopting what we have only since come to consider as the techniques of postmodernist and trauma fiction. Specifically, we shall see that, in their effort to evoke yet preserve the encrypted past and show the interruptions and disruptions wreaked by the traumatic, they deliberately reproduce the vying of narrative voices that has inadvertently marked not

---

[152] Cathy Caruth and Deborah Esch (eds), *Critical Encounters: Reference and Responsibility in Deconstructive Writing* (New Brunswick, NJ: Rutgers University Press, 1995), 3.
[153] Anne Whitehead, *Trauma Fiction* (Edinburgh: Edinburgh University Press, 2004), 82.
[154] Whitehead, *Trauma Fiction*, 3.

only survivors' attempts to testify to the past, but apparently also a number of theoretical disciplines that have, consciously or unconsciously, attempted to respond to the Holocaust. All the characteristics of trauma as they are defined by modern-day trauma theory are present, including the delay and disjunction between experience and comprehension of traumatic latency, the ensuing collapse of temporality and destabilization of space and identity, and the resulting thwarting of any kind of linear progression or progress, and its replacement with repetition, disorder, and indirection. However, they are present not only at a thematic but also, and indeed especially, at a structural level, where they produce narrative structures that fail to evolve, that bifurcate, multiply, double back on, or appear to consume themselves.

As has been indicated, the proleptic nature of these first-generation Holocaust novels raises questions about postmodernism and trauma theory's relation to the past. Reacting to a personal crisis, the authors presented here were already anticipating how what we would only later come to think of collectively as the Holocaust would come to stand both as a singular catastrophe and as the culmination of a hyper-crisis of modernity and cornerstone of a postmodernity founded on a sense of living in an aftermath. Their response makes the responses of postmodernism and trauma theory appear as much symptomatic as diagnostic of their times. At the same time, I suggest that trauma theory taken in conjunction with a postmodernist view of representation has retroactively given us tools with which better to understand, or at least describe, the efforts of these writers of first-generation fiction, and which, if applied to their texts, may open up a fresh perspective on Jewish writing after the war as well as on our more recent responses to the past. While such an approach may appear anachronistic, I shall draw on postmodernist and trauma-theoretical thought and terminology only to detail what is already present in these early texts and capture how they play with the relationship between an unspoken event and the structural disturbances that follow in its wake.

What I am proposing is a reading of first-generation Holocaust novels in which the psychoanalytical figure of the crypt and the phantom are interpreted deconstructively, as that which must remain encrypted in order to be transmitted and which must be allowed to haunt the text without being forced to reveal its secrets. One obvious area of convergence between postmodernism and psychoanalysis, which will serve to elucidate the point I am making, is the deconstructionist interpretation of Abraham and Torok's work propounded by Derrida in his foreword to their *Cryptonymie*, as well as Derrida's own take on phantoms as encountered in a great deal of his writing, for example, in *Spectres de Marx.*[155] Derrida downplays the extent to which Abraham and Torok advocate the recovery of meaning in a clinical setting in their studies. The figure of the spectre as conceived of by Derrida is 'a figure of the other, of the strange and the stranger, of that which in me is other than myself and that which outside me is more than I can know', and he believes that through an encounter with it an exchange with the dead is in fact possible, yet only if we regard it as 'a productive opening of meaning rather than a determinate content to be uncovered'.[156] While Abraham and Torok hold that the secrets of the phantom should be discussed and dispelled, Derrida feels that 'the spectre's ethical injunction requires us on the contrary not to reduce it prematurely to an object of knowledge', so that we may be able to encounter that which is 'strange, unheard, *other*' about it'.[157] As Davis puts it:

> For Derrida the ghost's secret is not a puzzle to be solved; it is the structural openness or address directed towards the living by the voices of the past or the not-yet formulated possibilities of the future. [...] The interest here, then, is not in secrets, understood as puzzles to be resolved, but in secrecy, now elevated to what Castricano calls 'the structural enigma which inaugurates the scene of writing'.[158]

In linking the theme of the ghost to the structural workings of literature, Derrida opens up the possibility of a haunted textuality in which the boundaries between self and other, past and present, inside and outside are disrupted. This form of textuality manages to convey the encrypted without decrypting it, by regarding it as a structure beyond the dichotomy of knowing and not-knowing. As such, it is characterized by the kind of writing which Derrida imagines, drawing on the language of *cryptonyms* described by Abraham and Torok, as one that shows as it hides:

> Tout se passe comme si la transcription cryptonymique [...] faisait l'angle d'un crochet pour dérouter le lecteur et rendre l'itinéraire illisible. Art de la *chicane*: de l'argutie juridique ou de l'âpreté ratiocinante d'un sophiste, mais aussi du stratagème topographique multipliant les simulacres de barrages, les portes dissimulées, les détours obligés, les changements brusques de sens, toutes les épreuves d'un jeu de patience pour séduire et décourager à la fois, fasciner et fatiguer.[159]

---

[155] 'Fors: Les Mots anglés de Nicolas Abraham et Maria Torok', in Abraham and Torok, *Cryptonymie*, 7–73; *Spectres de Marx: L'État de la dette, le travail du deuil et la nouvelle Internationale* (Paris: Galilée, 1993).

[156] Davis, *Haunted Subjects*, 76, 11.

[157] Davis, *Haunted Subjects*, 13; original emphasis.

[158] Davis, *Haunted Subjects*, 13.   [159] 'Fors', 62; original emphasis.

In this description, it will be suggested, Derrida unwittingly provides us with a retroactive paradigm for the writing of crypts and phantoms as practised by post-war Jewish authors who lived through the Holocaust.

In addition to trauma theory and the theory of deconstruction, I shall draw quite extensively on the very beginnings of trauma studies in the writing of Freud, with whom all my authors were, to a greater or lesser degree, demonstrably familiar. His thought has provided them with aspects of trauma theory *avant la lettre* that evidently chimed with the predicament they were trying to evoke. My readings are also informed by postmodern narrative theory more generally, especially by Brian McHale's definition of postmodernist fiction. McHale argues that when doubts about the possibility of attaining reliable knowledge (a typical modernist concern) become intractable in an author's work, epistemological uncertainty 'tips over' into 'ontological plurality', and a 'shift of dominant from problems of *knowing* to problems of *modes of being*' occurs.[160] In my authors' writing, this manifests itself, as I have indicated, by the fact that they do not try to explain or describe the incomprehensible origin of trauma but enact its impact structurally, by mimicking its continuing disruptive after-effects in the present on time, space, and self, as well as on the form of the narrative, and by passing the experience of these after-effects on to the reader.

In the analyses presented in Chapters 2–5, it will become clear that the decision of these first-generation authors to resort to fiction as a means of transmitting the encrypted was finally governed not only by personal predilection but by the sense that it might be the only form available that would provide them with a space in which to indicate what had fallen outside language/cognition. In consequence, their work not only becomes an example of 'a real fictitious discourse', to borrow part of the title of a text by Raymond Federman.[161] It also pre-emptively responds to Cathy Caruth's question:

> How can we think of a referential—or historical, or material—dimension of texts that is not simply opposed to their potentially fictional powers? How might the very fictional power of texts be, not a hindrance to, but a means of gaining access to their referential force?[162]

Reading these first-generation Holocaust novels requires a rethinking of notions of authenticity and reference. In a category of fiction where there

---

[160] *Postmodernist Fiction* (London: Routledge, 1987), 10–11; original emphasis.

[161] *Double or Nothing: A Real Fictitious Discourse* (Normal, IL: Fiction Collective Two, 1992).

[162] Caruth and Esch (eds), *Critical Encounters*, 2.

can be no narrative assimilation of events, where the past must be acknowledged but remain encrypted—and therefore be 'encoded' into the text—the 'theme' of the novel becomes its form; its content its structure. While the texts under discussion therefore unquestionably contribute towards refuting the 'myth of silence', the assumption that the Holocaust was not broached by the first generation, they do bear witness to the importance of silence as one facet of the response to the Holocaust and grapple with ways of incorporating that silence into their testimony: through the act of translating unnarratable trauma into a literary strategy of unnarrating.

2

Writing of Broken Time(s)

H. G. Adler, *Eine Reise, Die unsichtbare Wand*

> Tief
> in der Zeitenschrunde,
> beim
> Wabeneis
> wartet, ein Atemkristall,
> dein unumstößliches
> Zeugnis.
>
> (Paul Celan, *Atemwende*)

Hans Günther Adler, who would later abbreviate his first names because they were the same as a National Socialist functionary's, was born in Prague in 1910, to assimilated German-speaking Jewish parents. 'Das Elternhaus war jüdisch, aber fast alles Jüdische einschließlich dem Religiösen war kaum zu spüren', as Adler puts it.[1] It was the fact of persecution that drove him to identify with Judaism: 'Jude bin ich aus Schicksal.'[2] That 'fate' saw him sent to a forced labour camp in Bohemia in 1941 and then deported, with his wife and her family, first to Theresienstadt and in

---

[1] H. G. Adler, 'Nachruf bei Lebzeiten', in K. H. Kramberg (ed.), *Vorletzte Worte: Schriftsteller schreiben ihren eigenen Nachruf* (Frankfurt a.M.: Goldmann, 1985), 11–20 (12). Of his name, Adler says in the same piece: 'H. G. steht für Hans Günther, dies die Namen zweier jung verstorbener Brüder der Mutter, die alle drei zu verleugnen er nie wünschte, ohne doch noch diese Namen voll zu führen, nachdem Adolf Eichmanns Vertreter für das "Protektorat Böhmen und Mähren" in den Jahren 1939 bis 1945 eben so geheißen hatte' (12). For a concise biography, see Alfred Otto Lanz, '"Zu Hause im Exil": Biographische Skizze über H. G. Adler', in Heinrich Hubmann and Lanz (eds), *Zu Hause im Exil: Zu Werk und Person H. G. Adlers* (Stuttgart: Steiner, 1987), 139–46; or Franz Hocheneder, 'Vita H. G. Adler', in Heinz Ludwig Arnold (ed.), *H. G. Adler* (Munich: text + kritik, 2004), 98–106.

[2] In a letter to his first wife, Gertrud Klepetar, of 20 Oct. 1939. Cited in Marcel Atze, 'Adler, H[ans] G[ünther]', in Andreas B. Kilcher (ed.), *Lexikon der deutsch-jüdischen Literatur: Jüdische Autorinnen und Autoren deutscher Sprache von der Aufklärung bis zur Gegenwart* (Frankfurt a.M.: Suhrkamp, 2003), 2–4 (3).

1944 to Auschwitz, where his wife and his mother-in-law were sent to their deaths. Adler was transported on to Niederorschel and Langenstein-Zwieberge, subsidiary camps of Buchenwald, where he was liberated on 13 April 1945—liberated in name, for the rupture of the Holocaust, though survived, proved insurmountable in other respects. As Adler said with reference to the 'jüdische Katastrophe unter Hitler': 'Wohl habe ich sie überdauert, aber sie hat mich ereilt.'[3] When Adler returned to Prague after the war, he had lost his entire family as well as many friends and acquaintances. In 1947, in the face of the impending Communist take-over, he emigrated to London, where he remained until his death in 1988, working as a freelance author and scholar.

Though a prolific poet and novelist, Adler was for a long time, and is perhaps even today, known primarily as a witness and historian of the Holocaust: for being, as Theodor Heuss put it, 'aus dem Erlebnis heraus Historiker und Soziologe des Untergangs der Juden in Deutschland'.[4] His monograph on *Theresienstadt 1941–1945*, written between 1945 and 1948, and first published in 1955, was one of the earliest studies of its kind and continues to be invoked not only as a 'Pionierarbeit' but as a 'Standardwerk'.[5] Between 1955 and 1960, three further documentary volumes followed, as well as a second, revised, and extended edition of *Theresienstadt*.[6] Only in 1962 did Adler finally succeed in finding a publisher for a work of his literary prose. *Eine Reise*, which had been lying in a drawer since 1951, was in fact the third of six novel-length texts

[3] H. G. Adler, 'Zu Hause im Exil', in H. G. Adler, *Der Wahrheit verpflichtet: Interviews, Gedichte, Essays*, ed. Jeremy Adler (Gerlingen: Bleicher, 1998), 19–31 (19).

[4] 'Aus dem Erlebnis heraus Historiker', in Willehad P. Eckert and Wilhelm Unger (eds), *H. G. Adler—Buch der Freunde: Stimmen über den Dichter und Gelehrten mit unveröffentlichter Lyrik* (Cologne: Wienand, 1975), 19.

[5] Franz Hocheneder, '*Eine Reise*: H. G. Adlers wiederentdeckter Roman in neuer Auflage', *Literatur und Kritik*, 343–4 (2000), 86–8 (87); Otto F. Best, 'Panorama und Topographie: Anmerkungen zu Alfred Döblin, Peter Weiss, H. G. Adler und anderen', in Wolfgang Elfe, James Hardin, and Günther Holst (eds), *Deutsche Exilliteratur—Literatur der Nachkriegszeit: Akten des III. Exilliteratur-Symposiums der University of South Carolina* (Berne: Lang, 1981), 96–102 (99).

[6] *Theresienstadt 1941–1945: Das Antlitz einer Zwangsgemeinschaft (Geschichte, Soziologie, Psychologie)* (Tübingen: Mohr, 1955; rev. edn, 1960); *Die verheimlichte Wahrheit: Theresienstädter Dokumente* (Tübingen: Mohr, 1958); *Der Kampf gegen die 'Endlösung der Judenfrage'* (Bonn: Bundeszentrale für Heimatdienst, 1958); *Die Juden in Deutschland: Von der Aufklärung bis zum Nationalsozialismus* (Munich: Kösel, 1960). Several further volumes drawing on eyewitness accounts and on historical, psychological, and sociological data were published between 1964 and 1987, including *Der verwaltete Mensch: Studien zur Deportation der Juden aus Deutschland* (Tübingen: Mohr, 1974), the counterpart to *Theresienstadt* as considered from the perpetrators' perspective. For a more detailed bibliography, see Franz Hocheneder, 'Auswahlbibliografie zu H. G. Adler', in Arnold (ed.), *H. G. Adler*, 107–12. For a comprehensive list of primary publications, see Franz Hocheneder, 'Special Bibliography: The Writings of H. G. Adler (1910–1988)', *Comparative Criticism*, 21 (1999), 293–310.

that Adler had completed in at least draft form by the time the Theresienstadt study appeared. Three of these texts remain unpublished. On the others there exists still only little critical commentary, and scholarship tends to concentrate less on literary criteria and more on emphasizing the reciprocity between Adler's novels and his studies and on drawing out the testimonial aspect of his fiction.[7] The '"encyclopaedic" corpus' of his writings is treated as one great 'Gesamtkunstwerk'.[8] Thus we read in the *Lexikon der deutsch-jüdischen Literatur*: 'Mit seinem komplementären Schaffen stellt A.[dler] das personifizierte Gedächtnis des Holocaust dar.'[9] Peter Demetz has said of him: 'Ich sehe ihn, in der Epoche der *Shoah*, als Verbündeten Primo Levis und Elie Wiesels.'[10] *Panorama*, the most demonstrably autobiographical of Adler's literary works, has been described as 'a memoir rather than a novel'.[11] Indeed, Alfred Lanz's 'Biographische Skizze über H. G. Adler' makes a point of drawing attention to the parallels between it and Adler's life, though Lanz acknowledges in his monograph on the novel that Adler did not intend for it to be read as an autobiography.[12] Heimito von Doderer commented on *Eine Reise*: 'Was in dem Buche steht, ist [. . .] auch im Tatsächlichen durchaus richtig: es hat sich das alles begeben und genauso begeben, wie es im Buche steht. Verändert sind nur die Namen. Der Autor hat alles selbst erlebt.'[13] Adler's son, Jeremy Adler, refers to the three published novels in conjunction as depicting 'den persönlichen Weg' of the author: '*Eine Reise* (1962) schildert Deportation, Theresienstadt, Auschwitz und Befreiung [. . .]; *Panorama* (1968) beschreibt Arbeitslager, Auschwitz und Exil,

---

[7] The published novels are *Panorama: Roman in zehn Bildern* (written 1948–68) (Olten: Walter, 1968), republished with an afterword by Peter Demetz (Munich: Piper, 1988); *Eine Reise: Erzählung* (written 1950–1) (Bonn: Bibliotheca christiana, 1962), republished with an afterword by Jeremy Adler (Vienna: Zsolnay, 1999); *Die unsichtbare Wand* (written 1954–61), with an afterword by Jürgen Serke (Vienna: Zsolnay, 1989).

[8] Kathryn N. Jones, 'Fictional Representation of the Holocaust in H. G. Adler's *Eine Reise* and Georges Perec's *W ou le souvenir d'enfance*', in Jones, *Journeys of Remembrance: Memories of the Second World War in French and German Literature, 1960–1980* (London: Legenda, 2007), 73–89 (74); Jürgen Serke, 'H. G. Adler: Der versteinerte Jüngling, der ein weiser Mann wurde', in Serke, *Böhmische Dörfer: Wanderungen durch eine verlassene literarische Landschaft* (Vienna: Zsolnay, 1987), 326–43 (327).

[9] Atze, 'Adler, H[ans] G[ünther]', 4.

[10] 'Nachwort', in H. G. Adler, *Panorama* (Munich: Piper, 1988), 582–92 (582).

[11] Peter Demetz, 'H. G. Adler', in Demetz, *After the Fires: Recent Writing in the Germanies, Austria, and Switzerland* (San Diego, CA: Harcourt Brace Jovanovich, 1986), 30–4 (32).

[12] Lanz, 'Biographische Skizze', in Hubmann and Lanz (eds), *Zu Hause im Exil*, 139–46; Lanz, '*Panorama*' von H. G. Adler—ein 'moderner Roman': '*Panorama*' als Minusverfahren des Entwicklungsromans und Negation der Möglichkeit rationaler Welterkenntnis (Berne: Lang, 1984), 30.

[13] 'Die Schule des Lesens: Notizen zu H. G. Adlers Erzählung "Eine Reise"', in Eckert and Unger (eds), *Adler—Buch der Freunde*, 78–82 (78).

während *Die unsichtbare Wand* (1988) aus der Freiheit auf die Katastrophe zurückblickt.'[14]

The 'Verbundenheit des Erlebten und Geschriebenen' in all of Adler's texts is undeniable, as is the fact that both his non-literary and his literary works form part of a greater testimonial project.[15] By his own acknowledgement, Adler's approach to bearing witness to the past through his writing was twofold:

> Als es zu den Deportationen kam, habe ich mir gesagt: Das überlebe ich nicht. Aber wenn ich es überlebe, dann will ich es darstellen, und zwar auf zweierlei Weise: ich will es wissenschaftlich erforschen und in dieser Gestaltung vollkommen von mir als Individuum loslösen, und ich will es dichterisch in irgendeiner Weise darstellen.[16]

Yet while critics are unanimous in their agreement with Jeremy Adler that 'erst durch die Gesamtheit seiner Ausdrucksformen, der literarischen wie der gelehrten, konnte H. G. Adler seine Aufgabe als Zeuge erfüllen', few venture an opinion as to why this was the case.[17] What did the literary allow Adler to do that the non-literary apparently did not? The question is rarely even raised. Yet its exploration—and especially its exploration with regard to someone like Adler, as both a scholar and a poet of the Holocaust—could lead to a fuller understanding of the problematics of Holocaust representation in general and indirectly shed some light on the particularly ambivalent attitude held towards its literary treatment.

A TWOFOLD TESTIMONIAL PROJECT

For the most part, the difference between the literary and the non-literary in Adler's work is simply assumed to be one of degrees of objectivity. Jeremy Adler, for instance, speaks of the 'complementary handling of subjective and objective perspective in the scholarly and literary modes' and suggests that the novels supply 'die private Innenansicht' to complete the 'nüchterne Darstellung' of the studies.[18] Though on the face of it this

---

[14] 'Nachwort', in H. G. Adler, *Theresienstadt 1941–1945: Das Antlitz einer Zwangsgemeinschaft* (Göttingen: Wallstein, 2005), 895–926 (922). Future references to *Theresienstadt* are to this edition unless otherwise stated.

[15] J. P. Stern, 'Zum 75. Geburtstag H. G. Adlers', in Hubmann and Lanz (eds), *Zu Hause im Exil*, 147–50 (148).

[16] 'Es gäbe viel Merkwürdiges zu berichten: Interview mit Hans Christoph Knebusch', in H. G. Adler: *Der Wahrheit verpflichtet*, ed. Jeremy Adler, 32–55 (45).

[17] 'Nachwort', in H. G. Adler, *Theresienstadt*, 922.

[18] 'Good against Evil? H. G. Adler, T. W. Adorno and the Representation of the Holocaust', in Edward Timms and Andrea Hammel (eds), *The German-Jewish Dilemma:*

is what we might expect to find in a body of work straddling the art–science divide, such a view is not unproblematic, in as much as it promotes an alignment of the scholarly, understood as the logical and rational, with neutral, objective 'reality', while treating the literary as a personal, subjective response to that 'reality' and equating it with the non-factual, irrational, or even transcendental. As such, it affords too much scope for regarding Adler's literary oeuvre as the product of a purely personal attempt to come to terms with his traumatic past, or even as a conciliatory counterpoint to the 'unbearable objectivity' of his scientific project.[19]

This tendency is especially prevalent in, though by no means exclusive to, the earlier reviews of Adler's fiction. Roland Wiegenstein describes *Eine Reise* in terms that make its writing sound like an involuntary acting-out of trauma: 'Das beginnt umständlich, zögernd, in langen Sätzen tastet sich der verstörte Geist an eine Erinnerung heran, die mit plötzlich einfallenden, jähen, kurzen Sätzen ihn stellt.'[20] Benno Reifenberg refers to the same work, somewhat disconcertingly, as 'eine radikale Gewissenserforschung'.[21] Such a stance suggests a view of the trauma of the Holocaust as a personal psychological disturbance which the afflicted individual can be helped to overcome, allowing him or her to master the past, re-establish continuity, and even mend severed ties with non-Jews. Eberhard Bethge said of Adler that he was striving to overcome 'die Sprachlosigkeit zwischen Juden und Christen' and that the address of *Eine Reise* to its readers is an 'Anrede, die zu verändern beginnt, die weitet und beglückt und tröstet'.[22] As such, Bethge felt, the literary was a means for Adler to convey 'so etwas wie eine Auferstehung der Hoffnung'.[23] Elias Canetti also invoked the notion of hope in respect of *Eine Reise*, in a letter to Adler shortly after the latter had completed his first published novel: 'Die furchtbarsten Dinge, die Menschen geschehen können, sind hier so dargestellt, als wären sie schwebend und zart und verwindlich, als könnten sie dem Kern des Menschen nichts anhaben. Ich möchte sagen, daß Sie die *Hoffnung* in die moderne Literatur wieder

---

From the Enlightenment to the Shoah (Lewiston, NY: Mellen, 1999), 263; 'Nachwort', in Adler, *Theresienstadt*, 922, 919.

[19] Jeremy Adler, 'Good against Evil?', 263.

[20] 'Eine sanfte Stimme beschwört den Massenmord', in Eckert and Unger (eds), *Adler—Buch der Freunde*, 75–8 (75).

[21] 'Eine radikale Gewissenserforschung: Zu Adlers Erzählung "Eine Reise"', in Eckert and Unger (eds), *Adler—Buch der Freunde*, 74.

[22] 'Dichter und Deuter in unserer Zeit', in Eckert and Unger (eds), *Adler—Buch der Freunde*, 29–40 (38).

[23] 'Dichter und Deuter in unserer Zeit', in Eckert and Unger (eds), *Adler—Buch der Freunde*, 31.

eingeführt haben.'[24] As is so often the case with Holocaust literature of the first generation, these reviewers treat Adler's fictional works as monuments to their author's survival, and, by implication, to the resilience of the human spirit, rather than as texts in their own right. If his scientific studies provide a record of the reality he witnessed, his fictional works, by turning that reality into a tale, are viewed as evidence that the past can be transcended. By the simple fact of their literary form, they are thus perceived as tempering the unrelentingly factual account of the studies. Their very existence is consolation, not only to the early reviewers of Adler's novels. *Die unsichtbare Wand*, published only after Adler's death, in 1989, is (mis)advertised as a 'Roman über die Liebe und die Heimkehr ins Leben' on its back cover. Wendelin Schmidt-Dengler, apparently taking inspiration from this, comments in his review of the novel: 'Adlers Rede von der Hoffnung [. . .] nährt sich von der Empirie eines gelebten Lebens, in dem die Liebe [. . .] die Enttäuschungen tilgte.'[25]

Occasionally, dichotomizing views of the objectively non-literary and the subjectively literary in Adler's work are couched in terms worse than inadequate. Theodor Sapper, who is one of the few critics to attempt a more systematic exploration of the difference between the two modes, argues that Adler's scientific studies offer a 'kausale Begründung' of the functioning of the deadly National Socialist bureaucratic apparatus, which operates according to a 'Logik' that is 'eindeutig ersichtlich', whereas the reactions of its victims to this logic are the preserve of fiction because they are 'akausal':

> Wo jedoch, die Kausalität transzendierend und das Begriffsarsenal des Rechtsphilosophen überfordernd, das *Mystische* beginnt, das allein vom Dichter Auszusagende, dort zeigt sich äußeres Geschehen [. . .] durch eine Schilderung der zugehörigen Innenvorgänge ergänzt [. . .]. Im Innenleben der 'zu Tode verwalteten Menschen' kommt es zu psychischen Reaktionen, deren Gestaltung der Rechtsphilosoph Adler dem Dichter Adler überlassen mußte.[26]

Sapper then goes on to intimate that these individual psychological processes, which he likens to a cancer of the mind, are disproportionate to the reality that triggered them and are, ultimately, evidence of psychosis. Today, what

---

[24] Letter of 22 Nov. 1952; cited in Eckert and Unger (eds), *Adler—Buch der Freunde*, 72–3 (73); original emphasis.

[25] 'H[ans] G[ünther] Adler: Die unsichtbare Wand', *Literatur und Kritik*, 245–6 (1990), 277–8 (278).

[26] '"Der Dorn des Abfalls": Einheit von Idee und Bild im Werk H. G. Adlers', *Literatur und Kritik*, 84 (1974), 205–9 (206, 207); original emphasis.

Sapper terms psychosis would almost certainly be classified as a traumatic stress response.[27] Notwithstanding, Sapper comes uncomfortably close to implying that the 'psychische Reaktionen', but not the context out of which they arose, are disordered:

> Nicht die gleiche sinnfällige Eindeutigkeit kommt jedoch den Innenvorgängen zu, die in den Psychen einiger Opfer gleichsam metastatisch zu wuchern beginnen. Ihre durchaus 'akausal' zu nennende Art könnte als eine negative Mystik bezeichnet werden. [...] jene Reaktionen, in denen die Opfer auf das sich zusehends überstürzende Übermaß ihrer Qual innerseelisch antworten, bewirken ein Sich-Verrücken der Maßstäbe des Urteilens und Wertens, ein Sich-Verschieben der Proportionen, die zwischen dem von außen Herankommenden und der Art, wie es innerlich zu verarbeiten versucht wird [...], bestehen. Zuletzt ist es dann der Mechanismus der Psychose, der es allein noch vermag, eine bis zum Äußersten unerträglich werdende Realität zu interpretieren.[28]

According to Sapper, it was 'dieses rational nicht mehr faßbare Geschehen [...], diese Disproportion zwischen dem von außen her oktroyierten Quantum des Leidens, und dessen Beantwortetwerden im innerseelischen Prozeß' that could only be captured by literary means in Adler's oeuvre.[29] While the implications of Sapper's argument, or certainly its phrasing, are questionable, its curious mix of scientific and metaphysical vocabulary would appear to suggest that it is driven by the same impetus responsible for the vocabulary of consolation and redemption favoured by the majority of reviewers of Adler's literary works: the need to believe that the trauma of the Holocaust is a sickness with a (belated) cure.

A comparison of Sapper's comments on the mechanism of psychosis in a concentrationary context with Adler's own, made in his monograph on Theresienstadt, not only reveals the gulf between their perspectives, but in doing so sheds light on what Adler may have felt his fiction could convey that his scholarly works could not. When Adler speaks in the Theresienstadt study of apparently psychotic disturbances manifested by victims of the Holocaust, he concludes that the psychosis-like dissociative signs they might display were not symptoms of individual psychological disorders or, in other words, of a break *with* reality, as much as a reaction to a break *in* reality. It was less the individual than the 'Wirklichkeit' itself that

---

[27] On the question of where, if anywhere, psychosis falls on the spectrum of responses to a traumatic event, see Anthony P. Morrison, Lucy Frame, and Warren Larkin, 'Relationships between Trauma and Psychosis: A Review and Integration', *British Journal of Clinical Psychology*, 42 (2003), 331–53.

[28] Sapper, '"Der Dorn des Abfalls"', 207.

[29] Sapper, '"Der Dorn des Abfalls"', 207.

was 'ver-rückt'.[30] Any psychosis arising in response to this 'reality' was therefore

> keine echte klinische Psychose [...], sondern ein das Bewußtsein aufspal-tender Reizzustand im Bereich der unentrinnbaren psychischen Affektion, wo der Mensch, verwirrt und zerworfen, sich gleichsam schizoid betragen mußte, um die elementaren Zerwürfnisse im angeborenen und anerzogenen Weltbild mit dem unablässigen Flackern irritierender Erscheinungen müh-sam auszugleichen. Es ist gewagt, trifft aber besser die Verhältnisse, wenn wir sagen, daß die Psychose in der Außenwelt feststand, denn die Wirklichkeit selbst war schizophren gespalten und zerfallen.[31]

Though made with reference to the particularly pronounced split that characterized the 'Musterlager' Theresienstadt, where the rift between the facade created for propaganda purposes and the 'reality' experienced by the inmates produced an 'einmalige Wahnwelt', Adler's comments, as he points out, apply to existence in any of the concentration camps: 'In jedem Lager [...] ging es wahnhaft zu.'[32] He concludes:

> So war es eine 'pervertierte' Psychose in der objektiven Welt; die subjektiven Entartungen waren nur ihr Reflex. Aus diesem Grunde dürfte man nicht ohne weiteres behaupten, daß die Menschen wahnhaft empfunden und gehandelt hätten. Nur insofern taten sie es oft, daß ihre Reaktionen erken-nen ließen, wie die Wirklichkeit ihr Auffassungsvermögen einfach überbot. Jeder Wert, jedes Merkmal, jede Eigenschaft hat seine ursprünglich gültigen Bedeutungen eingebüßt oder verändert.[33]

The disturbances caused by trauma or even psychosis in an individual can, at least theoretically, be overcome, because the 'parameters of "normal" reality, such as causality, sequence, place and time', though violated where the individual is concerned, objectively speaking still apply.[34] Once they are re-established in the individual's existence, he or she is considered cured. Adler's characterization of the experience of the Holocaust as a rift in the external, objective world, as well as the self, suggests a fundamental dislocation of the parameters we consider 'normal', and thus a sense of an insurmountable rupture, which is underscored by his use of the perfect tense in the final sentence of the excerpt. The disruption, in Adler's view, is not just psychological but epistemological.

Stylistically, the passages evoking this 'Dasein an schneidenden Rän-dern, über ungewohnten Klüften' depart from the neutral, matter-of-fact

---

[30] *Theresienstadt*, 665.　　　[31] *Theresienstadt*, 666.　　　[32] *Theresienstadt*, 187, 666.

[33] *Theresienstadt*, 666.

[34] Shoshana Felman and Dori Laub, *Testimony: Crises of Witnessing in Literature, Psychoanalysis, and History* (New York: Routledge, 1992), 69.

tone that marks the greater part of the Theresienstadt study.[35] Apparently, rather than the representation of individual psychoses, it is the attempt to convey what happens 'wenn eine Welt aus den Fugen gerät' that sees Adler resort to a more literary idiom, even in his scholarly texts.[36] This sense of an out-of-joint reality causing not only individuals but an entire world view to founder is the 'rational nicht mehr faßbares Geschehen' to which straightforward factual descriptions alone do not appear to be able to do justice. This is especially evident when Adler speaks of the final weeks of Theresienstadt in April of 1945, when any semblance of structure in the ghetto was crumbling as transports from the extermination camps had started to pour in. The men and women arriving from places such as Auschwitz, where Adler himself had also been, were long past any pretence of order. As he attempts to convey the dissolution of all structures and points of reference that ensues when the 'anerzogenes Weltbild' and the reality experienced are hopelessly beyond reconciliation, Adler's account slides, over the space of two paragraphs, from scholarly report to literary evocation, and we read:

Etwa 400 Tote haben die Elendstransporte bereits ins Lager mitgebracht, wo sich das Sterben an Erschöpfung und Krankheit fortsetzte, vor allem an Flecktyphus, obwohl es gelang, die Sterblichkeit bei dieser Infektion unter 25 % hinunterzudrücken. Viele freiwillige Helfer steckten sich an, manche konnten nicht gerettet werden (s. 16. Kap.).

Jetzt galt keine Ordnung mehr, nicht einmal eine Lagerordnung; dazu waren die Entwürdigten nicht mehr bereit. [...] Wo der Mensch an jenem Ende steht, das ihn als ein unversöhnlicher Abgrund umringt [...]—wer will da noch ein Mindestmaß von Zucht und Ordnung beschwören [...]? [...] Alles war ausgelöscht, alles entwertet. [...] Es war das Ende—Ende als Untergang, als Weltgericht—als *Nichts*. Und es gab keinen Bestand mehr. Wer diese Vernichtung nicht an sich selbst erfahren hat, weiß es nicht, wird es nie wissen. Er hat zu schweigen. Er hat anzuhören [...]. Wer aber durch diese letzte Verzweiflung, durch die Nacht der Nächte, durch den namenlosen Untergang geschritten ist, ihn überdauert hat [...], der soll seine Stimme erheben und sagen, wie es wirklich war. Er soll die Wirklichkeit verkünden, [...] jenseits von allem theatralischen Grauen noch lebender Verwesung und toter Knochenberge, die nichts von der inneren Wahrheit enthüllen, da sie nur Schandmäler sind, aber nicht die Wahrheit selbst. Nein, die Wirklichkeit gilt es zu nennen, [...] die Wirklichkeit des *Nichts*, die weder denkbar, noch nachfühlbar ist, denn nicht zu denken und nicht zu fühlen ist das Nichts, nur ungeschaffen ist es [...] zu leiden.[37]

---

[35] *Theresienstadt*, 667.   [36] *Theresienstadt*, 674.
[37] *Theresienstadt*, 212–13; original emphasis.

What starts out as a factual testimony shifts to an invocation of the necessity of telling the 'real truth', beyond the documentable secondary evidence, and finally culminates in an acknowledgement of the impossibility of conceptualizing and lending shape to that truth.

What we encounter in this passage is another enactment of the contention between narrative voices that Lawrence Langer has identified in oral witness testimony, but which, as I have argued in Chapter 1, may affect any attempt in any genre to give a chronological, factual account of the events and effects of the Holocaust: between the voice that tries to speak from and of a 'life after "death" called survival' and that which interrupts from a 'life within death for which we have no name'.[38] The narrative current of the former, which draws on 'a vocabulary of chronology and conjunction', is stemmed by the 'durational persistence' of the Holocaust, which calls for 'a lexicon of disruption, absence, and irreversible loss'.[39] In Adler's passage, this struggle is carried out between the voice that attests to the possibility of traversing the 'Untergang' and coming out the other side, and the voice addressing us from within an insuperable 'unversöhnlicher Abgrund' that is all around. The former speaks in facts, figures, and percentages, documenting the visible 'Schandmäler', and it establishes structures: in its subject matter but also within its own form, for example through intratextual reference to other chapters. The latter dismisses all of this and undermines it by evoking the essentially unknowable formless void of the 'Nichts' that can only be suffered 'ungeschaffen'. The former can use the phrase 'gerettet werden', albeit in the negative and in a physical, not a transcendental, sense. The latter knows only 'Untergang'. The former unfolds as a sequential historical narrative. The latter mimics the irruption into the present of a traumatic past which cannot be integrated into any continuum, only (re)lived, and it reflects the structural upheaval caused by this. The former relies on the language of chronicle, the latter abandons it, and yet neither voice is restricted to a particular genre. The contention between the two may be present in any kind of text, simply weighted differently.

The passage just cited is the longest, and perhaps bleakest, example of its kind in Adler's monograph. Jeremy Adler refers to it in his epilogue to illustrate how: 'Ab einem bestimmten Punkt entzieht sich das Geschehene jedem Verstehen, jeglicher Erklärung.'[40] However, what the passage also

---

[38] Lawrence L. Langer, *Holocaust Testimonies: The Ruins of Memory* (New Haven: Yale University Press, 1991), 35.

[39] Langer, *Holocaust Testimonies*, p. xi; Langer, *Admitting the Holocaust: Collected Essays* (New York: Oxford University Press, 1995), 16.

[40] 'Nachwort', in Adler, *Theresienstadt*, 925.

suggests is that the exhaustion of the scientific, discursive mode need not entail an overall silencing. That which is indescribable in the Holocaust, that which exceeds the sum of its parts, resists conceptualization, and explodes existing structures, may not be 'unsayable'; it may simply require a different, non-descriptive mode of reference, one capable of doing justice to that excess's refusal of the solace of continuity and form: a destructuring mode.

The struggle between narrative voices that we witness in these passages is thus also a struggle between forms of remembrance. Lawrence Langer has said that there are two reasons why we remember: 'in order to protect continuity or to verify disruption'. He argues that where the Holocaust is concerned, the former serves only to 'conceal'.[41] According to Langer, we continue to use 'a discourse of consolation about an event for which there is none' because 'no full-fledged discourse of ruin, more appropriate to our hapless times, has yet emerged'. Such a 'discourse of ruin' should not be mistaken for 'a statement about the permanent defeat of hope', but it does presuppose the admission 'that the Holocaust was not an illness from which its "patients" could be cured or a trauma from which victims "recovered"'.[42] Langer's argument is one-sided with provocative intent. Adler's work, in contrast, exemplifies the necessity of allowing for both discourses in our commemoration of the Holocaust. As Adler's research shows, the facts of the Holocaust can be situated on a timeline and in some respects even contextualized. By his own assertion, the Theresienstadt study aimed to explore

> inwiefern das Lager in Theresienstadt nicht mehr und auch nicht weniger war als nur ein Beispiel, allerdings ein besonders markanter und bis ins Irrwitzige grell übertriebener Sonderfall einer Gesellschaftsordnung im Zeitalter des mechanischen Materialismus, die unter dem entsetzlichen Druck übermächtigen Zwanges und doch heuchlerischer Verbergung dieses Zwanges ausgearbeitet ist.[43]

The destructuring mode, on the other hand, Langer's 'discourse of ruin', testifies to the insurmountability of the caesura of the Holocaust and to its challenge to attempts to come to epistemological terms with the cataclysm. In Adler's scholarly writing, the destructuring voice is, on balance, subdued. It does not serve the aim of the project, which is to establish facts and identify structures and causality. In his literary work, however, where he is not bound by the strictures of purpose and form imposed on the

---

[41] *Admitting the Holocaust*, 14.   [42] *Admitting the Holocaust*, 7.
[43] 'Warum habe ich mein Buch *Theresienstadt 1941–1945* geschrieben?', in H. G. Adler, *Der Wahrheit verpflichtet*, ed. Jeremy Adler, 111–14 (114).

scholarly, this second voice speaks uncensored, making this, if anything, the less, not the more, forgiving of Adler's narrative modes. Here it is the voice of continuity that, though present, is often drowned out, while the destructuring voice bears witness to the empirically experienced but conceptually impossible: an insurmountable traumatic break, which upsets notions of time, space, and identity, and irretrievably separates knowledge from experience and words from meaning.

Of Adler's two narrative voices only one has consistently been heard, in his non-literary but even in his literary works: that which looks for continuity, proceeds chronologically, and places the events of the past in a context. Adler's efforts to trace these events back to their origin and chart the path that led us to where the Holocaust could happen, coupled with the circumstances of his biography, have meant that he himself tends to be regarded as part of a continuity, albeit more often than not one that ends with him. Thus he has variously been referred to as 'einer der letzten Universalgelehrten des 20. Jahrhunderts',[44] as 'for the last time incarnat-[ing] the traditions of the Prague intellectual of Jewish origins',[45] and as 'one of the last representatives of the Czech-German literary tradition'.[46] All this is true. However, in regarding Adler too exclusively as the personification of the end of an era, we run the risk of overlooking that in his work which verifies a rupture with the past and tries to initiate something new. In what follows, I shall consider Adler's literary writing not only as the end of a tradition but also as the incipience of something not easily slotted into pre-existing categories. In a radio interview, given in 1980, Adler said of himself: 'Ich bin noch heute ungefähr eine terra incognita auf dem Felde der deutschen Literatur.'[47] A decade earlier, when asked to write his own obituary, he had predicted that at the end of his life it would be said of Adler the author that he is 'noch nicht angekommen'.[48] I intend to show that, to the extent to which Adler ventured into unknown territory, his literary work indeed remains 'terra incognita' and has perhaps not yet succeeded in getting through to us. To this end, I shall concentrate on the first and the last of his novels to appear: on *Eine Reise*, written between 1950 and 1951, first published in 1962, and on *Die unsichtbare Wand*, written between 1954 and 1956, published

---

[44] On the cover of the 1999 edition of *Eine Reise*.

[45] Demetz, *After the Fires*, 34.

[46] Jones, 'Fictional Representation of the Holocaust', 74.

[47] Cited in Franz Hocheneder, 'Nachruf und Nachlass bei Lebzeiten: Über die Schaffensbedingungen und Publikationsmöglichkeiten H. G. Adlers zur Zeit des englischen Exils', in Arnold (ed.), *H. G. Adler*, 86–97 (87).

[48] 'Nachruf bei Lebzeiten', 19.

posthumously in 1989.[49] The Holocaust as insuperable breach marks both content and form of all the published novels, but its effects are most comprehensively reflected on in *Die unsichtbare Wand*, while having their greatest structural impact on *Eine Reise*, which Jeremy Adler, in his epilogue to the novel's second edition, and with a nod to David Rousset, describes as the 'Kernstück' of Adler's 'Auseinandersetzung mit "l'univers concentrationnaire"' (309).

I have chosen to introduce the textual analysis section of this book with Adler, because he is the only one of my authors to have experienced the 'concentrationary universe' from the inside. Though direct victims of the Holocaust, the other writers discussed here were less immediate witnesses to it than he had been. Perhaps in consequence, his writing is more profoundly affected by the contention between the voice of continuity, looking for cause and effect, and the voice of disruption, disputing rhyme and reason. As will become clear in Chapters 3–5, the focus in the texts by my other authors has shifted from the struggle to comprehend and portray the event itself to an increasingly postmodernist and post-cognitive pre-occupation with its aftermath and with the shattering beyond repair of the instruments used to quantify and describe it. In Adler's literary oeuvre we observe this shift in the making. Where the painful facts of the past become an insurmountable caesura in the present in his writing—and this informs both content and structure of the texts—we witness an adjustment of narrative mode towards the postmodernist, grounded in a sense of a historical and cultural slide towards a postmodernity in which 'the disruption [. . .] of all the "points of reference used by individuals and groups in the past to plot their life courses" [. . .] seems to point to a total unraveling of centuries of progress in human affairs'.[50]

THE RETURN OF *APEIRON*

In his attempt in the Theresienstadt monograph to find words for the 'unversöhnlicher Abgrund', Adler introduces a revealing term: he speaks of 'Apeiron'.[51] As a concept, *apeiron* originates in ancient Greek philosophy. Anaximander identified it as the origin or principle of all things. *Apeiron*, meaning that which has no *perai*, or bounds, denotes a limitless,

---

[49] Reference will be made, in parentheses in the text, to the following two editions: *Eine Reise* (Vienna: Zsolnay, 1999); *Die unsichtbare Wand* (Vienna: Zsolnay, 1989).

[50] Steven M. Rosen, *Dimensions of Apeiron: A Topological Phenomenology of Space, Time, and Individuation* (Amsterdam: Rodopi, 2004), p. xiv. Rosen is citing Alberto Melucci, *The Playing Self* (Cambridge: Cambridge University Press, 1996), 2.

[51] *Theresienstadt*, 667.

indeterminate state of pre-differentiation. As that which is before and beyond all distinctions, *apeiron* is unbounded in both space and time. It has variously been viewed as 'the many; the moving; the ugly; the bad [...] the inchoate flux of opposites or contraries [...] the principle of disorder or disharmony'.[52] It is neither perceptible nor intelligible, for, in preceding individuation, it precludes objectivizing consciousness. As Steven Rosen puts it: 'In the unconstrained many of *apeiron*, there can be no *one*; in its chaotic multiplicity there can be no unity, no stable center of identity, no indivisible core of being, no *individual*.' It was the 'drive toward differentiated being or individuality, toward *individuation*' that allowed Western culture to be 'forged from the struggle of human reason with the irrational forces of nature'.[53] By thus 'stabilizing his position in relation to a stabilized world, "man", the detached subject' has been able to 'exert his influence over nature; [...] treat it as an object; [...] measure it with ever greater precision'.[54] However, according to Rosen, 'after being held at bay for over two thousand years', *apeiron* has now 'returned with a vengeance', exploding the 'ordering contexts of space and time' and all notions of coherent subjectivity. This Rosen identifies as 'the dilemma that underlies postmodernity'.[55]

To some extent, Rosen's theory recalls Adler's understanding of *apeiron*. Both regard its reappearance as the negative *telos* of modernity, though Rosen does not equate its return with the Holocaust. In Adler's assessment, the systematic effort of National Socialism to dehumanize and eradicate an entire people is ultimate evidence of the irreversible failure of the Enlightenment project, which has turned on the very individual it was meant to emancipate and liberate, striving instead to disempower and extinguish it: 'Man hat die Welt vergeblich um einen nicht mehr ersetzbaren Preis aufgeklärt, indem man das Unheimliche, das Abgründige, das Apeiron aus der Welt geschafft hat – nun ist es wieder erschienen.'[56] This view of a self-destructive Enlightenment, reminiscent of that put forward by Horkheimer and Adorno in *Dialektik der Aufklärung* (1947), has resulted in Adler being accused of being overly general and of shying away from addressing the true cause and perpetrators of the Holocaust: 'Dass es *Deutsche* waren, die *Juden* ermordeten, das kommt bei Adler nur andeutungsweise vor, dass es nicht *der Staat* oder *die Moderne* an sich war

[52] Peter A. Angeles, *Dictionary of Philosophy* (New York: Barnes & Noble, 1981), 14–15. Cited in Rosen, *Dimensions of Apeiron*, p. xiv.
[53] Rosen, *Dimensions of Apeiron*, p. xiv; original emphasis.
[54] Rosen, *Dimensions of Apeiron*, 3.   [55] Rosen, *Dimensions of Apeiron*, p. xiv.
[56] *Theresienstadt*, 667.

[. . .], leider gar nicht.'[57] He has been reproached with undertaking a 'Sprung ins gänzlich Abstrakte' as an evasive strategy, 'als Ausweichen'.[58]

In fact, Adler's impression of the demise of the grand narrative of Enlightenment progress is inextricable from his sense of the irremediable disruption of his own life story. His indictment of modernity, and his choice of the term *apeiron* through which to convey this, are grounded in the first-hand experience of reality no longer corresponding to 'was gemeinhin Wirklichkeit gewesen war und was sie nach ursprünglichen Wünschen sein sollte'.[59] The connotations of *apeiron* in his writing are not merely abstract. In denoting a state in which subject and object, inside and out, world and self are indistinguishable, the term evokes the abrogation of individuality to which the interned were subjected in the concentration camps: 'Man war so zu Materie geworden, daß Materie fragwürdig wurde. Man durfte fast nur noch Objekt sein.'[60] In its unbounded incalculability, it alludes to the impression of the concentrationary universe as a parallel world existing outside the continuum of space and time. In signifying 'a chaos so total as to defy ultimate analysis', it shares traits with the unformed void of *tohu va-bohu*, but avoids any association with a state of God.[61] It brings to mind characteristics of the pre-conceptual, pre-objective *Sein* with which Heidegger correlated the term.[62] However, it is closer to the *il y a*—as the *apeiron* to which all things return—in Lévinas, who speaks of a post-Holocaust 'sensation de chaos et de vide', and a sense as if 'l'être même s'était suspendu' in an unbridgeable 'gouffre béant'; or to the radical disorientation of Blanchot's *désastre*.[63] The term is judiciously chosen, precisely because it resists being assigned a single, fixed meaning. As that which eludes comprehension and definition, is untellable, and knows no end, *apeiron* finally also stands for the Holocaust as insurmountable caesura. This is underscored by Adler's conception of the elimination of *apeiron* by the Enlightenment as a process of repression, as shown by his equation of *apeiron* with 'das Unheimliche' that is 'wieder erschienen'.[64] As will become apparent particularly in Chapters 3–4, the return of *apeiron*, understood as the

---

[57] Fabian Kettner, '*Die unsichtbare Wand*: Anmerkungen zu H. G. Adlers Werk', *Literaturkritik*, 10 (2004) <http://www.literaturkritik.de/public/rezension.php?rez_id=7477> [accessed 27 May 2007] (para. 6 of 7); original emphasis.

[58] Kettner, '*Die unsichtbare Wand*', para. 7 of 7.

[59] *Theresienstadt*, 666.   [60] *Theresienstadt*, 667.

[61] Jeremy Adler, 'Good against Evil?', 274.

[62] Martin Heidegger, 'Der Spruch des Anaximander', in Heidegger, *Holzwege* (Frankfurt a.M.: Klostermann, 1950), 296–343 (339).

[63] Emmanuel Lévinas, *Noms propres* (Montpellier: Fata Morgana, 1976), 179, 178; Maurice Blanchot, *L'Écriture du désastre* (Paris: Gallimard, 1980).

[64] *Theresienstadt*, 667.

return of the repressed in a Freudian sense, is also suggestive of traumatic re-experience as the inescapable reliving of something that is at the same time incompletely understood and distressingly familiar. Once the 'death-world' has entered the 'life-world', it 'continues to exist, for eternity as it were', and irreversibly upsets notions of linear development and progress both in an individual life and in the history of the world.[65] The result is a destructuring of narratives both petty and grand.

In his studies, Adler describes existence in the camps as a state of suspension, outside the flow of time, between life and death. He speaks, or cites other witnesses speaking, of a 'Herausgehobensein aus der Zeit', where 'Bestand und Unbestand' had become blurred and the interned were 'Gespenster', neither living nor fully dead.[66] These terms are echoed in Adler's literary works. *Eine Reise* recounts the deportation of a family by the jarringly ironic name of Lustig, initially to a camp in a town by the no-less-ironic name of Ruhenthal, in an unspecified country and period in time. In the camp, one of the deportees refers to a sense of 'ausgestochene Zeit' (108); another reports the impression 'daß sie gestorben sei, wenn auch nicht eigentlich tot; es war ein Verscheiden, das nicht tötete' (42). The persecuted and the interned are collectively referred to as 'ehemalige Menschen', 'Erloschene', or 'Geister' (33, 30, 69). This condition is not relieved by the dissolution of the camps. Even after his release, Paul, the sole surviving member of the family, struggles to resume life: 'Ist Paul abhanden oder ehemalig, ist er weggenommen oder leibhaft hier?' (279). The same applies to the main protagonist of *Die unsichtbare Wand*, which relates the post-war existence of one Artur Landau, who has survived the Holocaust and outlived his own end. After his return from the camps, first to Prague, then on to exile in London, Landau feels that he is 'abgeschafft und weggenommen, dennoch gelassen, dennoch da' and that his is a state where 'man tot ist und als toter Irrtum auftritt, ein Nachspiel seiner selbst' (54). Here, these terms refer exclusively to a time 'after' the camps. Evidently, the end of the war has not ended the abeyance of Landau's life. The past to him is not past, but a 'Todeswunde, von der ich nicht genesen war' (10).

On one level, this unhealed wound is indicative of personal trauma. Landau is assaulted by uncontrollably surfacing fragments of events he is unable to summon up consciously and intentionally and therefore cannot stop reliving: 'ich weiß, daß ich die Verfolgung nicht los werde. Das Ungeheuer springt einem immer auf den Nacken. Aber diese Erfahrung

---

[65] Edith Wyschogrod, *Spirit in Ashes: Hegel, Heidegger, and Man-Made Mass Death* (New Haven: Yale University Press, 1985), 34.

[66] *Theresienstadt*, 675, 667.

und die Erinnerung sind nicht dasselbe' (196). Such traumatic re-experience falls somewhere between event and memory, and resists any attempt at narrative recollection, (auto)biographical or historical. As Landau puts it: 'Das ist aber wieder lebendig und eigentlich nicht Geschichte. [...] Das eben hängt in der Mitte zwischen Geschichte und Geschehnis, ein krankhafter Zustand, nicht wahr?' (401). As a result of 'its structural resistance to integration into memory', the traumatic past is never truly past but welds itself to the present.[67] Landau refers to it as a 'festgefrorene [...] Vergangenheit, die dauerte und weiter Dauer über alle Zukunft weit hinaus verhieß' (238). Because it 'leaps out of chronology, establishing its own momentum or fixation', the 'constantly *re*-experienced time' of the Holocaust 'threatens the chronology of experienced time'.[68] It flies in the face of any historical rationalization seeking to transcend the subjectively and arbitrarily limited present moment in favour of an artificial linear continuity between the past and the future. Indeed, it calls into question the validity of the very notions of 'past', 'present', and 'future'. This is thematized in *Die unsichtbare Wand*, in a conversation between Landau and his wife, in which she observes that his sense of the chronological passage of time is disturbed:

'Siehst du, das ist genau das, was du nicht verstehst. Gestern, heute, morgen: eine Reihe, die sich fortsetzt jeden Tag. [...] Du willst es nie begreifen. Dein Zeitbewußtsein ist gestört.' 'Die Uhr, die Uhr, ich kann sie lesen!' Den Kalender, schau, ich zähle dir die sieben Tage der Woche ab, die greifen ineinander, Tag und Monat, sieben zwölf und sieben zwölf. Und jedes Jahr wird außerdem gezählt, ich weiß es genau. [...] Siehst du, Johanna, mein Zeitbewußtsein ist ungestört, intakt.' 'In keinem Takt. Du [...] stürzt mir alles durcheinander, tick und tack. Uhr und Kalender taugen nicht für dich.' (245–6)

The chronology of days, months, and years, measured by clocks and calendars, no longer holds for the survivor's life, as manifests itself in a wealth of phrases in Adler's novels testifying to an apparent disruption of the flow of time. In *Eine Reise* we read: 'Der Augenblick ist zähe geworden, er ist ein klebriger Brei' (47). Landau in *Die unsichtbare Wand* variously experiences time as 'zerzogene Zeit', in 'zerhackten Schüben' or as a 'verschwimmender Zeitenwirbel' (30, 35, 306).

However, although Landau suggests that this is a 'krankhafter Zustand', he also states categorically that the 'Verwirrung von Geschichte und

---

[67] Cathy Caruth, 'Introduction', in Caruth (ed.), *Trauma: Explorations in Memory* (Baltimore: Johns Hopkins University Press, 1995), 3–12 (4).
[68] Langer, *Admitting the Holocaust*, 15; original emphasis.

Gegenwart' is not evidence of a disorder purely on his part: 'Bitte glauben
Sie mir, das ist kein psychiatrisches Problem' (401, 404, 405). Not just his
perception of it, but the very notion of historical time, and all conventions
and constructs vital to modern Western culture associated with it, are
regarded as having been dealt a blow now that the Holocaust, conceived as
the return of *apeiron*, has given the lie to the humanist narrative of
progress. Adler's novels not only portray the disruption of individual
temporalities; they seek to challenge the specious causality and misguided
sense of security we derive from the 'unexamined article of cultural faith'
as Elizabeth Deeds Ermarth denotes the 'belief in a temporal medium that
is neutral and homogeneous and that, consequently, makes possible those
mutually informative measurements between one historical moment and
another that support most forms of knowledge current in the West'.[69]
One passage that shows this very clearly occurs in *Eine Reise*, as a number
of deportees, among them Paul, are marched from their camp to a forced
labour site. Paul reflects on their ghostly procession that if, in addition to
everything else, they were deprived of their sight and forced to march
blindly, they would be denied any remaining hope of ever extracting
themselves, if only in thought, from the abyss that is their world. Unable
to distinguish between day and night, they would lose all sense of the
passage of time, of time spans and measurable duration, and they would
become inescapably 'ins unmitteilsam Abgründige vertieft' (108). However, Paul's attempt to conjecture immersion in the abysmal is thwarted by
his inability to detach himself from, and gain a vantage point on, what he
is evidently already 'vertieft' in. What initially presents itself as mere
hypothesis in Paul's reflection reveals itself as an impossible, and ultimately self-undermining, attempt to cogitate the status quo. Paul's failure
demonstrates the actuality of what he initially appeared to be positing only
in the abstract: in the unlimited and unquantifiable abyss that is the world
after the return of *apeiron*, chronological time has been subverted, and
along with it any notion of causation, coherent space, and independently
cognizant subjectivity:

> Dann könnte die Zeit auslöschen; nur eine Richtung hätte die Reise, aber
> kein Ziel; sie würde währen und ginge doch nicht weiter. Unsinnig würde
> die Frage werden, wann einer geboren ist, weil sein Tod viel weiter zurück-
> liegen könnte als der Tag seiner Erschaffung. Habt ihr es noch nie empfun-
> den, wie in einer ausgestochenen Zeit alles durcheinandergeriet? Was ihr
> heute zu halten vermeint, wäre entfernt, euer verlogener Traum von Sicher-
> heit würde sich endlich von euch abwenden, denn Ersparnisse werden

---

[69] *Sequel to History: Postmodernism and the Crisis of Representational Time* (Princeton:
Princeton University Press, 1992), 20.

müßig, es gäbe keine Zinsen und Zinseszinsen, weil man auch nichts von einem Kalender wüßte, nichts von einem Datum, nur trübe rollte man durch trübe Masse hin, alles wäre gleichzeitig und in eins verbacken, doch wieder auch nicht, teils beisammen, teils auseinander, aber nicht fortgesetzt und kaum verbunden, aufgehoben der Grund, aufgehoben die Wirkung. Statt der gierig beschworenen und doch nie erschienenen Ursache bliebe nichts als das hingeworfene Meer verlorener Sachen, die ihr nicht sammeln könntet, weil ihr nicht wüßtet, wann zu sammeln; die Werte wären zerbrochen und zerronnen, bevor sie einer zu erretten vermöchte. Von jetzt an ist also keine Zeit. Doch von jetzt an? Sinnlose Rede. Wenn keine Zeit ist, war sie auch nicht und wird nicht sein, die Sprache zertrümmert ohne das Zeitwort, alles huscht durcheinander, verdorbene Reise. (108)

Chronological time is perhaps the foremost, but by no means the only, assumption informing liberal humanism to be denounced in this passage. The denouncement of 'the dialectics, the teleology, the transcendence, and the putative neutrality of historical time' implicates a number of other touchstones of 'Western discourse', such as

its obsession with power and knowledge, its constraint of language to primarily symbolic function [...], its categorical and dualistic modes of definition, its belief in the quantitative and objective, its [...] individual subject, and above all its common media of exchange (time, space, money) which guarantee certain political and social systems.[70]

The end of historical time signals the end of the human(ist) age: 'da den Menschen die Zeit entrückt ist, hat das tierische Zeitalter begonnen' (108). Gone are the days when 'Menschen und Dinge noch in einem faßlichen Zusammenhang beruhten und alles sich ineinanderfügte und ergänzte' (111). All there is 'now' is a 'trübe Masse', a spatialized conception of time without direction or delineation, origin or aim, cause and effect: the world marked by the apeironic durational persistence of the Holocaust, or, to borrow Celan's term from the epigraph, by the 'Zeitenschrunde', as a gaping wound both in and to the very notion of time.

As space and time converge to form an indistinct, shapeless mass, the conventional view of chronological time as a line or arrow is superseded, and notions of life as a journey, with a clear beginning and end, are supplanted by images of eternal aimless wandering. This unmappable convergence of time and space can no longer be travelled in any straightforward, unidirectional sense. In this chronotope it is impossible to trace a path back to 'wo das Unheimliche die Kette zerriß und ihre frühen Glieder verwarf und vertilgte' (*Die unsichtbare Wand*, 98), or, for that matter, to

---

[70] Ermarth, *Sequel to History*, 14, 6–7.

blaze a trail to a future beyond the distressingly familiar yet not fully knowable *apeiron*. An 'invisible wall' prevents both return to any point of departure and arrival at any destination. Because they are unable to remember specific events consciously and at will, the protagonists of Adler's novels are at sea. Without 'klar herausgreifbare Erlebnisse' to guide him through the 'Zeitenwirbel', Landau notes, 'ist es arg, und mir fehlen die Leitpunkte' (306). The impossibility of moving on in time is reflected in an inability to arrive anywhere in space, or as we read in *Eine Reise*, with reference to the 'post'-Holocaust present:

> Jeder muß seinen Ort verändern, da er nicht die Zeit verändern kann. So ziehen die Wanderer in entgegengesetzte Richtungen [. . .]. Das Ziel ist unbestimmt. Gewiß ist nur, daß es nicht hier sein kann, es ist woanders [. . .]. [. . .] Sie werden wandern und keine Heimat haben, in denen sie die Ordnung ihrer Wünsche in die Tat verwandeln könnten. (225–6)

In mirroring the movements of the deportees during the Holocaust, who were marched from one location to another until it became impossible for them, but also for the reader, to tell which of these, if any, were contiguous and whether there was any pattern or logic to their displacements, this disordered wandering after the war reflects the trapped persistence of the 'past' in the 'present' and indicates existence in a chronotope beyond any kind of 'Ordnung'. To 'remember' in this trapped persistence is to keep going over already covered ground and be subjected to arbitrarily and uncontrollably surfacing fragments of a past (perceived spatially) that can only be endured but not retained, and certainly not contained: 'nur wechselnde Schauplätze leuchten da und dort auf. Sie verlöschen. Ich [. . .] kann sie nicht halten. Nichts mehr ist so, was es war, auch wird es nicht mehr werden' (640). The phrasing 'auch wird es nicht mehr werden', instead of, as we might expect, 'und wird es auch nicht mehr werden', has implications beyond the impossibility of things returning to the way they were: it calls into question the very possibility of a future time, as well as perhaps recalling the German expression 'das wird nicht wieder', suggesting general irredeemability.

Without temporal and spatial continuity, there can be no coherence of self. Thus Landau speaks of 'mein Ich in Unbestand zerronnen', and states: 'Ich habe kein Teil an einem Kontinuum' (54, 45). Time, space, and self are not absolute but coextensive; each is a function and product of the others, as becomes apparent, for instance, from Landau's reference to himself as 'ich, der keine Grenzen mehr hat, aufgelöst in da und dort jäh aufblitzende Wirklichkeitspunkte, denen ich schnell und doch so plump zutaumle, daß ich sie nie erreichen kann, weil sie inzwischen verloschen sind' (188). As the passage showing Paul's failed attempt to reflect on his own situation demonstrated, this kind of split and plural self-in-flux bears no relation to the stable Cartesian subject congenial to empiricism. Its mode of existence is closer to Heideggerian *Dasein*: grounded in temporality and relative to position, not transcendent, autonomous, and detached from space and time. In the Cartesian model of cognition, the 'object is *what* is experienced, the subject is the transcendent perspective *from* which the experience is had, and space is the continuous medium *through* which the experience occurs'.[71] In *Die unsichtbare Wand* and especially in *Eine Reise*, perspective is multiple and shifting, and the distinction between subject and object becomes blurred. In the latter we read: 'Es ist nichts so besonders, als daß es sei oder nicht sei. Ihr seht es nur verschieden an, oder ihr seht es auch gar nicht an. Jedenfalls geht es vorüber, und ihr werdet vorübergeleitet. Oder ihr selbst seid ohne Bewegung in steinerner Erstarrung, und alles wird an euch vorübergeleitet' (70). In the former, Landau comments: 'Der Tag ist stehngeblieben, oder ich bin stehngeblieben. Es läuft auf dasselbe hinaus' (122).

Once the boundary between subject and object has collapsed, a self can no longer be sure whether it is master of its own mind or whether it, and the thoughts it forms, are in fact merely the object of another subject's cogitation, and so forth, potentially ad infinitum. Landau observes that every once in a while, when his presence is acknowledged by other people, he believes himself to be real and is tempted to agree with 'jenem Philosophen [. . .], der verwegen aus seinem bloßen Denken schließen wollte, bereits auch selbst zu sein, einfach zu sein'. In fact, Landau concludes, his existence is 'eher [. . .] ein Zustand, in dem einer gedacht wird, und dieser eine bin ich' (12–13). The origin of that thought is impossible to determine, and Landau repeatedly refers to himself as Adam, man of no woman born, 'ohne Gefühl, vom Weibe geboren zu sein' (49).

Again, this sense of a self without origin and coherence is on one level symptomatic of personal trauma. The inability to return to the source of the trauma means that nothing seems to connect the self that has survived its death sentence with the self that experienced—and in spite of its survival in some respects succumbed to—the attempt on its life, let alone with any self before that attempt. The impossibility of integrating the traumatic event into a continuous life story of a single stable self may produce the guilt-inducing, and perhaps guilt-induced, impression on the part of the survivor of never really having been 'there' at all, of being an incomplete witness, with no right to claim the experience as his or her own. Landau says:

---

[71] Rosen, *Dimensions of Apeiron*, 12; original emphasis.

Ich weiß nicht, ob ich so unmittelbar dabei war. Ich bin doch nicht gestorben, und da weiß man es nicht. [...] Nur die Toten waren dort, weil sie allein geblieben sind. [...] So deutlich ich es auch vor mir sehe, es ist anders. [...] Erinnerung ist etwas ganz anderes. Sie ist die Identifikation mit der Verschickung und allen ihren Folgen, also mit der erlittenen Vernichtung. Das kann ich nicht. Ich bin bestenfalls zerbrochen worden, vielleicht zerschmettert, doch da ich hier vor Ihnen stehn kann, bin ich nicht vernichtet. [...] nur die eigene Vernichtung wäre die wahre Erinnerung. (196)

However, the inability to remember and the resultant struggle 'sich zusammenzuhalten, sich als Einheit zu begreifen' are, again, not regarded as merely an individual psychological affliction: 'Ich selbst, darunter versteh ich bei mir etwas Aufgespaltenes, aber nichts Krankhaftes' (197, 470). Rather, Adler's literary texts are pervaded by a more general sense of the end of the Cartesian *cogito* and the impossibility of knowledge. As we have seen, even the Theresienstadt monograph, with its exhortation to survivors to testify to the truth of the facts, and its prescription of silence for anyone without first-hand experience of them, concedes that the full extent of the 'Nichts' may not be known to, or knowable by, any living being. This position is adopted less equivocally in Adler's novels, which distinguish more explicitly between establishable facts and experience beyond comprehension. In *Die unsichtbare Wand* we read: 'Würde sich das Gedächtnis noch so sehr zurückbohren, so muß es doch verlöschen, ein Riß, und die Abgründe des ungeheuerlichen Unwissens werden auch von gedrängten Gipfeln gehäufter Gelehrsamkeit nimmer erlöst' (50).

This 'Riß', which, even within the sentence in which it appears, separates memory from the abyss and therefore knowledge from (re-) experience, is felt to spell the end of the epistemological as we know it. This finds striking evocation in a passage in *Eine Reise*, which conveys a sense of the world after/during the Holocaust as a post-traumatic, post-historical, post-cognitive bottomless pit:

Alles ist auf der Flucht und fährt, weil es nicht sein kann. Es fehlt ihm selbst der Grund, auf den es fallen könnte. Wenn jemand noch herumläuft, ist es ein Irrtum. [...] Abgehackte Hände liegen rings verstreut. [...] Schaut ein Auge auf die Hände, dann ist es ein verlassener Blick, der sich nicht kennt und nichts erkennt. [...] was die abgehackten Hände zeigen, hat keinen Sinn. Sie weisen nicht, es fehlt ihnen Gedanke; leere Richtung gibt kein Ziel an. So ist alles sinnlos. (216–17)

Spatial (and thus temporal) orientation is denied where the possibility of signification itself is precluded. Mind and body, subject and object, self and other, signifier and signified are indistinguishable once consciousness has ceased to be irreversible. All are maimed. This is the 'Abgründiges' of

Paul's failed hypothesis, the abysmal that is 'unmitteilsam' and therefore 'unmitteilbar'. The experience of the Holocaust as insurmountable traumatic caesura and the sense of modernity's self-destruction and all it entails are inextricably linked in Adler's works.

DIS(AD)VANTAGING THE READER

A corollary of this link is Adler's condemnation of the unthinking or even deliberate perpetuation of the grand narratives of progress and certainty on which the culture responsible for the return of *apeiron* was founded. One example of this is his criticism of a post-war politics of commemoration as forgetting, which smoothes over the caesura of the Holocaust and consigns the past to a hermetically sealed space separate from the present, or as we read in *Eine Reise*: 'Die Vergangenheit wird unter Denkmalsschutz gesetzt und kommt ins technische Museum. [...] aus der Gegenwart muß man sie bringen, damit sie keinen Schaden stiftet' (226). Such a musealization of the past ignores the effects events had, and continue to have, on people and focuses instead on the measurable and inanimate, on facts and artefacts. After one of the deportees in *Eine Reise* is sent on from Ruhenthal to an extermination camp, those left behind have a premonition of their belongings being turned into exhibition pieces after they have been transported to their death: 'Was wird mit den Schätzen der Verreisten geschehen? Alles kommt in Vitrinen, nachdem man es geputzt und konserviert hat, und saubere Aufschriften werden da sein und alles schön erklären. Grabbeigaben für Frau Ida Schwarz' (172). Such conservation, a lepidopterist's arrangement of pinned-down, lifeless remains under a display case, not only keeps the past safely in the past, but above all also preserves those epistemologies that permit unquestioning belief in the possibility of labelling and explaining and neatly filing away everything that has happened in the first place. It is no coincidence that the terms in which this practice is described bring to mind the commandeering and meticulous recording of Jewish belongings during the Holocaust, while the owners of these belongings were being 'disposed of' in the camps: the alignment points to a cultural continuity that renders those responsible for it complicit by association in the crimes of the past. This is particularly apparent where *Eine Reise* recounts Ida Schwarz's arrival at what we must assume represents the selection ramp at Auschwitz: 'Links die Menschen, rechts das Gepäck. Den Menschen machte man den Garaus, das Gepäck wurde ins Museum geschickt. Der technische Fortschritt durfte nicht aufgehalten werden, aber seine Geschichte wollte man aufbewahren' (175). Kathryn Jones has commented on this passage: 'Adler offers a biting critique of the inversion of the value of life over objects and the preservation of the history of technological progress rather than the remembrance of people.'[72] The inversion of values is indeed glaring here, and it is a means for Adler to show, as Jeremy Adler has noted, that 'technology, voyeurism, and consumerism are equally implicated in the catastrophe'.[73] At the same time, Adler's critique reminds us that the culture responsible for the Holocaust lives on in our upholding of its metanarratives.

However, what transpires beyond this from these passages is an awareness of the more fundamental difficulty of finding any mode of thinking and writing about the Holocaust that is capable of stepping outside the epistemological foundations of modernity, when the simple fact of observing the past—with the adoption of a detached vantage point by an independently cognizant subject implied by such observation—perpetuates the very discourse Adler is looking to subvert. Jeremy Adler makes a similar point for different reasons. He argues with reference to *Eine Reise* that because 'the very act of observing the past' turns the reader into a 'retrospective, if unwitting, accomplice', he or she 'falls victim to a double-bind' where she or he is forced 'to experience either the guilt of ignorance or that of knowledge'. Jeremy Adler's argument is grounded in a reading of Adler's work against Adorno's dictum in 'Kulturkritik und Gesellschaft' (1951) that to write a poem after Auschwitz is barbaric, and he concludes that 'the imperative for the reader' must therefore be 'to engage in active memory and respond to the texts not just aesthetically, but ethically'.[74] Though I agree with Jeremy Adler's point regarding the double bind in Adler's texts, I would argue that Adler's writing in fact gestures beyond this double bind, and that in order to go where he points, it is, on the contrary, essential that we not only respond to the texts ethically, but engage with their aesthetic.

Adler appears to have been very conscious of the fact that the attempt to break down narratives of progress, personal or historical, and convey a sense of the end of chronological time and independent stable subjectivity, through description and reflection, is an inherently self-negating undertaking, equivalent to Paul's endeavour to adopt a detached perspective on the abyss from within it. By remaining at the level of the discursive, any such attempt will simply produce a descriptive, and prescriptive, totalizing

---

[72] Jones, 'Fictional Representation of the Holocaust', 78.

[73] 'Good against Evil?', 276.

[74] In Theodor W. Adorno, *Gesammelte Schriften*, ed. Rolf Tiedemann et al., 20 vols (Frankfurt a.M.: Suhrkamp, 1970–86), x. *Prismen: Kulturkritik und Gesellschaft* (1977), 11–30 (30); 'Good against Evil?', 277.

narrative of its own. In academic writing, which is essentially epistemo-logical and reliant on the possibility of adopting a detached viewpoint and establishing chronology and causation, this is inescapable. What Adler's novels, and those of the other authors discussed here, can do, that his—or any—encompassing, explanatory, or descriptive representations of the Holocaust cannot, is pursue the challenge to metanarratives to its conclu-sion: by enacting their breakdown at a structural level and denying the reader a spectator's vantage point.

The main consequence of this approach is that content and discourse of the texts start to become inseparable. Their authors do not write *about* the Holocaust. Even *Eine Reise*, which speaks in part from inside the camps, is never straightforwardly descriptive. Rather, the texts come as close to reflecting the abyss from within as is possible, by evoking the enduring presence of the past as a by-product of the enactment of their failure to gain epistemological purchase—in approximation of both personal and historical trauma. Their primary subject matter becomes the breakdown of their own structures. As a result, a great deal of the imagery we encounter in these texts doubles up as a blueprint of their form. In Adler's writing this is evident in the excerpts I have already cited, not least in Paul's aborted speculation (108). Another example, which appears as an icon of the text in which we encounter it, occurs in the final pages of *Die unsichtbare Wand*. Here Landau's 'post'-Holocaust existence is summed up in a set of images combining the impression of time as disordered space with the absence of all knowledge and certainty, and the impossibility of signification, to create a chaotic chronotope without hope of orientation or escape, where the structures of the outside world mirror those of the mind attempting to navigate the Holocaust persistence, between them providing a model for and of the textual structures:

> Ein überlebter Mensch, an einer Wegmarke in tödlichem Schneesturm vom Unheil verschmäht; als der Sturm verzogen war, lagen alle Gefährten erfro-ren, die Wegmarke ist zersplittert, auf ihren Spänen sind keine Ziele mehr zu entziffern, die Wege selbst gibt es nicht mehr, Schritte nach rechts wie nach links, nach vorn und nach rückwärts entdecken nimmer die einst beschrit-tenen Spuren; rund herum können die Füße wohl gangbaren Boden berüh-ren, bloß sicher ist der Boden nicht, so erstaunlich er auch die Last des Schreitenden trägt. Aber jeder Wandel eines Vergessenen führt überall in die Irre. Keine Richtung verheißt einen verläßlichen Sinn, auch die Strecken der Zeit werden in stockender Verwirrung immer undeutlicher, Träume nagen an ihnen und narren die sichere Stunde. Schon gibt es keine Stunde mehr, die Reiche der Vergangenheit und der Zukunft sind zerschellt, sie sind nicht einzuholen und nicht zusammenzubringen [...]. Aller Ablauf ist zerschüt-telt und verbogen, da ist nichts mehr wieder zu erwerben. (640–1)

This disrupted 'Ablauf' in time, which proves impossible to retrace in space, also describes the novel's plot and our reading experience. In their attempt to mirror the development from chronological timelines to spatio-temporal persistence, the texts analysed here seek to undermine causality, continuity, and teleology. They do not unfold as narratives with a beginning, middle, and end. Time sequences appear jumbled and even layered, as we often cannot be sure if what we are reading belongs to the narrative present or the past of recollection, or if it is the mark of the past in the present. One passage that illustrates this in Adler's writing unfolds over a good fifteen pages in *Die unsichtbare Wand* (15–32). At the beginning of the passage, we are with Landau in his garden in London when he imagines a voice speaking to him from the 'past', reminding him that he has not escaped its clutches, and threatening to track him down. This triggers the memory of an earlier incident when Landau, already in exile, had received a summons to report to the immigration authorities. About this incident we are then told the following: on receiving the summons, Landau is terrified that the past is repeating itself, and he decides to flee the country and return to Prague. On his arrival there, in a Kafkaesque sequence of events, he is denounced, arrested, interrogated, and imprisoned. As the walls of his cell, literally, start to close in, Landau tries to dig his way out with his bare hands, metamorphosing into a caterpillar in the process. Just as his captors come for him, he abruptly finds himself, covered in soil, back in his garden in London. The entire sequence, which was presented as reminiscence, is retroactively revealed to have been a nightmare. However, on reading the next sentence, we realize that the garden in which Landau has 'woken up' is not the garden from which he drifted away in memory/dream: 'Mit Entsetzen merkte ich, daß ich zu bald triumphiert hatte, Haus und Garten waren von Polizei umstellt, Gewehre im Anschlag gegen mich gerichtet. Da schrie ich unmenschlich auf, und Johanna schüttelte mich aus dem Traum' (32). At this point, at the very latest, we expect the narrative to pick up back where it left off when it slid into the memory/dream sequence. However, instead of returning to what we assumed was the primary diegetic level of the first garden scene, the narrative returns only to the beginning of the memory/dream sequence and starts to recount Landau's experience with the immigration authorities. In consequence, we not only lose track of the main diegetic level, but we also start to lose sight of where recollection ends and nightmare begins, especially since, in terms of their content, the two are indistinguishable. We cannot be certain if what we have just read was a nightmare within a memory within the 'reality' of exile, or whether what we read as nightmare is 'reality', and the initial escape to the idyll of the garden no less a dream than the second one. The experience of reading such a text is akin to attempting to 'decipher' an Escher print, or a four-dimensional maze: if we try to trace its structure on the page, we find it refuses to add up. The structure only 'works' if we factor in the simultaneous presence of a second 'reality' or perspective.

This ambiguity is sustained over the entirety of the text. Indeed, *Die unsichtbare Wand* both begins and ends with an evocation of furnaces emitting a 'schwarze Rauchfahne' (7, 644). Ostensibly, the reference is to an industrial estate near the Landaus' home in exile, but the image of chimneys and smoke is never innocent in a world 'after' Auschwitz. The entire narrative present appears to be underlaid with a stratum from another time and place. At the end of the novel, Landau predicts that there may come a day when the smoke is barely visible any longer, but this remains speculative, and it applies to a future in which he does not exist. Not only its main character, but the text itself, and with it the readers, have covered years' and pages' worth of ground apparently without making any headway. The same holds true for *Eine Reise*, even though its very title would seem to indicate displacement from a point of origin to a point of arrival. However, the novel begins and ends in *apeiron*, after its characters' death sentence has already been pronounced, and before even those who survive its execution are able to move on. It is often suggested that the ending of *Eine Reise* is, if not positive, then certainly hopeful.[75] In a sense, this is true, for the text concludes with Paul standing at the station, waiting to catch a train in order to go on a journey of his own free volition, to a destination of his choosing. The final sentence of the text reads: 'Er glaubt, sie winken ihm zu einer guten Reise, weil der Abfall überwunden ist' (304). As Jeremy Adler has pointed out, the term 'Abfall' is 'theologically loaded', and he concludes: 'the novel asserts messianically: "der Abfall ist überwunden" ("the fall has been overcome").'[76] It should perhaps be borne in mind though that the term 'Abfall', in its meaning of refuse, is also used throughout the novel to refer collectively to the deportees, of whom the country is being 'cleansed'. Paul is, in fact, not certain if he really is being given a friendly send-off. Moreover, trains in a post-Holocaust context do not usually have connotations of a 'gute Reise', and even if this one does, the text ends before Paul can embark on it.

Rather than offer us a bird's-eye view, these texts expect us to pick our own path through the textual labyrinths they create. An illustration of this is the passage in *Eine Reise* in which Paul tries to recount the 'selection' of his sister on the ramp in Auschwitz, leading up to her execution. In a

---

[75] E.g. in Jeremy Adler, 'Good against Evil?', 286; Jones, 'Fictional Representation of the Holocaust', 75.
[76] 'Good against Evil?', 286.

further instance of disordered chronology, narration of the incident is delayed until after the war, when Paul comes to be haunted by the scene not witnessed when it first occurred. Jeremy Adler argues that the retrospective account by Paul 'in his attempt to grasp what has just occurred' after he is already 'on his way to freedom' allows him to 'free [...] himself from this repressed event'.[77] I would suggest that, far from being liberating, the delayed narration reflects the confusion that reigns in this ruptured reality and interrupted time, and, by mapping the sequence of events on the workings of the narrating protagonist's brain, replicates the deferred reliving of trauma which falls outside chronological succession. This reading would appear to be supported by the fact that Paul's narration is never completed but breaks off at the crucial moment, just as the side to which his sister was sent is about to be announced, and before any mention of her murder, leaving the narrative suspended in mid-air and demonstrating the impossibility of returning to the origin of trauma.

The account leading up to this point is not presented as description but takes the shape of a dialogue, ostensibly between Paul and an unnamed interlocutor. However, the shift from the narrator's account to the interlocutor's interjections or requests for clarification is indicated by dots or dashes only, and the entire extract could easily also be read as a single, rambling and self-correcting monologue, in which no one viewpoint is allowed to remain uncontested. As it is about to reach the crux of its matter, the dialogue/monologue cancels itself out by splitting into two forks, in both space and meaning, at the final, ambiguous word that signifies both various/varying and deceased:

Doch als wir ankamen...
   Doch als ihr angekommen seid...? Sprich weiter!—Doch als wir ankamen und aus dem Zuge stiegen, war es ebenso dunkel wie jetzt. Es war unendlich dunkel, dunkler als es je sein kann. Es war die Dunkelheit so dunkel, daß niemand sie sah. So war es, wenn auch grausame Bogenlampen an hohen Pfählen hingen und die zähe Dunkelheit bewarfen, daß es schmerzte...
   Also war es doch nicht dunkel. Es war bloß Nacht, doch sehen konnte man.—Nein, dunkel war es. Niemand konnte sehen, wir gewiß nicht; wir waren angeblendet, aber in der Finsternis. Die anderen haben wohl gesehen, doch das ist unbekannt, wenngleich es sich vermuten läßt. [...] Und dann ein Mann...
   [...] Er stand in Herrlichkeit und hatte eine Hand.—Die hat er immer.—Es ist eine Hand, wie es keine anderen Hände gibt. Sie zeigt, die Hand.—Wie hat sie gezeigt?—Dorthin... Verschieden. (229)

---

[77] 'Good against Evil?', 271–2.

The reader is in little doubt as to what has happened to Paul's sister. Indeed, the narrative relies on this awareness on our part. Yet ours is anything but a privileged position, for nothing is ever spelled out in the text. The dialogue/monologue reads like another example of a contention between narrative voices, as identified by Langer. As readers, we are closer to the perspective of the voice 'after death', urging the voice 'within death' to continue, looking for the narrative thread, expecting answers that will resolve all uncertainty. However, no answers are forthcoming. In consequence, we are forced to participate in the creation of meaning, while at the same time being made acutely aware that the final text will be a limited and partial construct mediated through us.

Though this is true for both of the novels examined in this chapter, it is compounded in *Eine Reise* by Adler's implementation of a complex focalization strategy. The excerpt just cited shows the vying of two perspectives. The text as a whole presents a manifold of viewpoints, none of which, in the absence of a single controlling perspective, is allowed to stand unquestioned. Kathryn Jones speaks of a 'polyvocal narrative perspective' in her analysis of *Eine Reise* and argues that 'continual shifts of focalization and the inclusion of other voices lead to a powerful dialogue and imply that, for Adler, no single perspective can suffice to represent the Holocaust'.[78] However, Jones then goes on to distinguish between focal points, suggesting that the 'reader is able to contrast the deportees' despairing views on their journey with those of the apathetic townspeople', while the 'hostile voices of the perpetrators addressing their victims provide a further conflicting element to the dialogue'.[79] As the main voice, Jones identifies 'a heterodiegetic narrator, who addresses the deportees as individuals or as a collective with the pronouns "Du" and "Ihr"', and thus sets up a 'linguistic opposition [. . .] between the narrator and the "wir" perspective of the deportees that highlights their marginalized status'. According to Jones, 'this device has a distancing effect, as the narrator remains a detached observer'.[80] In fact, the narrator only rarely appears as a detached observer, and it is often not possible to identify the focal point of a perspective in the text as unambiguously as Jones suggests. Even while addressing the deportees in the second person, the narrator frequently appears to take their side. Ambiguity arises because he tends to do this while focalizing them through the perspective of the perpetrators, as in this example:

---

[78] Jones, 'Fictional Representation of the Holocaust', 76.
[79] Jones, 'Fictional Representation of the Holocaust', 76.
[80] Jones, 'Fictional Representation of the Holocaust', 75–6.

> Niemand hat euch gefragt, es wurde bestimmt. Man hat euch zusammenge-
> trieben und keine lieben Worte gesagt. Viele von euch haben versucht, einen
> Sinn zu finden [...]. Doch es war keiner da, der geantwortet hätte. [...]
> nur die Angst sprach, die konnte man nicht hören. Alte Leute haben sich
> nicht dareinfinden können. Ihr Jammern war ekelhaft, so daß sich vor das
> Bedauern der Unbetroffenen eine häßlich verkühlende Wand stellte, das war
> die Mauer der Erbarmungslosigkeit. (9)

The initial, internal perspective appears to align itself with the viewpoint of the deportees, but as soon as the focus pans to the outside, to the world's response to their response, it shifts to a hostile perspective, to the judgement passed on the deportees by the 'Unbetroffenen', even while remaining critical of this judgement. The deportees are marginalized less because their being addressed in the second person puts them at arm's length, but because it reveals the absence of a perspective out in the world for them to call their own. Whether the gaze directed at them is sympathetic or hostile, they are its object, never its subject. This mirrors the deportees' loss of subjectivity and self-determination: they no longer have the right to a point of view.

The only means for the narrator to focalize through their eyes is by ironically breaking the perpetrators' perspective. This is apparent in the very designations used for deporters and deportees in the novel. They are not identified in religious or ethnic terms but are referred to, for instance, as 'Helden', or as 'Unmündige' or 'Verbotene' (39, 15). A more extensive example of such narratorial irony is this:

> Jahre habt ihr hier zugebracht und wurdet gerne gesehen. [...] als wäre es
> eure Heimat, die euch ein Recht gab, was ihr, unwissend vor Habgier, gar
> nicht bemerktet und ohne Frage euch nahmt. [...] Man gewährte es euch in
> Großmut, und ihr habt es genossen. [...] man mußte euren Anblick
> ertragen. Doch wurdet ihr gern empfangen, man grüßte, man lachte euch
> an und fragte nach eurer Gesundheit, denn man liebte das Geld in eurem
> Beutel. (18)

Irony allows the narrator to side with the deportees, but the perspective adopted and vocabulary employed are those of the perpetrators.

This affects even the deportees' abortive attempts to adopt a perspective on their own situation. One passage that exemplifies this is the paragraph leading up to Paul's failure to reflect on the abyss from within, in which he imagines the procession of deportees being blindfolded. Paul finds that the only way for him to cogitate his own situation is exoperceptively, by sharing the perpetrators' perspective on it. As soon as he attempts to focalize isoperceptively, he finds himself already in the abyss, and the adoption of a perspective becomes impossible:[81]

> Es *würde* genügen, die Augen der ersten Reihe unverbunden zu lassen, die dann nichts anderes zu tun hätten, als auf den Weg zu achten und vorsichtig die Füße auf den Boden zu setzen. Die anderen *schlichen* hintendrein, die Hände auf den Schultern ihrer Vordermänner, die stumme Geisterbahn, die keine Geleise *braucht*, immer vorwärts durch den unbestimmten Hauch, mag es Tag sein oder Nacht, jedes Glied des Zuges nichts als unverwandtes Schreiten [...], ins unmitteilsam Abgründige vertieft und fast verloren. (107–8, my emphasis)

The slide from the perspectival to the aperspectival is signalled by a shift in tense and mood, from the conditional of hypothesis in the 'würde' of the first line, to the ambiguous 'schlichen', which can be read as either subjunctive or indicative, to the present-tense indicative of 'braucht', indicating the omnipresence and everlastingness of *apeiron*.

The same slide characterizes our reading experience. When we are offered an external perspective on events, it is aligned with that of the perpetrators, which forces us into an uncomfortable complicity with them. Where such a perspective is withheld, we are denied an epistemological handle and cannot be sure whose view we are sharing. A sentence such as 'An alles habt ihr euch gewöhnt, und so werdet ihr euch auch an die Reise gewöhnen' (18-19), which is cited by Jones as an example of the views of 'the apathetic townspeople', could in fact just as easily be the view of a perpetrator, the narrator, or even a deportee.[82] The ability to tell these perspectives apart would allow us to remain detached observers. However, not only are we denied the epistemological upper hand, but because of the sentence's direct address, we feel personally implicated. The text manoeuvres us into a position where we are either complicit subjects or implicated objects.

TERRA INCOGNITA

This absence of a stable perspective and detached vantage point is perhaps the most obvious respect in which the texts under discussion here differ

---

[81] I borrow the terms 'isoperceptive' and 'exoperceptive' (indicating, respectively, personal identity and personal diversity of the subject and object of a focalization) from Göran Nieragden, 'Focalization and Narration: Theoretical and Terminological Refinements', *Poetics Today*, 23 (2002), 685–97 (689–90). Nieragden in turn draws on Wilhelm Füger's distinction between 'autoperzeptiv' and 'alloperzeptiv'.

[82] Jones, 'Fictional Representation of the Holocaust', 76.

from the majority of German, and especially West German post-war texts by non-Jewish authors. The protagonists of the latter works, Böll's Robert Fähmel or Hans Schnier, Grass's Oskar, Koeppen's Keetenheuve, or Lenz's Siggi Jepsen, for instance, are not necessarily any less marginalized than, and often occupy similarly liminal, extra-societal spaces to, their Jewish counterparts. They may experience identity crises, feel threatened by public spaces, and be critical of official state memory discourses, causing them to withdraw to secluded locations, apartments, studies, even a billiard room or an asylum bed. However, these positions of liminality allow the protagonists of non-Jewish texts to act as chroniclers of their time. Though very often flawed individuals, they are nonetheless consciences of the nation, issuing 'Warnrufe vor den erkannten drohenden Gefahren der Restauration', and foregrounding the act of private memory in opposition to social commemoration.[83] Here the outsider's perspective tends to coincide with an epistemological as well as a moral vantage point, a privilege which is extended to the reader.

Where my authors' works differ from these predominantly modernist ones of their contemporaries, and where we most clearly perceive a slide towards postmodernism, is in their sense of the impossibility of gaining— and consequent refusal to grant—an epistemological advantage on their subject matter. This, to recall Brian McHale's definition of postmodernism outlined in Chapter 1, leads to a 'shift of dominant from problems of *knowing* to problems of *modes of being*' in their writing.[84] In Adler's texts, this manifests itself, for instance, in the fact that 'the time of the individual mind no longer functions as an alternative to social time' but social time 'is subject to the same divisions and fragmentations that affect the worlds and identities of individual characters'.[85] Though modernist discourse may feel overwhelmed by, or be critical of, the world around it, it nonetheless 'respects primarily the constraints of an "objective reality" that, from a postmodern context, appears to be the mediated construct of a founding subject'.[86] In a modernist narrative, inconsistencies and instability in a reality portrayed can often be attributed to the limited, unreliable, or untrustworthy perspective of the narrating consciousness. In a postmodern narrative, such recuperation is difficult and problematic, and 'the weakening of individual *as well as* social and historical time as parameters for organizing narrative is the most crucial problem the postmodern novel

---

[83] Ralf Schnell, *Geschichte der deutschsprachigen Literatur seit 1945* (Stuttgart: Metzler, 1993), 286.

[84] *Postmodernist Fiction* (London: Routledge, 1987), 11.

[85] Ursula K. Heise, *Chronoschisms: Time, Narrative, and Postmodernism* (Cambridge: Cambridge University Press, 1997), 7.

[86] Ermarth, *Sequel to History*, 18.

articulates in its multiple formal experiments as well as many of its thematic concerns'.[87]

Though scholars of postmodern writing such as Ermarth, Heise, and McHale focus in their studies on texts written later, and in some cases considerably later, than those of the authors discussed here, many if not most of their comments can be applied equally to these. In the texts examined in Chapters 3–5, the formal experiments are even more prominent than they are in Adler's work. Increasingly, the strategy of these texts will be ontological—or hauntological—rather than epistemological, and therefore focused more on structure than on content, as they seek to undermine narrative linearity, enact their own breakdown, project where they cannot portray, and engage the reader in their creation. Where Adler ventures into unknown territory is in his realization that bearing witness from within the 'Zeitenschrunde' has to involve a rethinking of reference, and that the shortfalls of linear, chronological, descriptive writing when it comes to evoking 'life within death' can be compensated for (though not overcome) by drawing attention to them and enacting their collapse formally. In this respect, a reappraisal of Adler's literary work is crucial for our appreciation of literature of the Holocaust by authors who did not witness the camps from the inside. What Adler's literary texts show is that we should not be too quick to assume that an author of non-realist Holocaust fiction was what Alvin Rosenfeld has termed a 'fabulist' of the Holocaust simply by default, out of lack of knowledge about the facts of the event.[88] In the absence of such a reappraisal, texts such as those produced by the authors discussed here will continue to suffer the fate of Paul's literary, non-realist rendition of his sister's final days, which is turned down by every publisher to whom it is offered in *Eine Reise*, with one of them commenting 'Das ist unmöglich. Das ist Wahrheit, das ist keine Dichtung. Für Wahrheit ist mein Haus nicht eingerichtet', and the other countering 'Das ist unglaublich, zu viel Phantasie. Die Zeit ist anders und begehrt die reine Wahrheit, doch nicht Dichtung' (231).

---

[87] Heise, *Chronoschisms*, 7; my emphasis.
[88] *A Double Dying: Reflections on Holocaust Literature* (Bloomington: Indiana University Press, 1980), 76.

3

The Unhoused Past

Elisabeth Augustin, *Auswege*;
Jenny Aloni, *Der Wartesaal*

Sometimes I still scurry through the city like a bedraggled weasel that
has managed to make it through a big extermination drive. I start at
each sound or sight, as if the scent of faltering memories were
assailing my calloused, sluggish senses from the other world. Here
and there, by a house or street corner, I stop in terror, I search around
with alarmed looks, nostrils flaring, I want to flee but something holds
me back.

(Imre Kertész, *Kaddish for an Unborn Child*)

This chapter is dedicated to texts by two authors: Elisabeth Augustin and
Jenny Aloni. The texts were produced thousands of miles and almost a
decade apart. The authors had no knowledge of each other's work or even
existence. Their common ground, beyond any coincidences or divergences
of biography and geography, is the experience of the Holocaust past-in-
the-present from which there is no escaping, and the strikingly similar way
in which this translates itself into their writing.

Elisabeth Augustin was born Elisabeth Glaser in Berlin in 1903, to a
Jewish mother and Roman Catholic father.[1] Growing up in Leipzig,
before moving back to Berlin, Augustin began at an early age to write
poems and short stories. From 1923, her pieces were being printed in local
newspapers. Ten years later, her first novel, *Der Ausgestoßene*, was accepted
by Kiepenheuer & Witsch. Due to appear in 1933, the book was prevented from being published by the political climate, and later that same
year, Augustin left Germany for the Netherlands. Unlike many exiles, she

---

[1] For a biographical outline, see 'Elisabeth Augustin', in Klaus Hermsdorf, Hugo Fetting,
and Silvia Schlenstedt, *Exil in den Niederlanden und in Spanien* (Leipzig: Reclam, 1981),
55–6; or 'Elisabeth Augustin', in Renate Wall, *Lexikon deutschsprachiger Schriftstellerinnen
im Exil 1933–1945* (Gießen: Haland & Wirth, 2004), 19–21.

already spoke the language of her adopted country, through her husband who had grown up in Holland and with whom she had translated a number of Dutch authors into German. In the Netherlands, Augustin's novel was taken on by a Dutch publisher and appeared, in her own translation, under the title *De uitgestootene* in 1935.[2] Three further novels followed between 1935 and 1938, all of which were composed in Dutch and were, remarkably, received almost without question as the works of a native Dutch author, so much so that Augustin developed qualms about thinking of herself as an 'Emigranten-Schriftstellerin'.[3] In 1938, Augustin's parents fled Germany and joined her in exile, but in 1942 her father died, and in 1943 her mother was deported to Sobibór and gassed. In response to the experience of persecution and the murder of family and friends, Augustin's writing came to bear the traces of a Judaism with which she never identified in any religious or cultural sense: 'viele starben mir | ich streute ihre asche | auf die noch feuchte schrift | meiner lieder'.[4] *Auswege*, her first novel since the German occupation had curtailed her publishing activities, is a striking example of this. Informed by the Holocaust in a fundamental, but not immediately obvious, way, its style is unlike that of any of her previous novels. It is the only one of her works of fiction that is self-avowedly part autobiographical and at the same time the only one of her exile novels to go back to a German manuscript, though it appeared first in Dutch, under the title *Labyrint*, in 1955 and did not come out in its German version until 1988.[5] Augustin's memoirs, on the other hand, which were published two years after *Auswege*, were composed in Dutch and have never been translated.[6] Though she continued to write poems, short prose fiction, and radio plays almost up to the end of her life, Augustin died in Amsterdam in 2001 having never completed another novel.

Unlike Augustin, Jenny Aloni did identify with Judaism, and increasingly so in the face of Germany's rising anti-Semitism. She was born Jenny

[2] *De uitgestootene* (Amsterdam: Van Kampen, 1935). For bibliographical details, see 'Bibliography', in *The Elisabeth Augustin Reader*, ed. Robert Lyng (Krimpen aan den Yssel: Proza, 1978), 71–7.

[3] Elisabeth Augustin, 'Eine Grenzüberschreitung und kein Heimweh', in Hans Würzner (ed.), *Zur deutschen Exilliteratur in den Niederlanden 1933–1940* (Amsterdam: Rodopi, 1977), 33–43 (35). The three novels are *Volk zonder jeugd* (Amsterdam: Van Kampen, 1935), *Moord en doodslag in Wolhynië* (Rotterdam: Nijgh & Van Ditmar, 1936), and *Mirjam* (Rotterdam: Brusse, 1938).

[4] *Meine sprache, deine sprache: zum gedenken Else Lasker-Schüler* (Gelsenkirchen: Xylos, 1985). Cited in Alexander von Bormann, 'Der deutsche Roman in den Niederlanden: Formsemantische Überlegungen', in Sjaak Onderdelinden (ed.), *Interbellum und Exil* (Amsterdam: Rodopi, 1991), 225–49 (233).

[5] *Labyrint* (Amsterdam: Holland, 1955); *Auswege* (Mannheim: Persona, 1988). Subsequent references to the German edition will be made in parentheses in the text.

[6] *Het patroon: Herinneringen* (Amsterdam: Arbeiderspers, 1990).

Rosenbaum in Paderborn in 1917 to an observant Jewish family.[7] In 1935, she joined the Zionist movement and left Paderborn in order to get ready for *aliyah*, first at a preparation camp in Brandenburg, and from 1936 in Berlin where she learned Hebrew. In 1939, Aloni left Germany for Palestine and enrolled at the Hebrew University of Jerusalem. Her parents and sister, who had stayed behind, were deported in 1942, and murdered in Theresienstadt and Auschwitz. That same year, Aloni enlisted in the Auxiliary Territorial Service (ATS) of the British armed forces and served in a military hospital in Palestine until the end of the war. She then trained as a social worker and, after serving again as a medical orderly in the 1948 Arab–Israeli War, took up youth work. Between 1963 and 1981, she volunteered at a psychiatric hospital in Beer Yaakov. In 1993, Aloni passed away in Ganei Yehuda, Israel. Though, like Augustin, Aloni was fluent in the language of her new country, she continued to write almost exclusively in German, as a result of which publishing opportunities were scarce, and a great deal of her work appeared only with a significant delay. Between 1956 and 1983, three novels, three volumes of short stories, and two volumes of poetry came out, some in West Germany, some self-published in Israel. Only between 1990 and 1997 did there follow an edition of her collected works, including two previously unpublished novels, with Schöningh in Paderborn.[8] The year 2006, finally, saw the publication of diaries she had kept from 1935 to her death.[9] Of the five novels in the *Gesammelte Werke*, the first three—*Das Brachland, Zypressen zerbrechen nicht*, and *Der blühende Busch*—deal principally with Aloni's experiences after emigration. The two later texts—*Der Wartesaal*, written between around 1962 and 1964, and *Korridore oder das Gebäude mit der weißen Maus*, written between 1966 and 1969—are Holocaust novels in the same sense as the other works discussed here: imbued with traces of a past that cannot be straightforwardly recollected and recounted.[10] My focus here will be on the earlier

---

[7] For biographical information and a detailed bibliography of primary and secondary texts, see the section on Jenny Aloni under <http://www.juedischeliteraturwestfalen.de> [last accessed 18 Dec. 2008]. For a concise outline, see 'Aloni, Jenny', in Andreas B. Kilcher (ed.), *Lexikon der deutsch-jüdischen Literatur: Jüdische Autorinnen und Autoren deutscher Sprache von der Aufklärung bis zur Gegenwart* (Frankfurt a.M.: Suhrkamp, 2003), 10–12; or 'Jenny Aloni', in Wall, *Lexikon*, 12–15.

[8] *Gesammelte Werke in Einzelausgaben*, ed. Friedrich Kienecker and Hartmut Steinecke, 10 vols (Paderborn: Schöningh, 1990–7).

[9] *'Ich muss mir diese Zeit von der Seele schreiben...': Die Tagebücher 1935–1993: Deutschland—Palästina—Israel*, ed. Hartmut Steinecke et al. (Paderborn: Schöningh, 2006).

[10] *Gesammelte Werke*, ed. Kienecker and Steinecke, v (1992), viii (1996). Of the former there also appeared an earlier edition: *Der Wartesaal* (Freiburg i.Br.: Herder, 1969). Subsequent references to *Der Wartesaal* will be to the *Gesammelte Werke* edition and will be included in parentheses in the text.

Der Wartesaal, where the persistent effects of the Holocaust as traumatic rupture are particularly apparent.

Like H. G. Adler, both Augustin and Aloni conceived of the Holocaust as an insurmountable caesura and figured it as an inescapable chronotope. Like Adler, both also considered its traumatic upheavals to be more than just symptoms of an individual affliction. While in Adler's work the disruption of personal life stories is read sociologically, against the backdrop of a failed Enlightenment project and the demise of modern meta-narratives, in their texts the unbridgeable caesura manifests itself in, and through, family history: the trauma of the Holocaust takes the form of a disturbing familial legacy, an inexorcizable transgenerational haunting. In Adler, the Holocaust is aligned with the uncanny as the return of a repressed *apeiron*; Augustin and Aloni go a step further than this in that the uncanny in their texts is given bodily, or at least astral bodily, form: the past returns to haunt their protagonists in the guise of revenant ancestors, who serve both as traces of a former presence and as indicators of a present absence, as reminders of an un-past past and as placeholders marking the blanks of traumatized memory bequeathed by one generation to the next.

THE UNCANNY LEGACY

The transmission of Holocaust trauma to the offspring of survivors has been recognized as a clinical phenomenon and widely researched in psychology and psychiatry since the late 1980s.[11] Since the 1990s, it has also established itself as a concept in literary scholarship, where Holocaust writing in the second and third generation has become an exhaustively studied genre in its own right. In these fields, the exploration of transmitted trauma has either been restricted to generations born after the Second World War or has occasionally been extended to the 1.5 generation, as Susan Rubin Suleiman has termed survivors of the Holocaust who lived through it as children, too young to have an adult understanding of what was happening to them.[12] However, the authors under discussion here evoke the transmission of trauma at the very site of the traumatic occurrence, in the generation of the adult survivors themselves. In their texts, the survivors' trauma is already not entirely their own. The full extent of

[11] For an overview of scholarship in this field, see Natan P. F. Kellermann, 'Transmission of Holocaust Trauma: An Integrative View', *Psychiatry: Interpersonal and Biological Processes*, 64 (2001), 256–67.

[12] 'The 1.5 Generation: Thinking About Child Survivors and the Holocaust', *American Imago*, 59 (2002), 277–95.

the traumatic event is perceived as being known only to the dead, who in the writing of Augustin and Aloni return to haunt protagonists and text as the ghosts of the narrators' murdered parents.

A starting point for many of the studies devoted to exploring traumatic transmission, and/or its literary evocation, in later generations has been Nicolas Abraham and Maria Torok's theory of transgenerational haunting. As indicated in Chapter 1, Abraham and Torok distinguish between the survivor's original trauma as a *crypte*, an inaccessible, inexpressible site in the psyche of the traumatized individual resulting from a 'refoulement conservateur', or preservative repression, of the traumatic event, and the *fantôme*, the passing-on of such encrypted material to subsequent generations, where it haunts secondarily traumatized individuals as the spectral absent presence of an incident not repressed but never known. In Abraham and Torok's definition, the *fantôme* is

> une formation dans l'inconscient dynamique, qui s'y est installée, non du fait d'un refoulement propre au sujet, mais du fait d'une *empathie directe du contenu inconscient ou renié d'un objet parental*. C'est dire qu'il s'agit là d'une formation qui n'a pas été [...] le produit de l'autocréation du sujet [...]. C'est dire encore que le fantôme qu'il porte en lui lui est étranger. C'est dire enfin que les diverses manifestations du fantôme, que nous appelons *hantise*, [...] ne sont pas à confondre avec des retours du refoulé.[13]

Today it is generally accepted that even primary trauma is in fact characterized less by a 'successive movement from an event to its repression to its return', as Freud and indeed Abraham and Torok would have had it, than it is marked by the victim's 'inability fully to witness the event as it occurs', and that the 'experience of trauma [...] would thus seem to consist, not in the forgetting of a reality that can hence never be fully known, but in an inherent latency within the experience itself'.[14] The principal difference between trauma in the first generation and transmitted trauma in subsequent generations is now thought to reside in the question of mastery, which, while it may be impossible for the primary (non-)witness to trauma, is thought to become a possibility for, and thanks to, secondary witnesses. The realization that 'the historical imperative to bear witness could essentially *not be met during the actual occurrence*', as Dori Laub puts it specifically with reference to the trauma of the Holocaust, has in recent years led to a great deal of importance being attached to enabling 'the act

---

[13] *L'Écorce et le noyau* (Paris: Flammarion, 1987), 439; original emphasis.
[14] Cathy Caruth, 'Introduction', in Caruth (ed.), *Trauma: Explorations in Memory* (Baltimore: Johns Hopkins University Press, 1995), 3–12 (7–8).

of bearing witness [. . .] to take place, belatedly, as though retroactively', which in turn has led to great emphasis being placed on the role of the secondary witness and his or her task of listening for that which remains unsaid in a survivor's testimony.[15] In other words, it is felt that 'the history of a trauma, in its inherent belatedness, can only take place through the listening of another'.[16] In this constellation, 'the listener [. . .] becomes the Holocaust witness *before* the narrator does', and it is through 'the coming together between the survivor and the listener' that 'something like a repossession of the act of witnessing' is made possible.[17] Even if the trauma is passed on not to someone who deliberately exposes himself or herself to the risk of secondary traumatization, such as an analyst or interviewer, but to an unwitting or involuntary recipient, the very fact of transmission, by enabling testimony 'across the gap' left by the absent original event, is believed to represent the first step towards overcoming trauma.[18] To use Abraham and Torok's terminology, it is held that once the crypt has been converted into a phantom, it becomes mutable and can in theory be exorcized, in the presence, and with the help, of the secondary witness.

As we saw in Chapter 2, this belief informs not only psychoanalytic studies but also a great deal of research on second-generation Holocaust writing, which tends to assume that for the children of survivors, writing about the past entails using their imagination to fill in the blanks in their lives left by their parents' undisclosed memories of the Holocaust and that this acts as a curative measure. By overcoming the epistemological gaps through fiction, they are thought to be able to reconnect the aftermath in the present with its cause in the past and work through trauma in the second degree, or as Erin McGlothlin puts it:

> The writers of the second generation [. . .] attempt to negotiate the crisis of signification and their severed relationship to the Holocaust through the process of imaginative writing, in which they attempt to explore through language an event that they do not personally know but that they neverthe-less sense by its absence. Their imagination of the Holocaust past of the parents becomes a way for them to reconnect to the referent of the mark and thus to try to establish a link between experience and effect.[19]

[15] 'Truth and Testimony: The Process and the Struggle', in Caruth (ed.), *Trauma: Explorations in Memory*, 61–75 (68, 69); original emphasis.

[16] Caruth (ed.), *Trauma: Explorations in Memory*, 11.

[17] Laub, 'Truth and Testimony: The Process and the Struggle', 69; original emphasis.

[18] Laub, 'Truth and Testimony: The Process and the Struggle', 68; original emphasis.

[19] *Second-Generation Holocaust Literature: Legacies of Survival and Perpetration* (Rochester, NY: Camden House, 2006), 10.

In this view of second-generation Holocaust writing, the 'memory and identity marked by absence' evoked by the authors are conceptualized as 'open wounds which the recourse to writing helps to heal'.[20] Béatrice Damamme-Gilbert, in reference to the writing of Patrick Modiano, even speaks of mourning, of 'un deuil qui a pu enfin se faire'.[21]

Whether or not the writing of later generations can in fact be this unambiguously classified as the laying-to-rest of the ghosts of the past is, of course, a matter of debate. Certainly, the description does not extend to the writing of the first generation studied here. What we witness in this is not the encryption of trauma and its subsequent conversion into a phantom on the road towards potential recovery, but the transmission of a trauma that at the moment of its encryption in the traumatized is already felt to be a phantom, the ghostly trace of someone else's experience. The survivors in these texts consider themselves the keepers of a secret which is not theirs to divulge. What is more, the unmemory of the atrocities of the Holocaust in this first generation appears inextricable from a sense of guilt on the survivors' part—as apparently on that of their authors—at not having shared the fate of those who died. In another context, this impression of being an 'incomplete witness' to the cause of trauma might be read as simply an inherent characteristic of traumatic experience; here it is perceived as a mark of shame.[22] This, in turn, is felt to act as an ethical injunction: as an imperative to recall the past yet acknowledge that it is fundamentally unknowable to the living, and to respect and maintain the inherent insuperability of the traumatic event. The authors discussed here seek to reproduce and preserve the traumatic disruptions of the past, viewing the threat these pose to memory, self, and text not as an affliction that can and should be cured, but as an integral part of what it means to live after, and write 'about', the Holocaust, and regarding the refusal to let the wounds close as the only adequate and appropriate means of commemorating and communicating the past. Unlike ghosts as we conventionally imagine them, their spectres have no message to convey; they, and the upset to the fabric of time, space, and text caused by their repeated return and their suspension between absence and presence, *are* the message. They appear not in order to be put to rest,

---

[20] Samuel Khalifa, 'The Mirror of Memory: Patrick Modiano's *La Place de l'étoile* and *Dora Bruder*', in Andrew Leak and George Paizis (eds), *The Holocaust and the Text: Speaking the Unspeakable* (Basingstoke: Macmillan, 2000), 159–73 (160).

[21] 'Secrets, fantômes et troubles de la transmission du passé dans la pratique littéraire de Patrick Modiano', in John E. Flower (ed.), *Patrick Modiano* (Amsterdam: Rodopi, 2007), 109–30 (117).

[22] As it is by Primo Levi, who coined the term 'complete witness'. In *The Drowned and the Saved*, trans. Raymond Rosenthal (London: Abacus, 1989), 64.

but so as to demonstrate their unrest. Rather than open up the possibility of their secret being spelled out and dispelled, traumatic transmission here in fact ensures its preservation.

The consequence of this for the protagonists of the texts examined here is that the unremembered, untellable past is not only endlessly relived by those who survived it; its unknowable insurmountability is then passed on from parents to progeny, or in the case of the works considered in this chapter, from mother to daughter. In both texts, a female narrator suffers, but also inherits and transmits, trauma, and the impossibility of coming to terms with the past is underscored by the fact that the final recipient of the trauma in each book is a child who either may no longer be alive or was never even born. As we shall see, in Augustin's text, the child's suspension between life and death could be read as an indication that trauma has already taken hold in the second and even third degree. In Aloni, the insurmountability of the Holocaust appears to preclude the very possibility of a future generation. Like Imre Kertész's *Kaddish for an Unborn Child*, her entire text is addressed to a child the narrator will never have. As carriers of the 'death-world' legacy, these children are all in a sense stillborn. They will never atone for the sins their fathers or mothers did not commit, just as these are unable to exorcize their own dead parents' spectres, and therefore, by extension and conflation, the spectre of their dead parents.

In consequence, the narrators are haunted by a past that is 'unheimlich' in more than one respect: uncanny—in the sense that it is unknown, or encrypted, a traumatic effect severed from its cause, yet, because of its continual returns, distressingly familiar to those it haunts—but also unhoused—in the sense that it has no home, can be consigned to no final resting place. Those haunted by it will never know, yet nor can they ever forget, and they carry the past, indecipherable and inescapable, with them wherever they go. This is reflected in the spaces they inhabit, and in the texts constructed around them. Devoid of chronological sequence and causal chains, their worlds are portrayed as labyrinths without centre, periphery, or exit, boundless in space and through time. At any moment, the past may unexpectedly present itself; it may be behind them, but it is also always just around the corner. This manifests itself thematically, but it is above all also enacted structurally. In the writing of both authors, but especially in that of Jenny Aloni, the text itself comes to resemble an inescapable maze, mapped on the confused, and confusing, actual and abstract trails followed by those who pursue, and are pursued by, traumatic memory. The narrators' inability to master the past that possesses them is mirrored formally by the text's refusal to take command of the trauma which inhabits it. Instead of culminating in the uncovering of a secret, this kind of writing strives as far as possible to sustain unknowing. The product of this is a narrative construct that recalls Hélène Cixous's description of Freud's efforts to define the uncanny: as a 'search whose movement constitutes the labyrinth which instigates it'.[23]

LOSING THE PLOT:
ELISABETH AUGUSTIN'S *AUSWEGE*

The precise genesis of *Auswege* is unknown, but it would seem that the text achieved something very close to its present form between 1945 and 1952. Having begun work on it soon after the end of the war, Augustin refers to its writing as a drawn-out process spanning many years, in which she attempted to come to terms with the 'Schmerz [. . .], der mich jahrelang gequält hat, nachdem ich den Tod meiner Mutter in einer der Gaskammern im KZ von Sobibor erfahren hatte'.[24] From Augustin's correspondence with various publishing houses, it would appear that a very preliminary draft of the novel was nearing completion as early as 1946.[25] However, it was 1952 by the time the work had reached a final form, and a letter to Daamen publishing suggests that Augustin hoped to see it in print by the end of that or the beginning of the following year.[26] The timeline tallies with Augustin's own later estimate of having dedicated about seven years to its writing, though it was to be another three years before *Labyrint* finally appeared with Holland publishing in 1955.[27]

Not least because Augustin had adapted so quickly to the culture and language of her new country and even fostered the image of herself as a 'niederländische Schriftstellerin', her work remains largely unknown outside the Netherlands.[28] What consideration it has been given has often been restricted to the field of linguistics where Augustin makes an interesting case study for research into bilingualism, owing to the fact that she

---

[23] 'Fiction and Its Phantoms: A Reading of Freud's *Das Unheimliche* (The "Uncanny")', *New Literary History*, 7 (1976), 525–48 (525).

[24] 'Grenzüberschreitung', 38.

[25] Letter of 16 Apr. 1946 from Elisabeth Augustin to Brusse Uitgeversmij, Rotterdam, in *Collectie Augustin, Elisabeth*, Letterkundig Museum Den Haag, A00475 B1 (A–K).

[26] Letter of 21 Apr. 1952, to Daamen Uitgeversmij, Den Haag, Letterkundig Museum Den Haag, A00475 B1 (A–K).

[27] Letter of 11 Dec. 1974, to J. C. van Schagen, Letterkundig Museum Den Haag, A00475 B1 (L–W). In the letter, Augustin notes that she has doubts about the quality of the novel and attributes these in part to having taken 'too long' to complete it: 'Ik heb er te lang aan gewerkt, zeven jaar meen ik.'

[28] For instance in 'Grenzüberschreitung', 35: 'Ich hatte sofort versucht, eine holländische Schriftstellerin zu werden.'

not only wrote in two languages but occasionally produced versions of the same text in both Dutch and German.[29] *Auswege*, the only one of Augustin's novels to have come out in German, received scant though favourable attention around the time of its publication, but this has since all but dried up. In the Netherlands, *Labyrint* was more widely reviewed when it first appeared, and again on the occasion of its second edition in 1982, but it found little acclaim and tended to be unfavourably compared to Augustin's earlier, more realistic writing.

The difference between Augustin's final novel and her first four is indeed considerable. Superficial thematic differences notwithstanding, the earlier novels are very similar. They depict the lives of outsiders in rural or working-class environments, who experience hardship and marginalization, and they do so by means of a first-person narrator who tells the characters' story in a neutral, detached fashion, as one who personally witnessed, and is privy to every detail of, events but had no influence on their outcome. Alexander von Bormann associates these earlier novels with 'Heimatkunst', with the 'Dorfroman, wie er in den zwanziger und dreißiger Jahren in Deutschland eine gewisse Konjunktur hatte'.[30] Yet their style is not 'völkisch' but that of social realism, aiming for a 'präzise Darstellung des Milieus'.[31] Victor van Vriesland has commented on *De uitgestootene*: 'No mood is sought here, hardly an atmosphere. [. . .] One feels rather a certain partial uninvolvement of emotions that appears not so much as weariness or pessimism, but a hard, unbending, sober sense of reality.'[32] *Auswege*, on the other hand, is much harder to categorize. The author herself refers to its style as magic realism, 'magisch realisme', or, in another interview, somewhat misleadingly, as 'utopisch realisme'.[33] Some recent critics have placed Augustin 'in die Nähe der literarischen Avantgarde', or have aligned *Auswege* with the French *nouveau roman*.[34] Others,

---

[29] See e.g. Helga Hipp, 'Autor und Text im Spannungsfeld der Zweisprachigkeit: Elisabeth Augustins niederländische und deutsche Textfassungen', *Zeitschrift für Germanistik*, 11 (1990), 318–23; Heiko Stern, 'Sprache zwischen Exil und Identität: Die Konstitution von Heimat durch Sprache bei Elisabeth Augustin', in Pól O'Dochartaigh (ed.), *Jews in German Literature Since 1945: German-Jewish Literature?* (= *German Monitor* 53) (Amsterdam: Rodopi, 2000), 77–93.

[30] Bormann, 'Der deutsche Roman in den Niederlanden', 232.

[31] Heribert Seifert, 'Menschen im Labyrinth ihrer Zeit: Hinweise auf Leben und Werk von Elisabeth Augustin', *Neue Zürcher Zeitung*, 14 June 1988.

[32] Cited in M. H. Würzner, 'Introduction', in *The Elisabeth Augustin Reader*, ed. Lyng, 7–10 (7).

[33] John Albert Janse, 'Duitsland blijft mijn taalland', *Vrij Nederland*, 29 May 1993; Marianne A. van Ophuisen, 'Ik ben een onverbeterlijke optimiste', *De Nieuwe Linie*, 22 Nov. 1978.

[34] Thomas Günther, 'Flucht ins Labyrinth: Eine Begegnung mit der Autorin Elisabeth Augustin', *Süddeutsche Zeitung*, 14 Mar. 1992; Alexander von Bormann, ' "Wir sind nicht,

especially in the Netherlands, have taken an even vaguer view, commenting simply that the novel has 'a modern feel' to it, 'doet modern aan', and that its style is 'abstracter en met minder woorden', or just generally somewhat inaccessible, 'moeilijk toegankelijk'.[35]

One of the main criticisms levelled against the work, especially on the occasion of its first publication in the Netherlands, was its lack of a clear plot. One reviewer in 1956 laments that a proliferation of the reflective ('het beschouwelijke') in the text has stifled its 'dramatische compositie'.[36] Another speaks of a privileging of atmosphere over plot, a 'vooropstellen van de sfeer waar de handeling', and deplores that the novel's content is forced to take a back seat to its 'constructie'.[37] A third calls *Labyrint* simply 'onleesbaar': a confused and disorganized ('verward, wanordelijk') book, whose author needs to impose order on her material ('in zijn stof orde scheppen').[38] The reviewers' comments appear to be borne out by their abortive bids to identify and trace the thread of the narrative: their efforts to reconstruct the novel's plot exhaust themselves in the telling. The same holds true for the content summary on the back cover of the German edition of *Auswege*, where the petering out of the precis is even reflected typographically:

> Amsterdam, kurz nach dem Ende des zweiten Weltkriegs: Marianne und Paul, deutsche Emigranten, die zu Beginn der Hitlerzeit in Holland Zuflucht gesucht haben, fahren für ein paar Tage ans Meer. Sie fahren zusammen mit Viktor, einem Jugendfreund Mariannes, der bei ihnen während der Besatzungszeit untergetaucht war. Ein Ausflug, der Marianne die Aussöhnung mit Paul und die Lösung von Viktor bringen soll. Aber die Männer streiten sich, und Marianne, von bösen Ahnungen getrieben, besteht darauf, sofort zurückzufahren, um nach ihrer Tochter zu sehen. Dorle jedoch ist verschwunden...

This is almost word for word the same attempt at a summary that we encounter in the reviews of the novel's Dutch version, except that these

---

was wir sind." Nichtidentität als Erzählkonzept im deutschjüdischen Roman nach 1945', in Jens Stüben and Winfried Woesler (eds), '*Wir tragen den Zettelkasten mit den Steckbriefen unserer Freunde': Beiträge jüdischer Autoren zur deutschen Literatur seit 1945* (Darmstadt: Häusser, 1993), 31–52 (39).

[35] Anke Manschot, 'Elisabeth Augustin: Een schrijfster die vergissingen toegeeft', *Opzij*, Apr. 1991; Lucie Th. Vermij, 'Verloren tijd inhalen: Het patroon in het werk van Elisabeth Augustin', *Surplus*, 5/6 (1991), 18–20 (19); Paul Arnoldussen, 'Te serieus voor de lezer', *Het Parool*, 8 Jan. 2002.

[36] Ben van Eysselsteijn, 'Bezinning op deze wereld en een andere', *Haagsche Courant*, 4 Feb. 1956.

[37] Albert Buffinga, 'Vermindering van spanning', *Elseviers Weekblad*, 21 Apr. 1956.

[38] Jan Greshoff, 'Romanschrijver moet in zijn stof orde scheppen', *Het Vaderland*, 9 June 1956.

tend to omit any reference to the historical context and speak instead simply of a love triangle: the 'driehoeksverhouding' between Marianne, Paul, and Viktor.[39] What causes these 'summaries' to end when and as they do is not a desire to create suspense as much as the fact that this is as far as any recognizable and recountable plot in the novel goes. What we initially take to be the main storyline unravels into multiple filaments, and ceases to progress in any straightforward sense, after Dorle's disappearance, which is first reported at the end of the first chapter. From this point on, the initial semblance of a conventionally structured, linear first-person narrative is dissolved, and the text reveals itself as a polyvocal, polyperspectival narrative composite. The first chapter, which is presented from Marianne's point of view and bears her name as its title, is followed first by Paul's and then by Viktor's perspectives on their situation and the events to date. Though each individual protagonist's outlook is limited and biased in its own way, the reader is at this stage still able to piece together the different narrative strands to form a more coherent overall picture. Of the book's eight chapters in total, the fourth and seventh are also ascribed to Marianne, the fifth to Viktor, the final one to Paul, and the sixth to a deceased friend of Marianne's, Pierre. Narrative perspective appears to be clearly assigned throughout.

However, in the fourth chapter, appearances turn out to be deceptive. As we shall see, perspective ceases to be unambiguously attributable here, irrespective of the chapter heading, and chronology and narrative linearity are further subverted as it becomes difficult to distinguish present from past in the text, or indeed to differentiate between fact and conjecture or between reality and dream. What initially appeared as the epistemological upper hand is now denied us. After this point, according to Albert Buffinga, the focus on 'constructie' impedes any plot progression and there is no use even discussing the rest, for it is 'ook door de schrijfster te weinig begrepen en doordacht'.[40] Even the reader who, in Ben van Eysselsteijn's words, can muster the patience to follow Augustin along the manifold 'smalle kronkelwegen' of her text, which are more important to her than 'de hoofdweg der handeling', will be disappointed by the absence of, as Hans Warren puts it, an even remotely 'bevredigend einde'.[41] As Warren's remark shows, even after the second edition of *Labyrint* in 1982, the time was apparently not ripe for a novel that not only had an unsettling subtext (though this was surprisingly often ignored by reviewers) but also a disconcerting form. While the work fares better in

[39] Hans Warren, 'Labyrint', *Provinciale Zeeuwse Courant*, 5 Mar. 1983.
[40] *Elseviers Weekblad*, 21 Apr. 1956.
[41] *Haagsche Courant*, 4 Feb. 1956; *Provinciale Zeeuwse Courant*, 5 Mar. 1983.

the few German-language reviews dedicated to it, these tend not to comment at all on the question of its structure, and an in-depth analysis of the text in any language has yet to appear.

I maintain that while the cited reviewers' powers of observation cannot be faulted, the assumption that the favouring of structure over content, and style over plot, is an unhappy side-effect, as opposed to the intended outcome, of Augustin's literary project is fallacious. Rather, I shall suggest that, as in the case of the other texts discussed here, the privileging of form reflects the author's realization that her subject matter could only be conveyed structurally, not thematically, and that the form of the text would therefore have to double up as its theme. The key to what might constitute this subject matter is introduced at the very beginning of the book. The crucial incident, on which the remainder of the text rests, takes place in the space of the first two pages. The novel starts as Marianne, Paul, and Viktor, three German exiles living in the Netherlands, are about to take a drive to a seaside resort, leaving their daughter behind in the care of the nanny. The daughter is reluctant to let them go. According to Marianne, this is because 'Dorle hat es geahnt' (5). The 'es' happens soon after their departure when they, allegedly, narrowly miss colliding with a train at a railway crossing. Having supposedly cheated death and escaped unharmed, they go on to spend some time at their destination by the seaside but leave early, impelled by a sense of foreboding on the part of Marianne. On their return, Dorle has vanished. At first, Marianne in particular is distraught. However, once the initial shock has subsided, the remainder of the novel shows that, rather than investigate Dorle's absence, Marianne, Paul, and Viktor increasingly begin to question the reality of their own presence, until Paul eventually reaches the conclusion that they may not have avoided the collision after all but that: 'wir gestorben sind ohne es gemerkt zu haben' (48). The ambiguity with which the incident triggering the (perceived) unreality of the protagonists' existence is described has led reviewers to disagree as to whether it is an actual 'auto-ongeluk', in which the protagonists 'om het leven zijn gekomen' but which renders them clairvoyant ('helderziend') in the final seconds of their life, or merely a 'jäher Schrecken', causing them to relive 'die Ängste der jüngsten Vergangenheit'.[42] Warren complains that the unrelieved uncertainty as to whether the protagonists are dead or alive is a fundamental weakness of the text: 'Het zwakke punt nu van "Labyrint" is, dat de schrijfster onduidelijk blijft. [...] Dat is het onbevredigende, vooral omdat Elisabeth Augustin de beide mogelijkheden tot het einde toe

---

[42] Nico Verhoeven, 'De weg van het mede-lijden', *De Tijd*, 10 Mar. 1956; Seifert, *Neue Zürcher Zeitung*, 14 June 1988.

openlaat.'[43] With the notable exception of Heribert Seifert in the *Neue Zürcher Zeitung*, most reviewers ultimately decide that Augustin does in fact allude to a fatal car crash, and they infer from this that the novel revolves around the question of whether there is life after death. What is more, because this question remains unresolved in the text, they then conclude that, in her choice of topic, Augustin had bitten off more than she could chew, or loaded 'te veel hooi op haar vork', too much hay onto her pitchfork, as Warren puts it.[44] Jan Greshoff states bluntly that 'Elisabeth Augustin, die letterkundig gesproken niet de eerste, de beste is', has overreached herself, 'heeft te hoog gegrepen'.[45]

I would suggest that Seifert's interpretation of the incident as a shock, which causes the protagonists to relive events of the recent past, holds far greater promise, and that the state of suspension between life and death in which Augustin's protagonists find themselves, and their delayed and incomplete insight into what has happened to them, are not the product of the author's failure to be clear as to the fatality or merely potential fatality of the incident; they are an allusion to the experience of trauma. Indeed, the image of walking away seemingly unscathed from a train collision but belatedly starting to manifest traumatic symptoms is one we encounter in exactly this form in Freud, in the section on 'Latenzzeit und Tradition' of his essay on Moses and monotheism, where he uses it in order to illustrate traumatic latency:

> Es ereignet sich, daß ein Mensch scheinbar unbeschädigt die Stätte verläßt, an der er einen schreckhaften Unfall, z.B. einen Eisenbahnzusammenstoß, erlebt hat. Im Laufe der nächsten Wochen entwickelt er aber eine Reihe schwerer psychischer und motorischer Symptome, die man nur von seinem Schock, jener Erschütterung oder was sonst damals gewirkt hat, ableiten kann. Er hat jetzt eine 'traumatische Neurose'. [. . .] Man heißt die Zeit, die zwischen dem Unfall und dem ersten Auftreten der Symptome verflossen ist, die 'Inkubationszeit' in durchsichtiger Anspielung an die Pathologie der Infektionskrankheiten.[46]

Given that Augustin refers explicitly to Freud's writings elsewhere in *Auswege*, where she quotes from his 'Der Wahn und die Träume in W. Jensens *Gradiva*' (204), it certainly seems possible that the text's founding incident might also be an allusion to his work. We might even read the fact that the

[43] *Provinciale Zeeuwse Courant*, 5 Mar. 1983.
[44] *Provinciale Zeeuwse Courant*, 5 Mar. 1983.   [45] *Het Vaderland*, 9 June 1956.
[46] Sigmund Freud, 'Der Mann Moses und die monotheistische Religion: Drei Abhandlungen' (1939), in *Studienausgabe*, ed. Alexander Mitscherlich, Angela Richards, and James Strachey, 11 vols (Frankfurt a.M.: Fischer, 1969–75), ix. *Fragen der Gesellschaft/Ursprünge der Religion* (1974), 455–581 (516).

one direct quotation of Freud is from an essay which documents the
application of psychoanalytic theory to a work of literature as encouragement
for the reader to do the same.

Certainly, the protagonists' response to the incident at the railway crossing is suggestive in a number of respects of post-traumatic stress disorder,
which Cathy Caruth, expanding on the theory of traumatic experience
developed by Freud in 'Jenseits des Lustprinzips', has defined as being
characterized by

> a response, sometimes delayed, to an overwhelming event or events, which
> takes the form of repeated, intrusive hallucinations, dreams, thoughts or
> behaviors stemming from the event, along with numbing that may have
> begun during or after the experience, and possibly also increased arousal to
> [...] stimuli recalling the event.[47]

Marianne, Paul, and Viktor all voice a sense of leading a life somehow
numbed and suspended. Paul speaks of 'das Le... das scheinbare Leben'
(207), and he even becomes self-conscious about using the term 'erleben'
to describe an experience, having earlier been picked up on this usage by
Viktor (54), and corrects himself: 'daß ich das erle... wissen erfahren
durfte' (208). In both these instances, the impression of a hiatus is
mimicked typographically by the use of ellipses. Paul's conclusion that
there may have been a collision after all is reached only with substantial
delay and in the face of overwhelming evidence to suggest that something
has in fact happened to put their lives on hold. Marianne, who out of the
three is most acutely aware of the dimming of her existence, states: 'Aber
ich lebe nur noch halb mit abgeschirmtem Licht' (121), and finally
concludes: 'Wie gering ist der Unterschied zwischen Leben und Nichtle-
ben' (168). Another manifestation of their numbed state is that all three
protagonists have difficulty distinguishing between waking and sleeping or
reality and dream. Viktor asserts: 'Ich weiß ebensowenig ob ich wach bin
oder träume' (59), while in one of Marianne's chapters we read: 'Wirklichkeit Traum ist der Unterschied so groß? Für mich nicht mehr' (77).

The protagonists' sense of not being fully 'there', or present in the
moment, is largely attributable to the fact that their experience of the
present is continually interrupted by intrusions of a past that can be
neither consciously remembered nor therefore left behind, with the result
that the different time frames may become indistinguishably blurred. Both
Paul and Viktor are represented as struggling but failing to form a clear
memory of the incident they suspect must have taken place, while Marianne in particular is haunted by flashbacks of the (near-)collision. The

---

[47] Caruth (ed.), *Trauma: Explorations in Memory*, 4.

sound of a car horn, for example, reminds her of the whistle of a steam engine and for an instant transports her back to the railway crossing as she imagines a train heading straight towards her (12).

At the same time, the impossibility, where trauma is concerned, of consciously recalling the traumatic event itself, and of determining in any absolute sense the duration of the 'incubation period', opens up the further possibility that the incident depicted might in fact not be the original cause of trauma, but merely a later trigger, which in some way resembles, and thus provokes a reaction to, an earlier traumatic event. The text itself makes no explicit mention of any link to a previous trauma, but Augustin's choice of having a close encounter with a train cast the existence of her protagonists into uncertainty could not only be seen as aligning her work with Freudian thought but, in the post-Holocaust era, of course carries another, ominous connotation: that of having escaped the ill-fated trains that would otherwise have transported these German exiles to their death.

This connection first suggests itself immediately after the incident at the railway crossing, when Marianne, Paul, and Viktor are almost at their destination but are unable to find the driveway leading up to the hotel, and pull up in a nearby forest for Marianne to set off to find it on foot. As she approaches the back entrance of the building, the sight of a pile of refuse in the distance causes her to experience a flashback to the past:

> Auf dem Abhang [. . .] lag ein Knäuel rostigen Eisendrahts und etwas weiter weg etwas Schwarzes das leicht hin und her wehte. [. . .] Stoffetzen wahrscheinlich halb vermoderte Stoffetzen. Ich starrte hin und gleich verwandelten sie sich in Rußflocken die aus dem Rost eines Luftschachts flatterten. Es war der Luftschacht in der Küche der Großeltern in Berlin. [. . .] Ich blickte zu dem Luftschacht hinauf und ekelte mich vor den hin und her wehenden Rußflocken. Schwarze gekrümmte Würmer. Und auf einmal waren es keine Würmer mehr. Verkohlte Leichen waren es. Ich wußte daß einer von uns oder wir alle einmal verbrennen würden so vollständig daß nur Ruß übrigbleiben würde. (10–11)

In an intricate layering and blending of time frames, Marianne remembers a scene of the distant past, but at the same time views this memory through a retrospectively prophetic filter, as a result of which in that distant past she has what appears to be a vision of the recent-past-as-future of the Holocaust. Over the course of the novel it transpires that in this vision Marianne had, without realizing it at the time, accurately predicted the fate of her mother, who, much like Augustin's own, was deported from the Netherlands and murdered in a concentration camp. However, before the significance of the vision, which has become clear to her only in hindsight, can be spelled out, Marianne experiences a second flashback in which premonition, initial trauma, and subsequent traumatic trigger are superimposed and the link between them becomes evident:

> Im Hinblick auf Mama hatte ich keine schlimmen Vorgefühle [. . .]. [. . .]
> Erst nachdem es geschehn war nachdem ich davon wußte fielen die Ruß-
> flocken mir wieder ein brachte ich sie in Zusammenhang mit . . .
>
> Ein durchdringendes Tuten schreckte mich auf. Ich hielt mir die Ohren
> mit beiden Händen zu ich sah die Lokomotive wieder auf uns losstürmen das
> grelle Licht blendete mich. Aber dann kam mir die Wirklichkeit wieder zu
> Bewußtsein. Dieses Tuten war nicht der Warnruf einer Dampfpfeife es war
> eine Hupe die Hupe unsres Autos. (11–12)

The present is suffused with images of both the recent and distant past to form a palimpsestic realm outside chronological succession. Again, ellipsis, followed in this instance by a paragraph break, is used to recreate the irruption of the past into the present typographically, while at the same time marking the presence of an absence, an unspoken reference to the trauma of the Holocaust. The layering of time frames, and general blurring of boundaries, is underlined at a formal level by the fact that, throughout the text, words and clauses within individual sentences simply run on, with no punctuation separating them. In this realm, chronological, sequential time has ceased to apply, or as Marianne exclaims elsewhere in the book: 'Zeit? Einbildung nichts als Einbildung. Dehnbar wie Gummiband' (171–2). As in Adler's texts, time and space seem to have converged here to form a chronotope in which, as Marianne puts it, there is 'keine meßbare Zeit und keinen meßbaren Raum' and which, by dint of being unbounded, is also impossible to navigate in any straightforward sense, and impossible to escape in space or through time (171).

This becomes particularly apparent in an incident towards the beginning of the novel, when, during their brief stay at the seaside resort, Marianne happens to cross a site where before the war there used to be a maze and she suddenly remembers watching her mother trying in vain to get her bearings inside that maze, some time before being deported and murdered in the Holocaust. The remembered incident, though trivial in itself, is coloured by the same sense of foreboding that retrospectively has come to cloud Marianne's entire present, and the scene appears unduly weighty and ominous in her account as a result:

> Ich sah schwarz gegen den bleigrauen Himmel eine Schaukel aufragen. Zwei
> hohe Pfähle mit einem Querbalken. Sie erinnerten an einen Galgen. Ein
> Schauder überlief mich. Gleichzeitig wurde mir bewußt wo ich mich befand.
> Dort wo jetzt die Schaukel steht war früher ein kleiner Irrgarten angelegt.
> [. . .] In dem Irrgarten sah ich Mama herumtrippeln und so ängstlich nach

dem Ausgang suchen als wäre es kein Spiel sondern Ernst. Das Atmen fiel mir auf einmal schwer auch das Gehn. Es war als watete ich durch Wasser ich kam nicht weiter. [. . .] Ein Schleier legte sich vor meine Augen als blickte ich durch beschlagne Gläser. Ich war mir Mamas Anwesenheit bewußt. (13–14)

The text does not provide any direct explanation for why such portent seems to be attributed to this incident. As with the tale of the 'Ruß-flocken', the narrative breaks off and is redirected before it can touch on the unmemory by which the memory it does recount is informed. Only from the sum total of similar occurrences throughout the novel can we infer that the circumstances of her mother's death cause Marianne to see everything through the filter of the Holocaust past. The memory of precisely how her mother died is incomplete, unsayable, and indefinitely deferred, but it interpolates itself as a diaphanous veil between the incident in the present and the (in itself insignificant) remembered event in the past, and it impedes Marianne's progress as though she were attempting to navigate an actual maze. At the same time, the labyrinthine wanderings imposed on Marianne by a structure that, though no longer in place, has nonetheless left its mark on the present evoke the mental processes involved in navigating the persistence of the Holocaust past, which cannot be 'remembered' by travelling back in time, only arbitrarily and unexpect-edly re-experienced in the present. Finally, the actual and mental trails traced within the text in turn reflect, and are reflected by, the form of the narrative, which changes tack whenever it is about to touch on the origin of trauma, as in this maze passage, which concludes with Marianne remarking that everything there appears unchanged while their lives have been turned upside down, or indeed ended:

Für mich ist dort alles noch genauso wie vor Jahren. Und es stimmt mich bitter daß es dort so unberührt erhalten bleiben konnte während sie . . .
Der Weg am Hotel entlang erschien mir endlos. Es war als käme ich nicht weiter als stünde ich still. (15)

For Marianne, moving on in any sense, physical, mental, or narrative, appears to be impossible.

Yet a development seems to take place between the text's first chapter and its fourth, which is again recounted from Marianne's perspective. After the latest onslaught of traumatic visions, triggered by the near-collision at the railway crossing, Marianne starts to remember that she has experienced similar flashbacks before, after the end of the war, or, as I have suggested, after the first time she narrowly avoided a fateful encounter with trains. At the time, her inability, or refusal, to acknow-ledge what had happened provided temporary relief and helped get her through the initial crisis. Indeed, according to Cathy Caruth, the 'temporal delay that carries the individual beyond the shock of the first moment', as an essential feature of trauma, is what makes possible survival in the first place.[48] Ultimately, however, the unacknowledged traumatic events had come back to haunt Marianne with a vengeance:

> Es rächte sich daß ich die Wirklichkeit damals nicht ganz als Wirklichkeit empfand. Immer wieder entzog ich mich ihr und ließ mich von ihr ablenken. Es stimmt daß dieser Selbstbetrug mir viel Leid und Angst ersparte. Andererseits konnte ich dadurch die späteren Ereignisse kaum ertragen. Sie kamen wie ein Blitz aus heiterem Himmel sie sprangen mir in den Nacken wie eine Katze aus einem Baum. (75)

It is remarkable how closely Augustin's choice of phrasing here resembles that used by Adler's Artur Landau in his description of traumatic reliving in *Die unsichtbare Wand*, where we read: 'Das Ungeheuer springt einem immer auf den Nacken. Aber diese Erfahrung und die Erinnerung sind nicht dasselbe.'[49] Now, it would appear that Marianne stops resisting the intrusion of the past in her present. This is a gradual process, which begins by her listing a number of events she failed to acknowledge during the period of what she refers to as self-deceit: the war, the occupation, her father's death of natural causes, and losing their home in Germany (75). She mentions neither the murder of her mother nor the Holocaust as such. However, when she then describes the effects of the 'späteren Ereignisse', or rather of the events only belatedly acknowledged, catching up with her, her account revolves around the atrocities of the Holocaust and the fate of her mother:

> Der Krieg war vorbei [...] als es zum ersten Mal in mein Bewußtsein drang daß ich Mama nie wiedersehn würde. Da erst erkannte ich daß die Erde ein Friedhof ist auf dem wir herumspazieren. [...] Nicht nur der Boden unter meinen Füßen schwankte das Schwanken spielte sich auch in meinem Kopf ab. Ich begann an allem zu zweifeln was ich sah fühlte sagte tat ich zweifelte daran ob ich wirklich lebte ob die Stadt existierte in der ich herumlief [...]. Oh ich widersetzte mich. Ich versuchte mich selbst hinters Licht zu führen. Ich versuchte den Tod und die Peinigungen der Deportationen auf andre Weise zu sehn von einem andern Gesichtswinkel aus. Aber was ich auch tat es war stärker als ich es überrumpelte mich nachts wenn ich müde und nicht auf der Hut war. Dann tauchte es vor mir auf: Gedanken Vorstellungen Bilder ein Totentanz. Die Gaskammern und das Geschrei [...] die Peitschenschläge das Schießen auf Wehrlose als seien es Puppen in einer Schießbude. Das Entsetzen. Ich versuchte es zu zeichnen zu malen in der

---

[48] Caruth (ed.), *Trauma: Explorations in Memory*, 10.
[49] *Die unsichtbare Wand* (Vienna: Zsolnay, 1989), 196.

Hoffnung es würde mir helfen. Es half jedoch nicht oder nur für kurze Zeit. Danach kehrte alles umso deutlicher umso tastbarer zurück. (75–6)

Since her affair with Viktor, Marianne had been able to suppress these flashbacks again, up to the moment when the near-collision at the beginning of the book caused them to resurface.

Even now, as her failure to include her mother's death in her list of repressed memories would suggest, Marianne is apparently still not fully conscious of the origins of her trauma. Consciousness, or at least as complete an awareness as possible, is not achieved until the middle of the fourth chapter, almost exactly halfway into the book. Here, Marianne goes to visit her father's grave at the cemetery but comes face to face with the ghost of her mother. The encounter has a deeply unsettling effect on Marianne, caused by her uncertainty as to whether the woman she has encountered is dead or alive, but compounded by a sudden fear on her part that she might be in the presence of simply a 'geschickte Nachahmung Mamas', of 'ein Automat', which according to Freud, who in turn is drawing on the work of his precursor Ernst Jentsch, is one of the ways in which an uncanny effect may be produced.[50] Yet once the initial shock has worn off, Marianne runs after (the spectre of) her mother and they embrace, in the process of which their two figures appear to merge into one: 'Zwischen der kleinen Kapelle und dem eisernen Tor standen wir aneinandergeschmiegt. Ich sah den Schatten auf dem Kiesweg: schräg ausgestreckt die Silhouette *einer* Gestalt' (92, original emphasis). At this moment, it is as if Marianne, who in the past has made every effort to repress the traumatic flashbacks she has been experiencing, assumes the trauma, which is only partly her own and in part belongs to the dead, and takes on her mother's psychological wounds. Her acceptance of the haunting legacy is signalled by the fact that she becomes aware of the creaking hinges of the cemetery gate which remind her of the whistle of a train. She then reflects on what her mother must have witnessed, including 'Hunger und Entbehrungen Erniedrigungen Ängste und Folterungen' but also 'Transporte', 'Viehwagen', 'Morde', and 'Gaskam... mern' (93–4). Finally, Marianne asserts: 'Mir ist als sei ich Mama' (96). At this point, she ceases to reflect and apparently starts to relive, as the narrative, still in the first person, segues into an account of the experience of persecution, deportation, and internment that is presented as if from the perspective of her mother (97–116). It is unclear to the reader who is speaking, and whether we are being given someone's memories, a vision,

---

[50] Freud, 'Das Unheimliche' (1919), in *Studienausgabe*, ed. Mitscherlich, Richards, and Strachey, iv. *Psychologische Schriften* (1970), 241–74 (250).

dream, or hallucination of such memories, or present-day conjecture.
Marianne's account, if it is still Marianne's, reads like prosopopeia. For
instance, the voice that seems to be speaking from beyond the grave
describes being locked up in a cattle car: 'Und immerzu eingeschlossen
zwischen Toten und den Exkrementen der Lebenden. Man wußte nicht
mehr ob man noch lebte' (114–15).

At the same time, we are continually reminded—for example by means
of the ellipsis in the word 'Gaskam... mern', or by aborted sentences such
as 'Ich kann das Wort Gas...'—of the gaps in Marianne's knowledge, but
also of the collapse of witnessing in those who experienced events at first
hand (94, 110). Moreover, Marianne's presentation of her mother's
experiences, if we decide this is what it is, ends with her imagining her
mother committing suicide before her persecutors have a chance to kill her
(116). The actual memory of how her mother died is untransmitted,
cannot be reconstructed, and remains forever elusive. The central passage
of the text thus functions similarly within the narrative structure as a
whole to the blanks within individual words and sentences: as the mark of
a breakdown of testimony, and as a lacuna at the heart of a traumatic
account. Trauma of this nature, even when it is assumed, as here by
Marianne, is not owned, and therefore cannot be worked through and
mastered, but like a family heirloom is temporarily safeguarded by one
generation to be enduringly preserved in transmission to the next.

In the second half of the text, after the encounter at the cemetery,
Marianne stops fighting her flashbacks and dreams altogether and even
starts to welcome them. They become more and more frequent until she is
no longer able to distinguish between past and present or reality and
hallucination. She finally leaves the 'real world' behind for good when, in
the final chapter of the novel, death puts an end to her already suspended
life. The gradual blurring of the real and the imagined in the narrative's
content is again mimicked by its form in passages such as the following,
which presents a collage of half-remembered and half-fantasized images, a
palimpsest of past and present incidents and sensations somewhere between memory, experience, and vision, and between primary and vicarious trauma:

> Verkohlte Fetzen. Rußflocken. Schwarze Würmer. Leichen. [...] Überall
> nur Skelette Ruinen Rauch Flammen. Merkwürdig daß meine Augen immer
> noch brennen. Das Licht tut weh. Licht und Gefahr gehören zusammen.
> Das Licht der Lokomotive die auf uns losstürmte brannte. Auch in unsrer
> Wohnung brannte Licht als wir nachhause zurückkehrten und dich nicht
> mehr vorfanden Dorle. [...] Die Erinnerungen. Die Flamme die alles
> versengt und die auf der Haut brennt und die Augen blendet. Freilich die

Lampe über einem bei einer Operation ist noch heller. Ein Scheinwerfer.
Und die Narkose ein Vorspiel des Todes. Gasgeruch. Giftgas. (192)

Marianne's husband, a psychoanalyst by profession, views these streams of
semi-consciousness on her part as a symptom of a pathology, refers to her
'verminderte Fähigkeit die Wirklichkeit lückenlos in ihrer ganzen Dichte
wahrzunehmen', and comments on what he perceives as Marianne's state
of growing detachment: 'Jeden Tag schien der Schleier dichter zu werden
der ihr die Welt entzog' (160, 202). Marianne herself does not disagree
with Paul's assessment but is inclined to see her lacunary view of 'reality' as
a sign not of diminishing mental health, but of growing acuity of perception, as an indication of her ability to recognize and accept the presence of
the past in the present: 'Die Welt wird immer durchscheinender für mich
und das ist gut weil ich nun die Bilder der Vergangenheit umso deutlicher
vor mir sehe' (161). The past, she concludes, had always been there,
buried but—or perhaps: and therefore—perfectly preserved under more
recent impressions: 'Alles ist erhalten geblieben tief in meinem Innern ich
hatte nur nicht mehr daran gedacht. Es lag unter all den neueren Bildern
verschüttet' (161). However, conscious, deliberate attempts to dig up
these buried memories often amount to nothing; the revealing ones are
those that surface unbidden, as they do in her hallucinations and dreams:

> Oft ist es so daß alles Suchen und Wühlen nichts nützt. Erst glaubte ich ich
> müsse mir nur Mühe geben und gut nachdenken. Ich sah eine Menge
> Gegenstände eine Einzelheit nach der andern aber das alles erwies sich als
> unwichtig. Wieviel wichtiger sind die Dinge die von selbst auftauchen! (161)

Now that she is more receptive to these submerged images, Marianne suggests
that it is, on the contrary, more pathological to suppress them than to allow
them to surface, as they are not imaginary but more real than a 'reality' in
which they are denied, or as she puts it: 'Träume das sind die wirklichen Bilder
[…] Träume speichern Wirklichkeit gelebtes Leben' (200).

From this, as well as from other references throughout the text, it would
seem that Augustin was also familiar with Freud's writings on dreams.
Certainly, she appears to have been concerned with the same question that
had come to preoccupy Freud himself, after he had established his theory
of dreams operating as wish fulfilment: how to account for those dreams in
which the dreamer revisits a past reality and relives a painful traumatic
incident, thus apparently contradicting the idea of one's dreams representing realized desires. In the novel's final chapter, which is presented
from Paul's perspective, he cites a line, unacknowledged and supposedly chosen at random, from Freud's Gradiva essay, which reads: 'Nach

mühevoller Übersetzungsarbeit erwies sich dem Verfasser der Traum als
ein erfüllt dargestellter Wunsch des Träumers' (204).[51] The fact that this
interpretation of the function of dreams does not seem to tally with the
protagonists' experiences, not now that their lives have apparently been
suspended and they are haunted by the past in their dreams, causes Paul to
reflect: 'Solange man lebt ist es möglich daß der Traum einen erfüllten
Wunsch darstellt. [...] Aber wenn man tot ist wovon träumt man dann?'
(205). Freud himself accounted for the hallucinations and nightmares of
trauma sufferers by positing that, in some patients, the pleasure principle
is overridden by a 'Wiederholungszwang', a 'compulsion to repeat', whereby a subject actively engages in behaviour that mimics earlier stressors, or
revisits painful experiences in hallucinations or dreams.[52] This, Freud
argues, enables them to shore up their defences and so paves the way for
them to master their trauma and for the pleasure principle to come into
effect:

> Wenn die Träume der Unfallsneurotiker die Kranken so regelmäßig in die
> Situation des Unfalles zurückführen, so dienen sie damit allerdings nicht der
> Wunscherfüllung, deren halluzinatorische Herbeiführung ihnen unter der
> Herrschaft des Lustprinzips zur Funktion geworden ist. Aber wir dürfen
> annehmen, daß sie sich dadurch einer anderen Aufgabe zur Verfügung
> stellen, deren Lösung vorangehen muß, ehe das Lustprinzip seine Herrschaft
> beginnen kann. Diese Träume suchen die Reizbewältigung unter Angstent-
> wicklung nachzuholen, deren Unterlassung die Ursache der traumatischen
> Neurose geworden ist. [...] die obenerwähnten Träume der Unfallsneuro-
> tiker lassen sich nicht mehr unter den Gesichtspunkt der Wunscherfüllung
> bringen [...]. Sie gehorchen vielmehr dem Wiederholungszwang, der [...]
> durch den [...] Wunsch, das Vergessene und Verdrängte heraufzubeschwö-
> ren, unterstützt wird.[53]

Though we cannot be certain if Augustin was familiar with this aspect of
Freud's work, the idea of compulsively returning to incompletely remembered events from the past features prominently in *Auswege*. Not only is
Marianne unable to work through, and move on from, trauma, but at the
end of the text, when her suspended existence is finally relieved by actual

---

[51] Freud, 'Der Wahn und die Träume in W. Jensens *Gradiva*', in *Studienausgabe*, ed.
Mitscherlich, Richards, and Strachey, x. *Bildende Kunst und Literatur* (1969), 9–85 (13). The
exact phrase in Freud actually reads: 'Aber völlig konnte auch er nicht die Beziehung des
Traumes zur Zukunft verwerfen, denn nach Vollendung einer mühseligen Übersetzungsarbeit erwies sich ihm [dem Verfasser] der Traum als ein *erfüllt* dargestellter *Wunsch* des
Träumers, und wer könnte bestreiten, daß Wünsche sich vorwiegend der Zukunft zuzu-
wenden pflegen.' Original emphasis.
[52] Freud, 'Jenseits des Lustprinzips' (1920), in *Studienausgabe*, ed. Mitscherlich, Richards, and Strachey, iii. *Psychologie des Unbewußten* (1975), 213–72.
[53] Freud, 'Jenseits des Lustprinzips', 241–2.

death, the trauma she has assumed does not die with her but is transmitted to the next generation, where it will live on as cryptic unmemory in her daughter's mind. In the novel's final chapter, as Marianne is about to pass away, her daughter Dorle suddenly reappears out of nowhere to shoulder the burden. No conclusive explanation is given for her return, though Paul, who still believes he and Marianne were killed in the train collision, conjectures that Dorle, too, must have died in order for them to be able to see her again. From the point of view of traumatic inheritance, Dorle's uncertain existence between life and death would appear to suggest that the legacy has already taken hold in her. Indeed, the final words of the novel are a description of her as having adopted the 'Haltung eines Kindes auf dessen Schultern die Rechte und Pflichten eines Erwachsenen gelegt werden und das zeigen will des ihm geschenkten Vertrauens würdig zu sein' (217).

In this last chapter, Paul, remarking on the fact that, since the incident with the train, he has been haunted by a constant sense of déjà vu, but at the same time providing a comment both on traumatic transmission and on Augustin's narrative technique, states: 'alles alles kann nur noch Wiederholung sein. Eine Wiederholung zusammengesetzt aus zahlreichen durcheinander gewürfelten Fragmenten früher schon gedachter Gedanken schon erlebter Erfahrungen' (206). From this, he draws the conclusion: 'Unsere Hirnzellen sind [. . .] Sammelbecken von Erinnerungsfetzen die plötzlich wieder ins Bewußtsein treten können' (206). Given that other passages in Augustin's novel suggest that she was familiar with Freud's essay on Moses and monotheism, it is conceivable that she may have had in mind his theory of transgenerational memory traces here, whereby trauma may come to affect an entire people, encoded, as it were, as an 'archaische Erbschaft' into a person's brain, which would thus contain 'nicht nur Dispositionen, sondern auch Inhalte [. . .], Erinnerungsspuren an das Erleben früherer Generationen'.[54] The crucial difference to Freud's understanding of trauma is that, in Augustin's novel, the resurfacing of 'Erinnerungsfetzen', and the continual reliving of the past, do not achieve 'Reizbewältigung'; they merely perpetuate trauma.

By force of its transmission, the encrypted traumatic bequest, which is present as an absence even in those who originally suffered it, becomes collective trauma as it is handed down from one generation to the next. Thematically, this is indicated by the fact that the female figures start to blend into one another so that as readers we can no longer be certain which of the three is origin and which ghostly replica. More precisely, we lose any sense that there ever was an origin. For instance, Marianne tells us

---

[54] 'Der Mann Moses und die monotheistische Religion', 546.

about herself: 'Ich mußte immer in die Haut andrer schlüpfen. Dadurch erfuhr ich am eignen Leibe was diese andern empfanden und litten' (122), suggesting that she is both personally affected by the experience of trauma and does not feel as if she owns the cause of that experience. A few pages earlier, in the passage in which she lends her voice to her dead mother, she says almost the exact same thing, even though she is now in theory speaking as the primary witness, exclaiming first: 'Ich habs am eignen Leibe erfahren', but then qualifying this by adding: 'Es ist eine dumme Gewohnheit von mir in die Haut andrer zu kriechen' (97, 109).

Moreover, their respective narratives cancel out both each other and the existence of each other's narrator. The version of events given to us by Marianne states that her mother has been murdered, whereas the account presented from Marianne's mother's perspective has it that Marianne herself is in fact no longer alive, having supposedly died in childbirth long before the incident with the train, which negates not only Marianne's but also Dorle's existence at the time of narrating. The evidence adduced by the mother's narrative for Marianne's death is the argument that, had she been alive when her mother was deported, Marianne would have found a way to prevent the train from taking her to Germany: 'Wäre sie noch am Leben gewesen als ich im Zug saß hätte sie mir helfen können. Sie hätte verhindern können daß der Zug weiter fuhr als nach Amsterdam' (103–4). The deliberate uncertainty as to who is dead and who is alive, who haunts and who is haunted, produced by means of the mutually contradictory narrative strands, manages to imply a sense of both double and infinitely perpetuated guilt. It suggests that Marianne feels somehow responsible for her mother's death, or feels that she is alive at her mother's expense or in her stead, thus illustrating, as Marianne puts it, 'daß man sich nach einer unerwarteten Katastrophe schuldig fühlen kann' (66). At the same time, it also hints at the deadening effect of the traumatic legacy left by the mothers to their daughters. Marianne is guilty both of failing to save her mother and, like her mother before her, of failing to deliver her daughter. This constellation then repeats itself at the end of the novel, where, depending on how we read Dorle's reappearance, Dorle is either alive instead of Marianne, or Marianne's death, and the transfer of the uncanny legacy it entails, also suspend Dorle's life. Given the degree of blurring between the female figures in the text, it is even possible to read all three women merely as projections of one and the same self, with Marianne imagining herself both as a daughter losing a mother to a train and as a mother lost to a train by a daughter. However we choose to read it, the doubling of the mother–daughter constellation (with the suggestion, produced by the blurring of identities, of an infinite continuation), and the resulting doubling of the narrative, demonstrate the insurmountability of trauma.

Evidently, the collapse of boundaries between past and present, and self and other, has implications for both the content and the structure of the text, the foremost of which is that the two become mutually reflective and interdependent, or as Marianne puts it: 'Innen und Außen sind eins geworden erfahrene Wirklichkeit' (77). This is particularly striking in the fourth chapter of the novel, especially if we conclude that the section presenting Marianne's mother's tale in this chapter is in fact spoken by Marianne herself. Here, Marianne's adoption of her mother's perspective (according to which she herself is no longer alive) means that she essentially writes herself out of existence before she can reach the core of the tale, the original traumatic event of her mother's murder. The narrative, meanwhile, in erasing its own narrator, eclipses not only its origins but also the possibility of being given a conclusion.

For both theme and form, the (non-)narration of trauma entails an infinitely regressing structure, in which a story apparently without a source is, as it were, ghostwritten by a narrator who at the beginning of the text is already a spectre, and whose narrative refuses to be put to rest even when her existence ends for good. A miniature icon of such a story of infinite regress is provided by Viktor in his attempt to describe their lives since the incident with the train:

> Was geschah doch mit dem Mann der träumte ein Schmetterling zu sein? Er träumte er sei ein heiter flatternder Schmetterling der nichts von dem träumenden Mann wußte. Der Mann erwachte und erinnerte sich erschrocken daß er [. . .] Tschwang Tschau war. Da wußte er nicht mehr ob er nur geträumt hatte ein Schmetterling zu sein oder ob er ein Schmetterling war der träumte Tschwang Tschau zu sein. (58–9)

In trauma narration, there is no clear sense of origin or agency. The narratives it produces are tales without a narrator, peopled by replicated selves without an origin, and every person and word in them is, from the outset, already a ghost, a pale replica of an absent origin. However, the uncertainty does not end with the characters in the text. As Borges, who was fond of double inversions of this kind in his writing, and indeed constructs one of his short prose pieces around the very same parable of Chuang Tzu and the butterfly, has pointed out, the disturbing thing about this sort of set-up is the possibility of there being no ceiling to it: if the protagonists within a text have no way of knowing if they are doing the imagining or are being imagined, this opens up the possibility that we as readers might also exist only in someone else's imagination.[55] As Marianne

---

[55] Jorge Luis Borges, 'A New Refutation of Time', trans. James E. Irby, in *Labyrinths: Selected Stories and Other Writings*, ed. Donald A. Yates and Irby, trans. Yates, Irby, et al.

speculates: 'Vielleicht bin ich nur noch ein Instrument auf dem andre spielen eine Leinwand die von Unbekannten bemalt wird' (77).

The same spectre of infinite regress and absent agency haunts the form of the text. Like trauma itself, *Auswege* is characterized by an assortment of fragments that do not add up to a story. Its division into, broadly speaking, two parts, with the second part reading like a ghostly replica of the first, mimics the return of unresolved trauma. Within each of its halves, the trails traced by the narrative remind us of Adler's description of the irruption of the Holocaust as marking the moment 'wo das Unheimliche die Kette zerriß und ihre frühen Glieder verwarf und vertilgte'.[56] The narrative does not progress in a linear fashion but digresses and is diverted or silenced whenever it gets close to the origin of the trauma by which it is informed. Chronology is disrupted and perspective may be misleading, leaving us as readers in a similar position to the novel's protagonists, who struggle to situate themselves in space or time. All of this calls for a new form of writing, a form of art which is defined by Marianne as having to be 'beweglich und stereoskopisch', so as to be able to reproduce the temporal disruption caused by traumatic flashbacks and create depth perception to evoke the palimp-sestic persistence of the past in the present (153). The experience of being ensnared in a haunted text as readers may be as close as these authors can come to approximating for us the experience of being trapped in a traumatic past. Both are evoked in Marianne's mother's description of their existence 'after' the Holocaust:

> Nein von uns läuft keiner mehr weg auch nicht wenn alle Türen offen stehn. Man weiß doch daß es kein Entkommen gibt. Die Parkwege können noch so gradlinig und übersichtlich aussehn sie wurden doch so raffiniert angelegt daß man den Ausgang nicht finden kann. Ich irrte lange genug vergeblich zwischen den Sträuchern und Hecken umher. Wenn man sich einmal innerhalb der Umzäunung befindet ist und bleibt man gefangen. (99)

For both characters and readers, the experience of navigating the chrono-tope of the past in the present is akin to attempting to orient oneself in a labyrinth, prompting Marianne to comment on the confusing trails she is forced to follow, in actuality and in her mind: 'Eigentlich sollte man immer ein Knäuel Garn mitnehmen' (164–5). Neither in her life nor in these texts are such props ever forthcoming.

Regarding the novel's title, it has been suggested that the change from 'Labyrint' in the Dutch edition to 'Auswege' in the German one signals

---

(London: Penguin, 2000), 252–69. For Borges's comment regarding the disturbing nature of these inversions, see 'Partial Magic in the *Quixote*', trans. Irby, in *Labyrinths*, 228–31 (229).

[56] *Die unsichtbare Wand*, 98.

not only a new 'Rezeptionsstrategie' but also a 'gewandeltes Verhältnis der Autorin zu dem als traumatisch erlebten und in fiktionale Prosa verwandelten Stück Autobiographie'.[57] While the former assertion is to some extent supported by the conciliatory tone adopted in the blurb of the German edition, which proposes that 'Auswege sind möglich—jedem fällt ein anderer zu', the novel's themes and form as I read them simply do not bear out the latter. The very fact that its title is plural suggests to me that *Auswege* is more concerned with the process of searching for a way out, which turns out not to exist, than it is with the reaching of any resolution or conclusion. The text presents us with endless 'Wege' but no 'Aus'.

TEXTUAL LABYRINTHS: JENNY ALONI'S *DER WARTESAAL*

Like *Auswege*, Jenny Aloni's *Der Wartesaal* aims to evoke, but preserve, an encrypted traumatic past by demonstrating the insurmountability of its effects in the present.[58] Again, this thematic intention has consequences for the author's narrative technique. Even more obviously than *Auswege*, Aloni's text appears inconclusive and unresolved at the level of form as well as content. In her work, as in those analysed in Chapters 4 and 5, greater and greater emphasis is placed on the structural enactment of the disruptive impact of trauma. In the effort to convey the compulsion to repeat the traumatic past, which, because the trauma is not felt to be the surviving protagonists' to resolve, is necessarily interminable, these authors not only produce texts that resemble the 'search whose movement constitutes the labyrinth which instigates it', but increasingly concentrate on deliberately drawing out that search so as to stave off any resolution, not only within the narrative, but of the text itself.[59] More and more, inside and outside, and world, mind, and text, appear as a function and product of one another in this undertaking. In *Der Wartesaal*, this approach results in the creation of a seemingly unbounded network of mutually reflective symbolic, linguistic, and structural labyrinths. In these, past and present overlap at every junction and, as in an actual maze, any intersection may be repeatedly revisited in the course of what, in an elaborate evocation of

---

[57] Hipp, 'Autor und Text', 320–1.

[58] We know from an entry in her diary that Aloni completed *Der Wartesaal* on 17 Mar. 1964, but it is unclear when exactly work on the novel began. An editorial footnote by Hartmut Steinecke estimates: 'Wesentliche Teile sind wahrscheinlich erst ab dem Herbst 1962 entstanden, als Jenny Aloni begann, regelmäßig Kranke in der psychiatrischen Anstalt Beer Jakow zu besuchen.' In *'Ich muss mir diese Zeit von der Seele schreiben . . . '*, 435 and n.

[59] Cixous, 'Fiction and Its Phantoms', 525.

the complexities of living, remembering, and writing (after) Auschwitz, is an ultimately unresolved search for a way out.

As in the case of Augustin's *Auswege*, the Holocaust subtext of *Der Wartesaal* has received surprisingly little critical attention. Margarita Pazi, for instance, though acknowledging the novel's 'rückblickende Erwägungen', emphasizes its thematization of Aloni's professional experience as a volunteer-worker in a psychiatric institute: 'Im "Wartesaal" werden zunehmend autobiographische berufliche Erfahrungen in den Vordergrund gestellt.'[60] Sabina Becker even speaks of an 'Einschränkung der "Rückbezogenheit auf Auschwitz"' in Aloni's work, and describes *Der Wartesaal* as engaging 'fast ausschließlich mit Israel und der israelischen Gesellschaft', with the problems of acclimatization and acculturation facing Jewish exiles in Israel.[61] By Aloni's own assertion, inspiration for the novel was drawn at least in part from her place of work.[62] However, *Der Wartesaal* is more than a documentation of either the professional experience of encounters with mental illness or the personal experience of exile from Germany. Rather than *aliyah* or clinical insanity, I propose that the primary concern of this text is the experience of exile and psychological disruption in a much broader sense, as a loss of orientation and selfhood in a world marked by the traumatic persistence of the Holocaust past.

Aloni's novel, which is narrated in the first person as the account of one woman's reflections on the present and her attempt to remember the past, is commonly understood to be set about a decade and a half after the end of the Second World War, in an Israeli hospital, 'im psychiatrischen Milieu'.[63] However, while descriptions of the surrounding scenery, and references to the eccentric behaviour of some of the figures populating the eponymous waiting room, support this assumption, it is never explicitly confirmed in the text. The building referred to as the waiting room is presented as one of a cluster of barracks in an undefined military-style

---

[60] 'Jenny Aloni, eine deutschschreibende, israelische Autorin', in Jenny Aloni, *Ausgewählte Werke 1939–1986*, ed. Friedrich Kienecker and Hartmut Steinecke (Paderborn: Schöningh, 1987), 162–73 (167).

[61] 'Zwischen Akkulturation und Enkulturation: Anmerkungen zu einem vernachlässigten Autorinnentypus: Jenny Aloni und Ilse Losa', *Exilforschung*, 13 (1995), 114–36 (123). The phrase 'Rückbezogenheit auf Auschwitz' is borrowed from Pazi, 'Jenny Aloni, eine deutschschreibende, israelische Autorin', 166, though Becker mistakenly places it in another of Pazi's articles. However, Becker is citing out of context here, since Pazi is in fact arguing that, though Auschwitz is not the main focus of *Der Wartesaal*, its 'Assoziationseinwirkungen' in the text remain 'offensichtlich'.

[62] 'Nachbemerkung', in Aloni, *Gesammelte Werke*, ed. Kienecker and Steinecke, v. *Der Wartesaal*, 109.

[63] Claudia Schoppmann, 'Jenny Aloni', in Schoppmann (ed.), *Im Fluchtgepäck die Sprache: Deutschsprachige Schriftstellerinnen im Exil* (Frankfurt a.M.: Fischer, 1995), 184–92 (191).

compound, situated in an unspecified, vaguely Middle Eastern landscape. Its occupants, in keeping with the travel metaphor of the title, are identified not as patients but as either 'Passagiere' or 'Wartende'. Though both these designations, like the image of the waiting room, suggest only a temporary interruption of a journey, the people in this compound have in fact given up all hope of improvement and discharge, and are more like prisoners than either passengers or patients. This is underlined by the narrator's claim that they have 'Agenten' to guard them instead of doctors and nurses to treat them. The metaphor of life in the waiting room, commonly associated with the notion of exile as an interim solution in a finite time and place, for instance in Lion Feuchtwanger's *Wartesaal* trilogy, has come to represent an infinite, inescapable space here. In this space, travelling and standing still have become synonymous, or as the narrator puts it: 'Gang [ist] gleich Stillstand und Vorwärtsdringen gleich Beharren' (18).

In addition to being in spatial limbo, the occupants of the 'Wartesaal' are also suspended in time. In order to leave the waiting room behind and move on, they would have to be able to conceive of their existence as a journey, with a beginning and end. However, they are presented as having lost all access to the past, as a result of which they also cannot imagine a future and therefore are unable to pick up the thread of their lives. This, in turn, affects their sense of identity: incapable of regarding their existence as an uninterrupted progression from past to present to future, they are also unable to conceive of a continuous, coherent self. Their status as non-entities who are neither here nor there in time and space is reflected by the waiting-room compound itself. This is described as a remnant of one unspecified war left over for the next, and fenced in between barbed wire and dragons' teeth used for anti-tank defence—'zwischen Stacheldraht und Drachenzähnen'—with the sense of suspension mirrored linguistically, in the bracketing of 'und' between assonant syllables (17, 16).

The conflation of time, space, and self in the waiting room is clearly apparent in the narrator's assessment of their situation, though not all of the occupants are as conscious of their predicament as she is:

> Auf jeder Liegenschaft ein Ich, das sich verliert, in schon allzu langem Aufenthalt vergessen hat, daß es auf eine Fortsetzung der unterbrochenen Reise harrt, auch wenn manche meinen, daß sie wartend ihre Rückkehr vorbereiten. Sie haben es noch nicht begriffen, daß keine Züge in das Gestern fahren. (18)

The metaphor of the unleavable waiting room has been interpreted in a number of ways by reviewers and critics, only a few of whom view it as standing simply for 'das ewige Einerlei des Krankenhausalltags'.[64] Friedrich Kienecker, in the cover blurb for the novel's first edition, reads it in a general existential sense as a comment on the human condition: 'Der Mensch im Wartesaal Leben ist dazu verurteilt, auf den Tod zu warten [...], noch die Fürsorge des Pflegepersonals [...] dient nicht dem Widerstand gegen den Tod, sondern der Vorbereitung auf ihn.'[65] Christa Fenzl proposes similarly that 'symbolisch gesehen', the waiting room takes on 'die Dimension eines Raumes, der dem Menschen zugeteilt ist als Lebensraum', in which humankind is caught 'zwischen Erinnerung und Hoffnung', forever in the grip of a fear 'den Zug zu versäumen, der in eine bessere Welt führt'.[66]

While the limbo of the waiting room undoubtedly does conjure up images of an institutionalized existence, and even of life in abeyance in exile, and while it can certainly be read as a comment on the human condition more generally, the text makes it very clear that it is in fact not a fear of 'missing the train' to a more hopeful future that haunts the narrator of *Der Wartesaal*, but a sense of having missed a train in the past, and of being unable to go back in time to rectify this:

> Wir sind keine Toten. Noch nicht. Der Tod ist ein Ideal, das wir noch nicht erreichten. Wohl stimmt es, daß wir nicht mehr leben. Wir haben es hinter uns zurückgelassen, als wir den Stacheldraht passierten. Doch unser Ziel haben wir nicht erreicht. Der Zug ist ohne uns davongefahren. (32)

Having been left behind by the train, the narrator apparently feels that they have failed to reach what was supposed to be their destination. Because 'keine Züge in das Gestern fahren', the end of the line for which they were bound in that past now seems irretrievably out of reach (18). Rather than being condemned to the inexorable process of dying that is existence in the waiting room of life, as Kienecker suggests, these characters appear sentenced to continue existing indefinitely in their state of suspension somewhere between life and death. In view of this, but also in light of the fact that the waiting-room compound is, at least in the narrator's mind, more reminiscent of an internment camp, complete with guards and barbed wire, than it is of a hospital, the train evoked by the narrator would appear to carry connotations more specifically relevant to her, but also to her author, than is implied by either Kienecker's or Fenzl's reading. I would suggest that the narrator is, in fact, alluding to the trains

[64] Suse Drost, 'Das ewige Einerlei: Zu einem Roman der Droste-Preisträgerin Jenny Aloni', *Südkurier*, 9 Jan. 1993.

[65] 'Buchumschlag Originalausgabe', *Der Wartesaal* (Freiburg i.Br.: Herder, 1969).

[66] 'Die Nummer wird zum Schicksal: Mit wachem Verstand und heißem Herzen ein psychiatrisches Krankenhaus erlebt', *Main-Echo*, 21 Sept. 1993.

that transported people to their death during the Holocaust, and that her perception of the 'Wartesaal', and indeed of life in general, as one great insurmountable waiting room is informed by her compulsive reliving of a traumatic past that was incompletely witnessed when it first happened. Rather than being a simple figure of speech, the impression of having 'missed the train', and therefore being unable to move on, might then be read as an expression of survivors' guilt, and of the sense of 'unverdiente Gnade', as Aloni describes it, that accompanies this: 'Ich blieb verschont. Unverdiente Gnade, die schuldig macht. Auch wenn es nicht absichtlich geschah, meine Nummer übersehen wurde oder nicht genügend Zeit blieb. Das unterstreicht nur die Zufälligkeit meiner Existenz.'[67]

A closer look at what we learn in the text about the narrator's life before the waiting room lends further weight to this reading. As transpires over the course of the novel, Aloni's narrator is a Jewish survivor of the Holocaust but with a Nazi past. Having at first thrown in her lot with the National Socialists by concealing her Jewish roots and taking up a job as a secretary in charge of transcribing names, including that of her own mother, onto deportation lists, she is finally denounced by her non-Jewish husband, and interned in a series of concentration camps. In the waiting room, after the war, she spends her days trying to recall her past and narrating the fragments she remembers of it to an imaginary daughter, Lisa, who was never born and may never have been conceived outside the narrator's mind. In the course of the narrator's account, we learn that she does not feel she has earned the status of victimhood that the fact of her persecution and suffering in the camps might otherwise have bestowed on her: 'Unmöglich, die blaue Nummer der Opfer von meinem Arm zu tilgen. [...] Doch ich verberge sie beschämt unter dem Ärmel [...]. Ich bin nicht würdig, sie zu tragen' (88). She was a victim of persecution, but at the same time a perpetrator, and so she does not feel she has the right to count herself among the former. In a vision towards the end of the novel, she alludes again to the liminal existence into which her failure to be a 'true' victim has cast her, evoking what reads like an immolation, as a literal translation, and re-enactment through the imagination, of a holocaust that was and is denied her:

Ich darf nicht verbrennen und darf nicht fliehen. Festgenagelt bin ich auf dem Schlachtblock der Opfer und ersehne vergeblich den erlösenden Hieb der Axt. Feuer prasseln, lecken lüstern an Leibern und verzehren sie,

---

[67] Jenny Aloni, 'Ich blieb verschont', in *Ausgewählte Werke 1939–1986*, ed. Kienecker and Steinecke, 110–11 (110).

unzählig viele Leiber, nur den meinen nicht. Ich bin nicht wert, von ihrer
Glut vertilgt zu werden. (103)

On the face of it, the narrator's biography—as that of a woman who
supposedly 'als Mitglied der NSDAP bewußt ihre Mittäterschaft an den
Nazi-Greueln in Kauf nimmt, um nicht zu den Opfern zu gehören'—
could not be further removed from Aloni's own. However, the narrator's
sense of being torn between suffering and feelings of guilt, and of leading a
life in suspension, in fact closely approximates that of a Holocaust survivor
who, though never on the side of the perpetrators, feels guilty about not
having died at their hands like others who were persecuted.[68] Other
statements in the novel recall Aloni's phrase of the 'unverdiente Gnade',
for instance when the narrator exclaims that though she did end up a
victim of the National Socialists, this does not exonerate her: 'Daß jene
mich dann verwarfen, mir die Berechtigung absprachen, zu ihnen zu
gehören, ist nicht mein Verdienst' (88). Though 'zu ihnen' ostensibly
refers here to the perpetrators, this could just as easily be read as a
survivor's allusion to his or her evasion of the fate met by other victims
as to an undeserved good fortune. Moreover, the presentation of the
narrator's account as an address from a mother to a daughter may have
been chosen to recreate a constellation that preoccupied Aloni herself, as
becomes apparent from a note she wrote in 1967, in the period between
production and publication of her novel:

Ich habe oft darüber nachgedacht, wie kann ich es der Tochter sagen, wie ihr
erklären, daß ich lebe? [...] wie plausibel machen, daß ich überlebte, wo
andre starben, erschossen, totgeprügelt, vergast, verhungert, sie lernt es in
der Schule, Millionen andere, nur ich nicht. [...] warum? Warum gerade
ich?[69]

It would appear from this that it is primarily the guilt-inducing sense of
having failed to experience the full extent of the Holocaust past that
prevents its survivors from moving on and has caused the narrator to
become trapped between the pronouncement of her death sentence,
through sacrifice by fire on the 'Schlachtblock der Opfer', and its indefinitely deferred execution (103). Traumatized not least by the fact of their
survival, survivors may find themselves compulsively attempting to return
to the past, but unable to do so in the form of a willed and comprehensive
recollection. In *Der Wartesaal*, for instance, there is another inmate who is
described as having a similar number tattooed on her arm as the narrator

[68] Wall, *Lexikon*, 13.
[69] 'Ich habe oft darüber nachgedacht', in *Ausgewählte Werke 1939–1986*, ed. Kienecker
and Steinecke, 112–13 (113).

herself. Whenever the narrator catches sight of this number, she cannot help but think of the past, yet finds herself incapable of remembering it consciously and deliberately: 'jedes Mal, wenn ich [ihre Nummer] sehe, muß ich daran denken, auch wenn alles immer wie hinter einem Dunst verschwimmt. Es ist nicht abhängig von meinem Wollen' (88). Like the characters in Augustin's novel, the narrator of *Der Wartesaal* cannot go back in time. Rather, the past keeps returning to haunt her to the point where it appears to have become part of the fabric of the present, causing reality and traumatic flashback to become blurred.

In consequence, time, as in the other novels, no longer appears to unfold in a linear, chronological, and unidirectional sense but comes to be perceived as a labyrinthine chronotope. In this chronotope, imagery of disordered roaming abounds and figures on several levels, providing a map of meandering paths in space and through time as an exteriorization of the protagonists' disoriented mental processes. Accordingly, 'sich erinnern' in this chronotope is described as an attempt to navigate an inescapable maze while periodically being snagged by the thorns of a past that reopen old wounds, and coming face to face with the ghosts of those who have not survived:

Wandern zwischen hohen Hecken, sich in ihren Ranken verwickeln und alte Narben blutig reißen an den Dornen. Immer tiefer hineingeraten in das struppige Brachland der Seelen. Sich in gewesenen Pfaden verlaufen, die längst verfallen sind [...]. Verfallen, doch nicht ausgelöscht. (47)

Traces of the past remain embedded in the present and surface at random, as incompletely understood memory fragments in the protagonists' minds, and in the shape of spectres they encounter in their interminable wanderings. At the same time, inherent in the evocation of these confused and confusing trails, there is a blueprint for the structures and strategies of the text. In order to preserve the traces of the encrypted past and the full force of its blow to comprehension, the narrative aims to recreate the labyrinths of the protagonists' world and minds, and to reflect their inability to retrace their steps to the past and their consequent failure to exit the labyrinth of the present. As far as possible, the text therefore tries to avoid any direct reference to the origin of the protagonists' trauma, while at the same time making itself appear as non-linear and interminable as possible. Where the protagonists are unable to find closure, the text strives to refuse it. As one of the protagonists reflects regarding the possibility of conveying the unspeakable experience of a (presumptive) concentration camp, this is a feat that can be achieved, though only indirectly, but it requires the creation of a textual construct that has no centre and therefore offers no exit: 'Es stimmt, der Kern ist unbeschreibbar. Nur wer seine Qualen an sich selbst erfahren hat, kann ihn benennen. Doch warum sollten die Worte, die sein Gehäuse beschreiben, unaussprechlich sein?' (92).

As a result of the author's effort to produce such a construct without a core, single centred meaning in the text is replaced by a theoretically infinite amount of associative nuclei, each of which may condense a number of meanings, belonging to multiple time frames and locations, into one image, causing the narrative to split and branch off into different directions at each one. One example of such a junction, where the text ostensibly refers to a situation in the narrative present, but at the same time evokes the Holocaust past, occurs when one of the inmates of the waiting room is prevented from committing suicide, and the narrator comments with bitter irony:

> Es gilt, das Prinzip zu schützen. Deshalb ist es verboten, dem eigenen Leben ein Ende zu bereiten. Deshalb bestrafen sie den mißglückten Versuch [. . .]. Anderes Leben zu vernichten mag erlaubt sein, besonders dann, wenn es en masse geschieht. Wer en gros handelt, erhält Vergünstigungen. Für Mord im Dienste von Ideen und Interessen lassen sich Berechtigungen erfinden. (13)

In examples such as this, the confluence of past and present connotations means that it is often not evident to which time frame or associative field the comment applies primarily. No relations of dominance are established between the then and the now, as is underlined by frequent switches from the narrative past to a universalizing present tense. A further example is the narrator's cremation, as she puts it, of insects which have fallen prey to a spider and have been reduced to 'leere Hüllen'. Again the underlying field of reference is implicit but obvious, and the past appears far from over, as the narrator exclaims: 'Die Kremation von Leichen ist nicht gestattet? Was du nicht sagst! Wo doch überall soviel getötet und verbrannt wird' (22).

Because time is perceived spatially, and there is no chronological hierarchy, we lose all sense of temporal sequence and cause and effect. As in Augustin's novel, the persistence of the past in the present means that even an apparently trivial event, such as here an innocuous pre-Holocaust train journey, remembered from the vantage point of a post-Holocaust present, may take on a universalizing and retroactively prophetic quality. Again, this is compounded by a shift in tense from the narrative past, used to describe the memory up to the moment of departure, to the present, and by occasional pronoun switches from first-person singular to plural:

> Dann packte ich die Koffer und fuhr nach Hause. [. . .] Wir torkeln durch das Labyrinth der Schienen. [. . .] Kein Zug erreicht das angegebene Ziel. Alle verlieren sich in der Wildnis. [. . .] Kreuzung der Wege, Bündel möglicher Richtungen. [. . .] Es ist nicht gestattet, sie selbst zu wählen.

Andere, auf die ich keinen Einfluß habe, bestimmen sie. Auch ob ich überhaupt noch weiterfahren werde. (58–9)

Suddenly, the scene is laced with ominous suggestion: 'Dann beschleunigt der Zug seine Geschwindigkeit. [...] Aus einem unsichtbaren Schlot schlägt rote Lohe. Wir sind in dem Bezirk der Hochöfen angelangt' (61). At the same time, references to a disoriented stumbling through a labyrinth with many intersections and no clear destination are emblematic of both the narrative technique of the novel and our reading experience. They suggest that we are involved in the creation of a text in which at each junction we are confronted with a 'Bündel möglicher Richtungen', in space and through time, without knowing which direction to follow or if any of the tracks lead anywhere other than on to a further cryptic allusion.

However, passages such as this one, which can be read both analeptically and proleptically, implicate us beyond merely relying on us to make our own way through, and bring our own knowledge to, a text that makes no outright mention of the word National Socialism. This is particularly apparent in the recounting of the narrator's (possibly imagined) initiation into the Nazi party during a summer solstice celebration:

Schwarz ist die Nacht. Kein Stern durchbricht sie. Pechfackeln flammen auf. Blutrot wehen unsre Fahnen. Ein dumpfes Trommelwirbeln. Feuer fliegen durch die Finsternis. Scheiterhaufen lodern zum Himmel auf. Unterbrich mich nicht. Ich sagte Scheiterhaufen, nicht Sonnenwendfeuer. Was kümmert uns die Sonne, ob sie sich wendet oder feststeht. Jetzt werden sie in allen Dörfern wissen, daß wir den Schwur ablegen, dem Führer bis in den Tod zu dienen. Bis in Millionen Tode. Doch das wissen wir noch nicht. Das kommt erst später. (73)

Although this excerpt is presented as a memory of the narrator's past, it is also, again, prophetically forward-looking in hindsight with its visionary tone, its substitution of stakes for bonfires, and its mention of millions of deaths. Yet the use of the present and even the future tense, and of the first-person plural, not only suggests that the incident could be read as retrospectively prophetic but opens up the possibility of it being understood as a premonition of the past repeating itself in the narrator's, or even in our own, future.

Like junctions in a real labyrinth, any of these nuclei of intersecting connotations may be revisited in the text. What links the different time frames and associative fields they comprise—even when it is unclear whether the reference is to a memory or to an incident in the narrative present or the future—are the themes of betrayal and pursuit or persecution. In place of a sequentially unfolding narrative, the text presents an achronological associative network, in which any given signifier may give rise to, or recall, another elsewhere in the text. The narrator's denunciation by her husband to the National Socialists, for instance, is given an equivalent in an earlier, pre-war betrayal which saw him leave her for another woman (78, 57). These betrayals in turn provide a model for, and replica of, the narrator's own betrayal of her mother (75). After each of the betrayals, the narrator feels haunted by ghostly visions of those who have wronged her and whom she has wronged, bringing to mind Freud's comment that whatever reminds us of our compulsion to repeat will be perceived as uncanny: 'daß dasjenige als unheimlich verspürt wird, was an diesen inneren Wiederholungszwang mahnen kann'.[70] It is, however, impossible to determine which, if any, of the three incidents in the text is the origin of the narrator's trauma, and which merely remind her of it retrospectively and cause her to relive it. As variations on a theme, the betrayals reflect, and are reflected by, one another in a seemingly infinitely regressive specular system. Following each incident, the narrator both is haunted by, and chases after, a phantom of either her husband or her mother. Moreover, this double status as hunter and prey in its turn appears to mirror the processes of a traumatized brain in vain pursuit of comprehension, and haunted by flashbacks unavailable to conscious recall. The first instance of betrayal leads to the narrator having continual phantom sightings of her husband with the woman for whom he has left her, and setting off after the two without ever catching up with them. The account of the second betrayal, in the course of which the narrator becomes responsible for her mother's deportation, is introduced by a ghostly sighting of another kind: the narrator speaks of how, since her waiting-room existence, a vision of her mother, of whom she had not thought in years, has come back to haunt her dreams, and how she reaches out but is unable to touch this apparition: 'Meine Mutter! Jahrelang aus meinem Gedächtnis vertrieben, kehrte sie zu mir zurück, wandert Nacht um Nacht durch meine Träume. [...] Ich strecke meine Hand aus, immer wieder. Doch ich erreiche die ihre nicht...' (72–3). Again, this also reads like an exteriorized enactment of the breakdown of conscious recall after a traumatic event. The account of the third betrayal, finally, the husband's denunciation of the narrator, refers to the narrator's own imprisonment, interrogation, and internment, and to her ensuing journey from one prison compound to another, all of which in turn recall the waiting room where she has ended up inescapably detained. However, instead of describing the individual stations of the journey, which escape willed recollection, she speaks of how, throughout it, she is relentlessly

---

[70] 'Das Unheimliche', 261.

pursued by a shadowy figure which would appear to represent her husband but is cryptically referred to as 'der Erzfeind' (86). In all three accounts, the narrator is both pursuer and pursued as she betrays and is betrayed, and chases after a memory but sees it slip through her fingers as a mere spectre of a former presence. None of the incidents establishes itself clearly as the original cause of trauma.

In addition to such first-degree mirroring, each reflection we encounter generates a host of further images which cast their web over the text. Every agent and visitor in the 'Wartesaal', as well as cats (13), microbes (e.g. 20), cranes (33), ants (35), and flies (94) are suspected by the narrator of being part of some great 'Mosaik der Spionage' (35) under the control of the 'Erzfeind'. The narrator's mother, on the other hand, belongs to a specular system that includes the 'leere Hüllen' left behind by the spider as miniature replicas of the empty vessels of the inmates, who in turn recall the 'Muselmanen', the walking dead of the concentration camps (e.g. 91). All of these reflections haunt the writing, just as they haunt the narrator in her every waking or dreaming moment, until the distinction between being asleep and being awake, between the past and the present, but also between living, reliving, and recounting is irreversibly blurred.

As with any signifier in the text, it is difficult to decide whether these visions conjured up by the narrator are visitations from the past or mirror images of the present. For instance, the various embodiments of both her mother and the 'Erzfeind' may at any given moment be either revenants or replicas, ghosts of others or projections of her own self as victim and as perpetrator, as experiencing and inflicting torment. The 'Erzfeind' could be read as personification of the narrator's guilt and constant reminder of her suffering, acting as a mirror image to the figure of her mother, personification of her suffering and constant reminder of her guilt. Indeed, when they were still together, the narrator's husband accused her of using him as a 'Spiegel deiner Selbstgefälligkeit' (67), and the narrator admits that what she loved in him was 'mein [...] Bild in seinen Augen' (50). Self-satisfaction has since given way to self-criticism, but the 'Erzfeind' has retained his mirror function, and has been joined by the spectre of the narrator's mother, in a hall of mirrors that ultimately may reflect nothing other than different versions of the narrator's self. This confusion between self and other is foregrounded in a passage where the narrator is roaming the streets—whether actually or mentally we do not know—looking for manifestations of her mother, but ends up only encountering herself:

> Vor allen Bettlerinnen beuge ich mich, weil sie ihr gleichen. Alle Bettelge-
> sichter taste ich ab [...]. Wer lacht da? [...] Mokiert sich der, der lacht,

über mich, die ich Erschlagene in Lebenden zu finden hoffe? [. . .] Ich selber
bin die Lachende. Einer der Wechselbälge meines Ichs. (87)

This collapse of boundaries between subject and object in these change-
ling selves, reminiscent of that which we encountered in Augustin's novel,
is underscored by the fact that, whenever the narrator tries to recall the
past and experiences these phantom sightings instead, she is described as
being on the other side of a reflective glass partition. She has visions of her
husband through the window of a train next to hers (60), on a street in the
rain when she is sitting in a café (62), or through the glass doors of a
supermarket (63). When she tries to reach out to the ghost of her mother,
this is described as being 'unerreichbar wie die Gestalt in einem Spiegel'
(73). In each instance, the narrator is painfully conscious that what is on
the other side is irretrievably out of her reach, or as she comments, on
seeing raindrops on one of these panes: 'Durch die Tropfen wird die
Scheibe sichtbar, hinter der ich sitze, wird entlarvt als Widerstand und
Grenze' (62). Not only does the reference to an interpolated semi-transparent
surface between the present and a glimpse from the past evoke traumatic
memory and the impossibility of returning to, or even getting a clear view
of, that past. The fact that the surface is at the same time reflective, and
that in her repeated attempts to return to the past the narrator therefore
only ever encounters herself in the ghosts of both her husband and her
mother, suggests that both she and, by extension, her narrative are also
only reflections and replicas, traces of an absent origin.

As the trace which remains of those in whose stead she is alive, above all
her absent mother, and as keeper of the unremembered, but insurmountable, secrets of the past, the narrator herself is, from the outset, already a
ghost, as evidenced, for instance, by her comment that her presence in a
train compartment does nothing to change the fact that this is empty: 'Ein
leeres Abteil. Mein Sich-in-ihm-Befinden ändert daran nichts' (58). As
such, she is also apparently unable to give birth, either as a mother or as a
narrator, to an independent creation, but is capable only of reproducing
further ghostly versions of herself. The blurring of origin and replica where
the self is concerned is therefore also extended to the narrator's ghost of a
daughter, as we see in the narrator's remark to her, in which all distinctions between self and other appear abolished: 'Ich bin du, und du bist ich,
und niemand fragt, wer du und ich sind. [. . .] Würmer, die den eigenen
Schwanz auffressen' (95).

This infinitely self-reflecting, and ultimately self-consuming, constellation in turn has implications for the narrator's tale. The fact that the
narrator never returns to the source of trauma, only ever to herself and to
her belated responses to it, suggests that, in fact, none of the incidents

recounted in the text constitutes the true cause of the trauma that is being preserved here, but that they are all merely secondary re-enactments of it, and that the trauma encrypted in the text may have nothing to do with any of the betrayals suffered or perpetrated by the narrator that are described in it. Thus, when the narrator refers to the self as having seemingly infinite 'Gehäuse', but no core, or as the narrator puts it: 'Masken und hinter ihnen kein Gesicht. Verhüllungen, die Kern geworden sind' (59), we can read this as emblematic of the protagonists' worlds and memory but, as we shall see, also of the text in which they appear. The 'Kern' of the self, like the present-as-absence 'Kern' of trauma encrypted in the mind, and finally therefore also the core of the text, is indefinitely dislocated, as becomes apparent from the reflection the narrator catches of herself in a train window: 'Neben mir [. . .] sitzen meine durchsichtigen Bilder, begleiten mich [. . .]. Hundert Bilder und nicht ein Ich' (59).

As well as affecting the self, and the themes, imagery, and structures we encounter, this proliferation of 'Gehäuse' without a 'Kern' is also acutely felt at the level of language in *Der Wartesaal*. Aloni stresses the absence of a single primary meaning in words, and plays with the bifurcation of the narrative thread that arises when a term progresses along a literal and a figurative trail simultaneously, without appearing to favour one over the other. This, in turn, contributes to the suspension of narrative linearity, or to cite Gérard Genette: 'L'espace sémantique se creuse entre le signifié apparent et le signifié réel abolissant du même coup la linéarité du discours.'[71] For instance, the narrator speaks of her life as 'ein aus Irrungen geknüpftes Netz', and we cannot, and are not meant to, be sure whether the reference to 'Irrungen' is to be understood literally, as aimless wandering, or figuratively, as the error of her ways, or if, in fact, the navigational difficulty is ours rather than hers and the phrase should therefore be read as a comment on narrative strategy (47).

The play between literal and figurative meanings is exploited throughout the text, and the narrator is very conscious of the fact that the meaning of words is not determinate but may vary according to the context in which they are used, as is manifested by several exchanges between her and a visitor in the waiting room who asks after her and whom she therefore suspects of being a spy:

'Also nochmals, wie geht es Ihnen?' 'Ich gehe nicht. Ich sitze, wie Sie bemerkt haben dürften.' [...] 'Also gut, wie ist Ihr Befinden?' 'Mein Befinden? Wissen Sie wirklich nicht, wo ich mich befinde? [...]' [...] 'Sie drehen mir jedes Wort im Munde um.' (15–16)

[71] *Figures II* (Paris: Seuil, 1969), 47.

Or at a later stage: '"Sie ziehen vielleicht die Hitze vor?" "Ich ziehe nichts vor und schiebe nichts nach." "Das ist nur so eine Art es auszudrücken." "Ich bin keine Zitrone." "Man pflegt so zu sagen." "Auch kein Mann."' (93).

On occasion, our passage from word to word of the text resembles labyrinthine meandering not just semantically but even phonetically. As well as being equivocal, language, through assonance and alliteration, engenders free association and acts as a generative mechanism that establishes networks of sound and imagery, and rhythmic patterns, all of which further condense the textual weave. For instance, when the narrator experiences what is either a flashback to, or a hallucination of, an erotic encounter with her husband, the entwining of her body with his is mirrored in the interweaving of semantic fields and lexical sets:

> Und während unsre Glieder sich verflochten, murmelte sein Mund: 'Gib die Weiche deines Leibes in das Hohle meiner Hand. Tauch die Glieder eines Müden in dein Übermaß der Lust. Gieß in meine düstere Seele von dem Licht, das dich erhellt.' Ich aber sagte: 'Komm und schließ die Wärme deiner Glieder über mich als einer Krypta Dach, daß ich zwischen ihren festen Säulen in dem Dämmer ihrer weichen Schatten mich verlieren darf und träumen.' Und er: 'Deiner Mädchenbrüste Füllen hängen wie die Trauben einer reifen Frucht aus der dunklen Wärme der Geäste in die Stille dieses frühen Morgens. Sie zittern, wie im Froste zu Eiszapfen erstarrte Wasser beben. Laß sie in die Dürre meines Mundes, auf die Brand gewordenen Lippen fallen.' (65)

Each of the binary opposites of soft and hard, concave and convex, liquid and solid, dark and light, warm and cold, fire and ice, wet and dry forms a miniature semantic thread that trails through the passage, shifts from one person to the other, and enters various combinations, some of which draw together semantic fields in a way that appears logically impossible, such as the breasts as bunches of grapes emerging from warmth as quivering icicles to quench thirst. Assonance and alliteration create their own webs, as does the syntax, through constructions such as the parallel imperatives of 'gib', 'gieß', 'tauch', 'komm', and 'schließ', or the chiastic placement of nouns and verbs in, for example, the sentence bracketed between 'Komm und schließ' and 'darf und träumen'. Between them, the arrangements of sound and syntax finally also produce a network of internal rhyme and sweeping, increasingly irregular rhythm to mirror the narrator's ecstasy. This passage, and to some extent the entire text, governed as they are by these associative symbolic, linguistic, and structural networks, read more like prose poetry than a novel constructed around, and driven by, plot.

Finally, as well as being enacted at a primary textual level, this approach to writing, the drawing-together of multiple temporal, spatial, semantic, and linguistic frames of reference, resulting in a labyrinthine structure, is repeatedly replicated *in nuce* in the novel, in which *mises en abyme* of narrative technique and the textual construct, but also icons of the patterns created by the writing, abound.[72] For one thing, labyrinthine imagery is everywhere, underpinning the impression of the labyrinth as dominant metaphor and structuring principle: in the ruins of a castle (50), in shadows cast by foliage (51, 52, 55), in flashes of lightning (56), in ice crystals and the scales of a fish (59), in oily puddles (61), in the aisles of a supermarket (64), in the noises and neon lights of the city (65), in the scars and bruises covering the body of the narrator's mother at their last actual encounter (85), and within the structures of the body itself, its organs and veins (19, 98, 92).

A more elaborate example of an icon of the text's non-linear associative structure and the way in which this draws together elements from seemingly unconnected spheres is the narrator's description of the appearance of the world when seen through a spider's web:

> Die Fäden ihres Netzes teilen den Rasen in Trapeze auf [...]. Der Fetzen eines Wasserstrahles verbindet sich mit einem Hosenbein, mit einem Stück Dach und einer Faust, die einen Griff hält. Dazu das Ende eines Gladiolenblattes und die Hälfte eines gelben Steines. Ein zweites Trapez [...]. Ein drittes [...]. Und so ein viertes und so ein fünftes und so fort. Hertha [i.e. the spider] trennt und verbindet rigoros, ohne traditionelle Verbindlichkeiten und Zusammenhänge anzuerkennen. (19)

At the same time, the image of the cobweb reflects, or is reflected by, the waiting-room compound, which is described as 'Netz der Nissenhütten', linked by meandering, intersecting paths, and monitored by the control centre of the agents' barracks, which, as the 'Sitz der grauen Masse des Agentenhirnes' (17), is inaccessible to the inmates, and from which the agents, like the spider from the centre of its web, observe the doomed wanderings of the 'leere Hüllen' caught up in the outer sections of their 'Netz'. In addition to reflecting each other, both images are also emblematic of the human brain and the convoluted workings of memory.

At the other end of the scale, the text as a whole, with its strategy of telling the 'Gehäuse' and thus evoking, but avoiding, the 'Kern', is placed

---

[72] The use of the term *mise en abyme* in literature to designate a miniature replica within a work which reflects either the work as a whole or a major theme of it goes back to André Gide, who borrowed it from the heraldic practice of having one quadrant of a coat of arms reduplicate in miniature the structure of the entire coat of arms in which it appears. In Gide, *Journal 1889–1939* (Paris: Gallimard, 1939), 41.

en abyme. In the process of retracing the narrator's personal past, including her 'Wanderung [...] von Gefängnis zu Gefängnis, von Stadt zu Stadt, von Lager zu Lager' (86), the narrative finally approaches her experiences of existence inside the camps, about fifteen pages before the end of the novel, and breaks off. From this point on, the narrator remembers nothing but a 'dichter, eintönig gelber Nebel', and in it 'Schemen, von denen ich annehme, daß sie Figuren sind, die einmal lebten, die aber ebensogut Schatten sein können, die niemals etwas anderes waren als immer nur ein Fehlen' (88). However, instead of being reduced to silence, the narrative interjects the narrator's report of an exchange between two other inmates, one of whom is a former concentration-camp prisoner like the narrator herself. During this exchange, the former prisoner takes the other woman on a journey through the past to show her that which has to be experienced because it cannot be described. She conjures up a vision of the 'langgezogene Holzhütten' of the camps, and leads the other woman past 'magere Gestalten mit kahl rasierten Köpfen', 'wandelnde Skelette', and 'Muselmanen' (90–2). She then asks her fellow inmate what else she can see, but the woman falls silent, even though, as her guide points out, she has seen only the 'Gehäuse' not the 'Kern'. Inherent in the *mise en abyme* is thus a condemnation of the refusal to represent the 'Gehäuse', which can and should be conveyed, as an act of cowardice: 'Du willst es nicht, weil du befürchtest, ihm dann nicht mehr entgehen zu können, diesem von Menschen erduldeten Unmenschlichen, diesem von Menschen begangenen Unmenschlichen' (92). Yet structurally, the suspended circuitous report is a scaled-down replica of the novel and its refusal to describe the 'Kern' in favour of an evocation of its traces. Though the 'Kern' is forever displaced, the impossibility of representing it is acknowledged, and brought to the reader's attention, by the *mise en abyme* marking its absence. This saves the text from falling silent, or from falling short by becoming one of the 'Kunstwerke, der Welt zum Fraß vorgeworfen' that Adorno had in mind when he wrote: 'Die sogenannte künstlerische Gestaltung des nackten körperlichen Schmerzes der mit Gewehrkolben Niedergeknüppelten enthält, sei's noch so entfernt, das Potential, Genuß herauszupressen.'[73] As the narrator in the text is haunted by the ghost of her mother, acting as a placeholder for an irrecoverable absent memory, so the text itself is haunted by the structural indication of a thematic absence.

As well as being a labyrinthine construction that comprises replicas of itself and of the patterns it creates, *Der Wartesaal* itself appears as a form of *mise en abyme* and nucleus in a much larger labyrinth: 'Diesseits und

---

[73] Theodor W. Adorno, *Gesammelte Schriften*, ed. Rolf Tiedemann et al., 20 vols (Frankfurt a.M.: Suhrkamp, 1970–86), xi. *Noten zur Literatur* (1974), 424.

jenseits der Stacheldrähte ist die Welt ein Tollhaus. Städte, Länder, Erdteile sind die Abteilungen in seinen Wartesälen. [...] Nur daß wir hier drinnen zumeist um unsern Zustand wissen und nicht mehr versuchen uns selbst zu belügen' (107). As with the *mise en abyme* within the text, the text as *mise en abyme* of the world has a decentring effect, causing the absent centre of the Holocaust to be shifted to the present and the world outside the narrator's waiting room, to the world of the reader. While fully familiar only to those who have experienced it to the core (and, arguably, therefore, are in no position to tell about it) the waiting-room existence in its broader sense—loss of selfhood and orientation in a bewildering labyrinthine world, haunted by a collective trauma that escapes the world's systems of thought and language and is therefore insurmountable—also appears more generally here as a post-Holocaust human condition.

Finally, in an ultimate blurring of the distinction between origin and replica, and micro- and macrocosms, the waiting room as both labyrinth with multiple nuclei and nucleus of a labyrinthine world not only contains and acts as *mise en abyme*, but writes itself into an abyss. The final image of the novel presents us with the narrator staring into the face of the 'Erzfeind', as he is coming for her, and seeing a reflection of the spider in the pupils of his eyes (108). If we read the 'Erzfeind' and the narrator as 'Verhüllungen' of the same absent 'Ich', and if we assume that, as creator of a web, the spider in turn forms part of this specular system, then the text has effectively guided the narrator to a reflection of her self in the eyes of another reflection of her self. Having already drawn attention to its refusal to reach a 'Kern' through a series of emblems and *mises en abyme* of its narrative technique, *Der Wartesaal* ultimately disappears into one of these and thus succeeds, if not in transcending, then at least in gesturing beyond the limits of its own expression and thus making itself interminable in abstraction if not in actuality.

Yet it is in more than one sense that the implications of the text are not contained by the words on the page. Before disappearing down a rabbit hole, the novel presents us with a further twist in its final passage in that this is introduced by the narrator's assertion that her allegiance with the National Socialists and her betrayal of her mother in the form in which these are described in the text are nothing but figments of her imagination, though the threat of the 'Erzfeind' remains very real to her:

> Und der Sommer, da ich mich verbündete mit den Bedrückern, weil ich selber nicht bedrückt sein wollte? Es hat ihn nie gegeben. Nichts war je wirklich, alles nur erträumtes Leben, alles nur Traum, der mich wie Leben dünkte.—Er nähert sich. Fast erreicht er mich schon. [...] Er wird mich

foltern, Traum oder nicht Traum. Auch geträumte Qualen haben ihre Wirklichkeit. (107)

Though this twist does not preclude a reading of the 'Erzfeind' as a personification of the narrator's guilt come to haunt her, it would appear to render that guilt an imaginary one by removing the reasons adduced for it within the text. However, given that, throughout the novel, the narrator is tormented by visions of her dead mother in her dreams, I would suggest that the 'geträumte Qualen' here are not imaginary, but the dreams, hallucinations, and flashbacks of traumatic reliving, and that though the reasons for it within the text are invented, the guilt associated with this trauma is very real. However, it is not guilt as a result of joining the ranks of the perpetrators in order to avoid becoming a victim, but guilt that is felt to have been incurred by having failed fully to join the ranks of the victims which causes the narrator, and perhaps her author, to feel that it is incumbent on them to preserve the encrypted phantoms of the past and not allow them to be exorcized.

Where the literary presentation of inherited trauma by later generations is concerned, it is generally assumed that writing about the absent memory of the Holocaust entails encircling, and attempting to outline, it in a concentric movement around a single centre. Thomas Nolden, for instance, has argued: 'Die nachgeborenen Generationen können sich diesem zentralen Ereignis in der Geschichte des modernen Judentums nur durch eine Bewegung nähern, die hier [...] als eine "konzentrische" Bewegung bezeichnet wird.'[74] The narrative techniques adopted in the first-generation texts discussed here, in contrast, are closer to what in *Der Wartesaal* is evoked as a 'systematisches Tohuwabohu', a strategy which makes the trauma of the Holocaust readable without deciphering it, not by encircling the void at its origin but by indefinitely dislocating and deferring it in a construct that is presented as unformed and disordered by design (35).

Indeed, despite being published over a decade after Augustin's novel, *Der Wartesaal* has, perhaps unsurprisingly, been the target of very similar criticism to *Auswege* and, to some extent, to all the texts explored here. One reviewer quite rightly observes that 'Leben im Sinn von gerade noch lebendig sein' is one theme in the novel, which also depicts a torturous 'Zustand der Unentschiedenheit', but he takes issue with the form and structure of the text, lamenting with reference to the author: 'Anstatt einen minuziösen, auf Genauigkeit bedachten Bericht zu geben, gelingt es

---

[74] *Junge jüdische Literatur: Konzentrisches Schreiben in der Gegenwart* (Würzburg: Königshausen & Neumann, 1995), 10.

ihr nur, eine [. . .] Irgendwie-Geschichte zu erzählen.'[75] In Chapters 4 and 5 of this book, the structural enactment of the insurmountable trauma of the Holocaust by means of an unresolved 'Irgendwie-Geschichte' will become even more important. In their effort to convey the impossibility of mastering the past by means of their texts' refusal to take control and reach a conclusion, these authors will demonstrate their conviction that, to cite the words of one of Wolfgang Hildesheimer's narrators, 'die Zeit des Gelingens ist vorbei, so wie auch die Zeit derer, die Gelungenes wollen'.[76]

---

[75] Lothar Romain, 'Eingesperrt zum Sterben: "Der Wartesaal"—Roman von Jenny Aloni', *Frankfurter Allgemeine Zeitung*, 29 Sept. 1969.

[76] Wolfgang Hildesheimer, *Gesammelte Werke*, ed. Christiaan Lucas Hart Nibbrig and Volker Jehle, 7 vols (Frankfurt a.M.: Suhrkamp, 1991), ii. *Monologische Prosa*, 348.

4

The Past Encrypted

Erich Fried, *Ein Soldat und ein Mädchen*

> To omit a word always, to resort to inept metaphors and obvious
> periphrases, is perhaps the most emphatic way of stressing it. That is
> the tortuous method preferred, in each of the meanderings of his
> indefatigable novel, by the oblique Ts'ui Pên.
>
> (Jorge Luis Borges, *The Garden of Forking Paths*)

Like H. G. Adler, Erich Fried, who was born in Vienna in 1921, adopted
London as his home in exile. Unlike Adler, Fried was able to flee before
the war; he left Vienna in 1938, following the annexation of Austria and
the murder of his father by the Gestapo.[1] As in the case of the other
authors discussed here, Fried's 'apprenticeship to Judaism' was performed
'under the gaze of the Other'.[2] The experience of prejudice and persecution, from being taunted as a Jew during his childhood to being hounded
as one in the Third Reich, formed Fried's sense of Jewishness in a way that
no religious or cultural influences had: 'Ich fühle mich nicht als Teil des
jüdischen Volkes [...]. Mein Judentum ist durch die Erziehungsschick-
sale meiner Kindheit geprägt und dadurch, daß Hitler mich in eine
Gaskammer geworfen hätte, wenn er mich erwischt hätte.'[3] Even after it
was averted, the destiny that would have seen him dead continued to loom

---

[1] For a concise biography, see Volker Kaukoreit, 'Erich Frieds Lebensdaten', in Erich
Fried, *Gesammelte Werke*, ed. Kaukoreit and Klaus Wagenbach, 4 vols (Berlin: Wagenbach,
1993), iv. *Prosa*, 655–90.

[2] I borrow this phrasing from Alain Finkielkraut, who derives the concept from Sartre
and uses it to distinguish Jewish survivors, who had their Jewish identity thrust on them by
the experience of persecution, from Jews of the second and third generation, who cast
themselves in a fictitious identity in the absence of such an experience. See Alain Finkielkraut, *The Imaginary Jew*, trans. Kevin O'Neill and David Suchoff (Lincoln, NB: University
of Nebraska Press, 1994), 15.

[3] See Hans J. Schütz, *Juden in der deutschen Literatur: Eine deutsch-jüdische Literaturgeschichte im Überblick* (Munich: Piper, 1992), 230. Cited in Katrin Schäfer, *'Die andere
Seite': Erich Frieds Prosawerk: Motive und Motivationen seines Schreibens* (Vienna: Praesens,
1998), 273–4.

as a hypothetical over what was now perceived as life in reprieve. Written and reworked repeatedly over an extended period of time, between 1946 and 1960, his post-war novel *Ein Soldat und ein Mädchen*, as we shall see, may be considered as a reflection both on and of this experience.[4] Much like the other texts referred to here, it is profoundly, though not immediately recognizably, a text that has arisen out of, and is shot through with traces of, the Holocaust.

From 1939, exile organizations such as the Austrian Centre and the Freier Deutscher Kulturbund provided Fried with publishing opportunities, but, although he succeeded in making a name for himself as a writer within the exile community, he remained for many years largely reliant on unskilled labour to earn a living.[5] After the war, Fried wrote for British re-education and POW journals, but it was thirteen years before a volume of his work, a collection of poetry entitled *Gedichte*, appeared in West Germany in 1958, and a further two years after that before the publication of his novel. In 1952, freelance work Fried had been doing for the 'German Service' of the BBC since 1950 turned into a permanent position as political commentator, which he held until 1968. Though in 1953 Fried finally returned to mainland Europe, on the occasion of a trip to Berlin, he did not go back to Vienna until 1962, and London remained his home by default until his death in 1988. To this day, Fried is known primarily for his politically engaged poetry and his translations of works by, among others, Shakespeare, T. S. Eliot, and Dylan Thomas, but he also wrote a number of short stories and essays, as well as, of course, *Ein Soldat und ein Mädchen*. Indeed of the latter he says in the 'Nachwort' to the novel's first edition: 'In all den Jahren hat mir dieses Buch mehr als irgendeine andere Arbeit bedeutet, ausgenommen einzelne Gedichte' (205).

'TO OMIT A WORD ALWAYS...'

Ein Soldat und ein Mädchen is usually presented as an account of the love affair between the eponymous soldier, a German-Jewish exile, who

---

[4] Erich Fried, *Ein Soldat und ein Mädchen* (Düsseldorf: Claassen, 1960; 2nd edn, 1982), and in *Gesammelte Werke*, ed. Kaukoreit and Wagenbach, iv. 5–211. References will be to the *Gesammelte Werke* edition and will be included in parentheses in the text. Though this is Fried's only published novel, his estate includes a manuscript of an early novel, from 1937, titled *Der Kulturstaat*. See Schäfer, *'Die andere Seite'*, 54–66.

[5] See Volker Kaukoreit, *Vom Exil bis zum Protest gegen den Krieg in Vietnam: Frühe Stationen des Lyrikers Erich Fried: Werk und Biographie 1938–1966* (Darmstadt: Häusser, 1991), or Steven W. Lawrie, *Erich Fried: A Writer without a Country* (New York: Lang, 1996), for details regarding Fried's exile and literary career.

emigrated to America before the war and returned to Germany with the US occupying forces, and the girl Helga, a German concentration camp guard on death row. Pól O'Dochartaigh has called it 'eine deutsch-jüdische Romeo-und-Julia-Geschichte'.[6] The girl is supposedly modelled on the historical figure of Irma Grese, a young German Nazi who was sentenced to death in the Belsen trial in 1945, at the age of 22, and who received a great deal of press coverage because of her defiant stance in court, and her striking and supposedly stereotypically 'Aryan' appearance. Fried's soldier spends the last night of the girl's life with her and suffers a mental breakdown after her execution. The novel's 'plot' is summarized accordingly on the cover of the second edition:

> Helga, die junge und schöne KZ-Lagerwärterin, ist von einem Gericht der Besatzungsmächte zum Tode verurteilt worden. Am Tag vor der Hinrich-tung äußert sie einen letzten Wunsch: die Nacht mit einem Mann zu verbringen. Ihre Wahl fällt auf den zufällig in der Zelle anwesenden ameri-kanischen Wachsoldaten, einen jüdischen Emigranten, der darauf eingeht. Der Soldat kann Helgas Hinrichtung nicht verhindern und erlebt einen psychischen Zusammenbruch, von dem er sich schreibend zu erholen ver-sucht.

Yet although the book is commonly described as featuring as its 'central story' the encounter of 'two star-crossed lovers', only a small part of it is in fact devoted to the development of this alleged main storyline, which remains, figuratively and literally, in the margins of the text.[7] The bulk of the novel is made up of the soldier's own writings, an assortment of prose vignettes and occasional poems, some of which he produces during and after his time in a 'Mental Ward' of an American army hospital after his collapse, and some of which date back to before he met Helga. These 'Schriften des Soldaten' are framed, in Parts I and III of the novel, by the account of a second narrator, another Jewish exile, who recounts how he met the soldier in London, after the latter's discharge from the army, and who presents us with the soldier's stories, interprets them, and provides background information. It is this second narrator who supplies the report of the soldier's affair with the girl in his frame narrative, and who sets out to tie the soldier's own writings to this encounter. He incorporates into his framing account the soldier's cryptically allusive descriptions of the night before and of the morning of the girl's execution, and he claims of the 'Schriften des Soldaten', which constitute the substantial middle section of

---

[6] 'Erich Fried: Poetik des Menschseins', in Norbert Otto Eke and Hartmut Steinecke (eds), *Shoah in der deutschsprachigen Literatur* (Berlin: Schmidt, 2006), 280–5 (281).

[7] Ilse Newbery, 'Erich Fried's *Ein Soldat und ein Mädchen*', *German Life and Letters*, 42 (1988), 46–59 (46).

the novel: 'im Grunde sind alle Manuskripte, die der Soldat nach der Begegnung mit Helga geschrieben hat, ja sogar einige schon früher entstandene Arbeiten, Beiträge zum Verständnis dieser Geschichte' (55). In fact, the soldier's texts in Part II make no explicit, and only some implicit, mention of the encounter with Helga. The section is subdivided into four parts, titled 'Fünf Umschreibungen einer Begegnung', 'Aus den letzten Kriegsjahren', 'Aus dem Mental Ward', and 'Vom Weiterleben', and not even the first of these subsections specifies the nature of the 'Begegnung' to which the fragments contained within it refer. Notwithstanding, the second narrator continually seeks to forge links to the soldier's one-night stand with Helga, and thus to impose coherence and some form of overarching narrative on the individual pieces. He does this mainly by adding comments or appending footnotes to the soldier's texts, comments and notes in which he offers interpretations of the texts, stresses patterns and leitmotifs that run through them, and generally attempts to relate the soldier's writings to his own frame narrative by casting them as 'Umschreibungen', as oblique references all supposedly periphrasing the encounter with the girl (e.g. 72). Very often, the links the second narrator establishes in this way are patently tenuous, and his efforts to channel the soldier's fragments into a story arc feel contrived and heavy-handed. This has prompted one reviewer to conclude: 'Den weitaus größten Teil des Buches [...] füllen [...] die sogenannten Schriften des Soldaten [...], die Erich Fried in den anhängenden Kommentaren mühsam auf jene Schicksalsbegegnung umzudeuten versucht.'[8] Worse still, the second narrator's technique has been described as 'banal and condescending', as 'the reader is given the impression of the narrator leaning over his shoulder and guiding him to an appreciation of the very artificially constructed and largely unconvincing connections'.[9]

Ein Soldat und ein Mädchen undeniably appears as a collection of at best loosely connected fragments: the makings of a *Novelle* with the supposedly true 'unerhörte Begebenheit' of the soldier's one-night stand with the girl, intermixed with more or less tangential further prose pieces, and footnotes expanding on or qualifying these, with poems and poetological reflections, intertextual references, free association and wordplay, references to myth and fairy tales, biblical allusions, and historical and autobiographical material drawing on the lives of both narrators as well as on Fried's own background. Hardly any of these fragments tell any kind of story. Rather,

---

[8] Heinz Beckmann, 'Kommentar statt Dichtung', *Zeitwende/Die neue Furche*, 32 (1961), 199–200 (200).
[9] Steven W. Lawrie, '"Etwas Romanartiges": Erich Fried's Novel *Ein Soldat und ein Mädchen*', *German Life and Letters*, 48 (1995), 199–221 (210).

they constitute a series of what the soldier calls 'Mikro-Beobachtungen', miniature reflections or vignettes, which touch on topics as apparently diverse as human ritual sacrifice, dragons and knights, a city being consumed by fire, being trapped in an apartment by an anthropomorphous mouse, exhuming the dead, or wandering through Hades. As the narrator explains, these miniature reflections are 'die kleinen und kleinsten Beobachtungen [...], die er [der Soldat] als Rohmaterial des Schreibensbetrachtet' (143). What critical attention the book has received has consequently tended to focus on the question of whether *Ein Soldat und ein Mädchen* even warrants Fried's categorization of it as a novel. Where critics have concluded that it does not, they have blamed factors such as the piecemeal genesis of the book, in the course of which a number of independently published short stories were drawn together and embellished to form a more substantial volume, or Fried's lack of first-hand knowledge of his material. An early reviewer suggests that the reason for the soldier's writings having 'nur weniges oder gar nichts' to do with the events related in the frame narrative is 'daß Erich Fried hier verstreute Arbeiten aus seiner frühen Zeit zusammengefaßt hat'.[10] Steven Lawrie proposes that the tenuous thematic link is the result of an attempt to provide 'depth rather than a continuation of the narrative' in the main body of the text in order to compensate for 'the author's ignorance about events and places in Germany'.[11] In this view, the second narrator's dubious elaborations and 'elucidations' are considered proof that Fried himself felt that the book failed to cohere as a novel, and the second narrator is regarded as a tool to which Fried resorted in a vain attempt to smooth over the cracks in his narrative construct, or at least to forestall criticism of his approach: 'Where Fried as author has doubts about aspects of his novel or anticipates objections from a reader, narrator II is used to appease these.'[12]

It is certainly true that Fried was very conscious of the fragmentary nature of his work and of what might be considered the drawbacks of its narrative technique. He acknowledges its lack of cohesion in comments both on and in the text. For instance, he refers to the book as 'Stueckwerk' and a 'Zwischending'.[13] He has the second narrator speak of the text with his contributions as 'ein Fragment, unverläßlich und unangenehm' (17). He then has him quote the soldier comparing his narrative technique to

[10] Horst Bienek, 'Literarische Scherben', *Frankfurter Allgemeine Zeitung*, 17 Sept. 1960.
[11] 'Etwas Romanartiges', 207, 215.
[12] Lawrie, 'Etwas Romanartiges', 214.
[13] The former in unpublished notes on the novel from Fried's literary estate; the latter in 'Den Leser einbeziehen', *Deutsche Zeitung*, 24/25 Sept. 1960. Both cited in Schäfer, *'Die andere Seite'*, 337, 15.

Aristotelian drama and conceding that his approach is a far cry from any conventional drawing-together and releasing of different strands of plot to create tension and resolve it in a denouement, that in his writing 'von einer Handlung oder gar vom Schürzen und Lösen des Knotens, wie wir das in der Schule gelernt haben, keine Rede sein kann' (59). The text also allows for the view that the individual components that constitute it are held together by the sheer force of the second narrator's dogmatism and that their signifying power, and the reader's assessment of them, may be limited by his prescriptive approach. In a prefatory remark to the soldier's writings of Part II, the second narrator reports a conversation between himself and the soldier in which he points out this potentially problematic aspect of his explanatory appendices but is shot down by the soldier: 'Meinen Einwand, durch erklärende Zwischentexte werde den Arbeiten etwas von ihrem Eigenleben geraubt, ließ er [der Soldat] nicht gelten' (59). Statements such as this have been read as a disingenuous ploy on the part of the narrator (and by extension the author) to head off criticism of his own shortcomings at the pass, without actually doing anything to address the underlying problems. Lawrie considers it an indication that Fried recognized the weaknesses of his approach 'but lacked the self-discipline which would have demanded alteration'.[14]

Other critics praise the formal discontinuity of Fried's novel and regard the work's open, fragmentary nature as an asset, or even try to render it politically productive. Alexander von Bormann, for instance, speaks of Fried's 'plurales Erzählprogramm' in the context of the cold war and proposes:

> Frieds Roman steht gegen Phantasmen oder Ideologien der Einheit, der Identität, wie sie im kalten Krieg neu aufgelegt wurden. [...] Wenn Fried den verfolgten Juden und die KZ-Wärterin *ein* Fleisch werden läßt, so nicht 'essentialistisch', als Rekurs auf *eine* beide umfassende/tragende Natur, son-dern als Konzept einer Versöhnung, die Begegnung mit dem Anderen voraussetzt, die Fremdheit zuläßt, einer Identität/Einheit, die ihr Anderes aushält, ja aufsucht, ohne dieses dialektisch 'aufheben' zu wollen.[15]

Nadya Luer reads the novel as similarly programmatic, albeit in a broader modern(ist) existential sense: 'Thematisiert wird vor allem die [...] indivi-duelle und soziale Erfahrung der Unbeständigkeit und Zerrissenheit. In diesem Sinne bleibt der Roman Frieds welthaltig und damit politisch. So

---

[14] 'Etwas Romanartiges', 214.

[15] '"Wir sind nicht, was wir sind": Nichtidentität als Erzählkonzept im deutschjüdischen Roman nach 1945', in Jens Stüben and Winfried Woesler (eds), '*Wir tragen den Zettelkasten mit den Steckbriefen unserer Freunde': Beiträge jüdischer Autoren zur deutschen Literatur seit 1945* (Darmstadt: Häusser, 1993), 31–52 (36); original emphasis.

kann die Vielschichtigkeit [. . .] des Romans als Programm gelesen werden.'[16] However, the device of the second narrator tends to be viewed no less critically in this latter camp of Fried criticism than in the former. Though the second narrator's comments introduce an element of (self-)reflection into the writing, which would conform with notions of a progressive 'plurales Erzählprogramm', Fried's perceived use of them as a reductive means of explaining and justifying his approach to the reader, described by Fried's own publisher as a 'den Leser allmählich verärgernde dauernde Selbstinterpretation', is here deemed to undermine his efforts to create an open work.[17] Karl Wagner, for example, declares:

> Irritierend bleibt, daß die selbstreflexiven und erläuternden Partien Ausdruck und Dementi eines offenen Kunstwerkes sind. Sie sprechen vom Fragmentarischen und Offenen und schränken es zugleich ein, indem sie die ausgesparten Verweisungszusammenhänge erläuternd determinieren.[18]

A very small number of critics in this camp disagree and maintain that the narrator's commentaries are 'absolut nicht schulmeisterlich'[19] but, on the contrary, offer vital clues precisely because, as Katrin Schäfer puts it, 'die komplexen Texte des Soldaten seine Gefühle und Situationen "nicht schildern, nicht erzählen, sondern nur 'umschreiben' können"'.[20] She goes on to say: 'Mit den kommentierenden Texten gibt Fried dem Leser eine Art Dechiffrierhilfe, um die symbolhaften oder parabolischen Texte aus der Sphäre der literarischen Fiktion in seine eigene Wirklichkeit zu übersetzen', and that in doing so he provides 'Anleitung zum richtigen "Gebrauch" seiner Lektüre'.[21]

Regardless of whether critics consider the openness of Fried's work to be incidental or deliberate, and his use of narrative commentary embarrassed and defensive, imperious and restrictive, or essential and effective, they all evidently place a great deal of faith in the assertions of this second narrator: they take him at his word, and they seem to view him, for better or worse, as a mouthpiece not only for the soldier but for Fried himself. Crucially, they assume that the periphrastic approach to narrating, which speaks in analogies not actualities and about which the soldier says 'man

---

[16] *Form und Engagement: Untersuchungen zur Dichtung und Ästhetik Erich Frieds* (Vienna: Praesens, 2004), 85.

[17] Letter of 21 June 1960 from Eugen Claassen to Erich Fried, in the Claassen-Archiv, Deutsches Literaturarchiv. Cited in Lawrie, 'Etwas Romanartiges', 210.

[18] 'Ins Innere des Schreckens: Erich Frieds Roman "Ein Soldat und ein Mädchen"', in Heinz Ludwig Arnold (ed.), *Erich Fried* (2nd rev. edn, Munich: text + kritik, 1997), 65–9 (68).

[19] Herbert Bornebusch, 'Umschreiben des Unbeschreiblichen: Die Grenzen des Schreibens als Thema des Romans', in Arnold (ed.), *Erich Fried*, 61–4 (64).

[20] Schäfer, *'Die andere Seite'*, 333, citing Fried, *Gesammelte Werke*, iv. 62.

[21] Schäfer, *'Die andere Seite'*, 333, 334.

sagt was Ähnliches, eine Umschreibung, damit man nur ja nicht das Eigentliche sagen muß', is limited to the soldier's manuscripts (14). But what grounds are there for believing that Fried intended us to treat the second narrator as any more omniscient or infallible, or even just more upfront, than the soldier-narrator? Surely this is a hierarchical convention that is consistently overturned in Modernism and after (though it has been known to be long before then), and as modern-day readers we should be used to texts in which the framed protagonist contradicts the framer or the framed story reframes the frame. Certainly Fried's text gives no indication that it expects us to assume that the frame has authority over the framed. On the contrary, it suggests that whatever insight we do gain into what is left unsaid by the 'Umschreibungen' we are meant to arrive at not thanks to but in spite of the second narrator's interventions. This becomes apparent further on in the passage cited earlier, containing the soldier's assessment of the second narrator's technique, which has the soldier conclude: 'Mein Lieber, sogar die dicksten Wälzer zur Erläuterung von Werken der Kunst und Literatur versagen mit nachtwandlerischer Sicherheit an allen wirklich wichtigen oder schwierigen Stellen. Also werden diese Stellen auch Deine Kommentare überleben' (59). Not only is the crux of the matter, whatever this may be, presented as being inexplicable, and the purported exegesis as incapable of uncovering a way into it for us; the use of the term 'überleben' suggests that the narrative commentary is not only not instructive, but obstructive, making it more instead of less challenging for us to navigate the text. In what follows, I shall show that by regarding the second narrator's perspective as more authoritative than others arising out of the text, and his statements as carrying greater weight than the rest of the novel, we are missing the point of Fried's work. I submit that the second narrator was never meant to facilitate our understanding, or direct our appraisal, of the work. His main function in the text is not to guide the way, or, for that matter, to justify, to grandstand, or to inculcate, but to impede and misdirect, if necessary through a combination of all of these. This, in turn, aligns his narrative technique with the soldier's. If the soldier's modus operandi is to be allusive and oblique, I intend to show that it is the task of the second narrator to prevaricate around the soldier's prevarications. The question then becomes: if the second narrator's comments are not the key to deciphering the text but just another lock designed to prevent us from entering into it too easily, what is it that is being dissimulated in this text, and why? In attempting to establish this, I shall demonstrate that there is indeed a 'plurales Erzählprogramm' at work in Fried's novel, of which the narrator figure constitutes but one important aspect. However, I shall suggest that this programme came about less as a reaction against cold-war ideologies or even as a result of a general twentieth-century malaise around concepts of identity and subjectivity, but in response to the more specific and personal experience of National Socialist persecution and the threat of the Holocaust. In other words, I aim to show that Fried's novel is a Holocaust novel in the same category as those already examined here, and that its fragmentary form and narrative technique are, once again, the result of its author's conviction that his material could not be done justice in any straightforwardly descriptive, thematic way. As in the preceding chapters, the narrative strategy of encrypting the upheaval of the Holocaust structurally while avoiding any direct thematic reference to it produces a digressive, meandering, and inconclusive text: a text-as-labyrinth. In this, it also comes to read as a partial model of a famous prototype of a bifurcating narrative that takes the shape of what it intends to represent without mentioning it directly, and in the process challenges both fictional conventions and notions about time: the eponymous garden-of-forking-paths novel of the short story by Jorge Luis Borges, whose writing was an important source of intertextual connection for Fried. In Borges's story, the narrative strategy of the labyrinth novel is described as follows: 'To omit a word always, to resort to inept metaphors and obvious periphrases, is perhaps the most emphatic way of stressing it. That is the tortuous method preferred, in each of the meanderings of his indefatigable novel, by the oblique Ts'ui Pên.'[22] As will transpire, Fried's novel shares both aspects of the approach cited in Borges's story and the narrative's own practice of using mirroring and *mise en abyme* to signal beyond the limitations of language and the text itself.

But what is the 'word' that *Ein Soldat und ein Mädchen* omits always? The second narrator would have us believe that what the soldier is shying away from is direct reference to his one-night stand with Helga and her execution the following day. If we take him at his word, we may indeed feel compelled to concur with Bormann's reading, or to conclude with Herbert Bornebusch: 'Die vollkommene Sinnlosigkeit ist nicht mehr darstellbar, der Kern der Romanfabel—die Begegnung mit einer Schergin des Naziregimes und ihr Tod—entzieht sich der Beschreibung. [...] Aber gerade das Unaussprechlich-Unausgesprochene steht im Zentrum des Romans.'[23] It is not easy to argue with this, as taking issue with Bornebusch's assessment requires definition of an unspoken absence. The soldier's only actual account of his night with Helga, and her execution

---

[22] Jorge Luis Borges, 'The Garden of Forking Paths', trans. Donald A. Yates, in *Labyrinths: Selected Stories and Other Writings*, ed. Yates and James E. Irby, trans. Yates, Irby, et al. (London: Penguin, 2000), 44–54 (53).
[23] Arnold (ed.), *Erich Fried*, 62.

the following day, is included in the second narrator's frame narrative in Part I of the novel, in two prose pieces titled 'Die Nacht' and 'Das zweite Bleistiftmanuskript'. Even here, the term 'account' is misleading, for these are not factual reports, but dreamlike, impressionistic streams of free association, often triggered by semantic, linguistic, or phonic correspondences, or as the second narrator puts it: 'Der Soldat geht [...] von Lautverbindungen zu Gedankenverbindungen über, und seine Beschreibung hat eigentlich weder Anfang noch Ende' (50). When pressed for details concerning the incident, the soldier is unwilling, or unable, to be any more specific but keeps resorting to the same image to evoke his time with Helga in the final hours of her life. The image in question is that of a 'dead angle', the blind spot which cannot be seen, or penetrated by bullets, from behind the parapet of a trench because of its proximity to the armaments and source of fire: 'Auf alle weiteren Fragen des Erzählers hin sprach der Soldat aber nur immer wieder vom Toten Winkel' (47). In the soldier's application of the term, the dead angle stands for the space between the ejection of a projectile and its fatal impact, or in the case of the girl, between the death knell of the guilty verdict and the death blow of its—and her—execution. Its meaning here is both concrete and figurative to him: it refers to an actual site, the cell on death row where Helga spends her final hours, but also to the abstract state of being suspended in a limbo where death looms but cannot yet strike. He consequently describes his final night with the girl as 'im Toten Winkel des Todesurteils gelegen', and he associates being in this place and state of suspension with a sensation of numbness and of feeling 'gewissermaßen erstorben', no longer fully alive, but not yet fully dead (47). The image of the dead angle is, of course, apropos to the girl's situation. In addition, it also provides an apt metaphor for an experience that resists straightforward comprehension and description. Thoughts and words may try to home in on what lies in the dead angle, but they will never touch it. In the context of narrative technique, this would account for the adoption of an approach that resorts to 'Umschreibungen' instead of 'Beschreibung', for as the soldier puts it: 'verstehn Sie, was einem selber passiert, das kann der Mensch dann oft nicht sagen. Es fehlt ihm der Abstand. Und wo man keinen Abstand hat, dort kann man auch nicht scharf einstellen und anvisieren. Das ist so, wie mit dem Toten Winkel bei der Artillerie' (14). So far, there does not appear to be anything here to contradict Bornebusch's theory that the unspoken core of the novel is the soldier's 'Begegnung mit einer Schergin des Naziregimes und ihr Tod'.

Yet I suggest that the metaphor of the 'Toter Winkel' holds a significance for the soldier (and for his author) beyond his encounter with Helga and her execution. One indication of this in the passage just discussed is that, contrary to what we might expect, the soldier in fact uses the phrase 'gewissermaßen erstorben' in reference to himself. The girl's end is imminent, yet he is the one who is said to be feeling quasi-dead. Even in the account most directly concerning her and her death, it is apparently not the girl who constitutes the main focus of the circumlocution, but the soldier himself. If we take a closer look at other instances where the image appears in the text, this impression starts to crystallize. Prior to its application to the Helga story, we encounter the metaphor twice, and both times it is used explicitly to characterize the soldier's frame of mind and to convey that, without realizing it, he is, even before the Helga episode, no longer fully alive and in synchrony with the world but has somehow fallen out of step with his time and surroundings. In the second of the two passages, we are told about this 'Zerfallenheit mit Zeit und Umwelt': 'Als er davon sprach, erwähnte er abermals den Toten Winkel, jenen Raum im Schatten einer Batterie, den ihre Geschütze nicht bestreichen können' (37). Moreover, we learn that the soldier was not aware when he met the girl of the extent of his 'Zerfallenheit', and that he only became conscious of it in the wake of the encounter: 'Wie weit auch er selbst mit seiner Welt schon zerfallen war, das wußte der Soldat an jenem Tag noch nicht. Es war der letzte Tag, an dem er es noch nicht wußte' (37). In other words, when he meets the girl, he is already trapped in an extended, less clearly defined version of the state of suspension she experiences for a night in the run-up to her execution; he is just not conscious of it. In addition to standing for an actual space, an existential condition, and a textual lacuna, the image of the 'Toter Winkel' would, then, appear to characterize a psychological state in Fried's novel: in any number of ways it signifies a realm under the gaze of death, but at the same time it marks a blind spot in one's own vision, an impairment in one's self-awareness. In the 'Toter Winkel' you are a ghost, but without realizing it. The time spent with the girl in the period of limbo between the pronouncement and execution of her sentence was not what first brought about the soldier's disconnected state; it merely reflected it, and thus reminded him, or rendered him cognizant, of it. Her experience on death row is a condensed version of his existence.

What is it, then, that has caused the soldier to become suspended somewhere between the dead and the living even before the fateful night with the girl, and of which his encounter with her serves to remind him? The second narrator's report of how the soldier comes to meet the girl suggests an explanation almost in spite of itself. We learn that when the soldier returns to Germany on the occasion of the war crimes trials, it is as a revenant in more than one sense, as a thrice-uprooted 'deutscher Jude, heimatloser Emigrant und nun waffenklirrendes Gespenst in den Ruinen des eigenen Landes' (26). It is not his post-war encounter with Helga but his experience of persecution and terror, his original confrontation with National Socialism, that has taken his life without killing him outright. The murder of his parents and family, and the abrupt discontinuation of his life as it was up to that point and banishment to exile—'das Zunich-tewerden seiner eigenen Lebenspläne, das Herausgerissensein, das elende Leben in einem fremden Land'—have left him for undead (27). His life after the event that was meant to be the death of him is perceived as life on borrowed time, not all that different from Helga's final hours before the sentence hanging over her is carried out. Like the protagonists of texts discussed in previous chapters, the soldier finds that you do not really get over your own death sentence, even if its execution is indefinitely deferred, or as he puts it: 'Außerdem aber unterbricht nichts im Leben [...] den Menschen so deutlich wie sein Todesurteil' (23). The observation applies as much to his own life as to Helga's last night, except that in his case it is not clear when he will exit the dead angle. In indicating a life interrupted and dislocated, and by extension the disruption of notions of temporal and spatial continuity, as well as a breakdown in conceptualization and com-munication, the image of the 'Toter Winkel' is revealed as another in the long line of metaphors accumulated in literary and theoretical writing to convey the idea of the Holocaust as caesura.

'...TO RESORT TO OBVIOUS PERIPHRASES...'

As we have seen in previous chapters, this has implications for both the content and form of the text, the foremost of which is that the two become difficult to separate. At a thematic level, the soldier's ghost-like existence in a dead angle, and his delayed recognition and incomplete understand-ing of his own situation, is suggestive of traumatic latency. As in earlier chapters, statements such as '"Ich war zu nah dran, ich hab' gar nichts gespürt und gedacht. Erst nachher hat's mich erwischt", sagte er, "dafür aber desto gründlicher"' (37) bring to mind Freud's account of the structure of trauma in 'Der Mann Moses und die monotheistische Reli-gion',[24] according to which someone who survives a harrowing accident may only experience the event after a period of delay, 'in connection with

---

[24] Sigmund Freud, 'Der Mann Moses und die monotheistische Religion: Drei Abhand-lungen' (1939), in *Studienausgabe*, ed. Alexander Mitscherlich, Angela Richards, and James Strachey, 11 vols (Frankfurt a.M.: Fischer, 1969–75), ix. *Fragen der Gesellschaft/Ursprünge der Religion* (1974), 455–581.

another place, and in another time'.[25] We know that Fried had a keen
interest in psychoanalysis and was closely acquainted with the works of
Freud and Jung. He underwent analysis himself, on two separate occasions
between 1948 and 1952, with the Freud specialist Derrik Eastman, and
with Philip Metman, England's then leading Jungian analyst.[26] In 1955,
Fried even gave a broadcast for the German Service of the BBC on Freud
and psychoanalysis.[27]

In Chapter 3, we saw how Freud's example illustrating latency may well
have served as a template for the (near-)fatal train collision in Elisabeth
Augustin's *Auswege*. In *Ein Soldat und ein Mädchen*, we encounter a
similar borrowing. The soldier's 'Fünf Umschreibungen einer Begegnung', which allegedly revolve most closely around his encounter with
the girl, are heavily preoccupied with the themes of death, insensibility,
and the impossibility of mourning. The first two vignettes present us with
men who have survived what should have been the death of them, but are
left feeling deadened by the realization 'daß das Sterben nicht tödlich sein
muß' (66). In the first 'Umschreibung', the second narrator traces this
sensation back to the electric shock treatment the soldier received in the
American army hospital after Helga's death. The treatment is then described as a lesser version of death by electric chair, except that instead of
killing a person, it kills their memory of the incident and of those who
died in it. According to the second narrator, this is another reference to the
girl and to the soldier's guilt at having allowed the memory of her to be
erased: 'Er habe damals ein schlechtes Gewissen gehabt; er habe die
Vorstellung nicht loswerden können, Helga sei erst dadurch ganz und
gar getötet worden, daß er sie sich "wegschocken" ließ' (64). All of this is
heavily reminiscent of the notion of trauma as an event which leaves no
trace but only a void in the psyche as it occurs, and which causes its
sufferers to be haunted by something of which they have no memory. In
the third story, a man who receives news of the death of his beloved gets
up, leaves the room, and kills himself. The remainder of the piece
speculates about the possibility of reversing chronology and raising the
dead by thus backtracking to, and changing the outcome of, the original
incident. Again, we are encouraged to read this as a reference to Helga, but
the phrase 'Nachricht vom Tod seiner Geliebten' is intriguingly ambiguous, and the German term 'Geliebten', like the English 'beloved', can be

---

[25] Cathy Caruth, 'Introduction', in Caruth (ed.), *Trauma: Explorations in Memory*
(Baltimore: Johns Hopkins University Press, 1995), 3–12 (8).
[26] See e.g. Kaukoreit, *Vom Exil bis zum Protest gegen den Krieg in Vietnam*, 205.
[27] See Steven W. Lawrie, *Erich Fried: A Writer without a Country* (New York: Lang), 358.

read as singular or plural (68). The final vignette presents us with a man who wears a black band around his arm as a sign of mourning but is unable to access the area covered by the band, which as a result is perfectly preserved in its original condition. The armband is depicted in terms that make it sound like a tomb:

> Luft und Licht können nun das unter der Binde ruhende Stück Stoff nicht mehr erreichen, zumindest fällt es ihnen schwer, die Binde zu durchdringen, die es von allen Seiten umschließt und ein wenig überwölbt. Dafür ist aber dieses verborgene Stück Stoff dem Straßenstaub und dem Regen entrückt und von seiner dunklen Umhüllung weit besser geschützt als alles, worauf noch das Licht scheint. (71)

We are reminded here of Abraham and Torok's concept of a *crypte* as a site in the analysand's mind where unremembered and inarticulate experience resides inaccessible, a sort of artificial unconscious in the ego, allowing traumatic events and deceased loved ones to inhabit the subject without his or her conscious knowledge.

The most overt reference to traumatic latency, however, occurs in the fourth of the five fragments, interpolated between the occurrence of a trauma in the first three pieces and the impossibility of mourning in the fifth. The fragment is entitled 'Menschenwürde', and it constitutes a reflection on how people deal with the blows fate deals them, and how they respond in the period after the 'Hereinbrechen der Katastrophe' (68). According to the second narrator, the passage indicates that the soldier was embarrassed at his ignominious collapse immediately following Helga's execution. In fact, the passage reads like an evocation of Freud's account of latency, in terms echoing very closely Freud's own, such as reference to a belated response following an incubation period, but without specifying the nature of the catastrophe in question:

> Andere sind beim Hereinbrechen der Katastrophe [...] tapfer, gefaßt und großzügig. Sie stehen scheinbar über den Dingen. Später aber, nach Stunden, Tagen oder Wochen [...] packt sie der Jammer. Sie bleiben gleichsam mitten im Wort stecken, versuchen mit Hilfe der bewährten Gesten über den toten Punkt hinwegzukommen [...] und brechen schließlich zusammen. [...] Das Verhältnis des Ausmaßes der in Erscheinung tretenden Gefühle zu den tragischen Anlässen und zur Länge der heldenhaften Zwischenzeit oder Inkubationsfrist läßt sich nur schwer durch eine brauchbare Formel ausdrücken. (68–9)

Fried's term 'Inkubationsfrist' here recalls Freud's reference in his essay on Moses and monotheism to an 'Inkubationszeit', to which he alludes 'in durchsichtiger Anspielung an die Pathologie der Infektionskrankheiten', immediately before introducing the term *Latenz*.[28] Like the works encountered in other chapters, Fried's text manages, without mentioning even the possibility of a prior trauma, to suggest that perhaps the circumstances of the Helga episode—her execution (which the soldier does not witness directly, and which he feels he ought to have prevented), his survival in the face of her death, his impression that he has allowed the memory of her to be 'shocked' out of him—merely act as a stimulus, triggering a delayed response to an earlier trauma. As in previous chapters, the protagonist's situation would appear to be covered by the definition of post-traumatic stress disorder as

> a response, sometimes delayed, to an overwhelming event or events, which takes the form of repeated, intrusive hallucinations, dreams, thoughts or behaviors stemming from the event, along with numbing that may have begun during or after the experience, and possibly also increased arousal to [...] stimuli recalling the event.[29]

Considered from this angle, the soldier's actions, and, by extension, his writings, appear in a new light, as responses to stimuli recalling an earlier incident, or even as failed attempts on his part to return to the original source of trauma and bring about closure. The soldier tries to go about this in two different ways. On the one hand, he makes repeated reference to the notion of raising the dead by recovering the memory of them and thus, paradoxically, creating the possibility of mourning them and laying them to rest. Failing that, he, on the other hand, hopes at least to lay himself to rest by retroactively bringing about the destiny that was meant to be his to share with them. The former is attempted literally in one prose piece titled 'Die Ausgrabung', which depicts a vision of the soldier digging up a cemetery to unearth 'halbvergessene' dead acquaintances and family members, who have been murdered by National Socialists (127). Initially, he appears to succeed in bringing the bodies back to life, but in the end they are 'lebloser als zuvor' (128). In his 'Versuch, die Macht des Todes zu besiegen', he has become 'ein Herbeiführer des Todes' (129), which could be read as an indication of a more general sense on his part that his failure to die has made him complicitous in the death of those he has survived. Finally, the soldier admits defeat and lies down in a grave next to the bodies. His failure to raise and put to rest the dead apparently leads him to conclude that his own death would be the only cure. His life in the 'wake' of his survival now consists in waiting for the existence he is still leading to effect the death that was already meant to have eclipsed it. We get a sense

---

[28] 'Der Mann Moses und die monotheistische Religion', 516.
[29] Caruth (ed.), *Trauma: Explorations in Memory*, 4.

of this paradoxical reversal of affairs when the soldier defines the final culmination of the process of dying, 'das Sterben selbst', as 'die endgültige Einholung des Nichts durch das Sein' (38). This is further confirmed, for example, by the fact that his prose piece entitled 'Die Heimkehr' traces a return to death. The origin of the trauma that occasioned the survival he is attempting to reverse is, again, unclear. His assertion that everything is out of joint following his failure to die ostensibly relates back to the Helga episode: 'Vielleicht hätt' ich nämlich auch sterben sollen, gleich damals in Deutschland, statt zusammenzukrachen und mich pflegen zu lassen. [...] jetzt ist alles ein bissel aus dem Leim gegangen. Oder hätte ich damals selber Schluß machen sollen?' (201). However, the ambiguity of the phrasing ('damals in Deutschland') means that the statement could equally be read as hinting at a prior trauma. Because we know that the soldier was already a ghost when he met the girl, his encounter with Helga could then be seen as a reminder of this earlier traumatic survival, and as a failed bid on the part of the soldier to re-enact the original trauma in the hope of closing the loop of his post-mortem existence and ironing out the glitch this has caused in the fabric of the world. This reading is supported by the fact that, in going to see Helga, the soldier felt he was retracing the steps of his family and friends: 'Er empfand, daß er, indem er zu Helga ging, den gleichen Weg nahm, den seine zugrunde gegangenen Verwandten und Freunde genommen hatten' (36).

For the soldier's abortive attempts to return to the source of trauma and achieve closure there is, as we have seen, also a precedent in Freud, of which Fried was most likely aware, and which we already encountered in Chapter 3: in Freud's observation in 'Jenseits des Lustprinzips' that, in some patients, the pleasure principle is apparently overridden by a 'Wiederholungszwang', whereby a subject actively engages in behaviour that mimics earlier stressors, or revisits painful experiences in hallucinations or dreams.[30] Because the idea of revisiting traumatic events seems incompatible with the concept of the 'Lustprinzip', Freud posits the existence of a death drive independent of, but antagonistic to, this, which tends towards the '*Wiederherstellung eines früheren Zustandes*', the restitution of an inorganic state prior to life, and thus towards the destruction of the organism in which it is at work, as well as other organisms and the external world.[31] However, while Freud argues that continually returning to a traumatic situation may allow the subject to achieve mastery over the stimuli that have breached its defences, enabling it 'die hereingebrochenen

---

[30] Freud, 'Jenseits des Lustprinzips' (1920), in *Studienausgabe*, ed. Mitscherlich, Richards, and Strachey, iii. *Psychologie des Unbewußten* (1975), 213–72.

[31] 'Jenseits des Lustprinzips', 246; original emphasis.

Reizmengen psychisch zu binden, um sie dann der Erledigung zuzuführen', this kind of mastery is not an option for the soldier.[32] Because of the way trauma is experienced, or, rather, not experienced at the moment of its initial occurrence, its (re-)experience is conceived of by Freud as the return of the repressed, in the course of which the patient will be 'genötigt, das Verdrängte als gegenwärtiges Erlebnis zu *wiederholen*, anstatt es [...] als ein Stück der Vergangenheit zu *erinnern*', until such a time as he or she is in a position to form memories, restore events to the order of narrative, and work through the trauma.[33]

However, as in the case of other Holocaust survivors, a significant part of the soldier's trauma consists not so much in the fact that he repressed what he witnessed, but in that he lived through it and therefore feels he witnessed incompletely. Because the absence of memory, as a product of the 'failure' to die, is consequently perceived not only as symptomatic of, but as fundamental to, the soldier's trauma, no amount of repetition-compulsion will afford him mastery. We are reminded of Artur Landau's assertion in Adler's *Die unsichtbare Wand*: 'Nur die eigene Vernichtung wäre die wahre Erinnerung' (235). In compulsively returning to an incident—the Helga episode—which is not the original source of trauma, Fried's soldier finds not closure, only the constant reminder of his guilt-inducing existence beyond a death sentence. 'If', as Peter Brooks argues, 'repetition is mastery, movement from the passive to the active, and if mastery is an assertion of control over what man must in fact submit to – choice, we might say, of an imposed end', the soldier's survival, the fact that he irreversibly failed to meet the 'imposed end' he feels was his destiny, comes to stand for an insurmountable crisis.[34] In ways that bring to mind the other texts under discussion here, *Ein Soldat und ein Mädchen* is thus governed by the impossibility of the soldier ever working through his trauma.

At a thematic level, Fried's text, though manifestly influenced by Freudian thought, has clearly moved away from the notion of a repressed, but recoverable, trauma towards a view that unwittingly prefigures a deconstructionist take on Abraham and Torok's concept of the *crypte* of the unconscious as harbouring the traces of a trauma that cannot ever be recovered and recounted. In what follows, I shall concentrate on how this impossibility of recovering and recounting trauma, and the endless compulsion to repeat engendered by it, are reproduced by Fried at the level of

---

[32] 'Jenseits des Lustprinzips', 239.

[33] 'Jenseits des Lustprinzips', 228; original emphasis.

[34] Peter Brooks, *Reading for the Plot: Design and Intention in Narrative* (Cambridge, MA: Harvard University Press, 1984), 98.

narrative form and the reading experience, with the result that he essentially turns his entire text into a crypt, or, for that matter, a 'Toter Winkel'. I intend to show that the techniques Fried adopts to this end are remarkably close to Derrida's interpretation of Abraham and Torok's thought, while at the same time recalling his analysis of Freud's 'Jenseits des Lustprinzips', even though *Ein Soldat und ein Mädchen* substantially pre-dates both of Derrida's texts, and indeed the entire theory of deconstruction as well as modern-day trauma theory. Psychoanalytic considerations converge with postmodernist representational strategies as the text models itself on its protagonist's life and mind.

'THAT IS THE TORTUOUS METHOD PREFERRED . . .'

Because the soldier is unable to return to the origin of his trauma, and is therefore precluded from achieving closure, his existence in a dead angle appears to have neither a clear beginning nor a foreseeable end. Moreover, his compulsive returns to trauma mean that the past is never really past but has become part of the fabric of his present, or as the narrator puts it: 'Wo aber eine Gegenwart von ihrer Vergangenheit eingeholt wird, dort ist immer ein Wohnort des Todes' (18). This has fundamental repercussions for the soldier's sense of time, space, and being-in-the-world. Conventional notions of chronology no longer seem to apply: 'Die Zeit ist nicht mehr genau bemessen' (52). One of the soldier's pieces states, with reference to the difficulty of measuring time in an existence that has fallen outside the temporal flow, 'das Datum tut nichts zur Sache', and adds 'und außerdem ist er immer ein wenig peinlich, der Versuch, am Zeitlichen das Ausfallen aus der Zeit zu bestimmen' (130). We are reminded of Lawrence Langer's concept of the 'durational persistence' of the past, which supplants the view of chronological time as a line or arrow with a spatialized conception of time.[35] Within this space-time persistence, straightforward linear progression of any kind has become impossible. Imagery of 'Zickzackwege' comes to dominate the soldier's writing, as he no longer knows whether he is coming or going in time or space (142).

In this 'aus den Fugen gegangene Welt' (37), the soldier has lost all sense of direction and hope of egress, as he laments in a poem entitled

---

[35] Lawrence L. Langer, *Admitting the Holocaust: Collected Essays* (New York: Oxford University Press, 1995), 15; original emphasis.

'Klage', which is the final sample of his writing the narrator has chosen to include:

> Wie [. . .] kann ich mein Weiterleben berechnen, | das nach einer Hinrich-tung eine Richtung sucht, | zwischen der letzten Nacht und dem ersten Morgen, | [. . .], zwischen den abgebrochenen Tausend Jahren | und den nicht angebrochenen Tausend Jahren, | zwischen den Lebenden, die über-wuchert sind und sich vermindern, | und den Toten, die wuchern und sich vermehren, | zwischen dem Ende des Krieges und dem Anfang des Friedens, | zwischen der fremden Heimat und heimlichen Fremde | [. . .] zwischen der Freude der Seligen und der Qual der Verdammten—| zwischen Mitschuld und Mitleid in Mitleidenschaft gezogen? (197)

The reference to the 'Tausend Jahren', presumably an allusion to Hitler's Thousand-Year Reich, again suggests that the execution mentioned has implications, and the soldier's life in suspension a cause, that pre-date Helga's death sentence. Trapped between original and subsequent trauma, and between the 'Mitleid' of compassion, the 'Mit-Leid' of being a fellow sufferer, and a perceived 'Mitschuld' in the fate of those he has survived, he is caught in an endless compulsion to repeat, unable to move on in any sense. This liminality between 'life' and 'death', a state of hovering uncertainly between time periods, spatialities, and meanings, where linear, end-directed advance of any kind is inhibited and all resolution denied, is precisely what the text is charged with recreating for its readers.

The application of Freudian psychodynamics and the notion of repetition-compulsion to narrative design and to the reading experience is by no means new. In *Reading for the Plot*, Brooks turns to Freud's theory of the antagonism between the death drive and the pleasure principle to provide a model for the processes of narrative plot, and to demonstrate how these processes are intimately tied to the dynamics at work in a human life. Brooks argues that the same tension between the urge to reach an end and the desire to defer the end that structures our lives also rules narrative. In life, we feel compelled to repeat those events we find traumatic until we are able to master them. According to Brooks, this fascination with the ordering, sense-making power of closure is also what drives us to read, but closure is at its most fulfilling when it comes after the digressions and dilations we associate with plot, or as Brooks puts it: 'The desire of the text (the desire of reading) is hence desire for the end, but desire for the end reached only through the at least minimally complicated detour, the intentional deviance, in tension, which is the plot of narrative.'[36] If closure arrives too soon, we feel cheated. Our need to read is thus governed by the

---

[36] Brooks, *Reading for the Plot*, 104.

mechanisms of sexual desire, but that desire is ultimately 'subtended by the death instinct, the drive of living matter to return to the quiescence of the inorganic'.[37] As in Freud's conception of the compulsion to repeat, the repetitions of narrative could then be said to perform the process of what Freud has termed 'Bindung'. Freud means by this the retroactive development, through repetition of a traumatic experience, of a protective layer of anxious apprehension, which was lacking at the moment of the initial shock, but which will allow the subject to 'bind', and thus master, the flood of traumatic stimuli, the 'ankommenden Erregungsmengen', after the event.[38] Brooks applies this idea to narrative plot and contends that 'repetition in all its literary manifestations' may function in a similar way, acting as 'a binding of textual energies that allows them to be mastered by putting them into serviceable form, usable "bundles", within the energetic economy of the narrative'. By 'serviceable form' Brooks means devices such as 'repetition, recall, symmetry, all these journeys back in the text, returns to and returns of, that allow us to bind one textual moment to another in terms of similarity or substitution rather than mere contiguity'. What he identifies as 'textual energy', or in other words, 'all that is aroused into expectancy and possibility in a text', only becomes 'usable by plot' once it has been harnessed and channelled by 'any of the formalizations, blatant or subtle, that force us to recognize sameness within difference'.[39] By delaying the discharge of textual energy, and denying immediate gratification, the detours and deviations of plot tease the reader and are in some sense painful, but this is 'to ensure that the ultimate pleasurable discharge will be more complete'.[40] Indeed, according to Brooks, 'the most effective [. . .] texts may be those that are most delayed, most highly bound, most painful'.[41]

The application of Brooks's model to literary texts dealing in trauma is also not original. Anne Whitehead draws on it in her compelling study on trauma fiction, in the chapter on W. G. Sebald's writing, in which she identifies repetition as a crucial thematic and structural element in a number of Sebald's texts, where it is 'suggestive of the endless drive to repeat'.[42] In keeping with Brooks, Whitehead argues that, in Sebald's writing, 'repetition undoubtedly fulfils the function of textual binding', and she interprets this 'as an attempt to create patterns of constancy', which in turn

---

[37] Brooks, *Reading for the Plot*, 51.   [38] 'Jenseits des Lustprinzips', 241.
[39] Brooks, *Reading for the Plot*, 101.   [40] Brooks, *Reading for the Plot*, 101–2.
[41] Brooks, *Reading for the Plot*, 102.
[42] 'The Butterfly Man: Trauma and Repetition in the Writing of W. G. Sebald', in Whitehead, *Trauma Fiction* (Edinburgh: Edinburgh University Press, 2004), 117–39 (125).

'allows something stable to be recuperated'.[43] What, though, if, as I claim of
the works under discussion here, a text wants to convey the impossibility of
'Bindung', the failure of repetition-compulsion to result in mastery? What if
the text's form, in analogy to its content, therefore strives, as far as possible, to
withhold the 'ultimate pleasurable discharge' altogether and offer only post-
ponement without gratification? As Brooks points out, 'we are able to read
present moments—in literature and, by extension, in life—as endowed with
narrative meaning only because we read them in anticipation of the structuring power of those endings that will retrospectively give them the order and
significance of plot'.[44] Though plot is oriented towards an end, its journey
towards recognition and illumination therefore also implies a return to an
origin. The repetitions of plot as outlined by Brooks 'mov[e] us forward [...]
by taking us back, as if in obsessive reminder that we cannot really move
ahead until we have understood that still enigmatic past, yet ever pushing us
forward, since revelation, tied to the past, belongs to the future'.[45] Paradoxically, 'the end', is then also 'a time before the beginning', with plot standing
as a 'deviance' between these 'two moments of quiescence'.[46] In staving off
closure, a text seeking to approximate and preserve the experience of infinitely
revisited trauma thus also refuses to shed light on the moment of its origin,
striving, ultimately, to become as non-linear as possible and consist only of
'that middle which is the place of repetitions, oscillating between [...] origin
and ending', where trauma appears insurmountable because it always was and
always will be.[47]

The closest *Ein Soldat und ein Mädchen* comes to implicating the Holocaust as the underlying cause of the soldier's trauma is in the frame narrative, when the narrator likens the soldier's initial hatred for Helga to an
all-consuming furnace, a 'Feuerofen', and then compares this furnace to
the 'durch ihre Grauenhaftigkeit unvorstellbaren und fast schon sagenh-
aften Feueröfen der Vernichtungslager' (27). The phrase, placed at a multiple remove from what it denotes by the fact that it is used as a simile for a
simile, is a self-conscious acknowledgement of the failure of language to
do justice to a referent that has already become clichéd in everyday usage.
Used as a figure of speech in the present, it marks the site of a return not
to the original trauma, but to something like it. As such, it is also symbolic
of the soldier's encounter with Helga. Because this is not the original
but itself an attempted re-enactment of an earlier trauma, no amount of

43 Whitehead, *Trauma Fiction*, 125, 126.   44 Brooks, *Reading for the Plot*, 94.
45 Brooks, *Reading for the Plot*, 125.   46 Brooks, *Reading for the Plot*, 103.
47 Brooks, *Reading for the Plot*, 108.

compulsively returning to it will allow the soldier to bind the original trauma: it is a substitute liaison.

No direct attempt is ever made by the narrator to attribute the soldier's condition to the event behind his phrase. The signifier of his framing account is kept entirely separate from the signified of the soldier's writings. This both underlines the text's refusal to spell out the source of trauma and draws attention to the disparity between word and meaning, a disparity that is perhaps never more acute than when we try to speak of the Holocaust. This second point is further exemplified by one of the narrator's footnotes, which demonstrates how his purview is the self-consciously inadequate and already hackneyed reference, whereas the soldier's is the referent that defies categorization: 'Der Soldat sprach selten von Nationalsozialismus, Hitler usw., sondern sagte meistens "die andere Seite"' (129). Their working relationship, as I shall show, consists in the soldier acting out trauma in his texts, and the narrator attempting to talk through it in his comments, in an embodiment of the vying between the narrative voices of disruption and consolation identified by Lawrence Langer in oral witness testimony, and exemplifying the approach, respectively, of deconstructionists and of trauma theoreticians.[48]

In the soldier's writing, repeated allusion is made to instances of persecution, terror, and mass murder, but the origin and perpetrators of these are not named. One of his prose pieces, 'Der Wagen fährt durch die Straße', for example, evokes a non-specific 'Zusammenstoß einer Gesellschaft mit einem in sich geschlossenen Terrorsystem' through the metaphor of a military track vehicle making its way through a town, crushing everyone, and pulverizing everything in its path (182). The spread of terror is conveyed through the gradual shattering of all windowpanes in the town, which symbolizes the population's crumbling resistance, as the inhabitants of those buildings whose windows are not immediately broken by the reverberations of the vehicle's engine are seen as a threat and are executed. In his comment on the piece, the second narrator draws our attention to the prevalence of the motif of shattered glass and smashed windows not only in that particular text but in the novel as a whole. As is his wont, he tries to link the image back to the soldier's encounter with Helga and claims that, though it may not be immediately apparent, the leitmotif originates in the window broken by the soldier shortly before the girl's execution:

> den Zusammenhang mit dem zerbrochenen Fenster am Morgen von Helgas Hinrichtung empfindet man eigentlich nur, weil das Zerbrechen von Fenstern

---

[48] *Holocaust Testimonies: The Ruins of Memory* (New Haven: Yale University Press, 1991), 35.

in den Schriften des Soldaten so oft vorkommt. Er selbst sagte dazu [. . .]: 'Ein Gleichnis ist wie ein Schatten: je weiter er vom Gegenstand entfernt ist, der ihn geworfen hat, desto größer wird er, aber auch desto unbestimmter.' (182)

Lawrie has argued that this is yet another forced attempt on the author's part 'to overcome the fragmentary nature of the whole by supplying an element of continuity'.[49] I would say that it is actually a further example of the narrator drawing attention to the 'shadow' in order to distract from the 'object' that cast it. In this instance, I would suggest that we are being diverted from what surely must be the first association that comes to mind when we hear of a terror regime which announces its intentions through the smashing of windows and shattering of glass: that of 'Kristallnacht'. Rather than mediate between the soldier's words and the reader, the second narrator's deliberately and obviously contrived and heavy-handed approach may be meant to signal that something in the text is being left unsaid. Through the weft of the soldier's words, and the warp of the narrator's, we catch a glimpse of an unspoken other thread. The narrator pointedly tries to assert his narrative strand and impose it on the text as a whole, but as in Freud's mystic writing pad in psychoanalytic, or a palimpsest in narratological, terms, his record bears traces of an unacknowledged past-in-the-present, just as the soldier's does which it attempts to overwrite.[50] In consequence, the text vacillates between time frames, and between supplied, suggested, and possible implied meaning, thus creating the interpretive equivalent of a dead angle, and inhibiting the development of any single, linear, end-oriented plot. This allows Fried's writing to remain faithful to the impossibility of conscious assimilation of the Holocaust, by ensuring that the origin of the trauma remains outside the order of narrative, while nonetheless making us aware of its mark on and in the present and, by extension, the text.

Such 'flickering' between textual layers, without the option of privileging one over another, manifests itself throughout the novel.[51] The first example, which sets the scene for the text as a whole, occurs at the very beginning of the frame narrative. Here, the second narrator recounts how, on the occasion of their first encounter, the soldier asked him to read a poem of his in which he alludes to the town of Hamelin, where German

---

[49] Lawrie, 'Etwas Romanartiges', 208.

[50] Freud, 'Notiz über den Wunderblock' (1925), in *Studienausgabe*, ed. Mitscherlich, Richards, and Strachey, iii. *Psychologie des Unbewußten* (1975), 363–9.

[51] I borrow this term from Brian McHale, who uses it to describe the 'ontological oscillation' between 'permanently and irresolvably ambiguous' narrative spheres in the context of postmodernist literature. See McHale, *Postmodernist Fiction* (London: Routledge, 1987), 32.

war criminals were detained after the Belsen trial, and to the execution of a young woman (11–12). The poem marks the start of the collaboration between the soldier and his narrator, and it precipitates the second narrator's entire narrative project in the sense that this is founded on his claim that the poem and all other writings by the soldier are 'Umschreibungen' of the 'true story' of the soldier's encounter with the girl. Yet the soldier's own comment on the poem, cited by the second narrator, casts doubt on the narrator's assertion and essentially undercuts his entire enterprise from the outset:

> was weiß denn ich von Belsen, außer was alle wissen? [...] Ich bin nie im Leben dort gewesen. [...] Nein, mein Lieber, dieses Gedicht ist eine Lüge! Die letzte und gefährlichste Art Lüge: wenn einer schon ganz nah is' bei seiner eigenen Wahrheit, aber er will nicht oder er kann nicht und sagt dafür was anderes! [...] das, was wirklich war—, das hab' ich nicht schreiben können. (14)

If the soldier has in fact never been to Belsen, when, according to both the second narrator and the author, the war crimes tribunal he is said to have attended is based on the Belsen trial, and the figure of Helga on a woman condemned there, this calls into question the nature of the absent true incident around which the entire work supposedly revolves. Is this core really what the second narrator claims it is? Or is it actually that the soldier has not been to Belsen (or Auschwitz, or Buchenwald, or Dachau . . .) in a very different sense, and is this the original unspoken trauma that lies at the root of the soldier's undead existence? Neither the soldier nor his narrator allude to such a prior cause, but by mutually undermining each other's assertions, they permit the possibility of an unspoken alternative to glint through.

Because no forward-moving, sequential storyline is ever permitted to unfold as a result of this flickering between narrative layers, origin and intention, or cause and consequence, may appear blurred or even reversed in the novel. This is particularly apparent in the narrator's comments on those of the soldier's texts that pre-date his encounter with Helga. One example is the footnote appended to the piece 'Der Brand', which is markedly similar to 'Der Wagen fährt durch die Straße' in that it conveys metaphorically the inexorable spread of a terror regime, albeit this time through the image of fire engulfing a city. Unlike the later 'Wagen' story, 'Der Brand' was purportedly written towards the end of the war, before the Helga episode took place, which might suggest that it would be impossible for the second narrator to pursue his usual tack of tracing the origin of the piece back to the soldier's encounter with the girl. Indeed, the narrator does concede that this is 'eigentlich eine richtige Flüchtlingsgeschichte', evoking 'Bedrohung und

Zerstörung der Heimat, überraschende Einblicke durch die Gefährdung althergebrachter Zustände, Vorbereitungen zur Emigration und zuletzt Anfang einer ratlosen Flucht'. He even acknowledges that the fragment is in part inspired specifically by the soldier's experience of trying to flee Germany 'nach den Judenverfolgungen vom 10. November 1938', which, incidentally, would further support the idea of the Night of Broken Glass being a subtext in the soldier's writings (83). However, the piece also refers to a sensation of numbness, 'wie wenn einem ein Fuß eingeschlafen ist, nur eben nicht im Fuß, sondern in der Magengrube und im Kopf, und vielleicht nicht einmal dort, sondern irgendwo außerhalb' (82). This the second narrator identifies as a response to a traumatic incident, but he then immediately cites the soldier's encounter with Helga as its 'original' source by claiming: 'Die Beschreibung des Starregefühls beim Brand der Stadt ist eine spätere Einfügung des Soldaten in sein Manuskript', and remarking about such later additions that they 'dürften *Umschreibungen* von Beobachtungen des Soldaten bei seinem ersten Zusammenstoß mit Helga sein' (84).

From this it would seem clear that the Helga episode, far from being the 'Kern der Romanfabel' and the 'Unaussprechlich-Unausgesprochenes' at the centre of the novel, is itself simply another 'Umschreibung' for the text to deflect to so as to leave something else, the trauma of the Holocaust, unspoken. What at first glance appears to be the second narrator's version of a talking cure, imposed on the soldier's traumatized acting-out, might then be read as an indication that the second narrator, too, is in fact acting out. His attempts to establish patterns, impose coherence, and assign meaning are no more successful than the soldier's, because he no more returns to the true origin of the trauma than the soldier does. Indeed, by appointing himself as the 'Umschreiber' of the soldier's 'Umschreibungen', he is also making it more difficult for the reader to make sense of things. From this it would appear that the 'Umschreibungen' in this text in fact operate not as periphrases in the sense that we might initially be inclined to assume, but as deviations and displacements. Meaning is not encircled by them, but distorted and dislocated, as an earlier incident is first rewritten in analogous form by the soldier, and then ascribed to a secondary source by his narrator. Instead of considering their narrative technique as one of 'Umschre*i*bung', we should perhaps be thinking of it as '*Um*schreibung'. The soldier rewords meaning by writing parabolically or paraphrastically, and the narrator displaces meaning by swerving off at an angle and rerouting us. Though a primary source of trauma appears to suggest itself, the text itself makes no direct mention of it: it presents no origin, only difference and deferral (or *différance*?). Indeed, the second narrator acknowledges at one point that his own account has further

'verfälscht' the soldier's report, which was already not 'in allen Einzelheiten verläßlich' (21). Fried adds that the adoption of this narrative form has
'zwangsläufig' entailed a 'Zertrümmerung oder Relativierung und Ver-
dächtigung der Fabel durch den Autor selbst' (207).

By claiming to hold the key, but actually adding a defensive layer
through his contributions, the second narrator diverts our attention from
the elusive source of trauma to the stratagems involved in keeping it secret.
This would appear to confirm that what is at stake here is not the text's
inability to spell out, but its ability to encrypt, not the 'Unaussprechlich-
Unausgesprochenes' it hides, but the 'Unaussprechlichkeit' it exhibits. In
other words, what matters is not so much the impossibility of accessing and
recovering meaning as the manoeuvres involved in deferring meaning
and thus conveying that impossibility. As in the texts analysed in earlier
chapters, the emphasis, indeed the onus, therefore comes to rest on the
structure, which ceases to be a vehicle for expressing the content but itself
becomes that content.

'...IN EACH OF THE MEANDERINGS...'

By entailing a form of writing that is intended to be indicatory rather than
revelatory, marking the spot where something is buried in the text, but
refusing to de-crypt it, Fried's narrative strategy reads not unlike Derrida's
deconstructionist take on Abraham and Torok's concept of *cryptonymie*.
According to Abraham and Torok, the bearer of a trauma encrypted in the
unconscious cannot speak of this trauma but may inadvertently reveal its
presence in coded form, through what Abraham and Torok call *cryptonymes*. Cryptonymic utterances have no semantic relation with the encrypted term from which they derive but arise through phonic slippages,
in the course of which signifiers metonymically come to represent other
signifiers, without reference to the signified. In this way, a series of
substitutions or cryptonyms may be formed, which follows paths of
avoidance, alludes without unlocking, and through which the subject
engages in a process of 'le dire sans le dire', 'montrer-cacher', and 'promener un rébus et le donner comme indéchiffrable'.[52] Abraham and
Torok's theory appealed to Derrida, who assimilated it to his own notions
of *différance* and dissemination, according to which meaning is not inherent, but always already different and deferred, and is not reducible to a
single signification or even to the controlled plurality of polysemy. While

[52] Nicolas Abraham and Maria Torok, *Cryptonymie: Le Verbier de l'homme aux loups*
(Paris: Aubier-Flammarion, 1976), 115, 122.

Abraham and Torok's aim as psychoanalysts was to achieve decryption and restore the unspeakable to knowledge and speech, Derrida aligned what they considered a mere impediment to the restoration of meaning with his notion of a fundamental rupture between signifier and signified, and regarded the process of deciphering as open-ended and infinite. A 'transcription cryptonymique', as envisaged by Derrida, is, then, a form of writing in which every referent is always already encrypted, and no interpretation is ever a final truth, but itself another text to be deciphered. As we saw in Chapter 1, Derrida describes this kind of writing as an 'art de la *chicane*', which veers off at 'l'angle d'un crochet pour dérouter le lecteur et rendre l'itinéraire illisible'.[53] Though Fried's writing suggests the presence of a single underlying meaning, the text itself refuses to resolve ambiguity and give up its secret, and the Holocaust figures in it only as the always-already-encrypted and never-fully-spelled-out. Translated into German, Derrida's notion of 'faire l'angle d'un crochet' as a deliberate strategy of deception is perhaps most accurately conveyed by the term 'Winkelzüge machen', and the individual words in Abraham and Torok's cryptonymy, the *cryptonymes* or *mots anglés*, are translated as 'Winkelwörter' in the German version of their study. In addition to featuring dead angles as a trope, *Ein Soldat und ein Mädchen* has apparently adopted the idea of 'Winkelzüge machen' as a structural technique, to ensure that ambiguity of meaning is preserved in the text, and to abolish all coherence and linearity in the process. The very expression 'Toter Winkel' is an example of a term that refuses to be pinned down and that contributes to the disruption of narrative linearity by splitting into a number of possible meanings, each of which in turn may generate further interpretations.

Indeed, just as events are never anchored in a single time plane in the text, and tropes or figures may have several coincident meanings, individual words in *Ein Soldat und ein Mädchen* may oscillate between semantic fields, or shift from one lexical meaning or grammatical form to another, and refuse to be tied to just one. As a result, even a single word may cause the narrative thread to bifurcate. Linguistic manipulation is particularly prevalent in the writing of the soldier, who favours a technique he calls 'ernsthaftes Wortspiel'. The narrator describes this as a kind of 'Assoziationstechnik [. . .], der sich der Verfasser in Augenblicken großer innerer Spannung öfters überläßt' (41, 136). Fried's interest in such free association, as in any technique that might cause the text to flicker, was that it would allow the unconscious workings of the mind to come out in

---

[53] Jacques Derrida, 'Fors: Les Mots anglés de Nicolas Abraham et Maria Torok', in Abraham and Torok, *Cryptonymie*, 7–73 (62); original emphasis.

language, without his having to spell out and, in so doing, dispel the impression of an uncontrollably surfacing cryptically suggestive underside to conscious processes of thought and language. One example of this occurs in the short story 'Die Falle', where we are presented with a semantic slippage from the word 'Maus' to the term 'Mausoleum', via the expression 'mausetot', and the implied, but unspoken, alleged Hebrew for death, which the narrator claims is 'Mauß' (115, 121).[54] The narrator's dubious etymological derivation might be taken as a suggestion that the protagonists' predicament in the story—that of being persecuted and trapped alive in a building that comes to represent an inescapable 'Mausoleum'—stands for a trauma that is at its root 'Jewish', though this is never made explicit, and the supposed Hebrew origin of the word is not mentioned in the main body of the story. Once again, a return to the source of trauma is precluded, and so closure is endlessly deferred. The ambiguous remark made by the imagined narrator of another of the soldier's prose pieces, 'Es ist uns nicht gegeben, auf irgendeinem Weg fortzuschreiten, ohne uns zu vergehen', not only illustrates the soldier's propensity for wordplay, but comes to stand as a comment on both the protagonists' situation and on the reading experience, and thus as a statement of intent regarding narrative technique (165).

Because meaning is constantly dislocated and deferred in the text, and the source of trauma is never made explicit, the repetitions, or variations on a theme, with which we are presented do not appear to have a common denominator, as a result of which they do not gesture towards any kind of fundamental order, but seem to be left dangling. The present portrayed, and, by extension, the text, are shot through with traces of a traumatic past, but these cannot be attributed to a clear cause, and so no memory is formed, and no pattern crystallizes. As a result, the protagonists in, but also the reader of, the text may feel that the repetitions encountered are both inexplicable and inescapable. We are haunted by their arbitrary, unpredictable, and potentially infinite (re)appearances. The effect of this is again one that, in a psychoanalytic context, we find documented in Freud, who maintains that although the death drive and related phenomena can be explained rationally, they may give the impression of being allied to irrational forces in that the inexplicable, senseless repetitions they engender can make the subject feel that it is pursued by some evil fate, or in thrall to some demonic power, for which Freud coined the term of the

---

[54] As Katrin Schäfer has pointed out, the etymological derivation here is questionable, but even if we consider this to be evidence of 'mangelnde Hebräischkenntnisse' on Fried's part, we can nonetheless appreciate his intention to create a 'hebräisch-jüdisches Wortspiel'. See Schäfer, *'Die andere Seite'*, 377.

'uncanny'.[55] Once again, we are also reminded of Caruth's assessment that 'the pathology [of trauma] consists [...] solely in *the structure of its experience* or reception: the event is not assimilated or experienced fully at the time, but only belatedly, in its repeated *possession* of the one who experiences it'.[56]

One example of the soldier being simultaneously drawn to, and haunted by, something that is eerily familiar in this way is, of course, the figure of Helga, and he comments on this uncanny attraction by saying: 'Gerade dieses Grauen konnte einen Menschen, der in einer Welt, in der das Grauen eine wesentliche Rolle spielt, schon längst seinen Weg verloren hatte, auch anziehen und im eigentlichen Sinn des Wortes bannen' (38). In critical commentary, the attraction tends to be read as an indication of the soldier's desire and/or sympathy for the girl, and is either condemned as 'an apparently masochistic attraction to the former enemy' or, again, given a political slant.[57] Katrin Schäfer, for instance, speaks of the 'Friedtypische Intention [...], alles von der "anderen Seite" zu sehen', and suggests that we should read this inclination to put oneself in the shoes of, or identify with, the other as an 'Aufforderung sogar in dem uns Fremden und Andersartigen den Menschen zu sehen und ihm tolerant und unvoreingenommen entgegenzutreten'.[58] Although, as with any trope and figure in the text, it is in fact impossible to assign a single unambiguous meaning to the girl, I would argue that, as the use of the term 'Grauen' in the context suggests, the soldier feels drawn to her not primarily as a lover, but because of his compulsion to repeat. The text itself would appear to confirm this in that it aligns this identification with the 'other' with psychological phenomena, not a political agenda: 'Die Tendenz, sich mit der "anderen Seite" zu identifizieren, eine mehr psychologisch als politisch begründete Verhaltensweise, war dem Verfasser selbst unheimlich' (146). If anything, this would appear to indicate not love for that which is alien in the other, but fear of what is other and alien in oneself. In fact, the soldier is trebly haunted by the figure of Helga, who mirrors his own condition of life suspended, who reminds him of his perceived complicity in the death of people he has survived, and in whom he sees a post-war emissary of the regime intent on destroying him: his *Doppelgängerin* in more than one respect. As such, she is an instance of the repressed resurfacing, but, because the soldier is an incomplete witness and

---

[55] Freud, 'Das Unheimliche' (1919), in *Studienausgabe*, ed. Mitscherlich, Richards, and Strachey, iv. *Psychologische Schriften* (1970), 241–74.

[56] *Trauma: Explorations in Memory*, 4; original emphasis.

[57] Lawrie, *A Writer without a Country*, 232.

[58] Schäfer, *'Die andere Seite'*, 239. See also e.g. O'Dochartaigh, 'Erich Fried: Poetik des Menschseins', 281.

the trauma of the Holocaust is not fully his own, she also marks the site of a secondary trauma and substitute repression.

Again, the second narrator does his best to divert us from this last fact and proposes an alternative interpretation whenever we might be tempted to regard Helga as an uncanny reminder of people killed in an earlier traumatic event. One example of this is the figure of Erna, who is among the dead the soldier tries to resurrect in the story 'Die Ausgrabung', and who is said to have died 'gerade als er im Begriff stand, sich in sie zu verlieben' (129). In the soldier's text, Erna is described as having been trampled to death by a National Socialist soldier on horseback. The second narrator's commentary, however, claims she died in New York, after the war, and that she is an 'Umschreibung' of Helga, not the other way round. Ultimately, we find ourselves unable to determine with absolute certainty if Helga is Erna's double, or Erna is Helga's, which, again, suggests the possibility that both women are in fact spectres of people lost in the Holocaust.

Finally, Helga also figures as a double of the soldier's sister. This becomes apparent in the second narrator's closing remarks, where we learn of the soldier's motivation for travelling to London in the first place, and it tellingly coincides with the final appearance in the novel of the image of the 'Toter Winkel'. We are told that the reason for the soldier's trip, on the occasion of which he first met his narrator, was to see his sister, the only member of his family to have survived the concentration camps. She was involved in a car crash but died before he managed to get to her: 'Nach England geflogen war er nur, weil seine in London verheiratete Schwester, das einzige überlebende Mitglied seiner Familie, die zum größten Teil in Auschwitz vernichtet worden war, einen schweren Autounfall erlitten hatte. Aber sie war einige Stunden vor seiner Ankunft gestorben' (203–4). The soldier's resigned response to this is the observation: 'Das geht schon einmal so [. . .], ich war gar nicht überrascht. Wir stehen alle noch mit einem Fuß im Toten Winkel, mein Lieber.' He then adds: 'Das Komische daran ist, daß mich jetzt endlich keiner mehr fragt, warum ich die schwarze Armbinde hab'. Dabei hab' ich sie schon vorher die ganze Zeit getragen' (204). Earlier in the novel the second narrator had told us about the black mourning band the soldier was wearing on his arm: 'Eine Armbinde hat der Soldat lange getragen, auch noch, als ich ihn kennenlernte. Man nahm damals an, er trage sie zum Zeichen der Trauer um seine Schwester. In Wirklichkeit hatte er sie schon zuvor getragen; die Trauer galt Helga' (72). The situation is the same both times: a person to whom the soldier is close, and whose life has already been interrupted by a death sentence, is killed; he is not there to witness this and unable to save them; he is numb and in mourning, but it is not clear whom he mourns.

As ever, the narrator attributes the soldier's condition to Helga's death and names her as the original object of his mourning, and both the narrator and the soldier studiously avoid referring to a possible prior cause.

As in the case of the Helga-soldier and the Helga-Erna doubling, the relationship between the figure of Helga and that of the soldier's sister appears to be that of an infinitely regressive reflection. The sister's time in a dead angle between the car crash that spelled her death and her succumbing to her injuries mirrors Helga's time in a dead angle between her death sentence and her execution. However, neither of these mirror images is the original. The origin of their mutual reflection is the sister's time in a dead angle between the concentration camps and death, which is itself, of course, in turn a reflection of millions of other people's fate. Since the reflective surface of the origin interferes, the reflection of that origin is endlessly deferred. The origin is a mirror that is already doubled, is absent. At the same time, there is no end to the reflections in sight, as each mirror, in reflecting the other mirror, is a container of reflection, a reflection which is then re-reflected as content at a second, and again as container at a third level. Matters become even more complicated when we factor in the figure of the soldier and consider that the two-way reflections of the girl and the sister, or of the girl and Erna, may in fact be part of an infinite hall of mirrors, in space and through time, with every character in the soldier's writings representing a reflection of, and being reflected by, the soldier himself: an endlessly echoing host of mirror images of an absent origin. As such, this is, of course, also an exemplification of the 'Toter Winkel': an inescapable realm, where time, space, and the unity of identity are disrupted, and which stands for both a stay of death and a suspension of life. We are reminded how the *Doppelgänger* in Freud can be an insurance against the destruction of the ego, and, reversing its aspect, become the uncanny harbinger of death.

'... OF HIS INDEFATIGABLE NOVEL...'

This hall-of-mirrors effect, which further illustrates the soldier's compulsion to repeat, is not limited to the soldier and the characters in his writings but is reflected in (and reflects) the organization and structure of this second part of the novel. As ever, the second narrator's attempts to counter disorder and impose coherence, coupled with our inclination to treat his editorial comments as more authoritative than the soldier's contributions and be led where he takes us, mean that the recursive and (self-)reflexive nature of the structure may not be immediately apparent. The manner in which the narrator presents the four subsections of the soldier's writings suggests that he intends for us to consider them as stages of a development, supposedly charting a progression from the soldier's breakdown after the Helga episode to his release from the psychiatric institution and his efforts to get on with life. In fact, the order in which the subsections, and the individual prose pieces within them, are grouped and arranged, read against their actual rather than their purported themes, is suggestive of repetition-compulsion not only at an individual level, but also on a larger historical scale. Within the frame of the second narrator's account, the soldier's writings regress from the section 'Fünf Umschreibungen einer Begegnung', penned immediately after his encounter with Helga, to his writings just pre-dating it, 'Aus den letzten Kriegsjahren', then progress to what he wrote 'Aus dem Mental Ward' after the girl's death. The very fact that the soldier's writings are presented out of chronological sequence in this fashion implies an inability to move on, which is further reinforced by the central position accorded to the 'Mental Ward' section within the novel as a whole. In a way that recalls the function of similar sites-turned-metaphors in other texts, that of the waiting room/psychiatric hospital in Aloni's *Der Wartesaal*, for instance, the 'Mental Ward', a quintessential dead angle, emblematizes the impossibility of escaping a life interrupted, and a text encrypted, and is placed, literally and figuratively, at the heart of Fried's novel. At the same time, the interpolation of the second, pre-Helga section—which was written towards the end of the war and revolves around the themes of terror, persecution, and mass murder—between the soldier's encounter with the girl and his time in the psychiatric institution would appear to reinforce the idea that the Helga episode may not be the origin of, only a trigger for, the soldier's trauma, and that his path from Helga to his breakdown leads through the belated effects of earlier experiences.

The fourth and final section of the soldier's writings, which is entitled 'Vom Weiterleben', would initially appear to indicate a way out of the impasse of the first three in as much as the title the narrator has given it implies progress at a thematic level, and in that, again according to the narrator, it presents the soldier's attempts to find 'einen neuen *modus vivendi*' (158). It is tempting to take the narrator's assertions at face value. Schäfer, for instance, says of the soldier:

> In den Geschichten 'Vom Weiterleben' sucht er einen neuen *modus vivendi*—er versucht, Helga und sein Liebeserlebnis bei vollem Bewußtsein zu verarbeiten, [...] in Form künstlerischer Betätigung, um auf dem Weg durch den Mythos [...] oder mit Hilfe surrealer Geschichten [...] im Zustand der Raum- und Zeitlosigkeit seine Problematik analytisch erfassen

zu können, indem er sie symbolisch in Geschichten verpackt und sein Erlebnis dadurch überwinden kann.[59]

In fact, this section is no less preoccupied with the themes of death, guilt, and eternal persecution than the earlier ones, and it concludes with the aforementioned poem 'Klage', which sums up the soldier's liminal position and condition in a way that makes it very clear that his is not a transitional state or surmountable trauma, and that his 'Weiterleben' will almost certainly be founded not on any new and improved modus vivendi, but on variations of his old one. Indeed, the entire fourth section appears as a mirror image of the pre-Helga pieces 'Aus den letzten Kriegsjahren', reflected through the 'Mental Ward' section in the novel's centre, with, for instance, as we have seen, the story 'Der Wagen fährt durch die Straße' mirroring, and being mirrored by, 'Der Brand'. This suggests not only a personal compulsion to return to trauma but that history, too, will go on repeating itself—an idea which is supported by the fact that this last section is prefaced by a short poem of the soldier's containing the words 'mein Vater war der Krieg | der Friede ist mein lieber Sohn | der gleicht meinem Vater schon' (157).

The arrangement of the individual pieces within this final section further confirms, and reflects, the impression of unstoppable repetition. The first piece, 'Am Ufer', supposedly alludes to the soldier setting sail for the United States after the Helga episode and leaving behind the 'Reich der Schatten und des Blutes' that, to him, is post-war Europe (160). The narrator claims that, in spite of the past horrors evoked between the lines of the piece, the soldier is determined to look to the future, perhaps even 'unbekümmert um das, was er hinter sich zurückläßt' (160). However, the final text before the concluding poem 'Klage', 'Die verurteilten Kinder', shows a death sentence being passed down from adults to their children, whose entire existence is consequently spent 'im Schatten des Urteils', and who, if they have children before they die, pass the sentence on to these in turn (193). According to the narrator's footnote, the soldier's comment on this story about transgenerational trauma is: 'in meinem Fall wird man eben Sachverständiger für Todesurteile' (194). Indeed, leading both up to, and away from, the central piece 'Der Wagen', which evokes an unspecified generalized spread of terror, are further texts which seem to be casting about for analogies with which to evoke the sensation of living life in eternal suspension, under the auspices of death. One of them, 'Ein Wunder', shows a people living with a sword—truly a sword of Damocles—suspended by a single thread above their heads. Another,

[59] Schäfer, *'Die andere Seite'*, 289.

'Schilderung der Flucht', presents a figure on the run after his home town has been laid to waste. The man is described as 'mehr tot als lebendig', and his continuing existence becomes one long 'Irrfahrt durch das Totenreich', in the course of which he meets a number of figures from classical mythology, all of them condemned to Sisyphean tasks, but he cannot be sure if what he is experiencing is 'Wirklichkeit oder Traum' (183, 190). The movement of the body of the soldier's writings is replicated here in embedded form, both in the subsection as a whole and within this individual piece, just as his compulsion to repeat is mirrored in the man's interminable roaming through Hades, which is in turn reflected by the fruitless struggles of the figures he encounters there. Like its characters, the soldier's prose pieces appear caught in an infinite hall of mirrors, which mimics an insurmountable compulsion to repeat and, at the same time, compels the reader to participate in the repetition.

In addition to being endlessly self-reflecting, the soldier's texts are also self-reflective. 'Schilderung der Flucht' is a prime example of a piece that consciously explores and exploits the novel's themes. As cited earlier, Schäfer suggests that the soldier uses myth in the final section of his writings to make sense of his life and work through his problems. This idea corresponds to Brooks's understanding of plot as the 'binding of textual energies' through repetition intended to bring order and purpose to a text, and to a life: 'As well as having form, plots must generate force: the force that makes the connection of incidents powerful, that shapes the confused material of a life into an intentional structure that in turn generates new insights about how life can be told.'[60] I would argue that 'Schilderung der Flucht' in fact exemplifies how Fried's novel frustrates our need to impose order on confusion, and undermines conventional patterning and sense-making devices. The protagonist of the piece does not recognize the unnamed mythological figures he encounters on his way, and he tries to identify some kind of underlying design in his confused impressions. When he asks the Danaids, who are filling their leaky vessels with water, as to the 'Ursache, Zeit und Ziel' of their undertaking, he receives no answer: 'So wurde mir keine Antwort gegeben, und keine Erklärung als eine bald anflutende, bald verebbende monotone Litanei von Schuld und Mord und Blut und Wasser' (187). When Sisyphus tries to persuade him that this time he is certain to complete his task, the man is doubtful and admits to trying to arrive at a 'Deutung der Gesamtstimmung' of his own, by attempting 'allenthalben Verbindungen zwischen dem Nebel, der vom Tod gezeichneten Landschaft

---

[60] Brooks, *Reading for the Plot*, 282–3.

und den einzelnen Gestalten und Gruppen am Weg zu knüpfen', but he never quite manages (190). As readers, we are aware of the implications of the mythological imagery presented to us, but at the same time we are confronted with the realization that, in relation to the text as a whole, we are in a similar situation to this protagonist: the missing piece of the puzzle may appear tantalizingly close but is withheld, as a result of which no definite order ever establishes itself, and we are forced to keep going over the same ground in our reading. Thematically and structurally, the mythical repetition-compulsions in this text within a text within a text represent our reading experience placed *en abyme* multiple times over, with no closure in sight.

All things considered, Fried's textual enactment of the soldier's insurmountable repetition-compulsion is thus also reminiscent of the dynamics at work in the writing of Freud's own 'Jenseits des Lustprinzips', which has attracted critical attention for supposedly mirroring the theories he was advancing. Derrida felt that Freud's discomfiting, self-querying textual performance in his work on death drives and the compulsion to repeat was proto-deconstructive, and he says of it: 'La démarche même du texte est diabolique. Il mime la marche, ne cesse de marcher sans avancer, esquisse régulièrement un pas de plus sans gagner un pouce de terrain.'[61]

Moreover, the self-reflective and self-reflexive infernal movement without progression of Fried's writing extends beyond the soldier's texts and the figures populating the second section of the novel. In addition to presenting us with a host of doubles within the soldier's writings, the text holds up a further mirror to the soldier with the figure of the second narrator, and, again, this is enacted both thematically and structurally. We have already seen how the soldier's insurmountable acting-out of trauma, and the narrator's displaced, and therefore unsuccessful and interminable, attempts to work through it complement each other but are kept separate, exemplifying the rupture between signifier and signified where the Holocaust (or all meaning, as Derrida would argue) is concerned. Psychologically speaking, because the second narrator's ostensible talking cure is revealed to be just another instance of acting-out, he and the soldier might also be regarded as alter egos, or even as two halves of a single split personality, with the soldier's stories representing the unconscious contents of a crypt to which the ego of the narrator has no access, and which he can therefore reveal only in encrypted form. The hall-of-mirrors effect is thus expanded from the metadiegetic level of the soldier's stories to include the diegetic one of the narrator's frame narrative. Structurally,

---

[61] Jacques Derrida, *La Carte postale: De Socrate à Freud et au-delà* (Paris: Flammarion, 1980), 287.

the narrator's frame narrative, as has already become apparent, recreates the compulsion to repeat by introducing the 'Schriften des Soldaten' with an account of the soldier's encounter with Helga, and closing his frame narrative with the explanation, delivered after the fact, as to why the soldier had come to London in the first place: the death of his sister, and thus a repetition with a twist of what was already a dislocated repetition at the outset.

In their respective contributions to the text, both the soldier and his narrator therefore keep going over the same ground, the soldier in over-determined, and ultimately indeterminate, analogies, and the narrator in his failed attempt to impose a master narrative, each of which is suggestive of an interminable compulsion to repeat. However, this takes place within the confines of the text, and even the least teleological writing will eventually reach its final word, even if what it thematizes is infinite mirroring and insurmountable repetition. How can this be reconciled with the intent to produce a text consisting, as far as possible, only of a repetitive 'middle', oscillating between beginning and end? In other words, how can the inevitability of an ending be reconciled with the impossibility of closure? As in earlier texts we have encountered, Fried's novel attempts this by means of a recursive greater structure that opens up his writing even as this reaches a close, by conveying a sense of potentially infinite regress beyond its own boundaries.

The key to this lies with the mutually implicating and reflective relationship between soldier and narrator, as respective embodiments of the inability to return to the source and the concomitant inability to achieve closure. The narrator's comments on this relationship would appear to confirm the impression of a split (and therefore doubled) or doubled (and therefore split) personality. Though he presents the two of them as distinct individuals, he acknowledges that their identities have become a blur to him: 'Die Geschichte des Soldaten hat mich nämlich von Anfang an so sehr beschäftigt, ich möchte fast sagen, überrumpelt, daß ich heute oft kaum mehr zwischen ihm und mir selbst unterscheiden kann' (29). He emphasizes the fact that both during, and for years after, the war he was absent from Germany, in the relative safety of exile, and he refers to this as the one thing that reminds him that he and the soldier are separate entities:

> Nur indem ich mich immer wieder auf die einfachen Tatsachen meines Stubenhockerdaseins in England besinne, das ich von meiner Ankunft als Emigrant im August 1938 bis zu meinem ersten Flug nach Berlin im Januar 1953 nicht ein einziges Mal verlassen habe, wird mir wieder klar, daß nicht ich selbst es gewesen sein kann, der Helga gekannt hat. (29)

In fact, the narrator's rather disparaging reference to his own 'Stubenhock-erdasein' only serves to underline the similarities between him and the soldier, who is also an exiled and incomplete witness. It acts as a reminder of the sense of guilt the soldier and his narrator have in common, rather than the biographical circumstances they supposedly do not. The narrator insists that, their different backgrounds notwithstanding, he has become so tied up in the soldier's fate that the soldier's existence can seem more real to him than his own, and that he is profoundly troubled by the soldier's experiences: 'Weil ich mich aber in dieses fremde Schicksal nachträglich so tief verstrickt habe, daß mir die Wirklichkeit meines eigenen Daseins oft weniger Ich ist als das Ich des Soldaten, fällt es mir nur noch schwerer, diesen Bericht ohne Befangenheit zu Papier zu bringen' (29). He even remembers events the soldier has told him about as though they had happened to him: 'Manchmal ist es so stark, daß ich mich schon bei der deutlichen Erinnerung an Ereignisse ertappt habe, die in Wirklichkeit der Soldat erlebt hat, nicht ich' (21). The second narrator is thus also the soldier's double in that he is evidently affected, even afflicted, by a trauma not originally his, just as the soldier himself is in the grip of a trauma which, in addition to not fully owning, he also does not own completely because it is in part the preserve of his dead relatives. The narrator is the bearer of an encrypted trauma already encrypted in another bearer. If we choose to regard him as an alter ego of the soldier, and the girl as representative of the soldier's dead beloved more generally, statements such as the narrator's response to the perceived implication of the soldier in the girl's death take on a new poignancy: 'Ich weiß auch, daß es Augenblicke gibt, in denen ich ihn hasse [...]. Ich weiß, daß mir der Gedanke gekommen ist, man könnte diesen Mann vielleicht zum Selbst-mord treiben, weil er Helga nicht gerettet hat' (45). Does the narrator hate the soldier because he did nothing to save the girl, or does the soldier-narrator loathe himself because he was unable to do anything to save his family? The text flickers between alternatives, refusing to settle on either.

In doing so, it once again affords us a glimpse of a further, unspoken layer: that of the author's own story. When we are first introduced to the figure of the narrator, we learn that he is a writer (13), that he is familiar with London's 'Emigrantenmilieu' (10), that he went into exile after the murder of his father by the Gestapo (16), that he remained in England until a visit to Berlin in 1953 (29), and that, after the war, he worked in a factory in London which produced 'handgemachte Glasknöpfe, Ohrringe und Broschen' (22). In all this, he resembles the novel's author, and Fried even explicitly equates the figure of the narrator with himself in the epilogue of the novel's first edition:

Die biographischen Angaben, die ich im Text über mich gemacht habe, stimmen. Ich bin im August 1938 als jüdischer Emigrant nach London gekommen, wo ich immer noch wohne, und habe deutschen Boden erst wieder Anfang 1953 betreten. Auch die Angaben über den Tod meines Vaters [. . .] sind wahr, nur der Name des Mädchens ist verändert. (205)

Not only does the narrator closely resemble his creator, but so does the soldier. As well as being Jewish and a 'heimatloser Emigrant', and having lost much of his family in the Holocaust (26–7), the soldier's appearance and some of his character traits are apparently modelled on Fried's own. He is portrayed as 'ein gutmütiger, zur Traurigkeit neigender jüdischer Intellektueller' (45), who is 'nicht unsympathisch, nicht viel über dreißig', and whose physical characteristics are listed as: 'Mittlere Größe, kräftiger Brustkorb, der Kopf groß, starke, breite Stirne, kluge Augen. Aber die Nase zu breit, die Lippen zu wulstig' (16). The soldier and his narrator not only mirror each other, they are also reflective of their author, who, by implication, is associated with their trauma and, in a sense, comes to haunt his own writing.

Steven Lawrie has suggested that 'the dissolution of the boundaries between the figure of editor-narrator and soldier-narrator', and their closeness to the author himself, are a weakness of the text, the effect of which is essentially that of allowing Fried 'to carry on a monologue with himself in which he frequently finds his own views corroborated'.[62] I would say that, on the contrary, precisely because the second narrator's perspective is nothing but a variation of the soldier's, and, by extension, their author's, no one viewpoint is allowed to appear superior to the others, and any possibility of retreat and objective judgement is precluded, thus allowing the text to flicker between possible interpretations and afford a glimpse of an underlying implication, without having to de-crypt it. Between the soldier and his narrator, a third figure glints through.

This manifests itself at a formal as well as a thematic level. The soldier's narrator makes a point of drawing our attention to the fact that the soldier is in the habit of referring to himself in the third person in his accounts of his night with Helga, purportedly so as to distance himself from the painful memory: 'In beiden Arbeiten schreibt der Soldat von sich selbst in der dritten Person, als wolle er immer noch Abstand halten' (41). This, of course, has the added effect of placing the source of his trauma (which, in my reading, is already a source at a remove from the actual traumatic origin) at a further remove. Yet every so often, the narrator himself is suddenly referred to in the third person. Indeed, in the novel's first few

---

[62] *A Writer without a Country*, 213.

lines, the entire text is presented as a third-person account of a narrative
collaboration between a soldier and a narrator, as told by a third narrator.
The third narrator introduces the account we are about to read by
reminding us that the second narrator was only able to report it because
the soldier had told him the story in the first place, and that the second
narrator is therefore the soldier's narrator now, but that the soldier was
narrator to the second narrator then. Not only does the ambiguous way in
which this is phrased immediately blur the boundaries between the
identity of the soldier and that of the second narrator, but the addition
of this third narrative consciousness obscures who is speaking at the
diegetic level of the narrative. We are left uncertain as to who is telling
whom: 'Der Soldat war der Erzähler des Erzählers, und nun ist der
Erzähler der Erzähler des Soldaten geworden. Da gerät leicht alles durcheinander. Außerdem fehlt mir die Gabe, aus einer wirklichen Begebenheit
eine wahre Geschichte zu machen' (9). As well as containing another hint
that the 'wirkliche Begebenheit' (which remains unspecified) has not
entered the text directly, but has been 'um(ge)schrieben', the sentence,
by switching abruptly from the third person to the first, gives the impression that a third figure has inserted itself between the second narrator's
account and the reader. Though jarring, this impression is soon forgotten,
as the remainder of the introduction continues in the first person and
appears to report the encounter between the second narrator and the
soldier, as well as the soldier's encounter with Helga, from the second
narrator's perspective, with the third narrator apparently having with-
drawn himself from the narrative act. However, periodically, he appears
to reinsert himself, and the slippage between narrative consciousnesses is
repeated, as in this example from towards the end of the introduction,
when the second narrator is again referred to in the third person: 'Der
Erzähler hat es vermieden, darüber allzuviel mit ihm [dem Soldaten] zu
sprechen' (31). The narrative appears to take a step back at this point: the
account provided by the second narrator, whom we have come to accept as
the extradiegetic one, apparently switches from diegetic to metadiegetic
text, as we are reminded that he, too, is a protagonist of a narrative nested
in someone else's brain. The figure of the author (which is not necessarily
identical to the person of the author) manifests itself, and the possibility
suggests itself that the elusive trauma in the text, now at yet a further
remove, may in fact be his, or his as well.

As in the case of the mutual mirroring between characters in the
soldier's writings, the already-absent origin of the reflection, in this case
the figure of the author, has been absorbed by the soldier and his narrator,
two parallel mirrors, producing endlessly receding images of each other, or
as we read in the text's frame narrative:

zwei Spiegel im Londoner Nebel, einander gegenübergestellt, und eine
unendliche Reihe wechselseitiger Bespiegelungen, während sie langsam er-
blinden. '*Das ist im Grund der Herren eigner Geist, in dem die Zeiten sich
bespiegeln.*' Ich mich in ihm, er sich in mir, und die Zeit in uns beiden. (15)

Only the hint of a shift in narrative perspective gives away the presence of
a third narrative consciousness. Moreover, in addition to intimating an
infinite receding of the text's own boundaries, the third/second narrator's
comment positions the text as a whole within a greater infinitely regressive
network, by dislocating the core of his reflection into an intertextual
realm. The sentence in italics in the passage just cited is a quotation
from Goethe's *Faust I* and in its complete form reads: 'Mein Freund, die
Zeiten der Vergangenheit | Sind uns ein Buch mit sieben Siegeln; | Was
ihr den Geist der Zeiten heißt, | Das ist im Grund der Herren eigner
Geist, | In dem die Zeiten sich bespiegeln.'[63] The quotation, then, is a
further self-reflective comment on the text's own narrative strategy, which
attempts to do justice to the impossibility of knowing, and adequately
representing, the past by evoking it through refractions of the traces it has
left of itself in the present—or through the mark the present is leaving on
it. Unsurprisingly, intertextual references or allusions figure prominently
throughout *Ein Soldat und ein Mädchen*. We have already seen the
importance of Freud for Fried's writing. Other acknowledged or implied
sources and influences include Aichinger, Brentano, Canetti, Cervantes,
Eliot, Hemingway, Hoffmann, Ibsen, Joyce, Kafka, Kasack, Kubin, Mar-
lowe, Shakespeare, and Wedekind.

Finally, in an intriguing twist to the strategy of narrative embedding in
higher diegetic levels, the practice of providing a commentary on the
soldier's writings (which could be seen as representing a traumatized
subject's impossible attempt to work through a trauma it bears encrypted)
is replicated in Fried's 'Nachwort' to the novel's second edition: though
only a bit over three pages long, this second epilogue has a footnote
appended to it. Read against the text's practice of having the narrator of
one narrative level comment on the writings of the narrator of another,
this might be taken as a suggestion that the author of the epilogue, whom
we take to be Fried himself, is not the ultimate mastermind of the text.
The novel apparently has no final hyperdiegetic level.

The content of the footnote is, incidentally, also interesting, in that it
could be read as a response to critical commentary, which has so often
either praised or condemned Fried's novel for supposedly being 'a belated

---

[63] Johann Wolfgang von Goethe, *Werke: Hamburger Ausgabe*, ed. Erich Trunz, 11th
edn, 14 vols (Munich: Beck, 1981), iii. *Dramen I*, 575–9.

reconciliation with National Socialism'.[64] The footnote, however, reads: 'Ich bin nicht für drakonische Vergeltung, aber die altgewordenen Sünder von Majdanek hätte ich alle zu lebenslänglichem Freiheitsentzug verurteilt' (211). Not only does Fried's novel intimate the possibility of infinite regress by intratextual and intertextual means, its footnoted epilogue also opens the text up to the metatextual network of literary scholarship.

In addition to suggesting an infinite 'upwardly' mobile series of diegetic levels beyond the author's own brain, with no end in sight, Fried's novel also jumps 'downwards', beyond its own beginning. It does this by means of a representational strategy particularly popular with postmodernist authors seeking to foreground textuality, that of *mise en abyme*. We have already come across evidence of partial examples of this, but there are three instances in the text where *mise en abyme* is used to especially striking effect, in a reflection both of, and on, the structure and strategies of its matrix.

The most comprehensive of these instances occurs in the soldier's account of the morning of Helga's execution, which is embedded in the second narrator's frame narrative, and it functions as a miniature replica of the text as a whole. The passage revolves around the notion of retracing one's steps, which features prominently in the entire novel precisely because it is perceived as an impossibility. Here, an entire sequence of events is relieved of its intentionality and played both forwards and backwards, like a series of frames in a motion picture. Indeed, vocabulary borrowed from cinematography is employed throughout the novel. For instance, Fried repeatedly uses the image of a 'Film beim Aufspulen' (68). The 'scene' in question here takes place just prior to Helga's execution, when the soldier discovers that someone has traced a picture of a gallows onto a misted window, gets upset, puts his hand through the window, and is given a sedative before being driven to where the girl will be executed. This sequence is first played forwards and then, as we shall see, in reverse. In addition, it is presented as being viewed through binoculars, which take the place of a camera lens, interpose an additional refractive layer between the narrators and the reader, and presuppose a prior observing consciousness. The passage, which thus reads like a film scene nested in the soldier's mind, is embedded in the soldier's later account, which is embedded in the second narrator's frame narrative, which, as we have seen, is apparently embedded in a third narrator's diegesis and so on, potentially ad infinitum. At the same time, the implication (by means of the impersonal

---

[64] Lawrie, *A Writer without a Country*, 243.

'man') that the version embedded in the soldier's mind is already viewed through another party's eyes means that the series of embeddings has no clear beginning either:

Und man schwankt zwischen nächster Nähe und fernster Ferne und hält einen Feldstecher an die Augen, einmal mit dem richtigen Ende, aber einmal mit dem verkehrten [...]. Der Weg aber führt durch das neblige Feld und durch zwei stechende, schwarze, glotzende Mündungen aus dem Ende herein und zum Anfang hinaus. Also sinkt man hintüber ins Auto des Arztes, und das Auto fährt rückwärts, und der Arzt zieht einem die Nadel der Spritze aus dem Arm und füllt zwei Ampullen, deren Glashälse wieder heil werden, ehe sich ihre Schachtel schließt. Und der Schmerz in der Hand, von der sich der Verband löst, hört erst auf, als die heile Fensterscheibe wieder den Galgen trägt, und der Wutkrampf weicht dem ersten beklommenen Gefühl, denn man atmet seinen dampfenden Hauch wieder ein, und also sieht man noch nicht den Galgen an der kalten Scheibe. Und weiter und weiter geht es, und näher und näher, rückwärts taumelnd durch Korridore, deren hallendes Echo sich unter die Fußtritte verkriecht und schweigt. [...] Und irgendwo im Kommenden läßt man gepflegte Offiziere gähnen und Beamte hüsteln und zwei unrasierte Soldaten Wache stehen, Nachtwache, hohl und grau, eine beklemmende Vorahnung. (53)

Revealingly, the sequence in forward motion that precedes this passage stops just short of describing the actual execution and unravels into a disordered accumulation of free-associative wordplay, out of which emerges this sequence in backwards motion, which in turn stops short of the pronouncement of the death sentence. By failing to trace its steps back to the origin of life suspended (trauma) and also failing to reach its end (closure/death), the scene as a whole constitutes an icon of the soldier's life—and of Fried's novel. It replicates in miniature an inescapable space, a dead angle, within which perspective, distance, and scale are all equally uncertain, linear, teleological chronology is exposed as an artificial construct, and notions of cause and effect are undermined. Events seem to be founded at once in a past reality and a possible future. The retrogressive passage cited culminates in a premonition of what has just happened being about to happen again, thus conveying the impossible future equivalent of a trace of the past in the present, which upsets the sequence of cause and consequence and suggests the possibility of interminable repetition. However, the culmination in a premonition also allows for another reading. Considering that everything else in the passage that was negative or broken when it was played forwards was made whole when the scene was reversed, the fact that the eerie premonition should persist is striking. As well as implying that the entire sequence is on a turning point and about to tip the other way, retrace its path, and compulsively repeat the whole motion all over again, it manages to suggest that the premonition is in fact a foreboding of something to come if we continue on this reversed track: a prior traumatic incident 'irgendwo im Kommenden' of the past, and as such a hint at an origin that precedes, and eludes, the presented sequence, but is nonetheless implied by it. The two extremes of the sequence's movement, the not-quite-dead and the not-yet-pronounced-dead, thus also recreate the two-way reflection suggestive of the same interminable repetition-compulsion caught between failing to return to a source and failing to achieve closure that we encounter throughout the novel.

Finally, this dense and detailed instance of *mise en abyme* might even be interpreted as replicating the text's propensity for positioning itself in an intertextual realm. The idea of toing and froing in a dead angle between two instants of death (or quiescence, to return to Brooks's application of repetition-compulsion to narrative plotting) is an image with which we are familiar from Kafka's work, for instance, from 'Kleine Fabel', where the mouse says 'dort im Winkel steht die Falle, in die ich laufe', and the cat behind it replies, 'Du mußt nur die Laufrichtung ändern'.[65]

Intertextuality is also the principle feature of this next instance of *mise en abyme*. The piece, which positions itself, and, by extension, Fried's novel, in a larger intertextual network, by placing intertextuality as narrative strategy *en abyme* in his text, is the first half of the bipartite 'Die Wahrheit über Don Quijote und den Ungetreuen Hirten' (153–5). This is presented as a response to Kafka's 'Die Wahrheit über Sancho Pansa'.[66] While Kafka's text suggests that Sancho Panza turned his demon into Don Quixote, Fried's Don Quixote turns himself into his own demon by commissioning Cervantes to write him a fictional alter ego. Fried's Don Quixote proceeds from the rational reflection that seeing an exaggerated, irrational version of himself on the page will allow him to distance himself from himself, and help him resist the temptation to tilt at shadows. However, after repeatedly reading his own story, the 'real' Don Quixote, according to an unnamed 'alte Quelle', feels more and more haunted by, and closer to, his fictional alter ego, and, so the piece suggests, finds himself turning into it, compelled to fall back into already established behavioural patterns (153). It is only then that he becomes Don Quixote as we know him. The same is true for the Kafka version, though here Sancho Panza is able to get the alter ego that haunts him off his back by

---

[65] 'Kleine Fabel', in Franz Kafka, *Sämtliche Erzählungen*, ed. Paul Raabe (Frankfurt a.M.: Fischer, 1970), 320.

[66] 'Die Wahrheit über Sancho Pansa', in Kafka, *Sämtliche Erzählungen*, ed. Rabe, 144.

making him the figure he was always meant to be. In both their versions,
as in that of Cervantes, Don Quixote only becomes the 'real' Don
Quixote, that is, Don Quixote, the literary creation, by reading about
what he will turn into. Yet the 'origin' of the two-way reflection between
the Kafka piece and the Fried piece—Cervantes's *Don Quixote*—is not
mentioned. It shines through between their mutually contradictory versions of the same story, and in the soldier's allusion to the prior source of
an 'alte Quelle'. In this, Fried's version mirrors the 'original' *Quixote*,
which had already presented itself as relying on old, forgotten source texts
and, in so doing, established an intertextual framework for itself at the
outset. However, as well as apparently copying a (reproduced) original,
Fried's piece at the same time manages to imply that his soldier's Don
Quixote pre-dates his Spanish ancestor, by having his author create the
fictional version of himself that would come to haunt him and establish
itself as the 'original' Don Quixote. Not only is there no end to the
amount of literary heirs a Don Quixote might have, but Fried, like
Cervantes and Kafka, subverts the very notion of origin, by suggesting
the possibility that each Don Quixote already exists as a fictional character
in someone else's mind. The boundaries between prototype and copy,
between the 'real' Don Quixote and his 'fictional' version(s), but also
between creator and character, are irremediably blurred. In this, Fried
plays with the question, as Borges would later put it: 'Why does it disturb
us that Don Quixote be a reader of the *Quixote* [. . .]? I believe I have
found the reason: these inversions suggest that if the characters of a
fictional work can be readers [. . .], we, its readers [. . .], can be fictitious.'[67] 'Die Wahrheit über Don Quijote' is thus yet another piece that
replicates in miniature form the way in which, both at the hypodiegetic
and at the hyperdiegetic level, Fried's text appears to be receding towards a
vanishing point, while also managing to implicate the reader in this
infinitely recursive structure. We are reminded of the second narrator's
comment on the soldier's narrative strategy. According to him, what the
soldier can show us is: 'Keinen Ausweg. Den gibt es nicht. Auch keinen
Weg *durch* das Geschehene *hindurch*, sondern *in es hinein*' (60).

From the preceding it has become apparent how Fried has attempted to
convey, through intertextuality and *mise en abyme*, that there is no
'horizon' to his novel: no closure, even after the writing comes to a halt,
but also no fixed point of origin. A final example of this is the prose piece
'Der Drache', a fairy tale embedded within the soldier's tale, and also the

---

[67] Jorge Luis Borges, 'Partial Magic in the *Quixote*', trans. James E. Irby, in *Labyrinths:
Selected Stories and Other Writings*, ed. Donald A. Yates and Irby, trans. Yates, Irby, et al.
(London: Penguin, 2000), 228–31 (229).

central story of the novel's central 'Mental Ward' section. Far from being a conventional 'Märchen', 'Der Drache' constitutes a self-reflexive, and self-reflective, speculation on the new mode of writing we encounter in the text as a whole. It starts out, as we have come to expect of fairy tales, with the description of a knight, who is setting out to slay a dragon, but after just a few lines the story in the soldier's piece ends, and we hear that this is because the book that contains the story (which is contained in the soldier's story, which is contained in a book) has had its pages ripped out after the first few words. As a result, it is 'fast als wäre ein neuer Geschichtenerzähler da, der sich an nichts halten muß, was man nur mit den altgewohnten Worten erzählen kann' (141). The rest of the piece mixes desultorily appearing fragments of a 'neues Märchen' with a narrative commentary enacted between two parties, a toad and snake, as well as with reflections both on the form of this new kind of writing and on the experience of reading it. The diegetic level of the story is impossible to pinpoint, and the tale has no clear beginning or ending: after the first few lines, it starts over, preventing any storyline from developing, and it ends with the dragon having a premonitory dream that might herald his death, but waking up. We are told about the fragmentary form of the writing:

> der Verlust der Blätter aus dem Märchenbuch [. . .] hat eine Bresche in die ritterliche Welt geschlagen. Sie ist nun ihrer festen Wehr beraubt und kann keine Fragen und Gedanken zusammenfassen oder gar beantworten. So werden die verstreuten Gedanken und die losen, belanglosen Fragen noch einen Augenblick lang laut, dann zerflattern sie. (141)

The readers of the story are said to have mixed reactions: 'Unter den Hörern Entrüstung, aber da und dort auch hingerissenes Gruseln' (141).

Thematically a reflection on, and formally a reflection of, the text as a whole, 'Der Drache' is both metatext and *mise en abyme*. Because of its position at the heart of the novel, the entire text disappears into the rabbit hole of its own abyss. Not only is there no 'ceiling' to the writing, but there is also no ground beneath our feet. The abysm really is a bottomless pit. As well as being haunted by phantoms of events, people, and inter-texts, the text as a whole haunts itself. As such, it is inescapable: a labyrinthine crypt or 'Toter Winkel', in which both protagonists and readers find themselves, as it were, buried alive, with theoretically no possibility of egress, and no escape from going over and over the same ground. Like the other texts encountered here, Fried's novel marks a watershed between individual trauma and collective memory, where the trauma of the past in the present is not converted into narrative, but is preserved in text. Writing of this kind cannot be reconciled with the trajectory of narrative plot outlined by Brooks. However, it might be argued that this is precisely what renders it effective as Holocaust literature, by allowing it to reflect the insight reached by the narrator at the end of the frame narrative: 'Ob der Soldat es je verwinden wird, und ob das wirklich wünschenswert wäre, das weiß ich nicht. Auch nicht, ob man alles verwinden soll' (204).

5

Design from Debris

Wolfgang Hildesheimer, *Tynset, Masante*

And so when the historians close their books, when the statisticians
stop counting, the memorialists and witnesses can no longer remember, then the poet, the novelist, the artist comes and surveys the
devastated landscape left by the fire—the ashes. He rummages
through the debris in search of a design. For if the essence, the
meaning, or the meaninglessness of the Holocaust will survive our
sordid history, it will be in works of art.

(Raymond Federman, *The Necessity and Impossibility of Being a
Jewish Writer*)

Like the other authors discussed here, Wolfgang Hildesheimer was ambivalent about Judaism and the question of his own Jewishness. Self-
consciously Jewish in some respects, he was also aware of a distance
between himself and a 'Judentum' he defined not in terms of faith or
race but as 'Zugehörigkeit zu einer Schicksalsgemeinschaft'.[1] Born in
Hamburg in 1916, he was descended from a family of prominent rabbis
and scholars in Berlin; his great-grandfather, Esriel Hildesheimer
(1820–99), had been 'einer der bedeutendsten Vertreter des orthodoxen
Judentums in Deutschland'.[2] Yet Hildesheimer's own upbringing was not
religious, or as he put it: 'Meine Vorfahren väterlicherseits waren Rabbi-
ner, einer nach dem anderen, nur mein Vater hatte keine Lust mehr und

[1] Wolfgang Hildesheimer, 'Mein Judentum' (1978), in Hildesheimer, *Gesammelte
Werke*, ed. Christiaan Lucas Hart Nibbrig and Volker Jehle, 7 vols (Frankfurt a.M.:
Suhrkamp, 1991), vii. *Vermischte Schriften*, 159–69 (159).

[2] Henry A. Lea, *Wolfgang Hildesheimers Weg als Jude und Deutscher* (Stuttgart: Heinz,
1997), 5. For further detailed biographical information see also Lea, *Wolfgang Hildesheimers
Weg*, 5–71. For a concise outline, see Stephan Braese, 'Hildesheimer, Wolfgang', in Andreas
B. Kilcher (ed.), *Lexikon der deutsch-jüdischen Literatur: Jüdische Autorinnen und Autoren
deutscher Sprache von der Aufklärung bis zur Gegenwart* (Frankfurt a.M: Suhrkamp, 2003),
243–7.

wurde Chemiker.'[3] Hildesheimer's parents were Zionists and had plans to emigrate to Palestine as early as 1929, though it was 1933 by the time the family finally left Germany for Jerusalem. Hildesheimer, who had lived abroad, in Holland and England, even before their emigration, adopted Palestinian citizenship in 1936. Having trained as a carpenter in Palestine, Hildesheimer moved to London in 1937 to attend the Central School of Arts and Crafts (now part of Central St Martins College of Arts and Design at the University of the Arts London). In 1939, he went back to Palestine to work for the British Public Information Office. After the war, Hildesheimer returned to London where he painted and did some graphic and stage set design before being asked to act as an interpreter and translator at the Nuremberg war crimes trials.

In later years, Hildesheimer would characterize his experience of the Second World War in terms that suggest that he viewed the persecution of Jews during the Third Reich from a position of greater remove than the other authors examined here. Having left Germany just before the rise of National Socialism, and having lost no close relatives in the Holocaust, he denied that his situation compared to that of his exiled German-Jewish contemporaries such as Peter Weiss:

> Peter Weiss war tatsächlich im Exil. [. . .] Ich habe in England nie das Gefühl gehabt, ein Emigrant zu sein. Ich habe Deutschland vor den Nazis verlassen und bin persönlich niemals in Kontakt mit den Nazis gekommen. Meine Eltern wollten sowieso schon weg. Das Exilbewußtsein oder Exilgefühl habe ich niemals verspürt. Das ist also etwas völlig anderes.[4]

According to Hildesheimer, his first exposure to the atrocities of the Holocaust was therefore in the form of a twice-removed witnessing of witness testimonies during the Nuremberg trials:

> Mit Judentum in seiner grausamsten Bedeutung, mit Rassenzugehörigkeit, Artfremdheit und all den Worten dieses Vokabulars, wurde ich erst konfrontiert, als ich Simultandolmetscher bei den Nürnberger Prozessen wurde; als sich hier, systematisch und schematisch, eine Geschichte aufrollte, die ich in den Jahren ihres Geschehens nur aus Berichten und Gerüchten gekannt hatte.[5]

Yet the professed detachment from the events of the past reveals itself as rather harder won than initially apparent in the remainder of the passage:

---

[3] Wolfgang Hildesheimer, 'Vita', in *Wolfgang Hildesheimer*, ed. Volker Jehle (Frankfurt a.M.: Suhrkamp, 1989), 17–21 (17).

[4] 'Ich kann über nichts anderes schreiben als über ein potentielles Ich: Gespräch mit Wolfgang Hildesheimer', in Manfred Durzak, *Gespräche über den Roman* (Frankfurt a.M.: Suhrkamp, 1976), 271–95 (272).

[5] 'Mein Judentum', 163.

Die Geschichte war entsetzlich, aber sie gehörte einer Vergangenheit an, deren Bewältigung schließlich nicht *meine* Aufgabe war. Die Frage der Schuld oder der Kollektivschuld überließ ich meinem Unbewußten und wartete auf den Entscheid von innen. Drei Jahre lebte ich als Angehöriger der Besetzungsmacht in einem großen Zimmer im Grand-Hotel in Nürnberg, das ich mir als Atelier hergerichtet hatte, um mich beim Zeichnen und Malen von dem Schrecken dieser ausführlich rekapitulierten Vorgänge abzulenken, was mir gelang.[6]

Here Hildesheimer presents himself not as a German Jew who finds out after the fact what the fate he fortuitously avoided would have held in store for him, but in an antagonistic role, as a member of the Allied forces. This allows him to imply that the events of the past with which he is confronted in the courtroom are otherwise nothing to do with him, that he is therefore not responsible for having to work through them, and even that he manages not to be unduly affected by them. As Lea, who cites this same passage in his monograph, points out, statements such as this make Hildesheimer seem 'merkwürdig unbeteiligt'.[7] However, doubt is cast on Hildesheimer's dispassionate stance partly by the allusion to his art that makes it sound like a form of displacement activity, but even more so by the reference to the 'Unbewußtes'. If what he was forced to witness through the imagination in court was in fact immediately relegated to his unconscious, this suggests (secondarily) traumatic encryption and unmastered preservation, rather than reflection on, and working through of, the past. Even the use of the word 'Schrecken' could be telling in this passage, if we decide it is employed in analogy to Freud's definition of the term in a psychoanalytic context. Freud conceives of 'Schreck', in contrast to 'Furcht' and 'Angst', as the particular type of shock associated with traumatic experience:

Schreck, Furcht, Angst werden mit Unrecht wie synonyme Ausdrücke gebraucht; sie lassen sich in ihrer Beziehung zur Gefahr gut auseinanderhalten. Angst bezeichnet einen gewissen Zustand wie Erwartung der Gefahr und Vorbereitung auf dieselbe, mag sie auch eine unbekannte sein; Furcht verlangt ein bestimmtes Objekt, vor dem man sich fürchtet; Schreck aber benennt den Zustand, in den man gerät, wenn man in Gefahr kommt, ohne auf sie vorbereitet zu sein, betont das Moment der Überraschung. Ich glaube nicht, daß Angst eine traumatische Neurose erzeugen kann; an der Angst ist etwas, was gegen den Schreck und also auch gegen die Schreckneurose schützt.[8]

---

[6] 'Mein Judentum', 163–4; original emphasis.
[7] Lea, *Wolfgang Hildesheimers Weg*, 22.
[8] Sigmund Freud, 'Jenseits des Lustprinzips' (1920), in *Studienausgabe*, ed. Alexander Mitscherlich, Angela Richards, and James Strachey, 11 vols (Frankfurt a.M.: Fischer, 1969–75), iii. *Psychologie des Unbewußten* (1975), 213–72 (222–3).

Characteristically for trauma, as we have seen in previous chapters, the traumatized individual, by force of his or her repeated reliving of the unmastered traumatic event, will keep being plunged back into a state of 'Schreck' until he or she manages, belatedly, 'die Reizbewältigung unter Angstentwicklung nachzuholen, deren Unterlassung die Ursache der traumatischen Neurose geworden ist'.[9] Though we cannot be sure if Hildesheimer did in fact have Freud's definition in mind when he used the term 'Schrecken' in the statement cited earlier, it is unlikely that he, who was acquainted with the writings of Freud and had himself undergone psychoanalysis, would have used either that or the term 'Unbewußtes' innocently in this context. Indeed, in the very piece containing the reference to the 'Schrecken' of the past, Hildesheimer describes himself as a 'Psychoanalysierter'.[10] Moreover, we shall see that, by Hildhesheimer's own acknowledgement, the idea of a constant return to a state of 'Schrecken', as a result of the failure to work through a traumatizing experience, informs both themes and form of the literary works of his discussed in this chapter.

After his involvement in the trials and in the editing of some of the court transcripts, Hildesheimer decided to stay in Germany and take up painting again. Instead, he found himself starting to write: short stories at first, but also poetry, plays, radio plays, essays, and, finally, more substantial prose works.[11] Because Hildesheimer was living in Germany when his writing career took off, and in 1951 was even invited to attend his first meeting of Gruppe 47, Stephan Braese, who refers to this invitation as Hildesheimer's '"Eintritt" in die westdeutsche Nachkriegsliteratur', has said of him:

> Kein anderer jüdischer Autor deutscher Sprache hat wie Wolfgang Hildesheimer versucht, in den Jahren des 'Neuanfangs' einer deutschen Gegenwartsliteratur nach 1945 an dieser Literatur teilzuhaben und das [...] Projekt einer Existenz als Schriftsteller an die Entwicklung und die Bedingungen des westdeutschen Literaturbetriebs zu knüpfen.[12]

This may be true for the first few years after his return, when it still seemed to Hildesheimer that things might be taking a turn for the better in Germany, or as he put it:

---

[9] Freud, 'Jenseits des Lustprinzips', 241–2.

[10] For details on Hildesheimer and psychoanalysis, see Lea, *Wolfgang Hildesheimers Weg*, 54.

[11] For a detailed bibliography of Hildesheimer's works, see Volker Jehle, 'Bibliographie', in Heinz Ludwig Arnold (ed.), *Wolfgang Hildesheimer* (Munich: text + kritik, 1986), 121–38; or Lea, *Wolfgang Hildesheimers Weg*, 369–99.

[12] *Die andere Erinnerung: Jüdische Autoren in der westdeutschen Nachkriegsliteratur* (Berlin: Philo, 2001), 237, 236. For further details on Hildesheimer's dealings with Gruppe 47, see *Die andere Erinnerung*, esp. 236–52.

die Möglichkeit bestand, dass alles sich zum Guten wende, und das Gefühl,
dass es mit Deutschland moralisch aufwärts gehe, war nicht abwegig. [...]
ich fühlte mich in Deutschland wohl, denn ich huldigte dem Glauben, dass
die Schuldigen in der Minderheit wären.[13]

However, at the time of writing the essay from which this quotation is taken,
Hildesheimer was already profoundly disillusioned, and the next sentence
reads: 'Heute weiss ich, dass sie in der Mehrheit waren.'[14] This was in 1963,
and Hildesheimer was no longer even living in Germany, having left it for the
second time six years previously and emigrated to Poschiavo in Switzerland,
where he was to remain until his death in 1991. Indeed, the piece in question
was originally intended for publication in a volume of essays, edited by
Hermann Kesten, entitled *Ich lebe nicht in der Bundesrepublik*, and Hildesheimer had called his essay 'Die vier Hauptgründe, weshalb ich nicht in der
Bundesrepublik lebe'.[15] In the same piece, which he ended up withdrawing
from publication, Hildesheimer states further: 'Ich bin Jude. Zwei Drittel
aller Deutschen sind Antisemiten. Sie waren es immer und werden es immer
bleiben', and he concludes by saying: 'Ich gehöre nicht zur Mehrheit, die
antisemitisch ist, und ich mag nicht zur Minderheit gehören, die eine solche
Mehrheit in Kauf nimmt. Kurz: ich mag nicht dazugehören.'[16] For all his
successful early efforts to establish himself as a writer in the Federal Republic,
as a result of which he has received far more—though not by any means
necessarily more positive—critical attention than the other authors discussed
here, it is probably true to say, with Lea, that even Hildesheimer is ultimately
'ein deutscher Schriftsteller [...] nur in dem Sinn, daß er auf deutsch
geschrieben hat'.[17]

Since the unexpected beginning of his writing career in 1950, most, if
not all, of Hildesheimer's texts were to some extent informed by what he
had heard and seen at Nuremberg, but after his second emigration in
1957, this became an increasingly important feature of his work. Braese is
absolutely right to speak of a 'kontinuierlich zunehmende Vergegenwärtigung der Verfolgungsgeschichte' in Hildesheimer's oeuvre, a 'Vergegenwärtigung' which, as Lea points out, culminates in the works produced in
the years after his arrival in Switzerland: 'Seine Schriften aus den ersten
Exiljahren, 1957–1973, konzentrieren sich beinahe ausschließlich auf die
unmittelbare deutsche Vergangenheit und Gegenwart.'[18] In both the life

---

[13] Cited in Braese, *Die andere Erinnerung*, 265.
[14] Braese, *Die andere Erinnerung*, 265.
[15] Kesten, *Ich lebe nicht in der Bundesrepublik* (Munich: List, 1964).
[16] Cited in Braese, *Die andere Erinnerung*, 265, and Lea, *Wolfgang Hildesheimers Weg*, 41.
[17] Lea, *Wolfgang Hildesheimers Weg*, 1.
[18] Braese, *Die andere Erinnerung*, 269; Lea, *Wolfgang Hildesheimers Weg*, 43.

and the writing of Hildesheimer, it is almost as if this second period of emigration belatedly made possible a (literary) response on his part to the traumatic past that could have been his, but which he had only experienced through witness testimony during the trials at Nuremberg. This response appears both as a further example of, and at the same time as an equivalent once removed to, that of the other authors examined here, whose reaction to the traumatic past was less mediated and delayed, but who, as we have seen, also already felt like witnesses at a remove. Unlike their trauma, Hildesheimer's is not only once but twice removed, triggered by witnessing the act of bearing witness. In as much as it is ever possible to quantify these things, he is less traumatized than an original witness, yet more directly affected than someone born too late to be considered, in the very broadest sense, a Holocaust survivor. As a result, he appears to be situated somewhere between the first generation of victims of the Holocaust and the second generation, whose trauma is wholly vicarious. Raymond Federman's image, cited in the epigraph, of the novelist 'rummag[ing] through the debris in search of a design' seems coined for Hildesheimer's situation more especially than for that of either memory or 'postmemory' authors.[19]

The doubly belated 'Vergegenwärtigung'—in the sense both of rendering conscious and of re-presenting—of the past, which becomes increasingly important in Hildesheimer's writing after 1957, finds its perhaps most striking enactment in the two works of what the editors of Hildesheimer's *Gesammelte Werke* have categorized as his 'monologische Prosa': the novel-length first-person prose narratives *Tynset* and *Masante*, first published in 1965 and 1973 respectively.[20] It is to these texts that I shall refer in what follows, though my focus in this chapter will not be on supplying a detailed stand-alone narrative analysis of works that in certain respects closely resemble those already encountered. Unlike for my lesser-known authors, a number of close critical readings already exist for Hildesheimer.[21] Rather, I shall aim to highlight the ways in which his approach differs from that of the previous authors, and to suggest how we

[19] 'The Necessity and Impossibility of Being a Jewish Writer' (2001), <http://www.federman.com/rfsrcr0.htm> [accessed 23 Apr. 2008].

[20] Subsequent references to these will be to Wolfgang Hildesheimer, *Gesammelte Werke*, ed. Christiaan Lucas Hart Nibbrig and Volker Jehle, 7 vols (Frankfurt a.M.: Suhrkamp, 1991), ii. *Monologische Prosa* and will be included in parentheses in the text. In addition to *Tynset* (7–153) and *Masante* (155–366), the volume also contains a selection of paralipomena (367–420), including a commentary by Hildesheimer on the earlier of the two texts, 'Antworten über *Tynset*' (384–7).

[21] See e.g. Christine Chiadò Rana, *Das Weite suchen: Unterwegs in Wolfgang Hildesheimers Prosa* (Würzburg: Ergon, 2003), for a compelling study of the treatment of time and space in the texts.

might therefore usefully consider his writing as a bridge between the survivor generation and generations born after the event, and what inferences such a consideration might allow us to draw about developments in form and function of the Holocaust novel across the board, and across boundaries and borders.

'JENES GROßE ERINNERUNGSPOETOLOGISCHE PROJEKT'?

Because they share a number of thematic and structural features, *Tynset* and *Masante* tend to be treated as an 'Interpretationseinheit' or even, in view of their focus on the 'Vergegenwärtigung' of the past, as two halves of a single 'erinnerungspoetologische[s] Projekt'.[22] In fact, neither of these assumptions is entirely borne out by a reading of the texts. There are significant differences of both theme and form between the earlier and the later work, and it is not least because of the progression evident from one to the other, though also because, once again, the past is not presented as past—and therefore not converted to memory—in them, that *Tynset* and *Masante* do not appear to fit squarely into a category of 'Erinnerungspoetologie'. As well as indicating aspects Hildesheimer's texts have in common with, and ways in which they differ from, those discussed in previous chapters, I shall consider how *Masante* has grown out of, but also moved on from, *Tynset*, and how, despite this development, the two texts between them might still be said to constitute an 'erinnerungspoetologisches Projekt' of sorts, even if, as in the works of my other authors, if not more so, the memory on which they are founded is present only as nonmemory.

Both *Tynset* and *Masante* are characterized by the fact that, as J. J. Long has pointed out, 'not a great deal happens' in them. The plot of *Tynset*, according to Long, can be summarized as follows:

> a middle-aged insomniac lies awake, and then takes a stroll around his house in the course of which the objects and sounds he perceives act as catalysts for the stories he tells about them [...] Most importantly, the narrator notices the town of Tynset in a Norwegian railway timetable, and throughout the night he periodically considers undertaking a journey to Tynset.[23]

---

[22] Günther Blamberger, 'Der Rest ist Schweigen: Hildesheimers Literatur des Absurden', in Arnold (ed.), *Wolfgang Hildesheimer*, 33–44 (39); Braese, 'Hildesheimer, Wolfgang', in Kilcher (ed.), *Lexikon der deutsch-jüdischen Literatur*, 245.

[23] 'Time and Narrative: Wolfgang Hildesheimer's *Tynset* and *Masante*', *German Life and Letters*, 52 (1999), 457–74 (457–8).

The plot of *Masante* is similarly restricted: 'the narrator arrives at a desert settlement called Meona. He rents a room in *la dernière chance*, an inn run by a couple called Maxine and Alain, and spends the day walking about between his room and the bar before strolling off into the desert.' Again, objects and names in the text 'function as goads to the narrative act'.[24]

The many micronarratives that are generated in this way in *Tynset* range from the narrator's indefinitely deferred plans to travel to the eponymous Norwegian town (e.g. 13, 19–20, 46, 152), to the time he triggered a dawn chorus of roosters in the Acropolis in Athens (25–6, 40–3), to the discovery of the corpse of an American evangelist (32–5), to tales of adultery and murder or lasciviousness and death that in centuries past took place in his antique summer and winter bed respectively (76, 136, 109–23). Phone books and timetables keep cropping up (e.g. 20–5, 10–12), as do a former female companion of the narrator's, who is never identified in detail and only named at the very end of the text (e.g. 46, 59, 143, 151–2), his housekeeper Celestina (e.g. 10, 149), and the ghost of Hamlet's father, who visits the narrator at night (e.g. 16). In *Masante*, the micronarratives touch on, among other things, the 'rat of Saloniki' (189, 330–1), St Augustine, who makes an appearance in discussions of four-letter words and sexual morality (213–14, 230–1), the discovery of a human ear (245, 261–2), the invention of the umbrella (268–70), and Bach's Goldberg Variations (337–40), all of which are interspersed with references to a saints' calendar and a box of index cards, the names and figures in which give rise to a wealth of further micronarratives (e.g. 168–72), and with details of the (imagined) life stories of two female figures, Maxine, one of the owners of *la dernière chance*, and Niki Almesin, an aristocratic art-history student from the narrator's past, both of whom he attempts to entice into an exchange of further micronarratives (e.g. 177–86, 239–46). In both texts, references to processes of ageing, decay, and ruin of the body, of buildings, of cities, and ultimately of entire civilizations abound (e.g. 9, 243–6).

However, the most important thematic nexus in both *Tynset* and *Masante* is made up of variations on the theme of persecution, which are played out in reference to an ever-growing assortment of so-called 'Häscher', shadowy persecutor figures from the past, who in *Tynset* bear names such as Malkusch, Obwasser, or Föttle, as in 'Föttle und Geiser', installers of gas ovens and gas chambers (39), but also Kabasta, who then reappears in *Masante*, along with a 'Fricke oder so ähnlich' (202), a Kranzmeier who was a 'Vergaser', a Stollfuß who had 'seine eigene

Methode' (291), a Motschmann, a Globotschnik, or a Perchtl. All of these continue to haunt the present, and the similarly proliferating cast of their victims, who go by the names of, for instance, Bloch, 'der sich buchstäblich sein Grab selbst schaufelte, und zwar unter Aufsicht von Kabasta' (39), Gerber, Felber, Lüning, or Weiszbrodt. The 'Häscher' of the past go about their lives in the present in complete impunity, as we see from passages such as: 'wo war es, daß ich Lampenschirme sah, aus heller menschlicher Haut, verfertigt in Deutschland von einem deutschen Bastler, der heute als Pensionär in Schleswig-Holstein lebt?' (81). Even the narrator's own father is included in the ranks of the victims in *Tynset*, and we are told about him: 'er ist nicht sanft ins Jenseits hinübergeschlummert, sondern erschlagen von christlichen Familienvätern aus Wien oder aus dem Weserland' (90).

In addition to the overt criticism of state and church evident in these examples, which was either a less immediate concern of, or took a more sociological than political form in, the works of the other authors examined here, we perceive another significant difference to the texts analysed in earlier chapters. In these, a personal reality was presented in the generalizing, depersonalizing guise of fiction (for instance, the experience of persecution and internment in Adler, or the deportation and death of the mother in Augustin). In Hildesheimer's texts, we encounter an increasingly 'un-real' fictitious discourse presented as an all-too-common personal reality. The narrator's father who was murdered by 'christlichen Familienvätern aus Wien oder aus dem Weserland' was not Hildesheimer's—though he could have been (90). The narrator's portrayal of the variations on the theme of persecution (with indefinite articles, modal particles, or in the conditional, in varying, sometimes multiple or mutually exclusive constellations, occasionally doubling back to correct himself) makes it clear that his victims and perpetrators are not to be read as specific historical individuals:

> Übrigens war das, denke ich, doch nicht Gerber oder Felber, der mit der Waffe [. . .]. Sein Name ist mir entfallen [. . .]. Wahrscheinlich lebt er nicht mehr [. . .]. Vielleicht ist er, trotz Waffe, einem Diethelm Fricke oder einem Wilhelm Motschmann zum Opfer gefallen, die wären schneller bei seinem Arm oder seinem Hals gewesen als er bei der Waffe—da gibt es viele Möglichkeiten. (212)

Though only generic embodiments in the texts, the 'Häscher' are, however, perceived as a very real and widespread past and present threat. As Hildesheimer said in 'Antworten über *Tynset*' in 1965:

> Obwasser und Kabasta existieren tausendfach, ich kenne sie, ich war Simultandolmetscher in Nürnberg, war auch bei außergerichtlichen Verhören

zugegen, und ich weiß auch, wer frei ausging und noch geht. Auch den Lampenschirm aus menschlicher Haut—und Schlimmeres—habe ich gesehen. Ob der Verfertiger heute noch in Schleswig-Holstein lebt, weiß ich nicht, halte es aber für wahrscheinlich. (384)

Indeed, their sense of menace is enhanced by the exemplary nature, and the resultant seemingly infinite number, of hunter–prey constellations we encounter. As Lea has pointed out with reference to *Tynset*: 'Wir stehen hier an der Grenze zwischen Persönlichem und Exemplarischem.'[25] This observation, I submit, holds true in an even broader sense for the themes and form of Hildesheimer's work than Lea suggests. Although, as we shall see, especially *Tynset* can still be read as an example of personal trauma writing, constructed in a similar vein to that encountered in earlier chapters, with *Masante*, Hildesheimer crosses the boundary between personal and exemplary, gradually leaving behind the former, though not the traces of a past which remain as much part of the fabric of his later text as they apparently do of the world at large.

'DER SCHRECKEN [IST] EIGENTLICH DAS HAUPTTHEMA'

In *Tynset*, we encounter a narrator who has cut himself off from the world in a cabin in the mountains, in a futile effort to access the absolute 'Nichts', 'wo nichts ist, wo nichts vergessen wird, weil nichts erinnert wird', 'gezogen' by his 'Sehnsucht, nirgends zu sein' (107). In this cabin, he lies awake at night and produces narratives, in a vain attempt to distract himself from uncontrollably surfacing fragments of the past. Yet his stories rarely progress much beyond their beginning before being cut off, at which point the narrator is forced to change direction and embark on a new narrative track. As in the other texts discussed here, it is possible to read this narrator's failure to turn micronarratives into metanarrative as reflective of his inability to achieve closure and bridge the gap of his life in post-traumatic suspension. The way in which the past returns to haunt him in the middle of the night is certainly reminiscent of the traumatic flashbacks experienced by the other authors' protagonists:

Es ist spät. Ich will versuchen zu schlafen, aber irgend etwas hat mich aufgestört, ich habe schon vergessen, was es war, und ich will versuchen, [. . .] sanft in andere Bahnen zu gleiten, an anderes zu denken, ich will hoffen, daß dieses andere nicht auch etwas Verstecktes enthält, das mich aufstört. (40)

[25] Lea, *Wolfgang Hildesheimers Weg*, 216.

Hildesheimer himself has made this link between traumatic experience and narrative in an interview with Matthias Prangel, in which he considers the consequences of that link for the structure of his text:

> immer dort, wo wir tatsächlich auf den Schrecken stoßen, kommt eine Zäsur: der Schrecken selbst. Die Beschreibung dieses Schreckens wird ausgespart, und es beginnt dann mit irgendeinem Divertimento, [...] in einer ganz anderen Ecke, einer ganz anderen Form. Dann werden wieder Themen ausgesponnen, wo man schon merkt: es zieht sich der Schrecken wieder ein. Und schließlich kommt es auf irgendeine andere Form des Schreckens. In *Tynset* ist der Schrecken eigentlich das Hauptthema.[26]

In 'Antworten über *Tynset*', Hildesheimer notes that though the 'Schrecken' itself is left out, the nature of the text's main theme—or of 'das Entsetzliche', as he also terms it—is revealed in the form of references to the 'Häscher' and their victims:

> das Hauptthema—das Entsetzliche, verkörpert durch [...] Kabasta, den Lampenschirm, die Mörder 'aus Wien oder aus dem Weserland', [...]—leuchtet nur auf, es wird nicht ausgeführt, ist nur kurzer Anlaß der Nebenthemen. Diese Nebenthemen—die verschiedenen Geschichten, Reminiszenzen, Rückblenden—stoßen sich daran ab. (385)

Yet the narrative complex to which the 'Häscher' belong in fact tells us no more about the narrator's personal trauma than the other micronarratives of the text do. As we have seen, the appearances of the past in Hildesheimer's texts, unlike those encountered in earlier chapters, do not mark flashbacks to an individual traumatic experience. This suggests that even the 'Häscher' fragments are not the actual manifestation of trauma, but merely a substitute for it, and that to some extent in *Tynset*, but increasingly so in *Masante*, the narrative fragments concerning Germany's National Socialist past are themselves simply part of the text's wealth of micronarratives, a story complex that is integrated into the overall weave like any of the others. This is also why the narrator does not give the impression of being helplessly exposed to their onslaught; on the contrary, he seems able to summon, and rearrange and manipulate, them at will, as he does all the other narratives—at least up to the point where they are interrupted by an actual flashback. The (non-)experience of persecution, which in previous texts has been the absent referent that generates a host of dangling signifiers, has entered the text in Hildesheimer's writing, but has entered it, in fictionalized form, as a placeholder. This, in turn, signals the absent presence of an unspoken underlying trauma which

---

[26] Cited in *Gesammelte Werke*, ed. Nibbrig and Jehle, ii. *Monologische Prosa*, 427.

would appear to consist precisely in the guilt-inducing *absence* of primary traumatization, resulting in the fact that the original experience, and the trauma caused by it, can only ever be recreated generically and imaginatively, and recalling, in a sense, Hildesheimer's own second-hand witnessing of (already incomplete) testimony.

Viewed in this light, the 'Häscher' complex would then be just one of a number of impossible attempts on the part of the narrator to return to a past he never knew. Another important embodiment of such a substitute trauma in the text is the town of Tynset itself, which, as an always distant location, both recalls the unreachable origin of trauma and, if considered as a metaphor or placeholder for something else, also indicates belated, vicarious traumatization, as characterized by the unreaching of what is already merely a substitute for the unreachable. How this unfolds over the course of the text becomes apparent if we pick out a few of the references to Tynset with which the writing is interspersed:

Von [...] Tynset dagegen weiß ich nichts (13)

Tynset, daran bin ich im Vorbeigehen haftengeblieben (19)

Tynset. Da liegt es, eine Saat zwischen die Gedanken gestreut, [...] so schlägt es Wurzel, [...] wuchert wie Unkraut, schlingt sich wie Schlinggewächse, erstickt die Gedanken außer den Gedanken an es selbst, es breitet sich aus, erobert Gelände (78)

Tynset läßt sich nicht verdrängen (125)

ob dieses Tynset nicht vor meinen Augen entschwindet oder in sich zusammensinkt wie eine fata morgana, wenn ich mich ihm nähere. (134)

ich schweife immer wieder ab, ich habe Tynset noch nicht im Griff, es entzieht sich mir, aber es kehrt immer wieder zurück [...] ich werde es von seiner Verzierung befreien, mit der ich es umzeichnet habe, es droht unter ihr zuzuwachsen. (139)

Ich werde nicht mehr nach Tynset kommen, ich werde es auch gar nicht versuchen, ich werde dieses Haus nicht verlassen [...].
Ich werde Tynset entfliehen lassen, werde es vergessen, verdrängen, [...] werde so tun, als sei [...] alles in schönster bester Ordnung. (152)

Since, by the time we reach the end of the text, we have already been told that Tynset 'läßt sich nicht verdrängen' (125), we rather suspect that the narrator's plans to release, forget, deny, or repress it in the future will fail, as they have failed up to this point. Only physical death would be able to put an end to this interminable process, and indeed the text ends on what appears almost as an enactment of the narrator's death:

in diesem Bett [. . .], in dem ich nun wieder liege [. . .], obgleich es Tag ist, liege und für immer liegenbleibe und Tynset entschwinden lasse—ich sehe es dort hinten entschwinden, [. . .] jetzt ist es entschwunden, der Name vergessen, verweht wie Schall und Rauch, wie ein letzter Atemzug— (152–3)

Yet the dash after the final breath (and, of course, the fact that the final breath is recorded in the first place) suggests continued existence, and indeed the narrator will reappear in the author's next work.

As something that can be neither repressed, nor returned to, grasped, and put into words, Tynset represents trauma, but it also signals the absence left by a prior trauma, as we can see from excerpts such as this:

Ja, Tynset ist ein guter Name für das Rätsel. Indem man dem Unbekannten einen Namen gibt, wird es zwar nicht bekannter, das Rätsel enthüllt sich nicht mit dem Namen, aber es ist benannt, es hat eine Bezeichnung erhalten, die das Rätselhafte, das es in sich birgt, zusammenfaßt, chiffriert [. . .]. [. . .] Aber was ist es denn, das ich mir unter Tynset vorstelle? Was?—Nichts, sei still, nichts. (138)

As soon as it touches on the question of an absent prior referent behind the (already unreachable) cipher Tynset, the narrative is silenced and diverted.

What this underlying trauma might consist in is perhaps hinted at in the narrator's association of the town of Tynset with the figure of Hamlet, as we see in statements such as: 'Tynset—klingt das nicht wie Hamlet? [. . .] seltsam, daß mir dies jetzt erst einfällt' (90), or 'Zu Tynset jedoch—das wird mir zunehmend klar—fällt mir nichts ein, nichts und niemand, außer Hamlet' (139). Periodically throughout the text, the narrator is haunted by the ghost of Hamlet's father, whom the narrator then compares to his own father. As in texts discussed previously, the return of a dead ancestor is tied here to a sense of guilt on the part of the living. The ghost is an exteriorization of their self-reproach for failing to compensate for the deaths of those who have left them an encrypted traumatic legacy to safeguard. Here, however, the relationship between the spectre of the past and the haunted survivor in the present, like the link between the narrator and the unspoken original trauma, is a doubly removed one. The ghost of Hamlet's father is asking the narrator to play a role he feels his own son was unable to assume. The narrator, in Hamlet's stead, feels reproached by the ghost of the father for being passive in the face of his unjust death: '[Hamlets Vater] sieht mich an, als wolle er mir bedeuten, daß ich ihm etwas schulde, aber er irrt, ich schulde ihm nichts' (16). The narrator denies feeling guilty, but he seems to protest too much, as we see in statements such as: 'ich trage selbst wenig eigene Schuld, sehr wenig' (18), or 'ich bin ohne Schuld—besser vielleicht, vorsichtiger gesagt: ohne

wesentliche Schuld—, daher auch ohne Pflicht. Ich habe nichts gutzuma-
chen, nichts reinzuwaschen, jedenfalls wüßte ich nicht was. Niemand hat,
soweit ich weiß, durch mich gelitten' (59). Finally, towards the end of the
text, he symbolically comes to assume a guilt that is not his (just as he, and
the characters of the other texts discussed here, are also the bearers of a
trauma not originally theirs), when he acts as confessor to his housekeeper,
who has mistaken him for a priest. The sins, the nature of which she never
reveals, are, however, not sins she has committed, but suffering inflicted
on her by others and which she is carrying around as a secret. It is
tempting to equate the housekeeper's undisclosed secret with the (already
encrypted) trauma of a primary witness, and to read the narrator's abso-
lution of her as a secondary (or if we read him as a placeholder for the
priest, a tertiary) witness's inheritance of the legacy of that crypt, not least
because, once he has relieved her of her 'Bürde', the narrator concludes:
'jetzt bin ich verdammt, das war ich zuvor vielleicht noch nicht' (131).

The effects of the narrator's abortive narrative project on both content
and structure of the text as a whole appear very similar to those we have
already encountered. Thematically, we have seen that the narrator's failure
to produce a metanarrative results in the text's refusal to stick with any one
storyline and allow it to unfold. Structurally, this results in a text that
swerves off at an angle whenever it approaches traces of the 'Schrecken',
and which might carry on down a path parallel to, but never identical
with, the one that would lead the reader to it. Once again, we are
presented here with a narrator who strives for closure and to reach the
'Nichts', but is caught up in an interminable compulsion to repeat, and a
text which mirrors this by seeking to avoid closure and to stave off its own
end, as a result of which the entire work, like the narrator's life, is held in
suspension. However, while in the texts examined in earlier chapters the
periodic flashbacks disrupting the protagonists' narrative hinted at the
nature of the traumatic event encrypted in it, here the 'flashbacks' to
persecution are an artificial construct, displaced phantoms without a
message, designed only to mark the absence of primary traumatization
in an approximation of the witnessing of traumatized testimony, rather
than of the traumatic event itself. Rather than compulsively returning to
the not-quite-past, the narrator here is caught up in endless not-quite-
returns to the not-quite-past.

'SPECULATIONS ON WAYS TO TELL THAT STORY'

This has consequences for both themes and form of the texts that, while
less immediately apparent in *Tynset*, are striking in *Masante*. In *Masante*,

we are reunited with the same narrator, who has since left his cabin (after which the second text is called) in the mountains and has retreated to a small outpost by the name of Meona at the edge of a desert, where he continues to produce fragments of narrative, and continues to fail to produce plot. The difference between the two texts is encapsulated in their very titles: in *Tynset*, the text and its narrator were writing towards an (admittedly unreached and unreachable) goal. In *Masante*, insight into the impossibility of arriving at that—or any—destination has resulted in the text being named after a place that has already been left behind (and with it the idea of closure it had promised but failed to deliver) and to which the narrator cannot return.

This difference manifests itself in a very similar way at the level of both the content and the structure of the text. While *Tynset* exhibits narrative processes that are labyrinthine and meandering, but keep returning to the (already-absent) origin of trauma, in a similar, though once-removed, manner to those encountered in previous texts, the narratives that make up *Masante* do not appear to have originated anywhere or to be headed for any destination. They proliferate in a thematically and structurally rhizo-matic pattern. The many references (far more than in *Tynset*) to the 'Häscher' of the past suggest that the fundamental trauma to which the writing never refers is, or at least once was, the same as in the earlier text. However, instead of constituting a single signifier for an absent referent, the 'Häscher' scenarios in turn produce metonymic chains of further examples of potentially traumatic constellations involving violence, op-pression, and the abuse of power, which shows that there are, and continue to be, 'Häscher' on every continent, and in every day and age. For instance, the narrator mentions an 'Oberst Ethos Mbagumbwe', 'im neugegründeten Staat Diamantenküste', who laughs while executing people (290), or a 'General Porfirio Figueras', the 'Indianer-Ausrotter' (328), but also the next generation of German and Austrian 'Häscher', 'Motschmann, Kranzmeier, Fötterle, jünger als heute, vielleicht auch eine andere Generation, doch unverändert, gestiefelt und gespornt, im Einsatz, wie man es nannte, nennt und nennen wird' (216). Again, these are, of course, fictitious characters, as we can tell not least from their ironic names, and, again, the very possibility of variation this allows for suggests that these are infinitely replicating figures that will never die out, and that even if they have not caught the narrator, and others like him, yet, they are bound to do so eventually: 'früher oder später würde er ihr Opfer werden' (225). With reference to this sense of pervasive and ever-proliferating threat, Hildesheimer has said of his narrator in *Masante*: 'die Be-wußtseinsebene des Ich-Erzählers hat sich geändert, meiner Meinung nach erweitert, und nun sind diese Elemente vorhanden, die in "Tynset" ja auch schon angedeutet sind: als Element der Angst'.[27]

The same pattern operates at the level of the text's structure. In the Prangel interview, Hildesheimer commented on the form of *Tynset* as being 'ja noch verhältnismäßig streng komponiert, nach einer Art Rondoform', in which the text keeps returning to the absent 'Schrecken' on which it is founded (427). The structuring principle of *Masante*, according to Hildesheimer, is somewhat different:

> Das ist bei *Masante* anders. *Masante* ist weniger streng komponiert. Aber der Mangel an Komposition ist natürlich auch in *Masante* ganz genau berechnet. Das Buch ist vielmehr Zettelkasten als *Tynset* und macht keinen Hehl daraus. Aus dem Zettelkasten ergibt sich eine anscheinend willkürlichere Komposition, die in Wirklichkeit gar nicht willkürlich ist. Ein Thema, das sich aus anderen ergibt; das oft waltende apropos-System, wo dem Ich-Erzähler bei irgendeinem Stichwort eine ganz andere Geschichte einfällt: das hat schon ein ganz bestimmtes Schema. Denn die Geschichte [. . .] wird nachher doch immer noch einmal erwähnt, so daß eigentlich ein zunehmendes Partitursystem entsteht, das zum Schluß in einer Engführung zusammengefaßt wird. (427)

While in *Tynset* the narrative would, at least at first glance, appear to mimic the compulsive returns (or attempts to return) to the past of a traumatized mind, *Masante* is much more obviously an enactment of the witnessing of testimony (rather than of any original event). The generating of further signifiers by a signifier that, from the outset, has no referent replicates how a secondary witness—and, by extension, all of us who come after the event—can always only respond to a reproduction of it, never to the event itself, which is especially true if that event was felt to have been incompletely witnessed in the first place. Formally, *Masante*, even more than *Tynset*, and more than any of the other texts we have encountered so far, reads like a postmodern text: like an example of Abraham and Torok's 'cryptonymic transcription' as understood by Derrida, in which every referent is always already encrypted, and no interpretation is ever a final truth, but itself another text to be deciphered.[28]

---

[27] Durzak, *Gespräche über den Roman*, 292. The use of the term 'Angst' here is noteworthy, in the context of the Freudian distinction between 'Angst', 'Furcht', and 'Schrecken', as a possible indication of an attempt to shore up one's defences in anticipation of the 'Schrecken' of the past repeating itself, though the fact that we are dealing with displaced trauma suggests that the attempt is doomed to fail, that the fear is without object, and that the 'Elemente der Angst', by failing to respond to a true cause, are simply becoming part of the tapestry of general post-Holocaust existence.

[28] Jacques Derrida, 'Fors: Les Mots anglés de Nicolas Abraham et Maria Torok', in Abraham and Torok, *Cryptonymie: Le Verbier de l'homme aux loups* (Paris: Aubier Flammarion, 1976), 7–73 (62).

As texts constructed entirely around the idea of responding to prior 'text', *Tynset* and even more so *Masante* exhibit a very high degree of narratological self-awareness. Both works foreground their own narrativity, and the narratological strategies employed in them, and, in so doing, they underline that the world represented in them is a verbal construct. This idea of the world as text is especially apparent in the many models and anti-models of their own form that both works provide. In both *Tynset* and *Masante*, the narrator draws comfort from timetables and calendars, or indeed any device designed to provide objectively reliable measurements, for these sometimes enable him to succumb to the illusion of ordered, structured chronology and post hoc causality, which are as lacking in his suspended existence as they are in that of all the traumatized protagonists we have encountered so far. On one occasion, the purposeful precision of cooking instructions ('ein Pfund', 'siebzig Gramm', 'zwei gestrichene Eßlöffel voll', 'fünf Minuten', etc.) conjures up a fleeting image for him of his life as a 'Station auf der Fahrt im Zuge der Zeit', as a 'Stück handfestlicher Gegenwart zwischen hungernder Vergangenheit und satter Zukunft', and a 'saftiges Stück Wirklichkeit' (72). If he were looking to tell this sort of linear, teleological life story or history, progressing from one clearly measurable and distinct, palatably bite-sized time period to the next, the narrator would be able to resort to the kind of writing stipulated by the timetables he finds so reassuring, and about which we are told:

> jedes wahre Kursbuch bietet ausschließlich gültigen Tatsachen Raum [. . .]. Seine Symbole sind einleuchtend wie Bilder für Kinder, verstecken sich nicht, sind, im Gegenteil, Vorbedingung zum Verständnis des Buches, offenbaren sich in klaren Zeichen und strenger Ordnung: jede Ankunftzeit und jede Abfahrtzeit steht für einen tatsächlichen, nachprüfbaren Vorgang: eine Ankunft, eine Abfahrt. Und mit jeder Zeile vergeht die Zeit, wechseln Zeit und Schauplatz des Geschehens. (11)

However, in order to evoke his own existence 'außerhalb allem, in einer anderen Dimension', he needs a model for a 'non-linear' form of writing capable of subverting the appearance of causality, teleology, and stability of meaning (141). Such a model is provided, for instance, by the inside of the desert bar in *Masante*:

> Die Bar [. . .], ein Raum im Stadium der Improvisation erstarrt [. . .]. Sie vereint vieles und ist nichts ganz; voller angetragener Gegenstände, aufgegebener Ansätze [. . .]. [. . .] Erinnertes sammelt sich, bildet Schichten, wechselt Form und Bedeutung [. . .]. [. . .] Reliquien, Fetzen, Reste. (176)

The interior of this bar, as a reflection of and on his text, represents the narrator's realization that:

die Zeit des Gelingens ist vorbei, so wie auch die Zeit derer, die Gelungenes wollen. Nur noch Fragmente, Dinge, die immer im Entstehen bleiben [...] ich habe immer Fertiges, Vollkommenes haben wollen—: mein Fehler. Damit bringt man es nicht weit. (348)

As the narrator puts it, 'nur die falschen Geschichten gehen weiter und entwickeln sich nach einem Gesetz oder Regeln der Kunst' (232).

We are familiar with the refusal of metanarratives, and with a high degree of self-referentiality, from texts discussed in earlier chapters, particularly those of Aloni and Fried, with their frequent use of *mise en abyme*. In these earlier works, the self-conscious emphasis on form and narrative technique was the product of the authors' efforts to replicate the effects of the trauma of the Holocaust on formerly unquestioned assumptions regarding time, space, self, and narrative, and to convey the persistence of the past in the present by developing narrative strategies designed to defer closure and convey the impossibility of returning to the traumatic event itself. However, even if they presented the origin of the trauma as being out of bounds, the texts were able to allude to the form it had taken in its enduring effects in the present. In Hildesheimer, the past is entirely 'exorbitant', to recall Robert Eaglestone's term.[29] A return to it is impossible even through traumatic (re-)experience, since this is created artificially by the narrator and does not take him back to a personal event prior to the testimony to which he is responding.

Rather than mark, as Long has suggested, 'a constant concern with modes of turning past experience into narrative and making sense of history', Hildesheimer's texts refigure fiction-making as the primary mode of consciousness.[30] We see this very clearly in *Masante*, where the act of narration is openly demonstrated, and the workings of the narrative are laid bare, as in this extended passage, in the course of which the narrator introduces an imaginary character and presents him first as a possible victim, to show how potentially threatening it is to be singled out as being different from a crowd. However, the narrator then recasts the same figure in the role of a further 'Häscher', and this time, he himself is the one who feels threatened:

In Augsburg war es [...], da saß ich beim Mittagessen im Hotel Goldene Krone oder Schwarze Post oder Roter Adler [...]. [...]
    da wurde ein Herr Otto Lüdig ausgerufen. [...] 'Herr Otto Lüdig, bitte zum Telefon!' Wahrscheinlich sollte der Mann erfahren, daß seine Frau

---

[29] Robert Eaglestone, *The Holocaust and the Postmodern* (Oxford: Oxford University Press, 2004), 191.
[30] Long, 'Time and Narrative', 458.

erkrankt, wenn nicht gar gestorben sei; oder auch etwas beruflich Drin-
gendes [...]. [...] Ich sah mich um und sah, daß auch andere sich
umsahen, und alle schienen befriedigt zu sein, daß sie nicht Herr Lüdig
waren, und ich war es auch. Plötzlich verspürten alle wir einsamen Esser
etwas Gemeinsames: unversehens waren wir in den Genuß einer Freiheit
gelangt, die dem abwesenden Herrn Lüdig, wenn er wirklich abwesend war,
nun auf irgendeine Weise beschnitten werden sollte. Kauend und schluck-
end und spülend, mit besonderem Behagen die Spekulation auskostend,
inwieweit dieser Herr Lüdig die Beschneidung seiner Freiheit selbst verschul-
det habe oder sogar verdienen möge, malten sich alle Tafler die Umstände
aus, unter denen sie selbst zum Telefon gerufen worden wären; daß es auch
sie hätte treffen können, aber das Los hatte, der Himmel sei gelobt, einen
anderen getroffen. Herrn Otto Lüdig hatten wir alle es zu verdanken, daß
uns das Essen plötzlich besser schmeckte, manch einer bestellte sich noch
einen Korn zum Bier, es war ein Leichenschmaus, bei dem die Lebenden mit
gesteigertem Genuß über dem Toten tafelten, dessen Heil sie nichts anging.
[...] schon begann ich mich dieser willkürlichen Gemeinsamkeit zu schä-
men; sie waren nicht meine Freunde, und plötzlich tat mir dieser Lüdig leid.
    Am Abend dieses Tages saß ich in Linz beim Abendessen. [...] Wieder
wurde jemand zum Telefon gerufen, [...] ich glaube, es war wieder Herr
Lüdig. Hier denn hätte eine Geschichte begonnen, in der mir Herr Lüdig
nicht mehr leid getan hätte: die Geschichte der Angst vor Herrn Lüdig, vor
allem aber vor den Männern im Hintergrund, die ihn nach vorn schickten.
[...] Seine Spur stand also in irgendeinem für mich rätselhaften, doch an
seiner Seite genau berechneten, Verhältnis zu meinem Weg [...]. [...]
    Wie auch immer: würde Herr Lüdig, jetzt, hier, in diesem Speisesaal in
Linz, aufstehen und zum Telefon gehen, so wäre die Verbindung mit dem
mittäglichen Ruf und mit mir eindeutig hergestellt, das Stück Erinnerung
würde zur Spekulation über unmittelbar Bevorstehendes, und meiner Furcht
wäre jenes Fundament endgültig und unmißverständlich entgegenge-
wachsen, das sie lange gesucht hat—wohlgemerkt: nicht ich selbst habe es
gesucht, sondern die Furcht in mir, die sich selbständig macht; so die
Geschichte, eine Geschichte mit Möglichkeiten. [...]
    Vielleicht hieß der Mann auch gar nicht Otto Lüdig, sondern Udo
Kranzmeier oder Diethelm Fricke, ja, das wäre plausibel— (191–6)

Once again, the one constant in a proliferation of otherwise unstable
meanings and mutually contradictory narratives is this sense of a pervasive
and unrelenting menace that may surface at any moment and in any
number of guises. The ostracism of the innocent Lüdig in the first version
of the narrative is cast in a particularly ominous light by the narrator's use
of the terms 'Beschneidung' and 'beschnitten' to refer to Lüdig's freedom
or liberties. Though employed in their primary meaning of curtail, the fact
that these terms also hint at the possibility of circumcision as a criterion
for ostracism is chilling in this context. What is further revealing in this

passage is the narrator's acknowledgement that his fear is looking for a foundation. This again suggests that the 'Häscher' to which he keeps returning in his narrative are not the actual cause of his belated experiencing of what is already characterized by latency, but merely a narrative approximation of trauma. Such an approximation cannot afford closure, and there is therefore always the risk that what has so far only been a substitute 'flashback' could in fact be a premonition of future events.

With reference to the foregrounding of repetition in Hildesheimer's narratives, Long has noted: 'Psychologically speaking, storytelling is a way of protecting the self from destructive impulses and fears, but foregrounded repetition also dramatises the repeated and progressive attempt to give form to a world of chaos and destruction.'[31] Lea even speaks of Hildesheimer's writing as 'ein psychischer Reinigungs- oder Klärungsprozeß' in which the author was able to come to terms with the past through literature.[32] In fact, repetition in Hildesheimer's writing appears to have the opposite effect. Storytelling in *Tynset* and especially *Masante* is not a way of 'protecting the self from destructive impulses and fears' but a means of exposing it to them, or, at least, to something akin to them. As such, it appears not as an attempt to 'structure [. . .] the represented world' but, rather, as an effort to destructure the text-as-world, by replicating the formal disruption of witness testimony and deliberately mimicking the effects of trauma apparently without a cause.[33]

What is more, Hildesheimer also engages the reader in this fiction-making process, as a result of which he is able to extend this approximation of traumatization, the experience of trauma through a reproduction of it, to us. Long demonstrates that an important device used by Hildesheimer to draw us into the text is 'the mentioning of names and episodes which, on their first appearance, are devoid of any specifiable referent'.[34] In this process, 'narrative seeds are planted and developed at later stages of the text'.[35] According to Long, one such example of the narrator dangling a cryptic reference to a new micronarrative before us and only returning to it later in the text is the story of his discovery of a human ear, or, as we read in the text: 'ich habe übrigens einmal ein Ohr gefunden, aber das ist eine andere Geschichte—' (245). As Long has put it, 'this device encourages a desire to read further by instituting expectation that the interrupted narratives will be completed at a later stage'.[36] A further example of this in *Masante* is the micronarrative of the rat of Saloniki. When it is first mentioned, we are simply told: 'Aber die Ratten sterben aus. Zwar fallen

[31] 'Time and Narrative', 470–1. [32] Lea, *Wolfgang Hildesheimers Weg*, 268.
[33] 'Time and Narrative', 471. [34] 'Time and Narrative', 467.
[35] 'Time and Narrative', 468. [36] 'Time and Narrative', 469.

nicht alle den Häschern zum Opfer, wie die Ratte von Saloniki, aber sie
verlassen unser sinkendes Schiff' (189). As Long has said of this example:

> Since '*the* rat of Saloniki' does not form part of the body of collective
> knowledge [. . .], the use of the definite article seems to assume knowledge
> on the part of the reader which s/he could not possess. Is it an occult cultural
> reference to some mythological rat? a reference to the narrator's personal
> past? The answer is indeterminable and such referential instability produces a
> disorienting effect, for as an exemplification the phrase is redundant at this
> point in the text. But it can be recuperated in the reading process by
> integrating it within the hermeneutic code: it becomes a mystery whose
> solution will be provided if we read further.[37]

However, while it is true that the narrator returns to the micronarrative of
the ear and the rat later in the text, the first reference to them does not
retrospectively appear as 'a mystery whose solution will be provided if we
read further'.[38] Rather, the 'enigma' posed by the narrative turns out to be
a *faux* enigma that is not actually solved. When we return to the ear, all we
get as an elucidation of the ear story is:

> doch ich fand ein menschliches Ohr, es war also vor kurzem noch etwas
> geschehen—es horchte hier noch, und auch ich horchte und spähte, ob der
> Mörder oder der Ohrenabschneider oder das Opfer vielleicht erst jetzt dort
> hinten auf der Gasse oder zwischen den Stämmen verschwänden, mir schien,
> als seien da von dem Luftzug der Flucht noch ein paar Äste in Bewegung. Ich
> begann zu pfeifen. (261–2)

The mystery it posed leads only to another mystery in the text. I would
suggest that the sequence as a whole in fact reproduces for us the
experience of witnessing trauma, for we see only the belated effects of
the original event (the severed ear), but are not afforded closure: we never
find out exactly what happened. Morevoer, the trauma enacted by the
micronarrative of the ear is then revealed as a mere placeholder trauma by
the fact that, on our return to it, we realize that it was another allusion to
the omnipresent threat of the 'Häscher': the mystery of what they have
done is never solved in the text, and so the threat and fear remain. This
becomes particularly apparent on the text's return to the rat-of-Saloniki
episode. The rat, it turns out, was a dead rat the narrator saw trapped
behind a store front:

> dem Schaufenster zugekehrt liegt sie auf dem Bauch, wie zu einem letzten
> tollen Sprung geduckt, die roten Perlaugen weit geöffnet: sie spiegeln das

---

[37] 'Time and Narrative', 467; original emphasis.
[38] 'Time and Narrative', 467.

erstarrende Entsetzen vor irgendeinem Anblick, der selbst das Herz einer
Ratte stillstehen läßt. Welcher Anblick? [...] Wie lange vorbei? [...]

Vor einer halben Stunde noch hätte ich hier die Ratte lebend gesehen,
hätte ihre Geräusche gehört, das Kratzen und Wischen und Quietschen,
wenn sie an der Scheibe hinaufspringt und wieder abrutscht,
aber ich hätte auch andere Geräusche gehört: Schritte. [...]

Im Fenster rast die Ratte, als spüre sie unter dem Elend ihrer Gefan-
genschaft die anschwellende Gegenwart von etwas Entsetzlichem. Jetzt kommen sie. [...] nur zwei, Stollfuß und Globotschnik [...].

[...] jetzt sehen sie auf die Ratte,
und die Ratte, zum Sprung gegen die Scheibe geduckt, sieht die beiden
Männer, Globotschnik und Perchtl, so wie auch Lüning sie von der Innen-
seite eines Ladens gesehen hat, sieht die Blicke aus den vier Augen auf sich
gerichtet, und ihr Herz setzt aus. [...]

Die Häscher entfernen sich, [...] allmählich wird die Luft wieder rein,
doch jetzt rieche ich ihre Spur, ahne noch diesen Gleichschritt, höre ihn,
wie er in andere Straßen abbiegt, und wieder in andere, irgendwo gehen sie
noch [...] fern und nah (330–2)

All of the elements in this story turn out to be substitutes at several removes
for someone or something. The feeling of being trapped like a rat is
one with which the narrator is acutely familiar, though here it also leads
on to further trauma, through the cryptic allusion to the parallel
experience of a further 'Häscher' victim, Lüning, and the ominous
suggestion of an imminent repetition at the end of the passage. The
dangling of cryptic narrative fragments in this extract constitutes both
an enactment of the witnessing of trauma (as the witnessing of symptoms seemingly without a cause) and a miniature replica of Hildesheimer's overall narrative technique. The two are inseparable: narrative
method and the transmission of trauma converge, as the structural
enigma created by one has become indistinguishable from the other.
Trauma is created through text, is text, in Hildesheimer's writing. As he
put it with reference to *Masante*: 'Das ist für mich die Realität, wie sie
nur in der Fiktion dargestellt werden kann.'[39]

Because the cause of trauma is absent from the text, and the return to
the origin of one trauma only ever leads on to another, never to closure,
Hildesheimer's text, as a reproduction of the experience of witnessing
trauma, is a text of cryptic references but no actual secret, or of *fantômes*
but no *crypte*. 'The interest here', to hark back to Colin Davis's comment
on Derrida's understanding of text, 'is not in secrets, understood as puzzles
to be resolved, but in secrecy, now elevated to what Castricano calls "the

---

[39] Durzak, *Gespräche über den Roman*, 294.

structural enigma which inaugurates the scene of writing"'.[40] While the texts discussed in earlier chapters were crypts preserving the origin of trauma, the crypt has been opened and revealed as empty in Hildesheimer's writing. The phantoms of trauma are spilling out and have become transmittable in and as text. However, in the absence of an underlying enigma, the attempt to enact such a transmission has, in this instance, perhaps by necessity, resulted in the act of 'contemplating a story which will be nothing more than the speculations on ways to tell that story'.[41]

---

[40] Colin Davis, *Haunted Subjects: Deconstruction, Psychoanalysis and the Return of the Dead* (Basingstoke: Palgrave Macmillan, 2007), 13.

[41] Raymond Federman, *To Whom It May Concern* (Normal, IL: Fiction Collective Two, 1990), 38.

Conclusion

What Comes 'After':
The 'Postmemory' Holocaust Novel

> Dennoch ist es mir bis heute, [. . .] als fiele von dorther, von diesen
> von mir gar nicht erlebten Schrecknissen, ein Schatten auf mich,
> unter dem ich nie ganz herauskommen werde.
>
> (W. G. Sebald, *Luftkrieg und Literatur*)

With Wolfgang Hildesheimer, my analysis of German-speaking first-generation novelists of the Holocaust is both brought to a close and opened up to what has taken its place: the popular and ever-expanding field of Holocaust literature written from a position of 'postmemory'.[1] With his clear sense that, though a member of the first generation, he was a witness at a remove, responding to prior testimony, not original experience or direct implication, Hildesheimer, even more so than the other authors discussed here, might be considered to bridge the divide that separates first-hand witnesses from most of us alive today, whose relationship to the Holocaust is determined by our coming to it after the fact, and so by the absence of recollection and the mediation of knowledge. In fact, however, such a bridging function is widely, and often tacitly, attributed not to Hildesheimer, or to any other German-Jewish writer of the first generation, but to an author who, though German, was neither Jewish nor, having been born in 1944, of an age to have any first-hand recollection of the time of the war: to W. G. Sebald.

Like Hildesheimer's, Sebald's writing is infused with traumatized effects that, even when they can be attributed to a specific event, generally fail to afford access to their original cause, and in both authors, these effects shape both content and form of the texts. Both authors' responses to the trauma of the Holocaust are coloured by a sense of what Mary Cosgrove

---

[1] Marianne Hirsch, *Family Frames: Photography, Narrative, and Postmemory* (Cambridge, MA: Harvard University Press, 1997).

has called their 'absenteeism' from it, though, for obvious biographical and chronological reasons, Sebald's distance is greater.[2] However, while Hildesheimer is consistent in demonstrating the vicariousness of trauma and absence of primary traumatization in his narrators and, by extension, himself, Sebald's writing, and especially his non-fiction writing, at times seems to betray an underlying 'desire [. . .] to reclaim past trauma' and may appear as 'a form of compensation for his own lack of access', or as 'a means of constructing [. . .] a (post)memory of the event'.[3] Yet even if, or where, this was not intended by the author himself, his work is surprisingly frequently interpreted as having, if not recovered history for non-witnesses, then certainly effected a recuperation of belated and mediated witnessing. Indeed, despite his lack of any experiential knowledge of what it was like to be a German Jew during the Holocaust, Sebald's writing is not just felt by many to have facilitated access to the survivor generation but for some actually seems to have become a substitute for the more immediate, or less belated, accounts, factual or fictionalized, provided by those who did know.

Sebald is widely accorded what Scott Denham has called the 'perceived status of a kind of Holocaust writer'.[4] His has been described as 'a mode of writing which appears to give literary expression to history's unfolding catastrophes, above all to the Holocaust as a defining caesura of 20th-century history'.[5] Moreover, he is counted among a very small number of non-Jewish German authors to have attempted to approach the past by focusing on the victims', not the perpetrators', experience. Helmut Schmitz even refers to his 2001 novel *Austerlitz* as 'a unique example of a literary effort from within the perpetrator collective to remember the suffering of Hitler's victims'.[6] In the same context, Sebald is also considered 'one of the key writers of contemporary trauma fiction', who is 'clearly conversant with the discourse of trauma theory'.[7] As Katja Garloff summarizes: 'It can hardly go unnoticed that Sebald's writings resonate with the contemporary discourse of trauma in psychoanalysis, philosophy,

---

[2] 'Melancholy Competitions: W. G. Sebald Reads Günter Grass and Wolfgang Hildesheimer', *German Life and Letters*, 59 (2006), 217–32 (217).

[3] Cosgrove, 'Melancholy Competitions', 221.

[4] 'Foreword: The Sebald Phenomenon', in Denham and Mark McCulloh (eds), *W. G. Sebald: History—Memory—Trauma* (Berlin: Walter de Gruyter, 2006), 1–6 (6).

[5] Anne Fuchs and J. J. Long, 'Preface', in Fuchs and Long (eds), *W. G. Sebald and the Writing of History* (Würzburg: Königshausen & Neumann, 2007), 7–9 (7).

[6] *On Their Own Terms: The Legacy of National Socialism in Post-1990 German Fiction* (Birmingham: University of Birmingham Press, 2004), 15.

[7] Anne Whitehead, *Trauma Fiction* (Edinburgh: Edinburgh University Press, 2004), 117; J. J. Long and Anne Whitehead, 'Introduction', in Long and Whitehead (eds), *W. G. Sebald—A Critical Companion* (Edinburgh: Edinburgh University Press, 2004), 3–15 (9).

and literary criticism.'[8] Garloff expands on this with reference to *Austerlitz*, noting how the text

> lists the symptoms of posttraumatic stress disorder resulting from the experience of persecution and flight during the Third Reich, and moreover, it incorporates the logic of trauma into the very form of the text. There is the protagonist's unwillingness or inability to talk about his life and origins, which at times widens to a general crisis of language. There is the indirect historical referentiality, the way in which history enters into the text at unexpected moments, in signifiers created through mechanisms of displacement and condensation. [...] And finally there is the idea of the temporal unlocability [*sic*] of traumatic events, the disjunction between experience and understanding Freud called *Nachträglichkeit*.[9]

Hartmut Steinecke has drawn on the narrative techniques of *Austerlitz*, as detailed by Garloff, to demonstrate how close the writing of a post-Holocaust non-Jew can come to approximating that of a second-generation Jewish author: 'Hier nähern sich Darstellungsformen der Shoah eines nichtjüdischen Autors den bei den jüdischen Schriftstellern [der "zweiten Generation"] beobachteten Techniken in erstaunlichem Maße an.'[10] In his evocation of historical trauma by means both thematic and structural, Sebald's approach in fact recalls not just narrative strategies employed by second-generation Jewish Holocaust writers but also those already encountered in the first-generation texts analysed in previous chapters, with the crucial distinction that, as a 'postmemorial' author, Sebald is illustrating the theory of trauma, not mimicking the experience, or even, like Hildesheimer, witnessing the witnessing of it. Indeed, Sebald's skill in putting theory into literary practice may also account for why he feels 'familiar', and 'authentic', to a scholar of Jewish Holocaust writing such as Steinecke.

However, Steinecke's observation is unusual. Far more commonly, Sebald's writing is felt to be practically a category unto itself, without precedent or certainly equal in either German literature or (Jewish) Holocaust writing internationally, as a statement by Michael Hofmann in the same volume suggests:

---

[8] 'The Task of the Narrator: Moments of Symbolic Investiture in W. G. Sebald's *Austerlitz*', in Denham and McCulloh (eds), *W. G. Sebald: History—Memory—Trauma*, 157–69 (158).

[9] Garloff, 'The Task of the Narrator', 158.

[10] 'Die Shoah in der Literatur der "zweiten Generation"', in Norbert Otto Eke and Hartmut Steinecke (eds), *Shoah in der deutschsprachigen Literatur* (Berlin: Schmidt, 2006), 135–53 (151).

Sebald hat in seinen zwischen Dokumentation und Fiktion kunstvoll glei-
tenden epischen Texten ein Modell literarischer Erinnerung entwickelt, in
dem die Nachwirkungen der Shoah an den beschädigten Lebensläufen
mittelbarer oder unmittelbarer Opfer der Judenvernichtung herauszulesen
sind.[11]

Between the phrase 'developing a model' and the use of the ambiguous
term 'Erinnerung', encompassing a range of meanings from remembrance
to reminder but also personal recollection, there is a sense here, as in a
great deal of Sebald commentary, not only that Sebald has entered wholly
uncharted territory as an author, but also that this has allowed him to
become a more eloquent spokesperson of the Holocaust and effective
guardian of its traumatic memory than anyone else, including its intended
victims, is supposedly in a position to be.

This outlook has manifested itself in a great deal of conflation, in both
the popular and the scholarly reception of Sebald's work, between the first
and later generations, between Jews and non-Jews, between victims and
non-victims, between the author and his characters, between primary and
secondary witnessing. Not all commentators stop at noting 'Sebald's
concern for past suffering and his empathic focus on the (Jewish) victims
of history's vagaries'.[12] Some imply his empathy was such that he was
practically Jewish himself. His Wikipedia entry at the time of writing
ambiguously reads: 'His concern with the Holocaust is expressed in several
books delicately tracing his own biographical connections with Jews.'[13] In
one review, by Richard Eder in the *New York Times*, Sebald is aligned not
only with the Jewish perspective but also with Holocaust survivors:
'Sebald stands with Primo Levi as the prime speaker of the Holocaust.'[14]
While hyperbolically phrased in this instance, the notion that Sebald was
somehow personally affected, even traumatized, by the Holocaust is not
an uncommon one. Ana-Isabel Aliaga-Buchenau, for instance, draws an
analogy between Sebald's characters and his own person(a): 'The Holocaust is the shadow that hangs over each one of the fictional lives as well as
the author's own life.'[15] Andreas Huyssen speaks of a 'transgenerational

---

[11] 'Die Shoah in der Literatur der Bundesrepublik', in Eke and Steinecke (eds), *Shoah in
der deutschsprachigen Literatur*, 63–84 (79).
[12] Fuchs and Long, 'Preface', in Fuchs and Long (eds), *W. G. Sebald and the Writing of
History*, 7.
[13] <http://en.wikipedia.org/wiki/W._G._Sebald> [accessed 9 Jan. 2011].
[14] 'Austerlitz', *New York Times*, 28 Oct. 2001 <http://www.nytimes.com/2001/10/28/
books/sebald-austerlitz.html> [accessed 22 Jan. 2011].
[15] '"A Time He Could Not Bear to Say Any More About": Presence and Absence of the
Narrator in W. G. Sebald's *The Emigrants*', in Denham and McCulloh (eds), *W. G. Sebald:
History—Memory—Trauma*, 141–55 (141).

traumatization without the experience itself' in Sebald's case.[16] However, the distinction between primary and secondary traumatization where Sebald's relationship to the past is concerned is not always made this clear. Rüdiger Görner acknowledges that Sebald's would have been a traumatization after the fact in his description of the 'unerträgliche Schwere der "späten Geburt"' that saw Sebald spend the first year of his life 'in der idyllischen Allgäuer Voralpenwelt' while 'weiter östlich die Hölle der Massenvernichtung wütete'. However, Görner refers to 'delayed' or 'belated', but crucially not secondary, trauma: 'Man kann im Falle Sebalds durchaus von einer verspäteten Traumatisierung sprechen.'[17] Since trauma is by definition characterized by a delayed response, the boundaries between generations, and between personal implication and mediated witnessing, are blurred here.

What is more, they are blurred in a way that Sebald's own comments on his background if not encourage, then certainly facilitate. For instance, he describes, in a statement closely echoed in Aliaga-Buchenau's analysis, how, even though he was too young to have any genuine first-hand memories of the war, he felt that he was a product of precisely the atrocities he did not experience:

> Bei Kriegsende war ich gerade ein Jahr alt und kann also schwerlich auf realen Ereignissen beruhende Eindrücke aus jener Zeit der Zerstörung bewahrt haben. Dennoch ist es mir bis heute, wenn ich Photographien oder dokumentarische Filme aus dem Krieg sehe, als stammte ich, sozusagen, von ihm ab und als fiele von dorther, von diesen von mir gar nicht erlebten Schrecknissen, ein Schatten auf mich, unter dem ich nie ganz herauskommen werde.[18]

Sebald is unspecific about the nature of the 'Schrecknisse' he did not experience, during a time of 'Zerstörung' he did not witness. Indeed, here as elsewhere, he is unspecific in a way that suggests he is referring to more than the bombing of German cities that is, on the face of it, his topic. This initiates a not-unproblematic alignment, developed in the next passage, of the long-term effects on later generations of the destruction visited on Germany with that wreaked by it, an alignment that can be identified on a number of occasions throughout the text, even as this emphatically stresses justified retribution and distinguishes between provoked and unprovoked

---

[16] 'On Rewritings and New Beginnings: W. G. Sebald and the Literature about the *Luftkrieg*', *Zeitschrift für Literaturwissenschaft und Linguistik*, 124 (2001), 72–90 (83).

[17] 'Im Allgäu, Grafschaft Norfolk: Über W. G. Sebald in England', in Heinz Ludwig Arnold (ed.), *W. G. Sebald* (Munich: text + kritik, 2003), 23–9 (26).

[18] *Luftkrieg und Literatur: Mit einem Essay zu Alfred Andersch* (1999; 5th edn, Frankfurt a.M.: Fischer, 2005), 76–8.

destruction, and between the experience of victims and perpetrators, in the first generation. The conflation does not end there. The never-experienced 'Schrecknisse' are presented as having had a far more lasting impact on Sebald than his actual childhood did. The former, not the latter, were felt to have cast a shadow from which he would never emerge. In fact, what Sebald sees projected over his life are not the horrors themselves but impressions gleaned from representations of these horrors. Moreover, these are delayed impressions, formed not at the time of the events but only belatedly, in adulthood, through the medium of, in this instance, photography and film footage from—or even just about—the war. Yet it is noteworthy that, in acknowledging the improbability, but not the impossibility, of his having retained any impressions from that time based on actual events, Sebald in fact allows for the exceedingly remote chance that he may have done so after all, a suggestion which is made even more explicitly in the preface to the published text, where he states that even though he was among those 'die so gut wie unberührt geblieben sind von der damals im Deutschen Reich sich vollziehenden Katastrophe', that catastrophe had 'dennoch Spuren in meinem Gedächtnis hinterlassen'.[19] First-hand experience, second-hand witnessing at the time of events, and belated, mediated witnessing after the fact are all condensed here. The gap left by scenes that Sebald would not have observed at first hand, and is hardly likely to have retained even if he had seen them in mediated form at the time, is filled with images to which he was exposed belatedly, and it is these images at a double remove that make him feel descended from a first-hand experience he never had.

In the next section, Sebald expands on the ambiguity between 'actually experienced' and 'having the quality of authenticity' inherent in the term 'real', an ambiguity that is implicitly already present in the passage just cited. He now fully reverses positions to assert that images of the never-witnessed destruction are more 'real' to him than the idyllic past he did see with his own eyes:

> vor meinen Augen [verschwimmen] Bilder von Feldwegen, Flußauen und Bergwiesen mit den Bildern der Zerstörung, und es sind die letzteren, perverserweise, und nicht die ganz irreal gewordenen frühkindlichen Idyllen, die so etwas wie ein Heimatgefühl in mir heraufrufen, vielleicht weil sie die mächtigere, übergeordnete Wirklichkeit meiner ersten Lebensjahre repräsentieren. Heute weiß ich, daß damals, als ich auf dem Altan des Seefelderhauses in dem sogenannten Stubenwagen lag und hinaufblinzelte in den weißblauen Himmel, überall in Europa Rauchschwaden in der Luft hingen,

---

[19] *Luftkrieg und Literatur*, 5.

über den Rückzugsschlachten im Osten und im Westen, über den Ruinen der deutschen Städte und über den Lagern, in denen man die Ungezählten verbrannte.[20]

Again, the images of destruction which for Sebald represent—and render present—the 'Ungeheuerlichkeiten im Hintergrund meines eigenen Lebens' are not restricted to the air war.[21] Though the events themselves are not equated, the smoke that rises across Europe rises equally from the battles, the bombings, and the camps, which implies that, for those who did not experience the fires, the experience of their fallout is equivalent. As a stock image for the aftermath of destruction in general, but especially in the context of the Holocaust—and as such not just a reproduction but a clichéd copy of earlier reproductions—the already metonymical 'Rauchschwaden' are, at best, a trace of an irrecoverable origin, if not a mere trace of a trace. Yet Sebald hints at a hierarchy of realities in which the smoke of the 'Zerstörung' he did not witness is the 'übergeordnete Wirklichkeit' of the time of his youth, and that, though not his reality, it is on this reality that his sense of belonging and identity is founded.

The notion expressed in this passage of an identity founded on an absent experience, recreated through the imagination, seems to betray what Peter Morgan, in his analysis of *Die Ausgewanderten*, has termed 'a wishful sense of belonging' on the part of Sebald, a sense of belonging that, according to Morgan, sees him identifying 'as a victim and exile rather than a perpetrator'.[22] However, based on the excerpts quoted earlier, I would argue that the desire for belonging in Sebald is in fact principally aimed not at the category of the primary, but at that of the secondary or 'postmemorial' witness. Indeed, the perceived impact of the not-witnessed 'übergeordnete Wirklichkeit' on his life, notwithstanding the tenuousness of his actual connection to the events behind the images, brings to mind Marianne Hirsch's assessment that, for the 'postmemory' generation, 'memory consists not of events but of representations', and that, supposedly, these representations can be 'so powerful, so monumental, as to constitute memories in their own right'.[23] What Sebald seems to be yearning for is not exactly a broadening of the concept of victimhood, but, rather, an expansion of the category of 'postmemory', which, though commonly extended well beyond the children of survivors for whom the

---

[20] *Luftkrieg und Literatur*, 78.   [21] *Luftkrieg und Literatur*, 76.
[22] 'The Sign of Saturn: Melancholy, Homelessness and Apocalypse in W. G. Sebald's Prose Narratives', *German Life and Letters*, 58 (2005), 75–92 (83).
[23] 'Surviving Images: Holocaust Photographs and the Work of Postmemory', in Barbie Zelizer (ed.), *Visual Culture and the Holocaust* (London: Athlone, 2001), 214–46 (218, 219).

term was initially coined, has by tacit agreement not included the descendants, in the broadest sense, of the perpetrators.

The same choosing of sides that informs Sebald's sense of biographical belonging is revealed in his view of his literary lineage. Here, too, he apparently positions himself on the side of the victims of the past, as a 'postmemorial' literary heir to Jewish writers, rather than as a descendant of the German post-war canon. What is more, Sebald seems to understand his 'postmemorial' role in the sense outlined by Hirsch, as being characterized not merely by its 'reliance on images, stories, and documents passed down from one generation to the next', but by the ability, through 'imaginative investment and creation', to witness, and even render productive, the traumatic traces transmitted from the first generation in a way the first generation itself could not.[24]

The most concrete examples of Sebald's literary self-understanding are provided by his treatment of two of the very authors discussed in this book: Wolfgang Hildesheimer and H. G. Adler. The former features in a scholarly essay in which Sebald compares and contrasts constructs of melancholy as a response to Germany's recent past in two texts published in the 1960s by members of the first generation: Hildesheimer's *Tynset* and Günter Grass's *Aus dem Tagebuch einer Schnecke*.[25] In this 'competition measuring the standard of authentic sadness', Hildesheimer 'wins hands down'.[26] Grass's 'Exkurs in die Trauer', according to Sebald, smacks of a 'historische[...] Pflichtübung', whereas Hildesheimer's *Tynset* seems to have emerged 'aus dem Zentrum der Trauer selber'.[27] However, as Mary Cosgrove has persuasively demonstrated, 'the absence of any academically sustainable argument to justify this victory is striking', and what ultimately carries far more weight than the 'highly valorized, at times questionable' literary criteria cited by Sebald are the non-literary ones of biographical background and generational and ethnic affiliation, that operate 'in a far more clandestine manner' in his evaluation.[28] These see him siding against Grass for reasons that would appear to include 'the troubled relationship to German identity as a member, or descendant, of the perpetrator collective', and the 'legacy of guilt and responsibility' bequeathed by the first German post-war generation to the second.[29] On the other hand, similarly non-literary criteria see him aligning himself

---

24 'Surviving Images', 222; *Family Frames*, 22.
25 'Konstruktionen der Trauer: Günter Grass und Wolfgang Hildesheimer', in Sebald, *Campo Santo* (2003; Frankfurt a.M.: Fischer, 2006), 101–27.
26 Cosgrove, 'Melancholy Competitions', 230.
27 'Konstruktionen der Trauer', 119.
28 Cosgrove, 'Melancholy Competitions', 230, 221, 227.
29 Cosgrove, 'Melancholy Competitions', 230, 231.

with Hildesheimer, whom he regards as a fellow exile and 'absenteeist', but also a potential victim and, thanks to Hildesheimer's belated and mediated witnessing of Holocaust trauma, one of the earliest representatives of 'postmemory'. Once all these unspoken factors are taken into consideration, Sebald's estimation of Hildesheimer's narrative mode of 'terminal melancholy', which precludes the possibility of the traumatic past being worked through and overcome, clearly says far less about Grass's oeuvre and outlook than it does about Sebald's own.[30] In praising in Hildesheimer's work an approach he has also adopted for himself, Sebald is not just validating his own craft and displaying 'a determined and exclusive affective commitment to the victims of history'; he is effectively positioning himself as an elective heir to the victim collective and assuming the (literary) legacy of Holocaust trauma.[31]

While he identifies with Hildesheimer on a 'postmemorial' level, Sebald's treatment of H. G. Adler is more complex. One thing Sebald particularly takes Günter Grass to task over in his 'Konstruktionen der Trauer' essay is the use Grass makes of documentary material regarding the fate of the Danzig Jews, material drawn from research supplied by the Jewish historian Erwin Lichtenstein. Sebald is critical of how Grass has come by this research, as it were, 'gratis' and uses it to lend an air of authenticity to his writing.[32] Despite the 'eindrucksvollen realen Details' provided, Sebald therefore suggests that Grass's borrowed representation 'still constitutes a repression and a personal evasion of the past'.[33] He concludes that 'vom realen Schicksal der verfolgten Juden wissen deutsche Literaten nach wie vor selber sehr wenig'.[34] What adds an interesting layer to Sebald's verdict is the fact that he himself, of course, draws extensively on 'real details' furnished by someone else's research in his 2001 novel *Austerlitz*, in which he inserts documentary and literary material borrowed from, among a large number of other sources, H. G. Adler.

Austerlitz, which Helmut Schmitz has summarized as 'a complex reflection on the continuity of historical damage among the victims of National Socialism, the destruction and painful recovery of memory, and a narrative critique of European enlightenment and civilization through the history of European architecture', 'tells the story' of one Jacques Austerlitz, an architectural historian, who belatedly learns that in 1939, at the age of 4, he came to Britain on a 'Kindertransport', and that his real

---

[30] Cosgrove, 'Melancholy Competitions', 217.
[31] Cosgrove, 'Melancholy Competitions', 218.
[32] 'Konstruktionen der Trauer', 111.
[33] 'Konstruktionen der Trauer', 111; Cosgrove, 'Melancholy Competitions', 229.
[34] 'Konstruktionen der Trauer', 111.

mother and father were Czech Jews who, respectively, were deported to Theresienstadt and disappeared without a trace in Paris.[35] More precisely, the novel presents an unnamed non-Jewish German narrator's account of the eponymous central character's account of his efforts to piece together scattered and fragmentary 'Erinnerungen, hinter denen und in denen sich viel weiter noch zurückreichende Dinge verbargen, immer das eine im andern verschachtelt'.[36] In this narrative history of a narrative history of an (at best) incompletely narratable history, memories, as well as unremembered traces of the past, filter through to the reader from a position of multiple remove and are mediated through plural perspectives. Indeed, the term 'Verschachtelung' is key not only to the contents of the incomplete and lacunary tales that make up the novel, but also to the narrative technique applied to these, a technique which, as in the pre-trauma-theory trauma writing of the first generation discussed in previous chapters, becomes as much the theme of the work as its form.

A further factor contributing to the 'Verschachtelung' in and of the text is that *Austerlitz*, like Sebald's earlier fiction, is characterized 'by a dense web of literary and cultural allusions that situate the work in a history of loss and destruction'.[37] H. G. Adler is by no means the only Jewish author to figure in this intertextual network, which also includes, among others, Jean Améry, Walter Benjamin, Saul Friedlander, Franz Kafka, Primo Levi, and Dan Jacobson. However, Adler is the most extensively cited, with sections of primarily his *Theresienstadt* study appearing in Sebald's novel in the form of, variously, reproduction, quotation, reference, and allusion.[38] Why such an extensive intertextual engagement with this one of all the possible (first-generation) Holocaust authors Sebald might have chosen?

Within the text, the detailed referencing of Adler is explained by the fact that Austerlitz turns to his *Theresienstadt* study to help him picture the ghetto and visualize his mother there, after he has previously tried, and failed, to get a sense of the past on site by visiting the Theresienstadt Ghetto Museum and documentation centre in Terezín. However, Austerlitz

---

[35] Schmitz, *On Their Own Terms*, 293.

[36] W. G. Sebald, *Austerlitz* (2001; 4th edn, Frankfurt a.M.: Fischer, 2008), 200. Further references to this edition will be included in parentheses in the text.

[37] Schmitz, *On Their Own Terms*, 293.

[38] See esp. the section on pp. 339–49, consisting of a single sentence, which contains multiple (near-)literal borrowings, including the reproduction of an actual page from Adler's documentary text. For a comprehensive analysis of Sebald's intertextual treatment of Adler's *Theresienstadt* study, see Marcel Atze, 'W. G. Sebald und H. G. Adler: Eine Begegnung in Texten', in Ruth Vogel-Klein (ed.), *W. G. Sebald: Mémoire, Transferts, Images/Erinnerung, Übertragungen, Bilder* (Strasbourg: Université Marc Bloch, 2005) (= *Recherches germaniques* 2), 87–97, which furthermore shows how *Austerlitz* is also apparently informed by other Adler texts, including *Eine Reise*.

finds that, despite poring 'Zeile für Zeile', and even 'silbenweise', over the wealth of authentic detail provided by Adler, he still cannot imagine 'wie es in Wirklichkeit war' (338, 350):

> trotz des von Adler mit solcher Sorgfalt niedergelegten und von mir bis in die letzten Anmerkungen studierten Berichts über die dortigen Verhältnisse, ist es mir unmöglich gewesen, mich in das Ghetto zurückzuversetzen und mir vorzustellen, daß Agáta, meine Mutter, damals gewesen sein soll an diesem Ort. (349–50)

Adler's 'real details' achieve more than the visit to Terezín did in that reading his text at least affords Austerlitz 'Einblicke [...] in das, was ich mir bei meinem Besuch in der Festungsstadt [...] nicht hatte vorstellen können', but they are not enough to make the past feel real to him, and he reproaches himself for not having gone to visit Adler before his death 'um mit ihm zu reden über diesen extraterritorialen Ort' (338, 339).

The intertextual incorporation of Adler's documentary text has been described as a device by which Sebald is able to lend his own text the semblance of authenticity ('scheinbare Authentizität').[39] Beyond this, Marcel Atze has praised the 'wertvolle Arbeit am kollektiven Gedächtnis' Sebald supposedly undertakes by reproducing the 'Informationen des Prätextes' yet presenting them 'auf neue Weise' so as to reach 'einen völlig anderen und wesentlich größeren Adressatenkreis'.[40] If these are indeed the uses to which Sebald meant to put the source material on which he draws, then the 'real details' in *Austerlitz* would seem to fulfil a very similar function to the one Sebald critically identifies in Grass. However, Austerlitz's comments on *Theresienstadt* clearly suggest otherwise. If even as comprehensive a study as Adler's 'nahezu achthundert enggedruckte Seiten umfassende[s] Werk', which describes the 'Ghettosystem' 'bis in das letzte Detail und in seiner ganzen Tatsächlichkeit', is unable to afford the kind of access to the past that Austerlitz is seeking, then what we are presented with here is not intertextuality as homage, or to fill an information gap, and certainly not to lend authenticity and invoke authority—at least not ostensibly, even though the fact that it is easily read this way may be a not-unwelcome side-effect, allowing Sebald, bluntly put, to have his cake and eat it (335, 339). Rather, Sebald's attempt to draw Adler into an intertextual dialogue suggests a view of their relationship as one of equals

---

[39] Hans-Christoph Graf v. Nayhauss, 'Adler und Sebald, Lichtenstein und Grass: Vom Umgang mit Dokumentationen bei der literarischen Produktion', in Gerhard Fischer (ed.), *W. G. Sebald: Schreiben ex patria/Expatriate Writing* (Amsterdam: Rodopi, 2009), 447–57 (454).

[40] '"Wie Adler berichtet": Das Werk H. G. Adlers als Gedächtnisspeicher für die Literatur', in Arnold (ed.), *W. G. Sebald*, 17–30 (27).

and perhaps even hints at a quasi-inversion of the relationship of primary to secondary witness. Rather than defer to the authority of the primary witness, Sebald seems to be calling into question—or calling for a complement or corrective to—the approach adopted to representing the past in *Theresienstadt*. As Lynn Wolff has pointed out, Sebald's works in general 'demonstrate a fundamental skepticism toward totality, upon which the explanatory function of traditional historiography is based, and they also challenge the hierarchy of significance and authority asserted in historical texts'.[41] This is evidently also true for *Austerlitz*, which 'reiterates Sebald's challenge to the nineteenth-century ideal of historiography to represent the past "as it was"'.[42] Both thematically and formally, *Austerlitz*'s narrative approach implicitly presents itself as an antithesis to the methodology required for producing a text with the kind of documentary ambition Sebald seems to attribute to Adler's *Theresienstadt* study.[43]

The complement and corrective to what Sebald seems to view as Adler's striving for a comprehensive metanarrative is provided by the open-ended narrative interplay between Austerlitz and his narrator. The unfinished product that emerges from their efforts is often regarded as the result of a therapeutic relationship, with the narrator operating as the therapist to Austerlitz's patient, and their narrative act is consequently considered as one of what Schmitz has called 'proxy-narration', in which the first-person narrator is a figure of authority 'to and through whom' Austerlitz tells his story.[44] In this view, 'Austerlitz needs a narrator who listens to him, records his stories, and puts his digression-filled narration into a cogent narrative'.[45] In fact, although the narrator is presented as 'the condition of the story', he neither controls the chance encounters between him and Austerlitz, encounters which allow Austerlitz's fragmentary recollections to surface, nor does he master these 'Erinnerungsfetzen' by turning them

---

[41] 'H. G. Adler and W. G. Sebald: From History and Literature to Literature as Historiography', *Monatshefte*, 103 (2011), 257–75 (p. 264).

[42] Wolff, 'H. G. Adler and W.G. Sebald', 265.

[43] Though see e.g. François Ottman's 'H. G. Adlers *Theresienstadt 1941–1945: Das Antlitz einer Zwangsgemeinschaft*: Ein gattungsübergreifendes Manifest für den Menschen', in Ruth Vogel-Klein (ed.), *Die ersten Stimmen: Deutschsprachige Texte zur Shoah 1945–1963/Les Premières Voix: Écrits sur la Shoah en langue allemande 1945–1963* (Würzburg: Königshausen & Neumann, 2010), 113–26, for evidence of how Adler's approach is far more complex than a simplistic reading of his study as a purely referential attempt to document the past 'as it was' would suggest.

[44] Schmitz, *On Their Own Terms*, 292.

[45] Karin Bauer, 'The Dystopian Entwinement of Histories and Identities in W. G. Sebald's *Austerlitz*', in Denham and McCulloh (eds), *W. G. Sebald: History—Memory—Trauma*, 233–50 (238).

into anything resembling the 'cogent narrative' of a talking cure (199).[46] As Katja Garloff has pointed out: 'if the novel invokes [...] the psychoanalytic idea of therapeutic narration, it also blurs the clear distinction between patient and therapist'.[47] This is underlined by the fact that not only Austerlitz but also the narrator is shown as being traumatized by the past, albeit one as a descendant of victims and the other as the son of a perpetrator. It receives further reinforcement from the way in which their accidental encounters, rather than comprise a process of acting out and working through, seem to 'mime the disjunctive rhythm in which traumatic memories come to the fore', as 'equivalents of the flashbacks and other manifestations of *mémoire involontaire* through which Austerlitz gains access to his repressed memories'.[48] As such, Sebald's transposition of 'the logic of trauma from intra-psychic processes to the interaction between narrator and protagonist' suggests that what he was interested in exploring was less the idea of a therapeutic narrative relationship than, at least in the realm of literature, the possibility of traumatic experience being transmitted between, and shared by, a primary (non-)witness and his secondary witness.[49]

At a formal level, this approach generates a necessarily unconcluded and inconclusive text, and a further example of the attempt to 'dramatize the ways that literary testimony emerges in spite of—or rather because of—the impossibility of fully recovering the traumatic past'.[50] Again, the absence of closure is also extended beyond the final page, by means of a further intertextual connection, this time to Dan Jacobson's *Heshel's Kingdom* (1998), another 'postmemorial' text that, according to Sebald's narrator, reflects (on) the necessity of tracing the 'Zeichen der Vernichtung' in the present in view of the impossibility of accessing the 'untergegangene Vorzeit' of the past (420). What is more, Sebald does not just include references to Jacobson's text in his own; he implies a two-way intertextual link by inserting himself into, or, more precisely, suggesting his presence in, a passage cited from *Heshel's Kingdom* at the end of *Austerlitz*. This last section of Sebald's novel shows the narrator revisiting Breendonk, a Belgian fortification of the First World War that was turned into a National Socialist prison camp in the Second, and spending a whole afternoon until dusk there reading the Jacobson text. Paralleling the narrator's own circumstances, the extract from *Heshel's Kingdom* referred

---

[46] Garloff, 'The Task of the Narrator', 166.
[47] Garloff, 'The Task of the Narrator', 162.
[48] Garloff, 'The Task of the Narrator', 166, 161.
[49] Garloff, 'The Task of the Narrator', 166.
[50] Garloff, 'The Task of the Narrator', 160.

to in this section deals with Jacobson's visit to Fort IX in Kaunas, Lithuania, an equally defunct fortress from the late nineteenth century that was converted into a concentration camp during the National Socialist occupation. Sebald's narrator recounts Jacobson's account of finding a number of last messages scratched into the fortification walls by former Jewish prisoners, including one that consists simply of a name and date: 'Max Stern, Paris, 18.5.44' (421). Yet Maximilian is also the name of Austerlitz's father, whose last-known whereabouts were in Paris, and Max is the name Sebald went by in England, and Sebald's date of birth is 18 May 1944. In a 'potentially problematic gesture of identification', as Garloff argues: 'The camp seems to become here the birthplace of the author, or at least the site of an uncanny proximity between him and his narrative subjects, thereby investing him with a new kind of authority to speak for the victims of the Holocaust.'[51] The alignment between 'Max' Sebald and Austerlitz's father again implies the possibility of a historical and literary legacy of trauma being transmitted across generational and cultural-confessional boundaries. It may even hint at a potential inversion of the relationship between first and second generation, and thus between the primary and the secondary witness, with the former handing over to the latter—or the latter taking over from the former.

Between its extensive use of intertextuality and its focus on the processes of, and possibilities inherent in, traumatic transmission, *Austerlitz* appears as a text principally preoccupied with questions of legacy and legitimacy. As such, it seems to be informed by a similar 'wishful sense of belonging' on the part of Sebald as the non-fiction essays discussed earlier: by a desire to be a 'postmemorial' witness, invested enough to believe he can feel the pain of the past almost as if it were his own, but belated enough to feel better equipped to preserve, or reproduce, its traces in the present than a primary witness.[52] By implicitly contrasting himself with Adler, or aligning himself with Jacobson, Sebald opens up intertextual lines of communication with the Jewish survivor and the Jewish 'postmemory' generation respectively, and creates a literary lineage into which to place himself and a legacy for him to assume. The moments of what Garloff, after Eric Santner, calls 'symbolic investiture', moments that 'confer upon the narrator—and the author—the authority to tell Austerlitz's story', are numerous in *Austerlitz*.[53] Of course, these moments are entirely of Sebald's own making. It is not strictly speaking true that the 'task of writing and preservation *falls* upon the German narrator'; it is

---

[51] Garloff, 'The Task of the Narrator', 168.   [52] Morgan, 'The Sign of Saturn', 83.
[53] Garloff, 'The Task of the Narrator', 166–7.

bestowed on him in Sebald's text.[54] Not only is the non-Jewish narrator chosen by Austerlitz to be a witness to his fragmentary testimony and to narrativize it (68–9), but this choice is repeatedly reinforced by symbolic gestures such as Austerlitz presenting the narrator with the keys to his house, where he may 'Quartier aufschlagen' whenever he wishes (414), or the fact that the narrator receives Jacobson's book—the book which is seen to legitimize him—as a present from Austerlitz (418). The choice is finally sanctioned when the narrator returns to Breendonk at the end of the novel. On the occasion of his first visit, the narrator found that being on site, and studying descriptions and maps designed to detail everything exactly 'as it was', not only failed to shed light on the 'Dunkel' of the past but actually made it more impenetrable (38–9). Returning to Breendonk, he is able to reconcile himself with the 'Dunkel', and even render it productive, by focusing not on his surroundings but on the work of 'postmemory' he is reading. This text, it is suggested, in acknowledging that the past of the author's family and people is an 'Abgrund, in den kein Lichtstrahl hinabreicht', and accepting that all that therefore remains are the 'Zeichen der Vernichtung', succeeds precisely by demonstrating its own failure (420). By extension and association, the same claim can, of course, be made for *Austerlitz* itself. The 'postmemorial' texts appear as better receptacles for the 'Schmerzensspuren' of the past than the historiographical text by one of its survivors (24).

In the final analysis, it is difficult to say where *Austerlitz* falls on a scale assessing the degree and legitimacy of his (literary) identification with, and possible appropriation of, a (hi)story that is not his. Is Helmut Schmitz right to call Sebald's work 'a concentrated effort to speak in the name of Hitler's victims without appropriating their story'?[55] Or is *Austerlitz* 'a novel that contests the possibility of ever fully understanding the victims', but nonetheless arrogates to itself 'the right to tell another's story', on the assumption that it is better equipped to do so than they are?[56] Garloff reminds us that we must distinguish between Sebald and his narrators and proposes that the appropriation that does take place in *Austerlitz* never extends beyond the realm of fiction because of Sebald's transparency about what she calls the 'encrypted wish to be able to speak for [the victims]': 'By narrating Austerlitz's story and simultaneously exploring the narrator's investment in his story, Sebald reestablishes the grounds of narrative legitimacy.'[57]

---

[54] Bauer, 'The Dystopian Entwinement of Histories and Identities', 239; my emphasis.
[55] Schmitz, *On Their Own Terms*, 291.
[56] Garloff, 'The Task of the Narrator', 169, 166.
[57] Garloff, 'The Task of the Narrator', 169, 158.

While some of Sebald's non-narrative texts suggest that this may be an overly generous interpretation, even an entirely ungenerous one could not fail to see that the 'underlying quest for legitimacy' that informs *Austerlitz* is in fact at least as much a characteristic of Sebald's reception as it is of his writing.[58] Indeed, it is not at all my intention here to detract from Sebald's qualities as an author, or to examine in greater detail whether he succeeded in recovering history from a 'postmemorial' position, or failed to do so, or succeeded by demonstrating failure, 'through a fictional representation of the inaccessibility of its occurrence'.[59] Ultimately, the problem lies not with Sebald's writing or his view of history, or even his self-perception, but with our tendency to take his 'subjectively valid position on the past' at face value and treat it 'not always as an intriguing phenomenon within a specific context [...], but as a context-creating discourse in itself'.[60] This tendency, which has seen Sebald treated not just as the rightful heir to the Holocaust in (German) literature, but, at times, practically as a witness in his own right, is perhaps rooted in some broader cultural and critical 'wishful sense of belonging'. Sebald's particular appeal, then, would appear to consist in the fact that he seems to be offering us if not access through the imagination, then at least a rehabilitation of our belatedness.

Time and again, there is evidence in the critical reception of 'postmemorial' authors in general, and of Sebald in particular, of the extent to which this has rendered us blind to the possibility of Holocaust literature before 'postmemory'. In Marcel Atze's assessment of Sebald's intertextual treatment of Adler, for instance, we, once again, see the inclination to treat a member of the first generation as a survivor and witness, not an author in his own right. Atze concludes his article with a comment on what he sees as Adler's 'Leistung', namely the creation of a repository of memory, a 'Gedächtnisspeicher' of details, in his texts, details of which Atze says: 'Es sind [...] jene Einzelheiten, die nur der Überlebende kennen konnte, die seine Erinnerung so einzigartig machen. Hätte er nicht überlebt, gäbe es Bücher wie die seinen nicht und auch nicht deren literarische Adaptationen.'[61] Though entirely well intentioned, such a statement omits that Adler himself had already produced such 'literarische Adaptationen' of his 'Erinnerung', and that these adaptations, moreover, also inform *Austerlitz*, albeit, unlike the documentary material, notably without explicit acknowledgement. In considering Adler's work as a simple 'Gedächtnisspeicher

[58] Garloff, 'The Task of the Narrator', 167.
[59] Ann Parry, 'Idioms for the Unrepresentable: Postwar Fiction and the Shoah', in Andrew Leak and George Paizis (eds), *The Holocaust and the Text: Speaking the Unspeakable* (Basingstoke: Macmillan, 2000), 109–24 (120).
[60] Cosgrove, 'Melancholy Competitions', 232.   [61] Atze, 'Wie Adler berichtet', 29.

für die Literatur', Atze implies that Adler's main achievement was to have survived and therefore be in a position to pass on the 'Einzelheiten' of his 'Erinnerung' to someone—in this instance Sebald—who would be able to adapt them to literature for the rest of us who did not witness what Adler did.

Other assessments of Sebald's work similarly regard him both as somehow part of a Jewish tradition of Holocaust writing and as a 'postmemorial' advancement on the first generation's response to the past. Katharina Hall, for example, has written intriguingly on the 'clear affinities' between Sebald's *Die Ausgewanderten* (1992) and the *Yizkor* or memorial books written by Jewish Holocaust survivors to commemorate their community's life and culture before the Holocaust and its destruction by National Socialism.[62] Hall states that, in its efforts 'to emphasise the importance of remembrance in the context of Jewish-German experiences of the Holocaust', and 'to rescue fragments of the Jewish history of the Holocaust', *Die Ausgewanderten* 'take[s] up the tradition of the *Yizkor* books'.[63] At the same time, the text 'moves beyond the parameters of the *Yizkor* format' in that the characters to whom its four narratives are devoted either 'cannot remember or have no desire to remember traumatic events, and if they do, are unwilling or unable to articulate those memories', which 'leaves it up to' the second-generation, non-Jewish narrator—whom Hall identifies with Sebald and who 'like the editor of the *Yizkor* books' functions as 'a mediator of the past'—'to assert the importance of remembering to counter the silences of the post-war era'.[64] In the final analysis, *Die Ausgewanderten* is described as remaining 'true' to the 'aims' of the *Yizkor* books while 'simultaneously exploring the Jewish and German legacy of the Holocaust in a radical and highly effective new way'.[65]

On balance, the notion of a 'postmemorial' improvement on past approaches to Holocaust literature always wins out over the exploration of literary continuities in Sebald criticism. As if literature, in the narrow sense of the term, of the Holocaust was simply not being written between the survivors' memoirs and their literary adaptations from a 'postmemory' perspective, Stefan Gunther, citing Andreas Huyssen, states with reference to *Die Ausgewanderten*:

---

[62] 'Jewish Memory in Exile: The Relation of W. G. Sebald's *Die Ausgewanderten* to the Tradition of the *Yizkor* Books', in Pól O'Dochartaigh (ed.), *Jews in German Literature since 1945: German-Jewish Literature?* (= *German Monitor* 53) (Amsterdam: Rodopi, 2000), 153–64 (153).
[63] Hall, 'Jewish Memory in Exile', 160, 161, 163.
[64] Hall, 'Jewish Memory in Exile', 157, 159, 160, 155–6, 160.
[65] Hall, 'Jewish Memory in Exile', 163.

I would like to argue that this book is emblematic of a shift from 'An obsessive focus on the unspeakable and unrepresentable, as it was compellingly articulated by Elie Wiesel or George Steiner [...] and as it informs the ethical philosophy of Jean-François Lyotard', toward a cautious expression of the need for uttering words that are appropriate, respectful, and, at the same time, mindful of the complex workings of memory and the process of remembering.[66]

As this book has shown, Sebald was not the first author to 'break through the unrepresentability of the Shoah' at the same time as providing 'a continuing testimony to its unsayability' 'through exploring the dynamics of trauma'.[67] However, the belief that he was has proven hard to shake, precisely because of the way in which he seems to speak to our own sense of 'coming after', while at the same time intimating the possibility of our nonetheless forming a connection to the past through this very afterwardsness. Arthur Williams inadvertently sums up this simultaneous sense of belatedness and desire for implication in the reception of Sebald—and in the age of 'postmemory' more generally—when he says: 'Sebald's project is in no sense a final reckoning with a past now behind us, it is rather about how we enter into responsible ownership of it.'[68] In light of this, it would seem that, for us, the challenge of 'responsible ownership' might consist precisely in not attempting to claim, belatedly, the original experience that remained deliberately unclaimed when it first took place: in the generation that lived through it, and wrote literature about it, and proleptically captured a very contemporary sense of living in a more generally post-traumatic age, before anyone was looking.

[66] 'The Holocaust as the Still Point of the World in W. G. Sebald's *The Emigrants*', in Denham and McCulloh (eds), *W. G. Sebald: History—Memory—Trauma*, 279–90 (290).
[67] Parry, 'Idioms for the Unrepresentable', 120.
[68] '"Das korsakowsche Syndrom": Remembrance and Responsibility in W. G. Sebald', in Helmut Schmitz (ed.), *German Culture and the Uncomfortable Past: Representations of National Socialism in Contemporary Germanic Literature* (Aldershot: Ashgate, 2001), 65–86 (72).

Bibliography

PRIMARY SOURCES

Adler, H. G., *Theresienstadt 1941–1945: Das Antlitz einer Zwangsgemeinschaft (Geschichte, Soziologie, Psychologie)* (Tübingen: Mohr, 1955; rev. edn, 1960).

Adler, H. G., *Die verheimlichte Wahrheit: Theresienstädter Dokumente* (Tübingen: Mohr, 1958).

Adler, H. G., *Der Kampf gegen die 'Endlösung der Judenfrage'* (Bonn: Bundeszentrale für Heimatdienst, 1958).

Adler, H. G., *Die Juden in Deutschland: Von der Aufklärung bis zum Nationalsozialismus* (Munich: Kösel, 1960).

Adler, H. G., *Eine Reise: Erzählung* (Bonn: Bibliotheca christiana, 1962).

Adler, H. G., *Panorama: Roman in zehn Bildern* (Olten: Walter, 1968).

Adler, H. G., *Der verwaltete Mensch: Studien zur Deportation der Juden aus Deutschland* (Tübingen: Mohr, 1974).

Adler, H. G., 'Nachruf bei Lebzeiten', in K. H. Kramberg (ed.), *Vorletzte Worte: Schriftsteller schreiben ihren eigenen Nachruf* (Frankfurt a.M.: Goldmann, 1985), 11–20.

Adler, H. G., *Die unsichtbare Wand* (Vienna: Zsolnay, 1989).

Adler, H. G., *Der Wahrheit verpflichtet: Interviews, Gedichte, Essays*, ed. Jeremy Adler (Gerlingen: Bleicher, 1998).

Aloni, Jenny, *Der Wartesaal* (Freiburg i.Br.: Herder, 1969).

Aloni, Jenny, *Ausgewählte Werke 1939–1986*, ed. Friedrich Kienecker and Hartmut Steinecke (Paderborn: Schöningh, 1987).

Aloni, Jenny, *Gesammelte Werke in Einzelausgaben*, ed. Friedrich Kienecker and Hartmut Steinecke, 10 vols (Paderborn: Schöningh, 1990–7), v. *Der Wartesaal* (1992); viii. *Korridore oder das Gebäude mit der weißen Maus* (1996).

Aloni, Jenny, *'Ich muss mir diese Zeit von der Seele schreiben . . .': Die Tagebücher 1935–1993: Deutschland—Palästina—Israel*, ed. Hartmut Steinecke et al. (Paderborn: Schöningh, 2006).

Augustin, Elisabeth, *De uitgestootene* (Amsterdam: Van Kampen, 1935).

Augustin, Elisabeth, *Volk zonder jeugd* (Amsterdam: Van Kampen, 1935).

Augustin, Elisabeth, *Moord en doodslag in Wolhynië* (Rotterdam: Nijgh & Van Ditmar, 1936).

Augustin, Elisabeth, *Mirjam* (Rotterdam: Brusse, 1938).

Augustin, Elisabeth, *Labyrint* (Amsterdam: Holland, 1955).

Augustin, Elisabeth, 'Eine Grenzüberschreitung und kein Heimweh', in Würzner (ed.), *Zur deutschen Exilliteratur in den Niederlanden 1933–1940*, 33–43.

Augustin, Elisabeth, *The Elisabeth Augustin Reader*, ed. Robert Lyng (Krimpen aan den Yssel: Proza, 1978).

Augustin, Elisabeth, *meine sprache, deine sprache: zum gedenken Else Lasker-Schüler* (Gelsenkirchen: Xylos, 1985).

Augustin, Elisabeth, *Auswege* (Mannheim: Persona, 1988).

Augustin, Elisabeth, *Het patroon: Herinneringen* (Amsterdam: Arbeiderspers, 1990).

Fried, Erich, *Ein Soldat und ein Mädchen* (Düsseldorf: Claassen, 1960; 2nd edn, 1982).

Fried, Erich, *Mitunter sogar Lachen: Erinnerungen* (Berlin: Wagenbach, 1986; rev. edn, 1992).

Fried, Erich, *Gesammelte Werke*, ed. Volker Kaukoreit and Klaus Wagenbach, 4 vols (Berlin: Wagenbach, 1993).

Fried, Erich, *Die Muse hat Kanten: Aufsätze und Reden zur Literatur*, ed. Volker Kaukoreit (Berlin: Wagenbach, 1995).

Hildesheimer, Wolfgang, *Tynset* (Frankfurt a.M.: Suhrkamp, 1965).

Hildesheimer, Wolfgang, *Masante* (Frankfurt a.M.: Suhrkamp, 1973).

Hildesheimer, Wolfgang, *Gesammelte Werke*, ed. Christiaan Lucas Hart Nibbrig and Volker Jehle, 7 vols (Frankfurt a.M.: Suhrkamp, 1991).

Sebald, W. G., *Die Ausgewanderten: Vier lange Erzählungen* (1992; 12th edn, Frankfurt a.M.: Fischer, 2008).

Sebald, W. G., *Luftkrieg und Literatur: Mit einem Essay zu Alfred Andersch* (1999; 5th edn, Frankfurt a.M.: Fischer, 2005).

Sebald, W. G., *Austerlitz* (2001; 4th edn, Frankfurt a.M.: Fischer, 2008).

Sebald, W. G., *Campo Santo* (2003; Frankfurt a.M.: Fischer, 2006).

OTHER WORKS

Aichinger, Ilse, *Die größere Hoffnung* (Amsterdam: Bermann-Fischer, 1948).

Améry, Jean, *Lefeu oder der Abbruch* (Stuttgart: Klett, 1974).

Anissimov, Myriam, *Comment va Rachel?* (Paris: Denoël, 1973).

Biller, Maxim, *Wenn ich einmal reich und tot bin* (Cologne: Kiepenheuer & Witsch, 1990).

Borges, Jorge Luis, *Labyrinths: Selected Stories and Other Writings*, ed. Donald A. Yates and James E. Irby, trans. Yates, Irby, et al. (London: Penguin, 2000).

Federman, Raymond, *To Whom It May Concern* (Normal, IL: Fiction Collective Two, 1990).

Federman, Raymond, *Double or Nothing: A Real Fictitious Discourse* (Normal, IL: Fiction Collective Two, 1992).

Goethe, Johann Wolfgang von, *Werke: Hamburger Ausgabe*, ed. Erich Trunz, 11th edn, 14 vols (Munich: Beck, 1981).

Kafka, Franz, *Sämtliche Erzählungen*, ed. Paul Raabe (Frankfurt a.M.: Fischer, 1970).

Kertész, Imre, *Kaddish for an Unborn Child*, trans. Tim Wilkinson (New York: Vintage, 2004).

Levi, Primo, *The Drowned and the Saved*, trans. Raymond Rosenthal (London: Abacus, 1989).

Rousset, David, *L'Univers concentrationnaire* (Paris: Pavois, 1946).

Thomas, D. M., *The White Hotel* (Harmondsworth: Penguin, 1981).

Weiss, Peter, *Das Gespräch der drei Gehenden* (Frankfurt a.M.: Suhrkamp, 1963).

Weiss, Peter, *Rapporte* (Frankfurt a.M.: Suhrkamp, 1968).
Wiesel, Elie, *La Nuit* (Paris: Minuit, 1958).

CRITICAL STUDIES

Abraham, Nicolas, and Maria Torok, *Cryptonymie: Le Verbier de l'homme aux loups*, foreword by Jacques Derrida (Paris: Aubier Flammarion, 1976).
Abraham, Nicolas, and Maria Torok, *L'Écorce et le noyau* (Paris: Flammarion, 1987).
Adler, Jeremy, 'H. G. Adler: A Prague Writer in London', in Charmian Brinson et al. (eds), *Keine Klage über England: Deutsche und österreichische Exilerfahrungen in Großbritannien 1933–1945* (Munich: Iudicium, 1998), 13–30.
Adler, Jeremy, 'Good against Evil? H. G. Adler, T. W. Adorno and the Representation of the Holocaust', in Edward Timms and Andrea Hammel (eds), *The German-Jewish Dilemma: From the Enlightenment to the Shoah* (Lewiston, NY: Mellen, 1999), 255–89.
Adler, Jeremy, 'Nur wer die Reise wagt, findet nach Hause', in H. G. Adler, *Eine Reise* (Vienna: Zsolnay, 1999), 307–15.
Adler, Jeremy, 'Good against Evil? H. G. Adler, T. W. Adorno and the Representation of the Holocaust', in Robert Fine and Charles Turner (eds), *Social Theory after the Holocaust* (Liverpool: Liverpool University Press, 2000), 71–100.
Adler, Jeremy, '"Die Macht des Guten im Rachen des Bösen": H. G. Adler, T. W. Adorno und die Darstellung der Shoah', *Merkur*, 54 (2000), 475–86.
Adorno, Theodor W., *Gesammelte Schriften*, ed. Rolf Tiedemann et al., 20 vols (Frankfurt a.M.: Suhrkamp, 1970–86), esp. x. *Prismen: Kulturkritik und Gesellschaft* (1977); xi. *Noten zur Literatur* (1974).
Agamben, Giorgio, *Remnants of Auschwitz: The Witness and the Archive*, trans. Daniel Heller-Roazen (New York: Zone, 1999).
Andersson, Björn, *Zur Gestaltung von Entfremdung bei Wolfgang Hildesheimer* (Uppsala: Almqvist & Wiksell, 1979).
Arnold, Heinz Ludwig (ed.), *Wolfgang Hildesheimer* (Munich: text + kritik, 1986).
Arnold, Heinz Ludwig (ed.), *Erich Fried* (2nd rev. edn, Munich: text + kritik, 1997).
Arnold, Heinz Ludwig (ed.), *W. G. Sebald* (Munich: text + kritik, 2003).
Arnold, Heinz Ludwig (ed.), *H. G. Adler* (Munich: text + kritik, 2004).
Attridge, Derek, Geoff Bennington, and Robert Young (eds), *Post-Structuralism and the Question of History* (Cambridge: Cambridge University Press, 1987).
Atze, Marcel (ed.), *'Ortlose Botschaft': Der Freundeskreis H. G. Adler, Elias Canetti und Franz Baermann Steiner im englischen Exil* (Marbach a.N.: Deutsche Schillergesellschaft, 1998) (= *Marbacher Magazin* 84).
Atze, Marcel, 'W. G. Sebald und H. G. Adler: Eine Begegnung in Texten', in Vogel-Klein (ed.), *W. G. Sebald*, 87–97.
Banner, Gillian, *Holocaust Literature: Schulz, Levi, Spiegelman and the Memory of the Offence* (London: Vallentine Mitchell, 2000).
Bauman, Zygmunt, *Modernity and the Holocaust* (Cambridge: Polity, 1989).

Bauman, Zygmunt, *Liquid Modernity* (Cambridge: Polity, 2000).

Becker, Sabina, 'Zwischen Akkulturation und Enkulturation: Anmerkungen zu einem vernachlässigten Autorinnentypus: Jenny Aloni und Ilse Losa', *Exilforschung*, 13 (1995), 114–36.

Beckmann, Heinz, 'Kommentar statt Dichtung', *Zeitwende/Die neue Furche*, 32 (1961), 199–200.

Bellamy, Elizabeth J., *Affective Genealogies: Psychoanalysis, Postmodernism, and the 'Jewish Question' after Auschwitz* (Lincoln, NB: University of Nebraska Press, 1997).

Berg, Nicolas, Jess Jochimsen, and Bernd Stiegler (eds), *Shoah—Formen der Erinnerung: Geschichte, Philosophie, Literatur, Kunst* (Munich: Fink, 1996).

Berger, Alan L., and Naomi Berger (eds), *Second Generation Voices: Reflections by Children of Holocaust Survivors and Perpetrators* (Syracuse, NY: Syracuse University Press, 2001).

Berger, Alan L., and Gloria L. Cronin (eds), *Jewish American and Holocaust Literature: Representation in the Postmodern World* (Albany, NY: State University of New York Press, 2004).

Berger, James, *After the End: Representations of Post-Apocalypse* (Minneapolis: University of Minnesota Press, 1999).

Bernhardt, Rüdiger, 'Fremd in den zwei Heimaten—die jüdische Schriftstellerin Jenny Aloni', *Exil: Forschung, Erkenntnisse, Ergebnisse*, 13 (1993), 17–26.

Best, Otto F., 'Panorama und Topographie: Anmerkungen zu Alfred Döblin, Peter Weiss, H. G. Adler und anderen', in Elfe, Hardin, and Holst (eds), *Deutsche Exilliteratur—Literatur der Nachkriegszeit*, 96–102.

Blamberger, Günter, *Versuch über den deutschen Gegenwartsroman: Krisenbewußtsein und Neubegründung im Zeichen der Melancholie* (Stuttgart: Metzler, 1985).

Blanchot, Maurice, *L'Écriture du désastre* (Paris: Gallimard, 1980).

Bloom, Harold (ed.), *Literature of the Holocaust* (New York: Chelsea House, 2004).

Boheemen-Saaf, Christine van, *Joyce, Derrida, Lacan, and the Trauma of History: Reading, Narrative and Postcolonialism* (Cambridge: Cambridge University Press, 1999).

Böll, Heinrich, *Frankfurter Vorlesungen* (Cologne: Kiepenheuer & Witsch, 1966).

Bormann, Alexander von, 'Der deutsche Roman in den Niederlanden: Formsemantische Überlegungen', in Sjaak Onderdelinden (ed.), *Interbellum und Exil* (Amsterdam: Rodopi, 1991), 225–49.

Bos, Pascale R., *German-Jewish Literature in the Wake of the Holocaust: Grete Weil, Ruth Klüger, and the Politics of Address* (New York: Palgrave Macmillan, 2005).

Braese, Stephan, *Die andere Erinnerung: Jüdische Autoren in der westdeutschen Nachkriegsliteratur* (Berlin: Philo, 2001).

Braese, Stephan, Holger Gehle, Doron Kiesel, and Hanno Loewy (eds), *Deutsche Nachkriegsliteratur und der Holocaust* (Frankfurt a.M.: Campus, 1998).

Brockmann, Stephen, *German Literary Culture at the Zero Hour* (Rochester, NY: Camden House, 2004).

Bronfen, Elisabeth, 'Entortung und Identität: Ein Thema der modernen Exilliteratur', *Germanic Review*, 69 (1994), 70–8.

Bronfen, Elisabeth, Birgit R. Erdle, and Sigrid Weigel (eds), *Trauma: Zwischen Psychoanalyse und kulturellem Deutungsmuster* (Cologne: Böhlau, 1999).

Brooke-Rose, Christine, *A Rhetoric of the Unreal: Studies in Narrative and Structure, Especially of the Fantastic* (Cambridge: Cambridge University Press, 1981).

Brooks, Peter, *Reading for the Plot: Design and Intention in Narrative* (Cambridge, MA: Harvard University Press, 1984).

Brumlik, Micha, Doron Kiesel, Cilly Kugelmann, and Julius H. Schoeps (eds), *Jüdisches Leben in Deutschland seit 1945* (Frankfurt a.M.: Athenäum, 1986).

Bullivant, Keith (ed.), *The Modern German Novel* (Leamington Spa: Berg, 1987).

Bullivant, Keith (ed.), *The Future of German Literature* (Oxford: Berg, 1994).

Caruth, Cathy, *Unclaimed Experience: Trauma, Narrative, and History* (Baltimore: Johns Hopkins University Press, 1996).

Caruth, Cathy (ed.), *Trauma: Explorations in Memory* (Baltimore: Johns Hopkins University Press, 1995).

Caruth, Cathy, and Deborah Esch (eds), *Critical Encounters: Reference and Responsibility in Deconstructive Writing* (New Brunswick, NJ: Rutgers University Press, 1995).

Caviola, Hugo, *In the Zone: Perception and Presentation of Space in German and American Postmodernism* (Basle: Birkhäuser, 1991).

Cernyak-Spatz, Susan E., *German Holocaust Literature* (New York: Lang, 1985).

Cesarani, David, and Eric J. Sundquist (eds), *After the Holocaust: Challenging the Myth of Silence* (London and New York: Routledge, 2012).

Chiadò Rana, Christine, *Das Weite suchen: Unterwegs in Wolfgang Hildesheimers Prosa* (Würzburg: Ergon, 2003).

Christolova, Lena, *'Die Zeit ist niemals in den Fugen gewesen': Raum-zeitliche Modelle in der poetischen Welt von Wolfgang Hildesheimer* (Konstanz: Hartung-Gorre, 1999).

Cixous, Hélène, 'Fiction and Its Phantoms: A Reading of Freud's *Das Unheimliche* (The "Uncanny")', *New Literary History*, 7 (1976), 525–48.

Clendinnen, Inga, *Reading the Holocaust* (Cambridge: Cambridge University Press, 1999).

Cohen, Arthur A., *An Arthur A. Cohen Reader: Selected Fiction and Writings on Judaism, Theology, Literature, and Culture*, ed. David Stern and Paul Mendes-Flohr (Detroit: Wayne State University Press, 1998).

Collier, Peter, and Helga Geyer-Ryan (eds), *Literary Theory Today* (Cambridge: Polity, 1990).

Connor, Steven (ed.), *The Cambridge Companion to Postmodernism* (Cambridge: Cambridge University Press, 2004).

Cosgrove, Mary, 'Melancholy Competitions: W. G. Sebald Reads Günter Grass and Wolfgang Hildesheimer', *German Life and Letters*, 59 (2006), 217–32.

Currie, Mark, *Postmodern Narrative Theory* (Basingstoke: Palgrave Macmillan, 1998).

Currie, Mark, *Difference* (London: Routledge, 2004).

Damamme-Gilbert, Béatrice, 'Secrets, fantômes et troubles de la transmission du passé dans la pratique littéraire de Patrick Modiano', in John E. Flower (ed.), *Patrick Modiano* (Amsterdam: Rodopi, 2007), 109–30.

Davis, Colin, *After Poststructuralism: Reading, Stories and Theory* (London: Routledge, 2004).

Davis, Colin, *Haunted Subjects: Deconstruction, Psychoanalysis and the Return of the Dead* (Basingstoke: Palgrave Macmillan, 2007).

Demetz, Peter, *After the Fires: Recent Writing in the Germanies, Austria, and Switzerland* (San Diego, CA: Harcourt Brace Jovanovich, 1986).

Demetz, Peter, 'Nachwort', in H. G. Adler, *Panorama* (Munich: Piper, 1988), 582–92.

Denham, Scott, and Mark McCulloh (eds), *W. G. Sebald: History—Memory—Trauma* (Berlin: Walter de Gruyter, 2006).

Derrida, Jacques, *De la grammatologie* (Paris: Minuit, 1967).

Derrida, Jacques, *L'Écriture et la différence* (Paris: Seuil, 1967).

Derrida, Jacques, *Marges de la philosophie* (Paris: Minuit, 1972).

Derrida, Jacques, 'Fors: Les mots anglés de Nicolas Abraham et Maria Torok', in Abraham and Torok, *Cryptonymie*, 7–73.

Derrida, Jacques, *La carte postale: De Socrate à Freud et au-delà* (Paris: Flammarion, 1980).

Derrida, Jacques, *Feu la cendre* (Paris: Des Femmes, 1987).

Derrida, Jacques, *Spectres de Marx: L'État de la dette, le travail du deuil et la nouvelle Internationale* (Paris: Galilée, 1993).

Diner, Dan, 'Zwischen Aporie und Apologie: Über Grenzen der Historisierbarkeit der Massenvernichtung', *Babylon: Beiträge zur jüdischen Gegenwart*, 2 (1987), 23–33.

Diner, Dan, 'Negative Symbiose: Deutsche und Juden nach Auschwitz', in Brumlik et al. (eds), *Jüdisches Leben in Deutschland seit 1945*, 243–57.

Diner, Hasia R., *We Remember with Reverence and Love: American Jews and the Myth of Silence after the Holocaust, 1945–1962* (New York: New York University Press, 2009).

Douglass, Ana, and Thomas A. Vogler (eds), *Witness and Memory: The Discourse of Trauma* (New York and London: Routledge, 2003).

Dunker, Axel, *Die anwesende Abwesenheit: Literatur im Schatten von Auschwitz* (Munich: Fink, 2003).

Durrant, Sam, *Postcolonial Narrative and the Work of Mourning: J. M. Coetzee, Wilson Harris, and Toni Morrison* (Albany, NY: State University of New York Press, 2004).

Durzak, Manfred, *Gespräche über den Roman* (Frankfurt a.M.: Suhrkamp, 1976).

Düwell, Susanne, *'Fiktion aus dem Wirklichen': Strategien autobiographischen Erzählens im Kontext der Shoah* (Bielefeld: Aisthesis, 2004).

Eaglestone, Robert, *The Holocaust and the Postmodern* (Oxford: Oxford University Press, 2004).

Eberhard, Pascale, 'Versuch einer Heilung', in Augustin, *Auswege*, 219–25.

Eckert, Willehad P., 'Jenny Aloni: Der Wartesaal', *Emuna: Horizonte zur Diskussion über Israel und das Judentum*, 5 (1970), 355.

Eckert, Willehad P., and Wilhelm Unger (eds), *H. G. Adler—Buch der Freunde: Stimmen über den Dichter und Gelehrten mit unveröffentlichter Lyrik* (Cologne: Wienand, 1975).

Eco, Umberto, *The Open Work*, trans. Anna Cancogni (London: Hutchinson Radius, 1989).

Eke, Norbert Otto, and Hartmut Steinecke (eds), *Shoah in der deutschsprachigen Literatur* (Berlin: Schmidt, 2006).

Elfe, Wolfgang, James Hardin, and Günther Holst (eds), *Deutsche Exilliteratur—Literatur der Nachkriegszeit: Akten des III. Exilliteratur-Symposiums der University of South Carolina* (Berne: Lang, 1981).

Emden, Christian, and David Midgley (eds), *German Literature, History and the Nation* (Oxford: Lang, 2004).

Epstein, Julia, and Lori Hope Lefkovitz (eds), *Shaping Losses: Cultural Memory and the Holocaust* (Urbana: University of Illinois Press, 2001).

Ermarth, Elizabeth Deeds, *Sequel to History: Postmodernism and the Crisis of Representational Time* (Princeton: Princeton University Press, 1992).

Eshel, Amir, *Zeit der Zäsur: Jüdische Dichter im Angesicht der Shoah* (Heidelberg: Winter, 1999).

Evans, Owen, *Mapping the Contours of Oppression: Subjectivity, Truth and Fiction in Recent German Autobiographical Treatments of Totalitarianism* (Amsterdam: Rodopi, 2006).

Ezrahi, Sidra DeKoven, *By Words Alone: The Holocaust in Literature* (Chicago: University of Chicago Press, 1980).

Federman, Raymond, *To Whom It May Concern* (Normal, IL: Fiction Collective Two, 1990).

Federman, Raymond, *Critifiction: Postmodern Essays* (Albany, NY: State University of New York Press, 1993).

Federman, Raymond, 'The Necessity and Impossibility of Being a Jewish Writer' (2001), <http://www.federman.com/rfsrcr0.htm> [accessed 23 Apr. 2008].

Fehn, Ann, Ingeborg Hoesterey, and Maria Tatar (eds), *Neverending Stories: Toward a Critical Narratology* (Princeton: Princeton University Press, 1992).

Felman, Shoshana, and Dori Laub, *Testimony: Crises of Witnessing in Literature, Psychoanalysis, and History* (New York: Routledge, 1992).

Finkielkraut, Alain, *The Imaginary Jew*, trans. Kevin O'Neill and David Suchoff (Lincoln, NB: University of Nebraska Press, 1994).

Fischer, Gerhard (ed.), *W. G. Sebald: Schreiben ex patria/Expatriate Writing* (Amsterdam: Rodopi, 2009).

Fliedl, Konstanze, and Karl Wagner, 'Tote Zeit: Zum Problem der Darstellung von Geschichtserfahrung in den Romanen Erich Frieds und Hans Leberts', in Friedbert Aspetsberger, Norbert Frei, and Hubert Lengauer (eds), *Literatur der Nachkriegszeit und der fünfziger Jahre in Österreich* (Vienna: Österreichischer Bundesverlag, 1984), 303–19.

Freud, Sigmund, *Studienausgabe*, ed. Alexander Mitscherlich, Angela Richards, and James Strachey, 11 vols (Frankfurt a.M.: Fischer, 1969–75).

Friedlander, Saul (ed.), *Probing the Limits of Representation: Nazism and the 'Final Solution'* (Cambridge, MA: Harvard University Press, 1992).

Fuchs, Anne, *Phantoms of War in Contemporary German Literature, Films and Discourse: The Politics of Memory* (Basingstoke: Palgrave Macmillan, 2008).

Fuchs, Anne, Mary Cosgrove, and Georg Grote (eds), *German Memory Contests: The Quest for Identity in Literature, Film, and Discourse since 1900* (Rochester, NY: Camden House, 2006).

Fuchs, Anne, and J. J. Long (eds), *W. G. Sebald and the Writing of History* (Würzburg: Königshausen & Neumann, 2007).

Fulbrook, Mary, and Martin Swales (eds), *Representing the German Nation: History and Identity in Twentieth-Century Germany* (Manchester: Manchester University Press, 2000).

Garloff, Katja, *Words from Abroad: Trauma and Displacement in Postwar German Jewish Writers* (Detroit: Wayne State University Press, 2005).

Genette, Gérard, *Figures I* (Paris: Seuil, 1966).

Genette, Gérard, *Figures II* (Paris: Seuil, 1969).

Genette, Gérard, *Figures III* (Paris: Seuil, 1972).

Genette, Gérard, *Nouveau discours du récit* (Paris: Seuil, 1983).

Genette, Gérard, *Métalepse: De la figure à la fiction* (Paris: Seuil, 2004).

Gide, André, *Journal 1889–1939* (Paris: Gallimard, 1939).

Görner, Rüdiger, 'Ins Innere des Wortes: Über H. G. Adler', *Literatur und Kritik*, 237–8 (1989), 298–304.

Görner, Rüdiger, 'H. G. Adler (1910–1988)', *Literatur und Kritik*, 293–4 (1995), 101–7.

Grass, Günter, *Schreiben nach Auschwitz: Frankfurter Poetik-Vorlesung* (Frankfurt a.M.: Luchterhand, 1990).

Greiner-Kemptner, Ulrike, *Subjekt und Fragment: Textpraxis in der (Post-)Moderne* (Stuttgart: Heinz, 1990).

Hahn, Hans-Joachim, *Repräsentationen des Holocaust: Zur westdeutschen Erinnerungskultur seit 1979* (Heidelberg: Winter, 2005).

Haines, Brigid, and Margaret Littler, *Contemporary Women's Writing in German: Changing the Subject* (Oxford: Oxford University Press, 2004).

Hamacher, Werner, 'Journals, Politics: Notes on Paul de Man's Wartime Journalism', in Hamacher, Neil Hertz, and Thomas Keenan (eds), *Responses: On Paul de Man's Wartime Journalism* (Lincoln, NB: University of Nebraska Press, 1989), 438–67.

Hartman, Geoffrey H. (ed.), *Holocaust Remembrance: The Shapes of Memory* (Oxford: Blackwell, 1994).

Hartman, Geoffrey H., *The Longest Shadow: In the Aftermath of the Holocaust* (Bloomington: Indiana University Press, 1996).

Heidegger, Martin, *Sein und Zeit* (1927; Tübingen: Niemeyer, 1979).

Heidegger, Martin, 'Der Spruch des Anaximander', in Heidegger, *Holzwege* (Frankfurt a.M.: Klostermann, 1950), 296–343.

Heise, Ursula K., *Chronoschisms: Time, Narrative, and Postmodernism* (Cambridge: Cambridge University Press, 1997).

Henke, Suzette A., *Shattered Subjects: Trauma and Testimony in Women's Life-Writing* (Basingstoke: Macmillan, 1998).

Hermsdorf, Klaus, Hugo Fetting, and Silvia Schlenstedt, *Exil in den Niederlanden und in Spanien* (Leipzig: Reclam, 1981).

Herzog, Hillary Hope, Todd Herzog, and Benjamin Lapp (eds), *Rebirth of a Culture: Jewish Identity and Jewish Writing in Germany and Austria Today* (New York and Oxford: Berghahn, 2008).

Hinderer, Walter, *Arbeit an der Gegenwart: Zur deutschen Literatur nach 1945* (Würzburg: Königshausen & Neumann, 1994).

Hipp, Helga, 'Autor und Text im Spannungsfeld der Zweisprachigkeit: Elisabeth Augustins niederländische und deutsche Textfassungen', *Zeitschrift für Germanistik*, 11 (1990), 318–23.

Hirsch, David H., *The Deconstruction of Literature: Criticism after Auschwitz* (Hanover, NH: University Press of New England, 1991).

Hirsch, Marianne, *Family Frames: Photography, Narrative, and Postmemory* (Cambridge, MA: Harvard University Press, 1997).

Hirsch, Marianne, 'Surviving Images: Holocaust Photographs and the Work of Postmemory', in Zelizer (ed.), *Visual Culture and the Holocaust*, 214–46.

Hocheneder, Franz, 'Aufzeichnungen einer Displaced Person: Werk und Nachlaß von H. G. Adler (1910–1988)', *Literatur und Kritik*, 329–30 (1998), 50–6.

Hocheneder, Franz, 'Special Bibliography: The Writings of H. G. Adler (1910–1988)', *Comparative Criticism*, 21 (1999), 293–310.

Hocheneder, Franz, '*Eine Reise*: H. G. Adlers wiederentdeckter Roman in neuer Auflage', *Literatur und Kritik*, 343–4 (2000), 86–8.

Hoffman, Eva, *After Such Knowledge: A Meditation on the Aftermath of the Holocaust* (London: Vintage, 2005).

Hoffmann, Daniel (ed.), *Handbuch zur deutsch-jüdischen Literatur des 20. Jahrhunderts* (Paderborn: Schöningh, 2002).

Hoffmann, Paul, 'Poesie und Engagement: Paul Celan und Erich Fried', in Paul Hoffmann, *Das erneute Gedicht* (Frankfurt a.M.: Suhrkamp, 2001), 69–98.

Hofmann, Michael, *Literaturgeschichte der Shoah* (Münster: Aschendorff, 2003).

Horowitz, Sara R., *Voicing the Void: Muteness and Memory in Holocaust Fiction* (Albany, NY: State University of New York Press, 1997).

Hubmann, Heinrich, and Alfred O. Lanz (eds), *Zu Hause im Exil: Zu Werk und Person H. G. Adlers* (Stuttgart: Steiner, 1987).

Hutcheon, Linda, *A Poetics of Postmodernism: History, Theory, Fiction* (New York: Routledge, 1988).

Hutcheon, Linda, *The Politics of Postmodernism* (London: Routledge, 1989).

Huyssen, Andreas, *After the Great Divide: Modernism, Mass Culture, Postmodernism* (Bloomington: Indiana University Press, 1986).

Huyssen, Andreas, 'On Rewritings and New Beginnings: W. G. Sebald and the Literature about the *Luftkrieg*', *Zeitschrift für Literaturwissenschaft und Linguistik*, 124 (2001), 72–90.

Imhof, Rüdiger, *Contemporary Metafiction: A Poetological Study of Metafiction in English since 1939* (Heidelberg: Winter, 1986).

Jehle, Volker (ed.), *Wolfgang Hildesheimer* (Frankfurt a.M.: Suhrkamp, 1989).

Johnson, Erica L., 'Unforgetting Trauma: Dionne Brand's Haunted Histories', *Anthurium: A Caribbean Studies Journal*, 2 (2004), 1–14.

Jones, Kathryn N., *Journeys of Remembrance: Memories of the Second World War in French and German Literature, 1960–1980* (London: Legenda, 2007).

Jopling, Michael, *Re-placing the Self: Fictional and Autobiographical Interplay in Modern German Narrative (Elias Canetti, Thomas Bernhard, Peter Weiss, Christa Wolf)* (Stuttgart: Heinz, 2001).

Kane, Martin, 'From Solipsism to Engagement: The Development of Erich Fried as a Political Poet', *Forum for Modern Language Studies*, 21 (1985), 151–69.

Kaukoreit, Volker, *Vom Exil bis zum Protest gegen den Krieg in Vietnam: Frühe Stationen des Lyrikers Erich Fried: Werk und Biographie 1938–1966* (Darmstadt: Häusser, 1991).

Kaukoreit, Volker, and Heidemarie Vahl (eds), *Einer singt aus der Zeit gegen die Zeit: Erich Fried 1921–1988: Materialien und Texte zu Leben und Werk* (Darmstadt: Häusser, 1991).

Kellermann, Natan P. J., 'Transmission of Holocaust Trauma: An Integrative View', *Psychiatry: Interpersonal and Biological Processes*, 64 (2001), 256–67.

Kettner, Fabian, '*Die unsichtbare Wand*: Anmerkungen zu H. G. Adlers Werk', *Literaturkritik*, 10 (2004), <http://www.literaturkritik.de/public/rezension.php?rez_id=7477> [accessed 27 May 2007].

Kiedaisch, Petra (ed.), *Lyrik nach Auschwitz? Adorno und die Dichter* (Stuttgart: Reclam, 1995).

Kilcher, Andreas B. (ed.), *Lexikon der deutsch-jüdischen Literatur: Jüdische Autorinnen und Autoren deutscher Sprache von der Aufklärung bis zur Gegenwart* (Frankfurt a.M.: Suhrkamp, 2003).

King, Nicola, '"We come after": Remembering the Holocaust', in Luckhurst and Marks (eds), *Literature and the Contemporary*, 94–108.

Klein, Judith, *Literatur und Genozid: Darstellungen der nationalsozialistischen Massenvernichtung in der französischen Literatur* (Vienna: Böhlau, 1992).

Klüger, Ruth, *Von hoher und niedriger Literatur* (Göttingen: Wallstein, 1996).

Köppen, Manuel (ed.), *Kunst und Literatur nach Auschwitz* (Berlin: Schmidt, 1993).

Kramer, Sven, *Auschwitz im Widerstreit: Zur Darstellung der Shoah in Film, Philosophie und Literatur* (Wiesbaden: Deutscher Universitätsverlag, 1999).

Krankenhagen, Stefan, *Auschwitz darstellen: Ästhetische Positionen zwischen Adorno, Spielberg und Walser* (Cologne: Böhlau, 2001).

Kremer, S. Lillian, *Witness through the Imagination: Jewish-American Holocaust Literature* (Detroit: Wayne State University Press, 1989).

Kren, George M., and Leon Rappoport, *The Holocaust and the Crisis of Human Behavior* (New York: Holmes & Meier, 1980).

LaCapra, Dominick, *Representing the Holocaust: History, Theory, Trauma* (Ithaca, NY: Cornell University Press, 1994).

LaCapra, Dominick, *History and Memory after Auschwitz* (Ithaca, NY: Cornell University Press, 1998).

LaCapra, Dominick, *Writing History, Writing Trauma* (Baltimore: Johns Hopkins University Press, 2001).

Lamping, Dieter (ed.), *Dein aschenes Haar Sulamith: Dichtung über den Holocaust* (Munich: Piper, 1992).

Lamping, Dieter, *Literatur und Theorie: Über poetologische Probleme der Moderne* (Göttingen: Vandenhoeck & Ruprecht, 1996).

Lang, Berel (ed.), *Writing and the Holocaust* (New York: Holmes & Meier, 1988).

Lang, Berel, *Act and Idea in the Nazi Genocide* (Chicago: University of Chicago Press, 1990).

Lang, Berel, *Holocaust Representation: Art within the Limits of History and Ethics* (Baltimore: Johns Hopkins University Press, 2000).

Langer, Lawrence L., *The Holocaust and the Literary Imagination* (New Haven: Yale University Press, 1975).

Langer, Lawrence L., *Holocaust Testimonies: The Ruins of Memory* (New Haven: Yale University Press, 1991).

Langer, Lawrence L., *Admitting the Holocaust: Collected Essays* (New York: Oxford University Press, 1995).

Langer, Lawrence L., *Preempting the Holocaust* (New Haven: Yale University Press, 1998).

Lanz, Alfred, *'Panorama' von H.G. Adler—ein 'moderner Roman': 'Panorama' als Minusverfahren des Entwicklungsromans und Negation der Möglichkeit rationaler Welterkenntnis* (Berne: Lang, 1984).

Lawrie, Steven W., '"Etwas Romanartiges": Erich Fried's Novel *Ein Soldat und ein Mädchen*', *German Life and Letters*, 48 (1995), 199–221.

Lawrie, Steven W., *Erich Fried: A Writer without a Country* (New York: Lang, 1996).

Lazarus, Joyce Block, *Strangers and Sojourners: Jewish Identity in Contemporary Francophone Fiction* (New York: Lang, 1999).

Lea, Henry A., *Wolfgang Hildesheimers Weg als Jude und Deutscher* (Stuttgart: Heinz, 1997).

Leak, Andrew, and George Paizis (eds), *The Holocaust and the Text: Speaking the Unspeakable* (Basingstoke: Macmillan, 2000).

Lentin, Ronit (ed.), *Re-presenting the Shoah for the Twenty-First Century* (New York: Berghahn, 2004).

Levi, Neil, and Michael Rothberg (eds), *The Holocaust: Theoretical Readings* (New Brunswick, NJ: Rutgers University Press, 2003).

Lévinas, Emmanuel, *Noms propres* (Montpellier: Fata Morgana, 1976).

Leys, Ruth, *Trauma: A Genealogy* (Chicago: University of Chicago Press, 2000).

Liska, Vivian, and Thomas Nolden (eds), *Contemporary Jewish Writing in Europe: A Guide* (Bloomington: Indiana University Press, 2008).

Long, J. J., 'Time and Narrative: Wolfgang Hildesheimer's *Tynset* and *Masante*', *German Life and Letters*, 52 (1999), 457–74.

Long, J. J., 'Power, Desire, Performance: Narrative Exchanges in Wolfgang Hildesheimer's *Masante*', *Neophilologus*, 85 (2001), 601–19.

Long, J. J., *W.G. Sebald—Image, Archive, Modernity* (Edinburgh: Edinburgh University Press, 2007).

Long, J. J., and Anne Whitehead (eds), *W. G. Sebald—A Critical Companion* (Edinburgh: Edinburgh University Press, 2004).

Lorenz, Dagmar, *Scheitern als Ereignis: Der Autor Jean Améry im Kontext europäischer Kulturkritik* (Frankfurt a.M.: Lang, 1991).

Lorenz, Dagmar C. G., *Verfolgung bis zum Massenmord: Holocaust-Diskurse in deutscher Sprache aus der Sicht der Verfolgten* (New York: Lang, 1992).

Luckhurst, Roger, and Peter Marks (eds), *Literature and the Contemporary: Fictions and Theories of the Present* (Harlow: Longman, 1999).

Luckscheiter, Roman, *Der postmoderne Impuls: Die Krise der Literatur um 1968 und ihre Überwindung* (Berlin: Duncker & Humblot, 2001).

Luer, Nadya, *Form und Engagement: Untersuchungen zur Dichtung und Ästhetik Erich Frieds* (Vienna: Praesens, 2004).

Lützeler, Paul Michael (ed.), *Spätmoderne und Postmoderne: Beiträge zur deutschsprachigen Gegenwartsliteratur* (Frankfurt a.M.: Fischer, 1991).

Lützeler, Paul Michael, *Postmoderne und postkoloniale deutschsprachige Literatur: Diskurs, Analyse, Kritik* (Bielefeld: Aisthesis, 2005).

Lyotard, Jean-François, *Le Différend* (Paris: Minuit, 1983).

Lyotard, Jean-François, *Heidegger et 'les juifs'* (Paris: Galilée, 1988).

McGlothlin, Erin, *Second-Generation Holocaust Literature: Legacies of Survival and Perpetration* (Rochester, NY: Camden House, 2006).

McHale, Brian, *Postmodernist Fiction* (London: Routledge, 1987).

McHale, Brian, *Constructing Postmodernism* (London: Routledge, 1992).

Malpas, Simon, *The Postmodern* (London: Routledge, 2005).

Marven, Lyn, *Body and Narrative in Contemporary Literatures in German: Herta Müller, Libuše Moníková, and Kerstin Hensel* (Oxford: Oxford University Press, 2005).

Mintz, Alan, *Hurban: Responses to Catastrophe in Hebrew Literature* (New York: Columbia University Press, 1984).

Morgan, Peter, 'The Sign of Saturn: Melancholy, Homelessness and Apocalypse in W. G. Sebald's Prose Narratives', *German Life and Letters*, 58 (2005), 75–92.

Morris, Leslie, and Karen Remmler (eds), *Contemporary Jewish Writing in Germany: An Anthology* (Lincoln, NB and London: University of Nebraska Press, 2002).

Morris, Leslie, and Jack Zipes (eds), *Unlikely History: The Changing German–Jewish Symbiosis, 1945–2000* (New York and Basingstoke: Palgrave, 2002).

Morrison, Anthony P., Lucy Frame, and Warren Larkin, 'Relationships between Trauma and Psychosis: A Review and Integration', *British Journal of Clinical Psychology*, 42 (2003), 331–53.

Newbery, Ilse, 'Erich Fried's *Ein Soldat und ein Mädchen*', *German Life and Letters*, 42 (1988), 46–59.

Nieragden, Göran, 'Focalization and Narration: Theoretical and Terminological Refinements', *Poetics Today*, 23 (2002), 685–97.

Nolden, Thomas, *Junge jüdische Literatur: Konzentrisches Schreiben in der Gegenwart* (Würzburg: Königshausen & Neumann, 1995).

Nolden, Thomas, and Frances Malino, (eds), *Voices of the Diaspora: Jewish Women Writing in Contemporary Europe* (Evanston, IL: Northwestern University Press, 2005).

O'Dochartaigh, Pól (ed.), *Jews in German Literature Since 1945: German-Jewish Literature?* (= *German Monitor* 53) (Amsterdam: Rodopi, 2000).

O'Dochartaigh, Pól, 'Erich Fried: Poetik des Menschseins', in Eke and Steinecke (eds), *Shoah in der deutschsprachigen Literatur*, 280–5.

Ofer, Dalia, and Lenore J. Weitzman (eds), *Women in the Holocaust* (New Haven: Yale University Press, 1998).

Orbán, Katalin, *Ethical Diversions: The Post-Holocaust Narratives of Pynchon, Abish, DeLillo, and Spiegelman* (New York: Routledge, 2005).

Parker, Stephen, Peter Davies, and Matthew Philpotts, *The Modern Restoration: Re-thinking German Literary History 1930–1960* (Berlin: de Gruyter, 2004).

Patterson, David, *The Shriek of Silence: A Phenomenology of the Holocaust Novel* (Lexington: University Press of Kentucky, 1992).

Paver, Chloe E. M., *Narrative and Fantasy in the Post-War German Novel: A Study of Novels by Johnson, Frisch, Wolf, Becker, and Grass* (Oxford: Clarendon Press, 1999).

Quendler, Christian, *From Romantic Irony to Postmodernist Metafiction: A Contribution to the History of Literary Self-Reflexivity in its Philosophical Context* (Frankfurt a.M.: Lang, 2001).

Rabinbach, Anson, and Jack Zipes (eds), *Germans and Jews since the Holocaust: The Changing Situation in West Germany* (New York: Holmes & Meier, 1986).

Renneke, Petra, *Das verlorene, verlassene Haus: Sprache und Metapher in der Prosa Jenny Alonis* (Bielefeld: Aisthesis, 2003).

Rosen, Steven M., *Dimensions of Apeiron: A Topological Phenomenology of Space, Time, and Individuation* (Amsterdam: Rodopi, 2004).

Rosenfeld, Alvin H., *A Double Dying: Reflections on Holocaust Literature* (Bloomington: Indiana University Press, 1980).

Roskies, David G., *Against the Apocalypse: Responses to Catastrophe in Modern Jewish Culture* (Cambridge, MA: Harvard University Press, 1984).

Rothberg, Michael, *Traumatic Realism: The Demands of Holocaust Representation* (Minneapolis: University of Minnesota Press, 2000).

Rothe, Anne, *Popular Trauma Culture: Selling the Pain of Others in the Mass Media* (New Brunswick, NJ: Rutgers University Press, 2011).

Royle, Nicholas, *The Uncanny* (Manchester: Manchester University Press, 2003).

Ryan, Judith, *The Uncompleted Past: Postwar German Novels and the Third Reich* (Detroit: Wayne State University Press, 1983).

Santner, Eric L., *Stranded Objects: Mourning, Memory, and Film in Postwar Germany* (Ithaca, NY: Cornell University Press, 1990).

Sapper, Theo, 'H. G. Adler: Panorama', *Literatur und Kritik*, 50 (1970), 633–6.

Sapper, Theo, '"Der Dorn des Abfalls": Einheit von Idee und Bild im Werk H. G. Adlers', *Literatur und Kritik*, 84 (1974), 205–9.

Schäfer, Katrin, *'Die andere Seite': Erich Frieds Prosawerk: Motive und Motivationen seines Schreibens* (Vienna: Praesens, 1998).

Scherpe, Klaus R., *Die rekonstruierte Moderne: Studien zur deutschen Literatur nach 1945* (Cologne: Böhlau, 1992).

Schier, Helga, *Going Beyond: The Crisis of Identity and Identity Models in Contemporary American, English and German Fiction* (Tübingen: Niemeyer, 1993).

Schlachter, Birgit, *Schreibweisen der Abwesenheit: Jüdisch-französische Literatur nach der Shoah* (Cologne: Böhlau, 2006).

Schlant, Ernestine, *The Language of Silence: West German Literature and the Holocaust* (New York: Routledge, 1999).

Schmid-Bortenschlager, Sigrid, *Konstruktive Literatur: Gesellschaftliche Relevanz und literarische Tradition experimenteller Prosa-Großformen im deutschen, englischen und französischen Sprachraum nach 1945* (Bonn: Bouvier, 1985).

Schmidt-Dengler, Wendelin, 'H[ans] G[ünther] Adler: Die unsichtbare Wand', *Literatur und Kritik*, 245–6 (1990), 277–8.

Schmitz, Helmut (ed.), *German Culture and the Uncomfortable Past: Representations of National Socialism in Contemporary Germanic Literature* (Aldershot: Ashgate, 2001).

Schmitz, Helmut, *On Their Own Terms: The Legacy of National Socialism in Post-1990 German Fiction* (Birmingham: University of Birmingham Press, 2004).

Schmitz, Walter (ed.), *Erinnerte Shoah: Die Literatur der Überlebenden/The Shoah Remembered: Literature of the Surviors* (Dresden: Thelem, 2003).

Schnell, Ralf, *Geschichte der deutschsprachigen Literatur seit 1945* (Stuttgart: Metzler, 1993).

Schoppmann, Claudia (ed.), *Im Fluchtgepäck die Sprache: Deutschsprachige Schriftstellerinnen im Exil* (Frankfurt a.M.: Fischer, 1995).

Schubert, Katja, *Notwendige Umwege—Voies de traverse obligées: Gedächtnis und Zeugenschaft in Texten jüdischer Autorinnen in Deutschland und Frankreich nach Auschwitz* (Hildesheim: Olms, 2001).

Schütz, Hans J., *Juden in der deutschen Literatur: Eine deutsch-jüdische Literaturgeschichte im Überblick* (Munich: Piper, 1992).

Semprún, Jorge, *L'Écriture ou la vie* (Paris: Gallimard, 1997).

Serke, Jürgen, 'H. G. Adler: Der versteinerte Jüngling, der ein weiser Mann wurde', in Serke, *Böhmische Dörfer: Wanderungen durch eine verlassene literarische Landschaft* (Vienna: Zsolnay, 1987), 326–43.

Serke, Jürgen, '"Die Toten, die uns hinterlassen hatten . . .": H. G. Adler und das Gedenken als die Pflicht zum Beginn', in Adler, *Die unsichtbare Wand*, 645–56.

Shedletzky, Itta, and Hans Otto Horch (eds), *Deutsch-jüdische Exil- und Emigrationsliteratur im 20. Jahrhundert* (Tübingen: Niemeyer, 1993).

Sicher, Efraim (ed.), *Breaking Crystal: Writing and Memory after Auschwitz* (Urbana: University of Illinois Press, 1998).

Sicher, Efraim, 'The Future of the Past: Countermemory and Postmemory in Contemporary American Post-Holocaust Narratives', *History & Memory*, 12 (2000), 56–91.

Sicher, Efraim, *The Holocaust Novel* (New York: Routledge, 2005).

Stanley, Patricia H., *The Realm of Possibilities: Wolfgang Hildesheimer's Non-Traditional Non-Fictional Prose* (Lanham, MD: University Press of America, 1988).

Stanley, Patricia H., *Wolfgang Hildesheimer and His Critics* (Columbia, SC: Camden House, 1993).

Steinecke, Hartmut, *Literatur als Gedächtnis der Shoah: Deutschsprachige jüdische Schriftstellerinnen und Schriftsteller der 'zweiten Generation'* (Paderborn: Schöningh, 2005).

Stephan, Alexander (ed.), *Exile and Otherness: New Approaches to the Experience of the Nazi Refugees* (Oxford: Lang, 2005).

Stern, Heiko, 'Sprache zwischen Exil und Identität: Die Konstitution von Heimat durch Sprache bei Elisabeth Augustin', in O'Dochartaigh (ed.), *Jews in German Literature since 1945*, 77–93.

Stoehr, Ingo R., *German Literature of the Twentieth Century: From Aestheticism to Postmodernism* (Rochester, NY: Camden House, 2001).

Stüben, Jens, and Winfried Woesler (eds), *'Wir tragen den Zettelkasten mit den Steckbriefen unserer Freunde': Beiträge jüdischer Autoren zur deutschen Literatur seit 1945* (Darmstadt: Häusser, 1993).

Suleiman, Susan Rubin, 'The 1.5 Generation: Thinking about Child Survivors and the Holocaust', *American Imago*, 59 (2002), 277–95.

Tal, Kalí, *Worlds of Hurt: Reading the Literatures of Trauma* (Cambridge: Cambridge University Press, 1996).

Thums, Barbara, *'Den Ankünften nicht glauben, wahr sind die Abschiede': Mythos, Gedächtnis und Mystik in der Prosa Ilse Aichingers* (Freiburg i.Br.: Rombach, 2000).

Trotter, David, *The Making of the Reader: Language and Subjectivity in Modern American, English and Irish Poetry* (London: Macmillan, 1984).

Vermij, Lucie Th., 'Verloren tijd inhalen: Het patroon in het werk van Elisabeth Augustin', *Surplus*, 5/6 (1991), 18–20.

Vice, Sue (ed.), *Psychoanalytic Criticism: A Reader* (Cambridge: Polity, 1996).

Vice, Sue, *Holocaust Fiction* (London: Routledge, 2000).

Vickroy, Laurie, *Trauma and Survival in Contemporary Fiction* (Charlottesville: University of Virginia Press, 2002).

Vogel-Klein, Ruth (ed.), *W. G. Sebald: Mémoire, Transferts, Images/Erinnerung, Übertragungen, Bilder* (Strasbourg: Université Marc Bloch, 2005) (= *Recherches germaniques* 2).

Vogel-Klein, Ruth (ed.), *Die ersten Stimmen: Deutschsprachige Texte zur Shoah 1945–1963/Les Premières Voix: Écrits sur la Shoah en langue allemande 1945–1963* (Würzburg: Königshausen & Neumann, 2010).

Wall, Renate, *Lexikon deutschsprachiger Schriftstellerinnen im Exil 1933–1945* (Gießen: Haland & Wirth, 2004).

Watanabe-O'Kelly, Helen (ed.), *The Cambridge History of German Literature* (Cambridge: Cambridge University Press, 1997).

Waugh, Patricia, *Metafiction: The Theory and Practice of Self-Conscious Fiction* (London: Methuen, 1984).

Weissman, Gary, *Fantasies of Witnessing: Postwar Efforts to Experience the Holocaust* (Ithaca, NY: Cornell University Press, 2004).

Wellbery, David E., and Judith Ryan (eds), *A New History of German Literature* (Cambridge, MA: Belknap Press, 2004).

White, Hayden, *Metahistory: The Historical Imagination in Nineteenth-Century Europe* (Baltimore: Johns Hopkins University Press, 1973).

Whitehead, Anne, *Trauma Fiction* (Edinburgh: Edinburgh University Press, 2004).

Wiesel, Elie, Lucy S. Dawidowicz, Dorothy Rabinowitz, and Robert McAfee Brown, *Dimensions of the Holocaust: Lectures at Northwestern University* (Evanston, IL: Northwestern University Press, 1990).

Winter, Hans-Gerd (ed.), *'Uns selbst mussten wir misstrauen': Die 'junge Generation' in der deutschsprachigen Nachkriegsliteratur* (Hamburg: Dölling und Galitz, 2002).

Wolff, Lynn L., 'H. G. Adler and W. G. Sebald: From History and Literature to Literature as Historiography', *Monatshefte*, 103 (2011), 257–75.

Wolfsteiner, Beate, *Untersuchungen zum französisch-jüdischen Roman nach dem Zweiten Weltkrieg* (Tübingen: Niemeyer, 2003).

Wrobel, Dieter, *Postmodernes Chaos—Chaotische Postmoderne: Eine Studie zu Analogien zwischen Chaostheorie und deutschsprachiger Prosa der Postmoderne* (Bielefeld: Aisthesis, 1997).

Würzner, Hans (ed.), *Zur deutschen Exilliteratur in den Niederlanden 1933–1940* (Amsterdam: Rodopi, 1977).

Wyschogrod, Edith, *Spirit in Ashes: Hegel, Heidegger, and Man-Made Mass Death* (New Haven: Yale University Press, 1985).

Young, James E., *Writing and Rewriting the Holocaust: Narrative and the Consequences of Interpretation* (Bloomington: Indiana University Press, 1988).

Zelizer, Barbie (ed.), *Visual Culture and the Holocaust* (London: Athlone, 2001).

NEWSPAPER ARTICLES

Arnoldussen, Paul, 'Te serieus voor de lezer', *Het Parool*, 8 Jan. 2002.

Bienek, Horst, 'Literarische Scherben', *Frankfurter Allgemeine Zeitung*, 17 Sept. 1960.

Buffinga, Albert, 'Vermindering van spanning', *Elseviers Weekblad*, 21 Apr. 1956.

Drost, Suse, 'Das ewige Einerlei: Zu einem Roman der Droste-Preisträgerin Jenny Aloni', *Südkurier*, 9 Jan. 1993.

Eysselsteijn, Ben van, 'Bezinning op deze wereld en een andere', *Haagsche Courant*, 4 Feb. 1956.

Fenzl, Christa, 'Die Nummer wird zum Schicksal: Mit wachem Verstand und heißem Herzen ein psychiatrisches Krankenhaus erlebt', *Main-Echo*, 21 Sept. 1993.

Greshoff, Jan, 'Romanschrijver moet in zijn stof orde scheppen', *Het Vaderland*, 9 June 1956.

Günther, Thomas, 'Flucht ins Labyrinth: Eine Begegnung mit der Autorin Elisabeth Augustin', *Süddeutsche Zeitung*, 14 Mar. 1992.

Janse, John Albert, 'Duitsland blijft mijn taalland', *Vrij Nederland*, 29 May 1993.

Manschot, Anke, 'Elisabeth Augustin: Een schrijfster die vergissingen toegeeft', *Opzij*, Apr. 1991.

Ophuisen, Marianne A. van, 'Ik ben een onverbeterlijke optimiste', *De Nieuwe Linie*, 22 Nov. 1978.

Romain, Lothar, 'Eingesperrt zum Sterben: "Der Wartesaal"—Roman von Jenny Aloni', *Frankfurter Allgemeine Zeitung*, 29 Sept. 1969.

Seifert, Heribert, 'Menschen im Labyrinth ihrer Zeit: Hinweise auf Leben und Werk von Elisabeth Augustin', *Neue Zürcher Zeitung*, 14 June 1988.

Strecker, Manfred, 'Reiches Leben, welthaltige Literatur', *Neue Westfälische*, 18 June 1994.

Verhoeven, Nico, 'De weg van het mede-lijden', *De Tijd*, 10 Mar. 1956.

Warren, Hans, 'Labyrint', *Provinciale Zeeuwse Courant*, 5 Mar. 1983.

Index

Printed and bound by CPI Group (UK) Ltd, Croydon, CR0 4YY